SUCCESS STORY

The Life and Times of S. S. McClure

❧ ❧

by PETER LYON

CHARLES SCRIBNER'S SONS, NEW YORK

SUCCESS STORY

The Life and Times of S. S. McClure

for Jane

A PREFATORY NOTE

This book is about an extraordinary editor. His vision and energy turned the literary, social, and political fabric of his own time inside out; the reach of his innovations still affects us all today; yet he has been forgotten.

S. S. McClure revolutionized American journalism by introducing syndicated material to metropolitan newspapers. He invented the Sunday supplement. He brought Robert Louis Stevenson, Rudyard Kipling, Conan Doyle, and Joseph Conrad to the attention of American readers, and so helped to make their fortunes. He created a vast new readership for serious literature (and for bilge, as well). He published and edited the first and best of the cheap American magazines. He was the first to print stories by O. Henry, Damon Runyon, Booth Tarkington, and a dozen others, and the first to bring Willa Cather, Stephen Crane, Jack London, and Frank Norris to national acclaim. The so-called muckrakers—Samuel Hopkins Adams, Ray Stannard Baker, Lincoln Steffens, Ida Tarbell, George Kibbe Turner, and others—wrote much of what they wrote at his direction and were in turn responsible for much of the remedial and progressive legislation in the years before the War of 1914–1918.

In his time, McClure was accounted a genius. The word keeps bobbing up in the letters, conversations, and memoirs of his contemporaries. It is hung round his neck, as accolade or albatross, by quite different sorts of people—by Rudyard Kipling and Willa Cather, by William Allen White and Ida Tarbell, by Ellery Sedgwick and Will Irwin, by Ray Stannard Baker and Samuel Hopkins Adams, by the English critic William Archer and the American editor E. S. Martin, and by several others whose opinion deserves respect.

Was McClure in fact a genius? The term must be defined. Of the many definitions—lexicographical, inspirational, monitory, or otherwise informed

—the one I prefer is that composed by George Bernard Shaw: "A genius is a person who, seeing farther and probing deeper than other people, has a different set of ethical valuations from theirs, and has energy enough to give effect to this extra vision and its valuations in whatever manner bests suits his or her specific talents." I believe that McClure qualifies by this definition. The question, then, is why he has been so soon forgotten. There are, I dare say, three reasons.

The first is that what suited McClure's vision and energy was journalism, and nothing dies quicker than yesterday's newspaper or last month's magazine.

The second is that McClure was an editor. Critics and readers confer immortality, and they are more interested in authors than in editors. Their preference puzzles editors, who know authors to be greedy, vainglorious, selfish, thankless, difficult creatures; but the fact remains that authors are remembered while the editors who helped to win them immortality are forgotten.

The third and perhaps the most telling reason for McClure's oblivion is that he lived too long. If he had died at the height of his powers and his fame, say in 1910, some biographer would have early told his story and (it is to be hoped) set the record straight enough so that subsequent historians of the muckraking period would not have slighted him so grievously. In the event, McClure lived on and on and on, while his powers abated and his good name was crazed and his considerable contributions were demeaned.

What follows is a belated attempt to make restitution and to correct some of the errors. Acknowledgment for the considerable help given me is made at the end. I cannot begin, however, without thanking Eleanor McClure, oldest daughter and literary executrix of S. S. McClure, who made available to me all his private papers and who was consistently helpful, not least by giving me a free hand to tell the story of McClure's life as I saw fit. His may not have been the model success story of the moralist, but it is representative of success on the American scene.

CONTENTS

SUCCESS STORY

The Life and Times of S. S. McClure

TO BEGIN WITH

1857 - 1884

[1]

In a grove near the country village of Hebron, in the northwestern corner of Indiana, folks were gathering for a celebration. It was the Fourth of July, 1866, the nation's ninetieth birthday, and farmers were coming with their families from miles around.

From one wagon there tumbled a boy with bright blue eyes and a shock of fair hair. He stood, charged with excitement, his head thrust forward, looking eagerly about. Everything was new to him: the wildflowers at his feet, the clean-boled sycamores and tall tulip trees, the sweep of prairie rolling limitless beyond: everything was strange and wonderful. Sparklers and firecrackers were going off all around him, the first he had ever seen or heard; a breeze stirred the flags set by the speaker's stand, with their brave stripes and (here he counted) their thirty-seven stars; someone thrust a cup of something cool and sweet into his hand, lemonade, the first he had ever tasted. The wooden benches before the speaker's stand were filling now; the boy was obliged to sit. But it took an effort: he could scarcely contain himself. Nothing, not even a dull speech, could disenchant him.

The orator for the day was the Hon. David Turpie, a local politician who had served briefly as United States Senator. Turpie uttered all the sentiments appropriate to the circumstances. He spoke of freedom, of opportunity, of equality. In his audience there were some who, for the occasion, had climbed again into their dark blue uniforms, so recently discarded; and to these bearded men the orator's perfunctory phrases may have glowed with meaning. But to the boy so intently listening the speech was surely more significant. For Turpie, with florid strokes, was sketching the American dream, and the boy's heart pounded.

Nowhere in the United States, it may be conjectured, was there on this day a more likely aspirant to the achievement of the American dream. Ideally

3

such a candidate must be young, poor, orphaned, and immigrant. To him America traditionally offers wealth, power, and status incomparable. On every count the boy qualified. Young: he was only nine years old, and small for his age. Poor: he had not a cent, his feet were bare of shoes, and the coat on his back was homespun. True, his mother was still alive, but his father was dead nearly three years. Immigrant: this day, this Fourth of July, 1866, was his first full day in America. He thrilled as to the music of a band. He sensed that here was something big and free. His eyes shone.

This eager, excited boy was born in County Antrim, Ireland, in February, 1857, the first of four sons born to Thomas and Elizabeth Gaston McClure, and he was called Samuel, for his paternal grandfather. His father's people were Scottish Lowlanders from Galloway: they were in Ireland because a Protestant king of England had, after the Battle of the Boyne in 1690, encouraged Scottish Protestants to colonize Ulster by granting them farmland. His mother's people were French Huguenot: they had fled to Ireland after a Catholic king of France had revoked the Edict of Nantes in 1685. Six generations after these historical events, the McClures and the Gastons, like most Ulster Protestants, still married only other Protestants. The intensity of the religious passions that had brought them here had abated, but a consciousness of it still lay uneasily under the surface of their daily lives.

Both families, McClures and Gastons, were large—Thomas McClure was one of seven brothers, Elizabeth Gaston one of fourteen brothers and sisters—and both worked their small farms hard to make a living. When first they married, Thomas was working for his father as a carpenter, Elizabeth for her father as a farmhand, and every night after work Thomas would walk a mile up the road from McClure's to eat his supper and spend the night with his wife at Gaston's. Young Sam was born in his grandfather Gaston's house.

A year or so later the young couple were able to buy their own little farm and move into their own home: two rooms, a roof of thatch, stone walls, a floor of earth. It was a house no better and no worse than the houses of most of the poor all over Ireland.

Nor was their life more or less narrow and hard. For a living, there was the farm, nine acres, most of it planted in potatoes; and Sam's father was able to find work fairly often in the neighborhood, now building a house or a farm building, now a cart or a wagon, now doing some cabinet work. He was a gentle man, accounted by those who knew him to have been singularly sweet and patient, and anxious as well to better his lot. In the evenings he used sometimes to hire a tutor to come to his home and give him lessons.

Apart from toil, the McClures' chief concern was religion. Their only three books were The Bible, The Pilgrim's Progress, and Foxe's Book of Martyrs. Until 1859 they were church-going Presbyterians, but in that year an evangelical movement swept over Ulster; both Thomas and Elizabeth were converted, by salvation, to the new sect. Its members claimed no name for their sect; they were known simply as the Brethren. They were a joyless group, stern and exclusive, abjuring even the simplest forms of service, condemning such lighthearted pleasures as dancing or music,* and wholly persuaded that those who had not found their particular salvation were doomed to the eternal torments of a quite literal Hell. It was a faith to match their toilsome life.

Commonplace people, living out a commonplace existence. And yet it was presently clear that their first child was by no means commonplace. What set young Sam apart was his extraordinary curiosity—about everything. He wanted to know, not only what and why as do most children, but also who and when and where and how. His family's three books fascinated him; his inability to read them vexed him.

In consequence Sam was bundled off to the National School—the equivalent of an American public school—when he was only four years old. He found education in every way delightful. It was at school, he wrote later, that "I first felt myself a human entity." † Certainly his career at school was as remarkable as his intense curiosity.

School lasted six hours a day, fifty weeks of the year. Despite this awesome schedule, there was never a day when he did not want to go to school. Since he would rather read than eat, he regarded breakfast as a nuisance. His mother had to devise schemes to get food into him. The one egg a day the family could afford was soft-boiled for his father's breakfast, and Sam was given the bit of white in the top of the shell as an appetizer. But he could never curb his impatience. His eagerness to get to school was matched only

---

* Sam McClure's mother later told a grandchild, with a reminiscent twinkle in her eye, that she was properly grateful she had not been saved until after she was twenty-two.

† The quotation is from My Autobiography, by S. S. McClure. Actually, My Autobiography was written by Willa Cather, to whom McClure acknowledged his debt in a brief foreword. The book was, in a way, a collaboration: he talked, she listened, later she wrote. Such a method imposes its own limitations; My Autobiography is notable more for what it does not say than for what it says.

by his reluctance to go home at the end of the day. Saturday found him disconsolate, for it was a half-holiday.

Naturally Sam did well in his studies. By the time he was seven he had passed through every class to the highest in the school, where his classmates were big boys, fourteen and fifteen years old. Here, moreover, he stood at the head of his class in every subject, week after week. What to do with him at the end of his fourth school year must have posed a problem. But events intervened.

One November afternoon Sam and some other boys were headed home from school. They were a carefree group and Sam was even more cheerful than usual. He was thinking of his good record in school and of how pleased his father would be to hear of it. His father was in Glasgow. Work had been slow in the neighborhood and Thomas McClure had concluded he must earn money elsewhere. Some weeks before, he had walked away, down his hill and over the next, with his wife and boys standing looking after him, to find a job in the shipyards on the Clydeside. Now Sam, as he strolled along the road with his companions, thought of the letter he would write to his father after supper.

Just off the road there was a patch of sweet Swedish turnips. One boy looked at another: they were all hungry. They scrambled through the hedge and into the field and began to eat, laughing and chattering. A man passing along the road heard them and, peering through the hedge, called out:

"Samuel—"

The laughter quieted.

"Samuel, your da is deid."

Bewildered and fearful, refusing to understand what the man had told him, the boy hurried home. His mother was not there. She had gone to Glasgow when first word came of an accident: Thomas McClure had tumbled through a hatchway and fallen clear to the bottom of the hold. Both skull and spine were fractured. Neighbor women moved about the house tight-lipped, caring for Sam's younger brothers. For three days the boy waited; at length his mother came home, and with her was his father's body, in a coffin. Sam found it hard to understand that his father was gone, never to come back; that all there was to show who he had been was a paid-up union card in the Clyde Branch of the Associated Carpenters and Joiners of Scotland, a certificate of registration of death, a receipt for delivering from Glasgow to Belfast one corpse, and a memory of a gentle man with a brown beard.

The coffin lay in the living room unopened, and the neighbors came to pay their respects. Sam looked into his mother's face, and then he went out alone and sat by the side of the road. He wished that he might find just sixteen pennies there, lying in a row, so that he might take them up and bring them to his mother.

They had been poor before, but now they faced bitter poverty. For a year his mother struggled, trying to farm her nine acres and at the same time raise her four sons, but it was an impossible task; at length she sold the farm back to her father-in-law and took her children to live in her father's house.

Here Sam was treated to a gratuitous lesson in family charity. Night after night he sat in a corner, listening to an interminable debate conducted amongst well-meaning aunts and uncles and cousins as to what was to become of him and his brothers. Why not send Sam to his Aunt Meg's? Couldn't Mary take care of Tom and John for a while? The baby must stay with his mother, but she must agree to work as farmhand for her board and keep and that of her baby.

Antithetical and meddlesome the talk ran on, and Sam's mother bridled as she listened. She was, moreover, suspicious: she felt she had been cheated in the distribution of her father's estate. One day she decided to take her case to a lawyer in Clough, three miles away. Since at nine years he was now the man of the family, Sam went with her. The lawyer's advice was discouraging. Sam and his mother went from his office to the graveyard at Clough, where his father was buried; they sought out his grave, and there they sat down and wept.

After that it was only a matter of time until his mother decided to come to America. She had two brothers and two married sisters who had already settled in Indiana; surely they would help; and so she could keep her family together.

They sailed in June, 1866; a strong and determined young woman of twenty-nine and her four sons, who were nine, eight, six, and one; from Londonderry to Quebec by steerage, a twelve-day passage. It was a miserable journey. The whole family was seasick for the first few days and convalescent for the rest; but no matter, for there was the wondrous excitement of seeing the shores of a new land at the end of it, a land where they could forget their sorrows, a land of promises. At Quebec they clambered on a train especially appointed for immigrants: other passenger trains, even fast freights, racketed past while they lingered, hot and frustrated, on sidings. They were seven days from Quebec to Valparaiso. At length, vexed by the cost of food along the way and by the long delays, they climbed wearily into Joe Gaston's wagon at Valparaiso and drove the fourteen miles south to the farmhouse where they were to spend the night. They were, so to speak, home.

On the next day, they were taken to their first Fourth of July celebration.

And Sam McClure, nine years old, listened to the oration. Here, as it seemed to him, was a promissory note handed to bearer, endorsed, certified, and guaranteed. Nothing remained but to cash it in.

[II]

But even inspirational literature, a very indifferent teacher, tells us that the virtuous do not achieve success so easily.

A superficial account of young McClure's first few years in this country is, as it happens, closely akin to the preposterous tracts of Horatio Alger or Samuel Smiles. The poor boy, struggling alone against overwhelming adversity, his eyes fixed always on an admirable goal, with no resources save thrift, industry, pluck, and grit—this is the picture sketched in by the Alger books and, as far as it goes, it is also the picture of McClure's youth. But the hero of inspirational literature is never required by his author to pay the price of his struggles in loneliness, privation, and despair; for McClure the case was different.

At first there was homelessness.

Sam was lodged first with one aunt, then with another, then—along with his baby brother—unceremoniously dumped back in his mother's lap. By that time his mother was working in Valparaiso as a sleep-in servant, but she could not keep her job and her children too. The first night, after wandering unhappily about the town, she came upon a commercial building that was being repaired; here she and her children found an empty room and went to sleep, a forlorn family of squatters. Next day a friendly foreman let her rent a room in the same building for a dollar a week, and she hired herself out at seven dollars a week as a washwoman for four different families. When she was evicted from the business block, one of her employers gave her the use of a basement room in return for her doing the family's washing. But with winter this family moved away from Valparaiso, and she was obliged to take her children back to her sister's tiny farm. Her sister had six children of her own; even without the four McClure children the small farmhouse was crowded; tempers frayed; Elizabeth McClure grew desperate. A half mile away, on a farm of one hundred acres, there lived a bachelor named Thomas Simpson, like Elizabeth an immigrant from the north of Ireland. Marriages of convenience are not arranged only among the very rich. Early in 1867 Elizabeth McClure married Thomas Simpson, to give her children a home.

Then there was grueling hard work.

When Simpson asked Elizabeth McClure to marry him, he must have weighed in the balance the consideration that two of her sons—Sam and Jack—would become his chore boys while a third—Tom—would work for his brother. Certainly Sam and Jack worked hard for their stepfather. Morning and evening they mucked out the stable and cowshed; they cut and split ten logs a day; they planted and cultivated corn by hand. By the time Sam was eleven years old he was doing a hired man's work, and it was the same for the next three years. The summer when he was fourteen, haying was late, and the heavy work came in very hot weather. At the end of the day he would drop exhausted to the ground. Thin, worn, sick with dysentery, he only considered that he was lucky that his stepfather, who was a kind if stupid man, did not in addition whip him, as most boys in the neighborhood were whipped, to improve their character.

His mother's drudgery was even harsher. Besides all the cooking and housework, she also milked the six cows and made butter for the Chicago market, somehow finding time as well to bear four more children. But she had never forgotten her first-born's passion for learning, and that summer, as she watched his strength breaking under the load, her expression was grim. He had, as she knew, gone as far as he could in the small country school; indeed, he had done the work several times over. She remembered how, when he had first heard there was a kind of mathematics in which letters were used rather than numbers, he had scoured the countryside until he could find an algebra textbook, so that he might grasp the matter by himself. She recalled his growing impatience with the lack of something, anything, to read, in a house where there were only mail-order catalogues and agricultural reports. And so in September she called him aside and spoke to him privately. He would, she told him, have to make a break. A new high school was to open in Valparaiso in a week or so; she could give him no more than one dollar to speed him on his way; he would have to work for his bed and board; but he must get on with school. He agreed. He left the same day.

After the farm, wouldn't Valparaiso be paradise? So Sam thought, as he looked down on the white houses of the little town, in the late afternoon. Surely in one of those houses there was a man who needed a boy to do chores, except during school hours. Probably there were several such, but the first on whose door he knocked was Dr. Levi Cass.

This Cass was at the time the richest man for miles around. He owned several farms, let out to tenants, and he could reckon his fortune in six figures. He had not made this money without the ability to strike a hard bargain.

Young McClure was told he would be given a bed in the basement and his meals in the kitchen. In return, he would wake at five every morning except Monday, make fires in four stoves, take care of the cow and the horses, and do any necessary marketing before going to school. After school, in the afternoon, he would work on the grounds and do other chores until supper-time. After supper, he might study his lessons for the next day. On Monday, he would wake at one in the morning so that he might help the two daughters of the house with the week's wash. If he didn't accept this splendid offer he was a wicked, ungrateful boy who would come to a bad end in a poolroom somewhere. McClure, like any naïve Alger hero, promptly accepted.

His troubles began on his very first day at school. When the teacher asked each pupil to give his name, McClure discovered that every other boy present had, in addition to the usual first and last name, a middle name. On the spur, Samuel McClure scrabbled around amongst some possibilities from his more recent reading: there was a subscription history of the Civil War, in which surely the most dashing hero had been General Sherman. . . .

"And your name?"

"Samuel Sherman McClure," he answered.*

And when Professor McFetrich asked which of the courses of study—arithmetic, history, Latin, algebra, geography, German, geometry, English composition—he wanted to take, young McClure chose all of them. Which could he afford to ignore? He was, however, persuaded to compromise on a sensible curriculum.

McClure had committed the schoolboy's unpardonable sin: he had revealed that he actually wanted to be taught. To make matters worse, he spoke with an outlandish accent; hence, he was a freak. Since he was small,

---

*Later McClure capriciously changed his middle name to Sidney. In any event, he was S. S. McClure from that first day in the Valparaiso High School, and so he signed his name everywhere, even in his schoolbooks.

he at once became the butt of every bully in the school and his hours at school became a time of torment.

Away from school, his hours were even bleaker. Cass considered labor to be a great character-builder, especially when he was not obliged to pay for it; he worked young McClure so hard that the boy had no time to find a friend. Sam's dollar was soon spent, nor could he find time to earn another; and so there was never a penny for clothes, much less for books. An Indiana winter can be severe, but he had no overcoat. "Speed," he wryly said later, "was my overcoat." Now, to the sense of homelessness and the endless routine of chores, there was added a helpless loneliness. At night, in his cellar room, he used to wake up and cry bitterly as he thought of his thatch-roofed home in Ireland and of his dead father.

Christmas fell on a Monday that year and, for a wonder, Sam was permitted to go away, on Christmas Eve, to visit his uncle, James Gaston, who was then living four miles north of the town. It was Sam's first holiday in years. When he overstayed his time, not to return till the following Monday, Dr. Cass kept the door locked in his face. But this was a stroke of luck, for he soon found a place with a family named Kellogg, and these good people truly tried to make a home for the boy. Theirs was, moreover, as he gratefully recalled it later, "a place with only one cow and one stove."

By that time, however, it made little difference where he lived, whether with kindly people or harsh, for young McClure was a bundle of tensions, keyed up, impetuous, impatient, impulsive. He was easily upset, and as easily plunged into fits of gloom; when this happened, he was irresistibly driven to the same way of allaying his tensions: he would run away.

This impulsive running away was overmastering; it was a pattern in his life; it was, indeed, as he said, "a necessity of my life. I could do without a bed, without an overcoat, could go for twenty-four hours without food; but I had to break away and go when I wanted to." It was not something that he did just once or twice; he ran away dozens and dozens of times, for a day, for two days, for a week, or for just a few hours. The tug of tension—he thought of it simply as restlessness—would pull him down to the railroad station, where he would hop the first freight train out of town. Freight cars in those days had at either end a small platform about a foot wide, where the brake-rod came down. Here he would crouch, a thin wiry boy with bright anxious eyes, his cap pulled down over his fair hair and a woolen scarf wound tight around his neck; and here he would ride for long hours at a time, or until the uncomprehended fit of despondency might abate.

Such erratic behavior could scarcely pass unnoticed. It won young McClure a reputation of being unstable and inconsequential; and this opinion of his character was reinforced by his cavalier attitude toward the jobs he took, whenever the chance was presented. One summer he engaged to teach a country school for three months, but he couldn't stick it for the third month. He clerked in a grocery store—for two months. He deviled for the printers of The Valparaiso Vidette—for two months. He tried his hand as a butcher, as a laborer in a railroad section gang, as a worker in an iron foundry; but he stuck to none of these jobs. The only anchor that kept him from drifting utterly aimless was his insistence on getting an education. In the fall of 1873, a year of financial panic and hard times, it seemed that even this passion would not avail; he was obliged to forgo school in order to earn a living; he even seriously considered hitting the road as a tramp. But once again events intervened.

A message came: he was to come back to the farm at once, for his step-father was dying of typhoid fever. Simpson left his farm to his widow and the one of their four children who survived him; since Sam was the oldest son, once again the man of the family, he had no choice but to stay and work the farm.

The three older brothers—Sam was sixteen, John fifteen, and Tom thirteen—thereupon undertook to do what Simpson had never been able to do: run the farm profitably enough to clear it of debt. It was one thing to be a stepfather's chore boy; it was quite another to turn up one's sleeves and run the whole shebang one's self. The brothers were understandably proud when, in the summer of 1874, they raised and harvested a bigger crop than had ever been produced on that farm. Sam had never worked harder nor with greater satisfaction. But still in the back of his mind lay the hunger to know more.

Late that summer the three brothers were working under a hot sun in the hayfield when they saw coming toward them a man they recognized as their Uncle Joe Gaston, whom they had not seen for years. He had gone off, they recalled vaguely, to study for the ministry at a college somewhere in Illinois; was it called Knox?

The three boys made their uncle welcome. Leaning on their pitchforks, they chatted with him. Sam eyed him enviously: here was a man who was studying in a college—Latin and Greek surely, perhaps even Hebrew. Sam asked Gaston about Knox, about studies at the college; but even before he heard the answers his mind was made up. He had to go to Knox, too.

His mother, remembering the boy of four who had trudged off down the hedged Irish lane on his way to school, smiled and agreed and set about making him a suit of clothes.

In September Sam left for Galesburg. He had eight dollars for his train fare and a heavy black oilcloth satchel filled with books and a few shirts and socks. His suit—he was wearing the only one he owned—embarrassed him painfully: the trousers were too wide at the cuff and too short to cover his cowhide boots. But he could have spared himself his embarrassment. In 1874, when a country boy went to college, he rarely had an Ivy League look.

Young McClure, as he surveyed the campus of Knox, found it sweet-smelling and fresh after a rain. He had only fifteen cents but this consideration, to a youngster who had known the bitterness of going for months without a penny, was trivial. Nor was he dismayed by the prospect of having to qualify for college by first studying three years at the Knox Academy. When one is seventeen, seven years does not seem a high price to pay for a good education.

The college buildings were before him, brick and ivied: here he would learn Latin and Greek. Once, he recalled, in Ireland, at a public house in Ballymena, he had seen a young priest bent over a book; with his characteristic lack of self-consciousness Sam had craned over the priest's shoulder, curious to know what should so interest another reader. The letters were recognizable, but they spelled no sense. "It is Latin," the priest explained. The word had been strange, but not the resolution to master it. The resolution was still fixed and now here was the moment.

The first installment on the promissory note was about to be paid.

[III]

Young McClure left his mark on the Knox College of his time. His contemporaries were aware that he was among them; indeed, they were hard put to ignore him.

"I have never seen," said one classmate, not entirely with admiration, "so much enthusiasm and life in such a small carcass." Another said, after reflection: "You can't help but like him, as he means well, and is a goodhearted

Irishman. We have never quarreled, for you can't quarrel with him, but I must own I've lost my respect for him." This disenchantment had come about over a disagreement about money. McClure, his classmate thought, lacked reverence for money, and one of his teachers was heard to murmur that he had not a just sense of debt and money matters: "It is constitutional, and he can't help it. All the Irish are so." Another professor thought him "conceited, impertinent, and meddlesome." Still another was awed by him; he seemed a volcano: "I every moment anticipate the volcano will send forth a stream of words. My anticipation is realized." A fourth remarked, "He is a genius—or would be, if he could stick to one thing." And a friend commanded: "Be *idle* once in a while! You will be all worn out and old before you are thirty-five."

But for some youngsters idleness is difficult. "I feel like a chained tiger," McClure wrote, and "I fret against my chains." He had no slightest glimpse of his destiny but whatever it was he was impatient to be at it. "The key to my character," he wrote, is that "if I want anything & there is *hope* to get it, I *can't help try*ing." In his sophomore year, he chose Enthusiasm as his theme for the class essay contest. "The essence of this principle," he wrote, "is intense desire. Under its influence, men overcome opposition that would otherwise be insuperable." As copy-book maxims, these statements cannot be faulted, and the temptation is to set them aside as the routine expressions of an ambitious and overly earnest youth. But as it happens they also stand as remarkable examples of insight. In his years at Knox he found something he desired intensely. His chances of getting it were bleak indeed, yet there was hope, and so he never ceased from trying. And more than anything else, it was his efforts to overcome his almost insuperable opposition that enabled him to leave his mark.

To those familiar with college life today, the Knox of eighty years ago would seem very odd indeed. Apparently one's only reason for enrolling was to get an education; in such pinched circumstances, the only way to win recognition, it would seem, was in scholarship. The campus hero was not the captain of the football team, for there was no football, nor any other sport, intercollegiate or intramural; not the president of the interfraternity council, for there were no fraternities; not the chairman of the prom committee, for there was no organized social life—no glee club, no theatricals, almost no extracurricular life whatever. To be sure, there was an undergraduate publication, The Knox Student, but it was forbiddingly literary; and there was the Adelphi Society, the severely intellectual sponsor of Knox's sole concession to intercollegiate rivalry, the Inter-State Oratorical Contest; * but in general this hopelessly backward institution offered its students only the search for knowledge as its own end, and the campus hero was the valedictorian of the graduating class.

Fortunately, in this state of affairs, the faculty included some remarkably able teachers. Professor George Churchill, who had charge of the preparatory school, was one; it was his task to mold a farmboy into a scholar. Professor Milton Comstock, the head of the department of mathematics, was another; he rejoiced in a beard to rival Father Time's. But perhaps the strongest man on the Knox faculty—its outstanding scholar, and probably one of the finest natural teachers in the country at the time—was Professor Albert Hurd. Since he taught Latin (as well as most of the natural sciences), Hurd was tagged by his students with the inevitable nickname, "the noblest Roman of them all"; but in his case the epithet was strikingly appropriate: he was a tall man, remindful of a Roman senator, clean-shaven, with a classic profile and a distant, chilly, marble manner. If his appearance was august, he knew how to use it: when taking recitations he sat always in profile, in the manner of Whistler's Carlyle. He affected a long black Prince Albert and a strict black ribbon of a bow tie. His great-grandmother, Barbara Heck, has been called the founder of American Methodism and, after seeing Hurd, after talking with him, diligent, simple, dedicated, clean-cut in his living as in his speech, the thing could be believed.

Under such men McClure studied in single-minded absorption. Beyond the brick walls that circumscribed his immediate concern, the nation was wracked with one severe crisis after another: an American President was fraudulently admitted to the White House; the national economy was plunged into a harsh depression; the prices of wheat, corn, and cotton fell sharply; workingmen, sorely tried, went out on strike and were bloodily repressed by Federal troops at a cost of death for dozens; there were violent riots, especially in Pittsburgh, where nearly ten million dollars' worth of property, including one hundred and twenty-six railroad locomotives, was destroyed; Andrew Carnegie and John D. Rockefeller were successfully designing the most enormous of the industrial trusts, and ruthlessly trampling out their competition in the logic of their process; the desperate legions of

---

* Over the years some youngsters on the threshold of tolerably illustrious careers won the Inter-State Contest. There were, for example, the elder Robert La Follette, Albert Beveridge, and Otto Harbach, the composer. In his year, however, the Boy Orator of the Platte, William Jennings Bryan, had to be content with second prize; he was beaten by one of McClure's former classmates.

Populism, of Greenbackery, of Grangerism and Free Silver were closing their ranks to do battle; in San Francisco, the angry Henry George was setting down the angry words of Progress and Poverty: "The gulf between the employed and the employer is growing wider; social contrasts are becoming sharper; as liveried carriages appear, so do barefooted children." At every hand there thrived political and commercial chicanery, lawlessness, jobbery, and graft. Since these facts were of the kind in which McClure would later be so surpassingly interested, it is the more remarkable that at the time he ignored them totally. "In seven years," he said later, "I scarcely read a newspaper."

His studies engaged his attention as they had always done; he would often assign himself trivial auxiliary tasks like reading every volume in the small Galesburg library, or assembling an etymological dictionary based on his translations of Homer. And he did well. When he graduated, with the class of 1882, he was an honor student, having failed by only a fraction of being the class valedictorian.* And yet it was not, after all, because of his scholastic excellence that he came to be well known at Knox. It was because he tumbled into love.

Quite probably McClure fell in love several times before at length it took, for he was starved for affection. He needed the warmth of someone's—anyone's—regard as direly as he needed food or drink. When, for example, he was nineteen and in his second year at the Knox preparatory school, he was boarding at the home of the Reverend M. L. Williston, Galesburg's Congregational minister. Louise Williston, his wife, was an unusually sympathetic woman of about thirty, and McClure, in his need, promptly fell in love with her. He was lucky.

"I believe," Louise Williston confided to a friend, "I used the most conscientious faithfulness in trying to chill and drive him from me, at first." But "the pangs he suffered were so genuine and great, I forbore in mercy. It was no use—he *belonged to me.*" She chose to believe that what he sought was a mother, but he made it difficult for her. "Sam had," she said, "a powerful effect on me. Proud as I am, reared in the most rigid aristocracy New England maintains, I am forced to own that I accepted from that boy what I have never taken from *anyone* before—vitality and help in that way. He could not pass my door but I felt the influence, nor sit in my room but,

---

* There was no chapter of Phi Beta Kappa at Knox in those years. When one was later organized, McClure was elected to it.

if I chose, I could draw from his vigor, and after I found how he cared for me I was willing to take it, and almost lived on its strength."

Such a Candida-Marchbanks relationship was bound to fall of its own weight, but on a morning in May of 1876, unwittingly, Louise Williston brought it to an end. What she did was to send McClure to invite a guest, a young girl, for luncheon. McClure first saw the girl standing on her porch, with an armful of flowers from her garden. She was very slender, with clear blue eyes and a look of serenity. In such a small town, how was it possible he had never seen her before? At luncheon he sat next to her, and he was lost. Mrs. Williston noticed and, as soon as she could snatch the chance, gave him some hurried advice. "Don't cry for the moon, Sam," she whispered. But it was too late. He had fallen again, and this time into a love affair that captured the imagination of both town and gown and would, before it was settled, occupy the time and attention of scores of curious gossips and correspondents all over the Midwest and even into Canada. Only in the sense that it was never the subject of newspaper comment could this concern be considered private; otherwise it was as public, and quite as fascinating, as the weather.

The affair was, from the outset, preposterous. She was Harriet Hurd, the older of Professor Hurd's two daughters, regarded by all who knew her as the most beautiful and gifted girl in town, gently nurtured, brilliantly responsive to her father's special efforts toward her education, a girl whose future was warm with promise. And he—he was an Irish immigrant, poor, unstable, with a future at best uncertain. As to his family, his mother had sold the farm and had come to visit in Galesburg, and even his good friend Louise Williston had found her difficult, a woman whose theology she described as "hideous." He had nothing to offer except his vitality, which was boundless. It was enough. After luncheon he offered Hattie his small autograph book. They looked at each other. She took his pen and wrote: "Proverbs XXII, 29. Hattie Hurd." McClure knew his Bible well enough to recognize the verse: "Seest thou a man diligent in his business? he shall stand before kings; he shall not stand before mean men."

They met again, and then again, at "sociables." His mother saw what was happening, and her mouth closed in a hard, thin line. No matter: on May 30 young McClure presented himself at the Hurd house for the awful ordeal of meeting Hattie's family and thereafter taking her away for their first formal date. He had for her a handful of wild flowers that he had gathered in the fields. He was painfully shy and strangely silent; he made a poor impression. Again, no matter: for they had a precious hour alone together and, although nothing ritual was said on either side, each was satisfied the matter was settled. There was love: a few ceremonial conventions would have to be observed: there would be marriage. He was ready to shout it from the housetops; although she was more sensibly restrained, she was as deeply moved.

But there were, in each case, affectionate parents. They were wholly unlike (to the satisfaction of each) but they were agreed that this budding affair was unthinkable. McClure's mother was the first to act: she proposed a trip back to Ireland, to be paid for from the proceeds of the sale of the farm. The bait, to a footloose boy, was irresistible; accordingly, early in June, and taking advantage of the special railroad rates, mother and son traveled from Chicago to Philadelphia (for eleven dollars), took in the Exposition of 1876, and then sailed for Ireland.

"Nineteen is a fine age, and Ireland is a fine country," McClure wrote, of the first day of his return after ten years. "It was a beautiful day late in June, with brilliant sunshine and a sky intensely blue, and everywhere the wonderful green of Ireland, like no other green in the world . . . the cleanness of the grass, washed by so many rains . . . the look of neatness and tidiness that I had always missed in Indiana and Illinois. The white houses, plastered and graveled outside and then whitewashed, glistened in the sunshine, and the rose bushes were everywhere in bloom about the doors . . . the rich green of the boxwood hedges about the gardens, and the dark laurel bushes that I had always loved when I lived among them . . ."

All this was powerful magic and presently, cooking an even stronger brew, his mother told him she planned to leave him to make his living amongst his relatives and neighbors, while she sailed back to America without him. This was a decision, flat and final, and, since she held the purse-strings, and since he was nearly four thousand miles from Galesburg and Hattie Hurd, that, she considered, was that. As well lead a stallion about with a silk ribbon. McClure reacted to his mother's fiat characteristically by running away. For two weeks he was gone on a long tramp along the North Channel from Larne as far as the Giant's Causeway, always keeping the water in sight, always puzzling how he was going to get back across it. Gradually his spirits revived. The solution had come to him, and it was so simple he wondered that he had ever worried. Of course: he would stow away back to America: as easy as that.

In Liverpool McClure found lying at dock the same steamer on which he had come over six weeks before. Confidently he marched aboard her, approached the baker and some stewards, and in all candor told them what he meant to do. They eyed him, doubtless wondering from what booby-hatch he had escaped, and at length nodded gravely. He would, they agreed, have no trouble at all. It never occurred to him that they were not taking him seriously. "Credulity," he admitted later, "was my native virtue."

After he had made himself thoroughly conspicuous for a day or two, he was summoned by the ship's first officer, who had tired of the fun, and ordered off the ship. In despair, McClure retreated to the dock. Presently the gods who have in charge innocent folly inspired him to get a bit of paper and a pencil and thereafter coached him as he composed one great whopper after another in a long letter to the first officer. The words flowed, and it seemed to their author that he was writing nothing but lean, hard truth. Indeed, when his need was great enough, McClure never in his life considered that what he was saying was not so. There are men who respect the truth so much that they rarely use it, but he was not one of them. McClure would never descend to deceit to achieve what he wanted; but, when his desire was imperative enough, he had the happy faculty of identifying what he said with truth. He was absolutely obliged, he wrote the first officer, to get back to America; he was, he wrote, well launched on a program of education designed to make of him a physician; after medical school in America, it would be back to Ireland to care for the needy; between his lines could be read the splendid altruism of an idealist, a servant of his fellow man, a selfless visionary. Having got a seaman to hand his letter to the first officer, McClure resigned himself to the inevitable.

But he underestimated his inspiration. He was summoned on board and given a berth as assistant to the ship's doctor. Moreover, since the ship was twenty-four hours at sea before the doctor could discover his utter inadequacy, his passage was assured. He had to work for it—swabbing out corridors, polishing brass, serving as mess boy for the officers' mess, and baking fifty pies a day—but once again his native enthusiasm lightened his load. He fancied himself a master baker and actually began to look forward to his daily stint. Making good pastry wasn't drudgery, he decided, but a skill worthy of a craftsman.*

* McClure delighted, years afterward, to recall this experience. In 1919 he was crossing the Atlantic again, this time on the Leviathan, and he bragged to her skipper of his skill. The skipper made inquiries of the first-class passengers as to their preferences and presently ad-

Back in Galesburg, he went straight to Hattie Hurd's house. And now see what love can do to logic:

McClure was not yet twenty years old; he had not a cent in his pockets, for his last dollar he had given to a student committee soliciting contributions toward the building of a new gymnasium; he had still a year to go in the preparatory school before he would be a freshman. Hattie was not yet twenty-one, but she was beginning her senior year at Knox, after which, presumably, she would be free to do with her life as she wished. They had seen each other six times in all; they had spent only an hour alone together. Oblivious, impetuous, hungry with need, he poured out his heart and asked her if she would wait seven years and then marry him. She was overwhelmed. She said she would.

Professor Hurd was less of a romantic. It is likely that in principle he was as proud as any man of the tradition that in America class barriers are not opposed to the ambitious youth, but for Hurd the case altered when the ambitious youth proposed to illustrate the tradition by marrying his daughter. Indeed, the very idea of his daughter's marriage rarely crept into Hurd's daydreams, and then never as a welcome guest. When Hattie was only eleven she was already making the charts he used in his geology lectures and classifying the fossil crinoids he found for the Knox museum; college Latin and Greek were familiar stuff to her by the time she was thirteen. "I confess," Hurd told her, "to the charge of being ambitious for you." He saw her as a maiden teacher, dedicated, like himself, to scholarship and culture.

"How can a sane person look at life in such a way?" Hattie exploded to McClure. "It just assumes that I have no capacity for affection, no love of home—that I am hardly a woman at all!"

Since Hurd's plans for her obviously distressed her, he forced himself to consider the distasteful alternative of her marriage. Meticulously he set down for her his specifications for the right man. "Character," he wrote, "is, of course, the first, the most important matter to be regarded. A man of integrity and rectitude based upon religion is the only man who can be unreservedly trusted. But a fitness in other particulars is necessary to happiness. A husband capable of making *you* happy should be a good man, an intelligent man, a man of some education & the more the better, and a man *who can support you.* . . . Beware of any *serious* entanglements with gentle-

---

dressed a memorandum to "Mr. S. S. McClure, Baker Extraordinary," challenging him to bake thirty-seven pies to order—twenty-four apple and thirteen mince. Bake them he did. And they were good, too.

men until you know that you can *prudently* venture to marry, should you have a chance to do so."

Any dutiful daughter, Hurd hoped, would realize that McClure fell so wide and short of this ideal that she might forever erase him from her mind. Lest there be any doubt, Hurd made clear that his opposition to her engagement was total. Any meetings, even any correspondence, with McClure would incur his withering disapproval. This was a decision, flat and final, and since he held the purse-strings, and since in the Hurd household of 1876 it was Hurd alone who presumed to lay down the law, that, he considered, was that.

And so the lovers entered upon a winter of that sweet anguish that has always afflicted star-crossed romantics. In her family's parlor, Hattie wrote McClure furtive notes, concealed under long, seemly letters to maiden cousins. In his dormitory room—he lived, that year, in a cramped tunnel of a building called the Bricks, only one story high and one room wide, so that the freezing Illinois weather could reach him impartially through floor, ceiling, and both outside walls—McClure tried to concentrate on his studies. It was hard work. Apprehensive about her father's unfriendly pressure, resentful over his mother's continued interference, he got stubborn: he refused even to take care of his own health. He would go to bed supperless rather than seek out chores to earn his keep. His studies were of some help. He was able to lose himself in Virgil's Aeneid, for example, perceiving as do precious few schoolboys that here was a tale of romantic love and stirring adventure. But his food was wretched and his room was fearfully cold. Night after night the pail of water he kept to wash with froze solid. Hattie knew of this, and when, on her twenty-first birthday, her father gave her five dollars, she gave it to McClure so that he might buy coal to burn in his fireplace. There was a solemn, rabbity divinity student, equally poor, who shared his room for a time. One Sunday during that bleak winter, when the two youngsters had only cold cornmeal mush for their dinner, the prospective clergyman shuddered. "O Lord," he said, through chattering teeth, "bless, we pray thee, this miserable food to our perishing bodies."

But spring came, and May evenings when, forbidden or not, lovers could snatch a few moments together in the warm darkness. After an embrace they would stare at each other hopelessly. What were they to do? Her father's hostility was implacable and her mother was scarcely more sympathetic. *His* mother, again a visitor in Galesburg, was equally determined that Sam should not marry. Even their friend Louise Williston counseled them to break it off for a year or two. In the face of this unanimous disapproval McClure was as incoherent and contradictory as have been many before him and many since. He began one letter to Hattie at noon: "I have been so miserable and sad. . . . My love is a living agony. . . . My own angel I am afraid that out of sympathy for me you are sinking your own self & sacrificing yourself on the altar of *my* love. Are you? Oh! Hattie tell me tell me & then let me go and die. . . . My life is at your feet. . . . Oh God! perhaps even now you are deciding to break the engagement. Hattie Hattie the thought kills me. . . ." By six in the evening he had found no comfort: "It seems as if you always lose sight of yourself & think only of me. . . ." And by nine the next morning, still adding to the same letter: "Tonight we'll break the engagement." He added: "Tomorrow I start for the West. I leave forever. Hattie if you love me as you say you do & as you wish to I won't go. We won't break the engagement." (All this was crossed out, but very lightly.) Then he went on: "Hattie this is goodby forever. God knows how terribly I suffer. . . . Oh Hattie why are you so unselfish so godlike as to break your heart to save mine?"

And so their engagement was broken, but it was still May when they patched it up again. "My own dearest Sam," Hattie wrote to him, "I know you fear that I will change again, but I tell you that you may put all your trust in me now, and I will never change again. . . . I tried hard to change, for I felt that I must, but I couldn't keep my word when I broke the engagement, and every time I tried it almost took my life. . . . You don't know how sick and worn out I am. But I'll never try it again. It is treason. . . . But it has been bitterly hard for me, for I loved you all the time. I tried to think I didn't, but when you would go, how I cried! . . . I tell you solemnly, I can never change."

And the next day, the anniversary of his first call at her house, she assured him again: "I can't bear to think what reason you have to doubt me. But I can *never* break the engagement again."

If she couldn't, her father could. Her commencement exercises were approaching; she was to be valedictorian, having achieved the highest marks in her course of study of any Knox undergraduate until her time. Her father waited, watchful. On the eve of commencement, she wrote another note to McClure: "Tomorrow is the dreadful day. If you'll send me a little bunch of pansies, only a *few, mind,* I'll be delighted to wear them. . . ."

McClure brought them in person. Hurd, always a frank man, was even chillier than usual. Nor was anyone else present more cordial. McClure proffered Hattie his handful of pansies and fled.

And then, in a torment of misery, he went back to his room in the Bricks and plunged into a fever of work. To no end: the school year was over. But he had one of his self-appointed tasks, the etymological dictionary, and into it he poured his bitterness. He would not eat. He pulled his mattress from its springs, tossed it on the bare floor, lay on it, and, day after day, pored over Greek and Latin dictionaries. Day after day he got weaker. Somebody saw him and told what he had seen. And so, presently, there came Mr. Bangs, a prissy little man whose wife was principal of the girls' seminary, a man at whom all the Knox students used to jeer, a man with a sense of fraternity for the woebegone. Bangs took one look, summoned a buggy, and hauled McClure off to the seminary, where he was put in an empty bedroom and cared for. For several days he could eat nothing but milk toast.

"And so you are sick!" Hattie exclaimed, in a letter she wrote early in July. "Ah, I am so sorry! If I could only do something for you! But I don't even know how you are. . . . I must see you before you go, although I am under promise as to what I shall say. If I hadn't promised I couldn't see you at all. . . . I will see you this once, Sam, I must do that, but not again. And you mustn't write to me or expect to hear from me, as long as I am dependent on my father. If I should bring his displeasure on me it would kill me. Oh, Sam, it is very hard to bear, but look constantly to God, and keep a brave, cheerful heart. . . . Be a very good boy, and *take care* of yourself. The next time we meet, it will be for good-bye. Oh! Sam, I am so sorry!"

When he could walk, he called at her house. She met him at the door in tears. Her father, she told him, was sending her away to graduate school: she was bound not to tell him where, she was bound never to see him again, she was bound never to write to him again.

And so he said good-by and turned around and walked away down the path.

[IV]

In the study of Roman history, one may encounter the phrase novus homo, a new man. It was used to describe the first man of a family to rise to the rank of senator, or praetor, or any other dignitary who by custom was permitted to sit on the curved, backless chair called a curule. In ancient Rome the phrase, as well, came to mean a man with pretensions above his station, an upstart. As soon as young McClure came upon the phrase, he wryly appropriated it for himself. It seemed to fit: a new man, an immigrant who presumed to be the equal of his fellows, a man who—McClure may well have thought—would one day make his detractors eat their words.

A novus homo also makes a fresh start, and so, after taking his painful leave of Harriet Hurd, McClure went back to the Bricks and packed his books and his clothes in a box. He was nailing it shut when his uncle Joe Gaston came into the room. Like Hattie, Gaston had just graduated; he planned to go on to a theological seminary in Chicago. McClure told him that he was quitting Knox, that he meant instead to go to Oberlin, that he could not imagine sitting in Professor Hurd's classes, that he wanted to be far from Galesburg and all its associations. Gaston grinned and took the hammer from McClure's hand. "Stay at Knox," he said, prizing off the lid of the box. "Stick to it. Make it hot for 'em." And he set McClure's books back on their shelf.

It was sensible advice. By then McClure was well enough known in Galesburg to be able to pick up jobs whenever he needed them, and well enough known, too, to the college authorities to sign notes for his tuition. (A year's tuition, it might be noted, cost forty-five dollars.) And the college could give him work as well: he was variously an instructor in algebra, the janitor for the college gymnasium, and an instructor in zoology; one year he and a brother cleared all their expenses by organizing and operating a second-hand bookstore. McClure never needed much money. In his freshman year, for example, he found that he was able to live adequately by buying his own food and cooking his own meals in his dormitory room. Expenses ranged from eighteen to seventy-four cents a week. (In those days, of course, a dollar was a fairly important sum of money.) And with Harriet Hurd out of town he was far less distracted and far more prudent in providing for himself.

In the summertime McClure worked to earn the money needed to meet his year's expenses. Since those years (1877–1882) were years of hard times, he did well enough. Only once was he obliged to take a year off from his college course: that year he taught school near Valparaiso at his mother's urgent behest; he stuck at the job until the first warm days of spring and then he deserted his small pupils without a qualm. By that time, he had hit upon a way of making money that was compatible with his footloose nature. He had become a peddler.

Once again his native enthusiasm pointed the way. Mr. Bangs, the finical fussbudget who had cared about McClure's welfare, was also a man of an inventive turn of mind. He had waved his wand and lo! he had created a coffee condenser. It was "a simple affair, so constructed that the coffee could be kept or boiled any length of time without losing its aroma." It could also be duplicated, apparently, by any smith at a hardware shop; whether or not Mr. Bangs, in those innocent days, had letters patent covering his invention was beside the point, for he had contrived a small die with which any moron could stamp PATENTED on each duplicate. The price was right, and McClure, when the idea was presented to him, glowed hot. He envisioned a coffee-condenser empire. He got Bangs to give him the general agency for Indiana, Ohio, and western New York; he would, as he saw it, commission sub-agents from the big high-school population at Valparaiso; with a sub-agent in every county and a factory established at Indianapolis (or Cleveland, or Cincinnati), a man could be wearing diamonds in no time. McClure vowed to pay Bangs a toothsome royalty, and took off into the hinterland.

The scheme had a flaw. Everybody who drank coffee already had a coffee-pot, and everybody who had a coffee-pot preferred his own, for this was before the days of modern advertising. But one thing led to another. After signally failing to sell the coffee-pot from Galesburg to Chicago to Valparaiso and northeast into Michigan, at length in New Buffalo McClure noticed a pair of pitchmen peddling lampwicks, pins, cheap hosiery, and handkerchiefs. He watched them for a time and then ventured one dollar's capital on a representative stock of their items. Since he and his brother, by working house to house for an hour or so, were able to make that one dollar grow into two, he was hooked. He was in a new business.

McClure reinvested his capital, now doubled, and at the same time got the address of the home office, a company in Chicago that consigned notions wholesale. He ordered from this firm five dollars' worth of gimcracks, paid for them C.O.D., and sold them for fifteen. Clearly this was better than work. For one thing, he could go wherever and whenever he listed, and at whatever pace, like the casual butterfly; he could pick up his business or drop it at a shrug of his shoulder. Should the burden of his tensions—what he called his "restlessness"—come upon him, he had only to pick up his pack of notions and be off, and he would even make money out of his troubled wandering. Then too, there was always the excitement of meeting new people, of talking to them, of finding out what made them tick, what interested them, what they liked to talk about—the people who lived in small towns and along winding, rutted country lanes, the people for whom an itinerant young peddler was a welcome change, a distraction.

In this fashion, sometimes on foot, sometimes with a horse and wagon, sometimes hitching a ride on a convenient freight train, sometimes on a Mississippi packet, he crossed and crisscrossed the Midwest again and again, from Ohio down to Missouri and up to Minnesota, soaking up its folkways, jawing with its people, learning its small towns, always eager, always with questing enthusiasm. Occasionally he was able to persuade a Knox classmate to go with him. One summer he sold microscopes, scarcely instruments of scientific value: cost to him at wholesale, twenty-five cents; retail price for the wide-eyed customer, one dollar. That summer his companion was his roommate, a slender, reedy boy from Davenport, Iowa, named Albert Brady, with whom he had struck up a close friendship. Brady soon showed McClure his business mettle. When the partners found that in such Minnesota cities as Brainerd and Duluth the police practice was to exact from street peddlers an exorbitant fee for a license, Brady promptly solved the problem by renting, for fifty cents, a vacant lot in the downtown business district where they might set up their pitch. Now no policeman could terrify them with demands to see their license; they were selling their dubious wares on their own rented property. If they were subject to taxes, they told a judge politely, they would be delighted to pay—at the end of the year. The judge grinned appreciatively and dismissed them.

Good times: sleeping in sweet-scented hayricks, joking about the size of Mississippi River mosquitoes (McClure tried to bottle one, he reported in a diary, so that he might "cart or freight it to Galesburg for the Knox Museum; but having nothing but a pint bottle for the purpose, we found the project impossible; the mosquitoes were too large"), broiling steaks on green sticks at campfires in hickory groves, traveling free and easy.

But always Harriet Hurd was at the back of his mind. Her friends had argued that he was inconstant, and surely there was evidence to back up the charge; but they failed to take into account his pertinacity, always particularly provoked by opposition. The fact was that the antagonism of Professor Hurd and of his mother had nourished his love for Hattie. "My feeling for her," he was to recall, "became a despairing obsession, as fixed as my longing to get an education had been." In short, he had got his Irish up. Every week of his freshman, sophomore, and junior years he read the society column of The Galesburg Register, fearful lest there might appear an announcement of Hattie's marriage to a lucky someone, somewhere. Late in his freshman year he overheard a snatch of conversation: a friend asked Professor Hurd where Harriet was, and Hurd answered that she was studying French at a school in Berthier, in Canada. McClure rushed to an atlas. Sure enough, there it was: on the St. Lawrence, north of Montreal. At once he wrote her a letter. She got it, but she was faithful to her promise; she never answered it.

He sent her another letter, in code, the year he dropped out of Knox to teach school, for he was worried that she might return and wonder where he had gone. In the spring of that year, a rumor reached him in Indiana that she had come back to Galesburg; at once he was off, two hundred miles by wagon road, to find if he could see her. She was there, her mother told him, but she did not wish to see him again, then or ever. That was final enough. He wrote her a note.

> Miss Hattie Hurd:
>   It now seems to me that the only honorable & advisable course is for me to free you formally from the engagement. This may seem useless but it is my earnest desire to undo all that may have been done un-wisely.
>   I also return your photograph. I can forget you more easily without it.
>   While in Ann Arbor I purchased Lord Derby's "Homer" expressly for you & saved it all year for you. I can't look at it now. *May* I give it to you?
>   Yours respectfully,
>   S S McClure

And then in September of his senior year he caught a glimpse of a girl. He was sure it was she although he hadn't seen her in more than four years. She was crossing the campus, some distance away. He ran to over-take her. When he was at her side he was out of breath and for a few mo-ments could only look at her, gasping. He was afraid, he said at last, that she was under some misapprehension about him. She was her serene, pleas-ant, friendly self, as if she had seen him only the day before. Misapprehen-sion? She knew of none. She felt that things had never changed between them. Unbelieving, he asked if he might call on her that evening. They met in the small, crowded parlor of the Hurd house, and it was as though they had never been apart.

In more ways than one: Professor Hurd's opposition to the romance was still implacable. In consequence, the lovers were obliged to contrive im-probable rendezvous; the most convenient was at a class in Anglo-Saxon, taught by a young instructor, Melville Anderson, who was to become their close friend.* Hurd was not taken in for an instant. Anglo-Saxon was not, he was confident, necessary to his daughter's training as a teacher. Although he would have preferred that she stay at home, he decided, because McClure was so perseveringly underfoot, that she would have to leave again, this time to take up her career. He cast about for openings. He had hoped she might find a post on the faculty of Vassar or Wellesley, but his hand was forced. He had to jump at what was available. There was a position open at the University of Nebraska, in Lincoln; there was another at Abbot Academy, in Andover, Massachusetts. Nebraska was too near and too readily receptive to a young man fresh from college, but Andover was near Boston, then the country's cultural capital; an Irish immigrant like McClure, Hurd reasoned, would hardly dare assault such a citadel of refinement. And so, like a man trying to turn off Niagara Falls with a spin of a faucet, Hurd sent letters to Andover.

McClure was acutely aware of these plans for Hattie. "we live in heart-beats, not in moments," he wrote her, in a hastily scribbled note. He was constantly fearful lest Hurd forbid her to see him again. And there were other distractions as well; for McClure had been, somewhat to his own astonishment, elected editor-in-chief of The Knox Student. This had come about not because his classmates had divined in him any special ability but rather because of campus politics. One faction was led by a youngster named Robert Mather; the other included McClure, Albert Brady, John Phillips, and Frederick Bancroft.† There had been a rumpus over a college essay contest; feeling had run so high that one boy, Bancroft, withdrew from Knox to attend Amherst instead. In their senior year, Mather and his faction seized control of The Student. One night soon afterward, some party unknown broke into the offices of the journal, made off with the subscription list and the account books, and turned them over to the opposition faction. McClure, Brady, and Phillips, displaying that harmony which would later stand them in such good stead, promptly incorporated the journal legally at the state capitol in Springfield; McClure was elected editor-in-

---

* Anderson concluded a distinguished career as chairman of the department of English Literature at Stanford University. Among his many achievements is a graceful translation of Dante's Divine Comedy.

† These are all names of more than passing interest. Mather, for example, was an exceptionally able man who became president of the Rock Island Railroad and was elected chairman of the board of Westinghouse. He was also for a time general counsel for McClure's publishing enterprises. Brady, first a newspaper publisher in Iowa, was later the business and advertising manager of McClure's Magazine. Phillips was for many years associated with McClure in both the syndicate and the magazine, and was later editor of The American Magazine. Bancroft became a historian of some distinction.

chief, Phillips literary editor, and Brady business manager. This last choice was the most important to the success of the piratical venture, for Brady had some contract blanks printed and at once signed up Galesburg's businessmen for a year's advertising. By the time Mather could recover and commence publication of a rival paper, The Coup d'Etat, he found that there was no advertising revenue to support him.

McClure took little joy in his work as editor. The responsibility was a bore and a nuisance; he was cross because it kept him from earning the money that might have got him out of debt. To be sure, there were occasional fringe benefits, as when he was praised: "Phillips," he wrote Hattie, "regards me as the readiest and easiest writer on the staff. . . . Many others, and myself, regard him as the best"; and at such times he could add, "I rather enjoy journalism"; but he would have hooted at the idea of making it a life work.

When it came to his plans for a career, no weathervane ever whirled about so rapidly. At one moment he was going off to the Dakota territory to take up a timber claim; at the next he was headed for post-graduate work at Columbia, or at Johns Hopkins, or at Leipsic; a sermon on the death of Emerson persuaded him he was destined to be a philosophical thinker and writer; when he was offered a job as a teacher it put him at once in mind of Horace Mann and Thomas Arnold. Or had he a vocation? He listened intently, but no voice called very insistently. He saw himself as judge, as international diplomat, as professor of political science, as physician, as philologist. His friends knew him better. "Many of the boys urge me to go into journalism," he wrote to Hattie. But for him, journalism seemed only a convenient way of getting free passes on the railroad.

In truth, McClure had only one fixed goal, and that was to marry Hattie. To this end he had set himself the task of getting two thousand dollars by June, 1883, a year after his prospective graduation. But how to do it? His brain teemed with schemes. In the fall of his senior year he conceived the notion of a western college songbook, but his editorial board squashed it. He was the more vexed when the idea was successfully taken up on another campus. By December he was planning an intercollegiate news bulletin: correspondents in various western colleges were to send him news of their campus activities, after which he would publish a weekly bulletin—and sell his information, as well, to The Chicago Inter-Ocean.* This led to the organization of the Western College Associated Press, of which McClure was elected

---

* The idea of such a service was not original with him. Some enterprising easterner had, in December, 1876, established a World's "College Chronicle," a weekly publication circulating for ten dollars a year, with correspondents in the twenty most important eastern colleges.

president, in May, 1882, by a convention of editors from colleges in seven Midwestern states. With his customary buoyancy he envisioned lush pickings from this and his next venture, a History of Western College Journalism. If he could sell enough advertising in the History, he wrote Hattie, "I can make from $3000 to $5000 this year."

These were, alas! undergraduate dreams of glory, but when she chided him for his inconstancy of purpose and his overweening ambition he grew hot. Her parents had ridiculed him to her; they had spoken of how he was egotistical and was prating of impossibilities. " 'Impossibilities.' *I* don't know any," he answered. "I will be slow to make a choice, but when I have made the choice, I'll put any amount of energy into the work. . . . I have no fear. I can't imagine why your people should think that I would remain poor. . . . The reason why so many think me egotistic is this: I talk of my plans in a straightforward way & more, I *do* things with an assurance of success that they imagine to be conceit. . . . It is nobody's business what I do. I *am* free & I *will* do what I think is right & necessary, & I don't care what anyone says or thinks. Because I happen to be poor, people deem it allowable to criticize me & my actions. Don't fear. I'll admit that my aims are rather immoderate, but I'll begin slow and sure. . . . *I'll get what I want* & you may depend upon it."

Hattie had gone in March to Andover, to teach at the Abbot Academy, for ten dollars a week. Throughout the spring she and McClure wrote each other nearly every day, counting the moments until, in late June, he should have graduated and could hurry east to meet her. Graduation day was June 22; by then she would be visiting with friends in Marcy, a small town not far from Utica, New York; their letters, as they prefigured the day of their reunion, were tense with yearning. "I've wanted you every minute," she wrote him on June 14; "the sweet time is so near at hand." He was in a boil of energy: worrying about his graduation, memorizing his speech, fretting over his History of Western College Journalism, prodding contributors, circularizing prospective advertisers, coping with printers, urging sales on thirty different campuses, corresponding with all to the total of five hundred, harassed by his final examinations, but most of all tormented by the prolonged separation from Hattie. She was busy; her obligations to her host and hostess, she wrote, kept her from writing as often as she wanted. "How I want to see you!" she assured him. "Oh, Sam, I am *very* lonesome. You can imagine that I am dreading to hear from my father. I don't want you to feel troubled about it, Sam. He can't do a thing in the world about it, but I couldn't keep from telling him. . . . I was very careful what I wrote him. . . . I don't really suppose he will say anything to you at all. . . . But it seemed to me wrong to keep it from him. He has always trusted me. It is chiefly that that makes me so worn out." That was on a Monday.

Three days later (the weather was sweltering hot) McClure stood on the stage of Galesburg's Opera House to deliver his commencement oration. Once again, Enthusiasm was his theme. By this time the criticisms of his contemporaries (and of Professor Hurd) were familiar, and, bristling, he incorporated them: "The Enthusiast has faults. He shocks our sensibilities. He is rude, forceful, careless of people's feelings. Too bad! The sun has spots. We won't receive his light and warmth, we want a perfect sun. Yes, but the spots of the sun are brighter than the brightest light men can make, and the faults of the true Enthusiast are superior to ordinary virtues. What has he to do with our conventionalities? Is he not destroying the false system that demands these customs? He lives in another sphere."

It was the custom in those days for their friends to present the graduating students with bouquets of flowers. McClure was tendered a dozen such. He was happily arranging them at the conclusion of the exercises, when Hattie's mother and younger sister came on the stage of the Opera House. Mrs. Hurd came over to face McClure but looked right through him and passed on without a word of congratulations. She joined Professor Anderson and began talking about the splendid opportunities for staking claims in Dakota timberland; her husband and younger daughter were, she said, leaving for the territory next Monday morning. Anderson was planning to go too. "We should take McClure along," he said. Mrs. Hurd glanced coldly at McClure. "If he comes," she said, "my husband and daughter will stay at home." She picked up her skirt and withdrew from the stage.

The culmination of eight years, while he had struggled to support himself and help support his younger brothers and at the same time get a good education—and in less than a minute whatever joy he had had in this climactic moment was trampled flat.

He walked away by himself. To the post office: maybe there was a letter from Hattie: but no. Three days had gone by without a letter. He talked it over with John Phillips: what had happened? A week ago she had signed herself, "Yours forever." Nothing could have changed her, could it? In so short a time? Money was coming in now, in every mail, the receipts from his History of Western College Journalism, but he could not abide the suspense. Phillips agreed to take care of his interests. McClure sent off a letter to Hattie ahead of his own departure: "Will be with you by July 4th or earlier if you say so. *I am so glad*. My dear, dear Hattie."

The day he left Galesburg, Hattie's long-awaited letter arrived. "Mr. McClure," she had written, "I have come to the unalterable conclusion that I have not and never can have any respect or affection for you. . . . I have no pleasure in you or in anything of yours. Of course you understand that since I feel in this way I wish never to meet you again. Harriet S. Hurd."

But McClure was gone. Still hopeful, still happy, he was on his eager way east to meet her.

[v]

The young man in the train going east in June, 1882, was twenty-five years old. It is an age when those fretful over the gap between aspiration and accomplishment are likely to exclaim in despair, "A quarter century on this planet, and what have I got to show for it?" McClure had, in truth, not much. In twenty-five years he had grown only five feet six inches, and this negative achievement galled him. He had grown a blond bristle of a mustache that somewhat camouflaged his stubborn lower lip, but this was scarcely an unparalleled exploit. To be sure, he could take pride in the fact that he was the first McClure of his family to win a college degree, and for the most part he had done it unaided; but in the process he had gone a few hundred dollars into debt, and the accomplishment had bred some sobering responsibilities, for he was now the chief reliance of his twice-widowed mother, his three younger brothers, and his half-sister; soon he would have to start sending them all money, or else finding them jobs. How was he to go about it? What was he to do? He had no idea.

In his pocket he had a little cash, his profits from his History of Western College Journalism. On the seat beside him was his valise; in it, a few clothes and a small stock of notions; at the worst, he could always fall back on peddling. All these thoughts were sufficiently melancholy. But the nub of his anxiety was Harriet Hurd and the state of her mind. Why had he not heard from her? He was sure her father must be to blame for her silence and for her change of—but surely her heart had not changed. It was unthinkable.

McClure reached Utica early in the morning. The first train to Marcy brought him, long before breakfast, to the door of the home where Hattie was visiting a friend, a former schoolmate at Berthier-en-Haut, Miss Angeline Potter. The inconvenience of the hour was not calculated to daunt him. He pressed the bell and presently Miss Potter came to the door to confront him.

Miss Potter was a strong-minded maiden, some years older than McClure, a woman who clearly would brook no nonsense. She informed him that Miss Hurd preferred not to see him. At his insistence, however, she ushered him into a severe front parlor, went to fetch her guest, and returned to keep him company until Hattie should arrive. During this painful interval the amenities were difficult. What, inquired Miss Potter, did he propose to make of his life now that he had graduated from Knox? McClure, who was dreadfully speculating about Hattie's reluctance to see him, could murmur only that he had thought his work might lie in "the field of popularizing some great and new life truths." "My dear young friend," said Miss Potter testily, "what the world needs for its elevation and regeneration is not a startling revelation of *new* truths, but men with souls rich in appreciation and combinations of the old ones."

His stomach empty, his mind encumbered with woe, and now faced by this complacent gorgon, McClure was at a sorry disadvantage. But matters could worsen. For Hattie entered the room and, with a wave of her hand, commanded Miss Potter to stay in her seat and witness the interview. She talked not so much to McClure as at him. Her phrases gouged and bit and tore. ". . . So little delicacy of honor as to tell a dozen confidential friends not only his own private affairs but those of any lady, however indifferent an acquaintance she may be . . . only a total lack of manliness . . . such treachery . . . I could say more, but I never shall!"

Sitting to one side, Miss Potter wondered at Hattie's withering words and pitied young McClure. And he, bewildered, had not even the presence of mind to take hold of her and shake her and demand to know what had got into her. Besides, how could he plead his case under Miss Potter's chilly gaze?

There was no mistaking the finality of Hattie's last words. "I do not love you," she said, "and I never can. Please," she added, "be good enough to return to me any of my letters that you may still have." Then she left the room and he, after directing upon Miss Potter one mute, hopeless glance, left the house.

There was no train from Marcy to Utica for some hours. McClure set off on foot along the railroad tracks, his valise awkwardly slung over his shoulder. "Once," he recalled later, "when I was walking along the bottom of a cut, I heard a train coming behind me; for a moment I thought it was not worth while to get out of the way."

At Utica the ticket agent told him the next train due would arrive in a half hour; it was bound for Boston. If that was as far away as he could go quickly, he would go there. He bought a ticket. When the train arrived, he looked about for his valise, which had within it everything he owned. It was gone. Still numb, he climbed aboard the Boston train and went on, empty-handed.

Fate, it would seem, had been at special pains to contrive for McClure a thoroughly hapless plight. He arrived in Boston late at night, in the middle of a violent thunderstorm. He was lonesome, heartsick, and wretched. He had only six dollars in his pocket and no prospects whatever for earning more. Within a radius of one hundred miles, there was only one soul he knew. And yet—for Fate dearly loves a good irony—in truth he was, all unwitting, on the brink of the career for which she had intended him all along.

His one acquaintance was Malvina Bennett, who had taught elocution at Knox; she lived in a Boston suburb, and he headed for her house like a homing pigeon. As it happened, the lamps were lighted; the family was up, for Miss Bennett's mother was sick. Nevertheless young McClure was made welcome; a bed was found and he stayed over the weekend. On the Monday, he traveled back to Boston where, with Fate's firm hand on his elbow to guide him, he went to 527 Washington Street. Here he paused, while she went inside to make sure that all was ready for his reception.

McClure was outside the offices of the Pope Manufacturing Company, the country's leading manufacturer of bicycles. The firm's prize product was the Columbia Roadster, a redoubtable machine with a front wheel nearly five feet high. In 1882 there were, after five years, still only a trifling twenty thousand bicycles in use in the United States, but the craze was about to catch on. In the next decade the bicycle would spread all over the country; roads would be improved because of it, songs would be written about it, clubs would spring up around it; it would be responsible for the first nationwide interest in outdoor sports. Colonel Albert Pope, the company's president—his title derived from a Civil War command—would in large part be able to take credit for this vogue. In 1876 he had bought the American rights to the basic patents from their European inventors. Already in 1882 he was persuaded of the benefits of advertising. He advertised wherever he could, in no matter how unlikely a medium. He had even written a note to McClure a month earlier, buying for five dollars a two-inch advertisement in the History of Western College Journalism, and it was on this slender connection that McClure now based his hopes of getting a job.

Inside, Fate having paved his way by putting the office boy in a good temper, McClure asked to see Colonel Pope. Without delay, McClure was ushered in to the office of the president.

When McClure explained that he was there because of an advertisement, Pope answered that he was buying no more advertising space that season. McClure said he wasn't selling any more, that what he wanted was a job. Pope shook his head. They were laying men off, he answered, not taking them on. But still McClure sat, on the edge of his chair. He had to have a job. If Pope turned him down, where would he go? Was there nothing at all he could do? Pope looked at him sharply. It was as though the president had recently read a Horatio Alger story. "Willing to wash windows and scrub floors?" he asked. McClure most certainly was. Pope summoned his office boy. "Has Wilmot got anybody yet to help him in the downtown rink?" he asked. The boy, previously alerted by Fate, said he thought not. "Very well," said Pope to McClure, "you can go to the rink and help Wilmot out for tomorrow." The next day was the Fourth of July, and an extra man was needed for that day.

At the downtown rink, McClure found that what Wilmot wanted was a man to teach beginners how to ride. He had never been on a bicycle in his life, nor even very close to one, but, as he later recalled, he "was in the predicament of the dog that had to climb a tree." In two hours he had forced himself to ride the fearsome wheel and was teaching other people as well.*

For his first day's work he was paid a dollar. Nobody told him to come back the next day, but on the other hand nobody told him not to, so he did, day after day; and at the end of the week Colonel Pope sent for him and put him in charge of the uptown rink. Mercifully for prospective beginners, McClure was not long on this job. He was summoned to the president's of-

---

* This was no inconsiderable feat. Teaching a beginner to ride the high, perilous wheel was like training an apprentice jockey to maneuver a balky giraffe. Instruction booklets of the time began by detailing how a teacher should get the machine in an upright position so that the neophyte might mount; after hopefully describing the first few turns around the practice rink, these manuals concluded by discussing the problems of Dismounting and Learning How to Fall, both tasks warranting all the space they got. McClure learned the hard way. Subsequently, so did some of his pupils. One of them, John Ewart, a former classmate at Knox, wrenched his shoulder so severely that both teacher and pupil were obliged to spend several hours in finding a doctor who might set it.

fice. Once again he perched expectantly on the edge of a chair. Pope told him that he was thinking of launching a special promotion; the time had come, he had decided, to publish a magazine devoted to the interests of bicycling enthusiasts, and to increasing their number. McClure had edited a college paper—did he think he could edit such a magazine?

"Yes, sir," said McClure quickly.

There was the sound of a slight whirring of wings: Fate, having completed her mission, was off about her other business.

"At least," McClure added, with an unwonted access of prudence, "I could edit a monthly. I hardly think I could manage a weekly."

The magazine was to be called The Wheelman. Pope was prepared to back the venture liberally; he wanted only "an interesting, valuable, and profitable magazine" that would "weave the bicycle into the best in literature and art." Here was a large order, and a queer one; but McClure vowed he could deliver it. He sent to John Phillips, in Galesburg, for copies of The Knox Student, to show Pope what he could do. He reminded Pope that a couple of years before the editors of The Century had run a long illustrated article entitled "A Wheel Around the Hub"; he was at once dispatched to New York to buy the plates of the article and the right to republish it. For three hundred dollars McClure not only got his first nineteen pages but he also solved his problem of make-up and typography, for, since it would have been absurd to dress the infant Wheelman from two different fonts, and since, moreover, The Century was at the time the handsomest of all American magazines, he simply cribbed its format. There is no flattery like imitation, and so Roswell Smith of The Century was impressed as well as astonished when he glanced at the first issue of The Wheelman.

Pope, too, was impressed with the way young McClure took hold of his new assignment. But he recognized that McClure needed help. The choice of an assistant was left up to McClure, and he thought first of John Phillips.

Phillips was a quiet, bookish, self-effacing boy, about four years younger than McClure. His home was in Galesburg, where his father held the post of city physician; in the Phillips house McClure had for the first time read magazines, Scribner's and The Century. What had chiefly struck him was the price: who had thirty-five cents to spend on a magazine? One May evening Phillips had come to McClure's dormitory room and they had read Faust together. Presently Phillips asked McClure if they might not work together after graduation. McClure was dubious. Later he privately noted that Phillips "hasn't an overplus of energy." Still, that had been May; now it was July, and from Galesburg, whence he had sent the requested copies of The Knox Student, Phillips also sent a letter. "You are the surest fellow I ever saw," he wrote McClure admiringly. "You always alight on your feet. I wish I had one half your push and business ability. Great Heavens, I wish I was with you. If you think I can make a living . . . I'll come. Couldn't your office boy become your assistant some time? Just say come & I'll do so. . . . Oh I *do* hope I *can* come. I'd give anything. . . ."

And so John Phillips was invited to come east, and so—for McClure was always alive to his family responsibilities—was Jack, his own next younger brother. Jack McClure was a merry, feckless youngster, with no particular talent to recommend him for the work, but the third of the brothers, Tom, had already found himself a job, while Robby, the fourth, was too young; so Jack got the call. By mid-August the three young men were established in offices a block away from those of Colonel Pope; by mid-September they had their own gratifying letterhead:

THE WHEELMAN

Editors,	Advertising Agent,
S. S. McClure,	A. J. Lansing.
J. S. Phillips.	Business Manager,
Editorial Contributor,	S. S. McClure.
Charles E. Pratt.	

Could a youngster less than two months out of college have dreamed a more dazzling dream? To be sure, McClure was paid only ten dollars a week, but was he not an editor-in-chief? He called on an editor at the offices of Houghton, Mifflin Company, a Mr. Smith:

Smith: Who's the editor of The Wheelman?
McClure: I am.
Smith: Oh? Who's in charge of the art department?
McClure: I am.
Smith: Who then is the publisher?
McClure: I am.
Smith: Umm. Isn't that a great deal to do, for one so young?

It was; it was, indeed. But despite the inexperience of the editor and his staff the magazine they turned out was professional and even lively, considering its odd parochial appeal. It sold for twenty cents a copy; its articles were, in the main, staff-written or contributed by clergymen, teachers, and physicians, who modestly concealed themselves behind pen names, and who were in most cases paid for their stint by being presented with one of Colonel Pope's alarming bicycles; and it was accorded a respectful critical reception by the leading journals of the day. "Among the most attractive of the monthly magazines," said The Nation's reviewer, and his comment was representative.

Such acclaim was the more impressive since it was tendered to a trio of youngsters fresh from the Midwest who yet dared to measure themselves against the Brahmins, and within the very bastion of cultural snobbery. Alas! poor Professor Hurd! He had confidently expected that this Irish immigrant, this novus homo, this presumptuous upstart so conspicuously lacking in breeding and culture, would surely butt his head in vain against that bastion. Instead here was McClure, a busy editor, now hurrying over to Beacon Street to beseech of Oliver Wendell Holmes—at any cost—a poem on bicycling, now bustling down to Newburyport to urge Harriet Prescott Spofford to write one of her popular stories for The Wheelman, now doing battle with The Century itself for the services of a Concord engraver, now attending festive affairs at which he sat at the head table and was called on to speak after the mayor and the eminent Catholic poet, John Boyle O'Reilly. Did Professor Hurd not have reason to grieve and to wonder wherein he might have failed, that he should be so sorely tried? At any rate, he was able to get a little of his own back: when complimentary copies of The Wheelman were sent to him, he refused them at the Galesburg post office.

And what of his daughter Hattie? After a summer spent visiting relatives in Canada, she had returned to Andover to resume her teaching career at Abbot Academy. In mid-September she sadly wrapped a package and wrote a letter.

> Mr. McClure:–
> I send you today the books belonging to you, all I have of yours. I hope you will not dispose of them, but keep them for yourself. . . .
> Respectfully,
> H. S. Hurd

For his part, McClure had never quite given up hope. All summer he had clutched at connections to Hattie, even to the point of corresponding with such fierce and didactic partisans as Miss Angeline Potter. Now he wrote to Miss Hurd: "I certainly shall not dispose of the books. It hurts me exceedingly to have you imagine that I would. You no doubt think me a coarse, vulgar nature, but the time will surely come when you will learn the real truth in this matter. Of course, what passed between us the last day of June utterly precludes any further intercourse. You certainly don't want it, & I *couldn't* speak to you again. It was the straw too much, the first time that my ability to forget & to forgive was ever overreached. But I can't think of you as having wronged me. . . ."

Poor Hattie had never been more miserable. "Mr. McClure," she wrote, "Please send the rest of my letters."

> I did not [she went on] ask you to keep the books because I thought yours was a coarse, vulgar nature. I was only thinking of my own impulse to put forever out of my sight the little book you sent back to me because of the cruel pain it caused me to look at it.

And then she added:

> I write to you in confession to-day. I did not tell you the truth last June, and I can never find peace till you know the truth. What I tell you now is the truth as it lies open before God's eye. My father told me last summer that he would never receive you as his son-in-law, and that if I married you he would not even admit you to his house again. I felt then that I *could not* disobey him, that it would be far easier to give up you than him. But I felt that you would take nothing as a reason for our separation, as long as you believed that I loved you—and so I gave you, falsely, the only reason that I knew would be valid in your eyes, that I no longer cared for you. But I perjured myself. . . . There is no excuse. . . . It is utterly irreparable. . . . I have no reproach to make you in any point. You never failed me in any smallest way. It is absolutely not your fault and I regard you altogether as I did before I left my home. . . . If you saw my heart. . . . On the last day of June I wronged and wounded Love and Truth and you. I loved you then, and love you still. But I obeyed my father. . . .
>
> I do not . . . *wish* you to forgive me, much less do I *ask* such a thing. . . . But I want you to know that I have never had a thought of blame for you, and that I am conscious of having wronged you and the integrity of my own soul as deeply as possible.
>
> Harriet S. Hurd.

In the face of such a handsome amends, McClure nursed his grievance as long as he could—one day—and then sped to Andover, once again to look into Hattie's eyes and to clasp her hands. "It seems so strange to be so happy," he said. Once again they were on the old footing; but this time, twice-burned,

McClure was thrice-shy. "I dread every mail," he wrote her, "lest you tell me never to see you again."

That fall McClure shared a garret with his brother and Phillips, spending only four dollars of his weekly ten-dollar salary, for he had to send some money west to his mother. He was busy, hustling to New York, to Philadelphia, to Baltimore and Washington, in search of contributors; he was fearful of Professor Hurd's influence on Hattie; and he was apprehensive, for his mother, still grimly opposed to his alliance with Hattie, had served notice that she was coming east to live with him in Boston. That winter these various pressures took their toll. He was seriously sick for three weeks of typhoid fever. When he recovered, there was his mother, his youngest brother, and his half-sister, all descended upon him, and, as he wrote Hattie, "it is dismal around here. Mother has come to the conclusion that I am engaged in an ungodly business in editing *The Wheelman*. She has had suspicions for some time & now she is fully persuaded. . . . She is just driving me distracted. . . . A heavy gloom is settling around us." Jack McClure sensibly withdrew from this cheerless menage and went to live with Phillips. "Mother [McClure went on, in a letter to Hattie] is very much depressed. Her melancholy is seemingly perpetual. . . . I'm getting to be a fine housekeeper. I suppose you know that I am not only purveyor-general, but head cook & oftentimes dish-washer. . . . I am homesick & no place to be homesick for. . . ."

Yet McClure's work on the magazine was unflaggingly enthusiastic. And it continued to attract notice: there were offers of jobs from both the Scribners and The Century, but he decided to reject them.

"So," said Lansing, the advertising manager, "the Scribners were after you."

"Yes," said McClure, "and they did not get me."

"The Colonel is mightily pleased that you stood by him. He means to help you a good deal."

But did he? Pope talked of giving McClure a third of the stock in The Wheelman, but this was a bookkeeping transaction, no more—worthless until the magazine should start to show a profit. And apparently Pope was quite content to take a loss, month after month, since he was being provided with invaluable promotion for his manufacturing business. McClure's weekly salary continued microscopic.

And so McClure's enthusiasm abated. Or rather, since it was impossible for that luxurious growth to shrivel, it commenced to flourish in another direction. His restless mind conceived the notion of a new magazine. It was to be called The Eclectic Magazine of Continental Periodical Literature, and it was to reprint articles from the leading French, German, and Italian journals. He talked his idea over with all sorts of people. In Newburyport, James Parton, at the time the country's foremost biographer, gave it his blessing. So did Thomas Bailey Aldrich, who had two years before taken over the editorial chair at The Atlantic Monthly from William Dean Howells. McClure even went to Cambridge to wait upon Charles Eliot Norton, a Brahmin of resounding reputation who had been an editor of The North American Review and had helped to found The Nation. Norton listened with grave interest and got it all wrong. He assumed McClure proposed to publish his articles without translating from the original. This demented notion nonetheless impressed him. McClure, woefully imposed upon by Norton's great prestige, actually inclined to adopt his view. He bubbled over. He began to spend his evenings in the Athenaeum, leafing through recent issues of European periodicals; he even drew up a budget of expenses.*

But presently McClure was distracted from these amiable chores by news affecting his plans for a June wedding. For Hattie, after much troubled reflection, had finally written to Galesburg to tell her parents that her mind was unalterably made up: she was determined to marry Sam; if not with their approval at home, then without it, in Andover in June. But marry him she would.

Here was a shock to rock the prairie. Hattie had given no slightest hint that she had reverted to her former fancy; Professor Hurd could have been forgiven for thinking McClure no more than a distasteful memory. Hurd was proffered a splendid opportunity to show sensibility and forbearance. He sat down at the desk in his study.

Dear daughter Hattie [he wrote, in his even, careful copperplate]:-

> Life is but a tangled skein,
> Full of trouble, toil, and travail;
> Knots that puzzle heart & brain,
> We must study to unravel;
>   Slowly, slowly,
>   Bending lowly
> O'er our task and trusting wholly
> Unto Him whose loving hand
> Helps us smooth each twisted strand.

---

* Based on his experience with The Wheelman, and estimating on a magazine comprising cover, one hundred quarto pages of letterpress, and ten pages of advertising, circulating to two thousand subscribers, McClure could figure, in 1883, that presswork, paper, binding, office rent, part-time bookkeeper, mailing, circulars, and salaries for editor and assistant editor would cost less than five hundred dollars a month. His net, he concluded hopefully, would be nearly two thousand dollars a year.

I have ever loved my two daughters and, with good reason, have always been proud of them. In my imperfect way I have tried to make them happy and to prepare them for usefulness & respectability in life, and have fondly cherished the hope that no wall of separation would ever arise between me and them. But, in part at least, my wishes are not to be realized. Last summer I gave you my opinion of McClure. . . . His personal appearance, his bearing, & his address are not pleasing to me; I think him conceited, impertinent, meddlesome, &c., &c., and, of course, would not choose him for your husband. I regard it as a misfortune that you ever made his acquaintance. I do wish you were about to unite yourself to some family which we, I & your mother & Mamy, could know, could respect, and could love. But your mother never desired even *an acquaintance* with *Mrs. McClure,* & we feel that you are going into a family which we can never enter. We fear you are making a sad mistake. . . . Nevertheless, Hattie, I shall not cease to love you, & to pray for your happiness. I wish you to come home during the summer & make us a long visit; and I wish you also to remember that our house will always welcome you whenever you desire to enter it. I hope you will not forget to love your old father & mother, and your sister, & that you will ever find it a pleasure to visit us as you have opportunity during the few remaining years we may live. . . . I have now said all I shall, in all probability, ever say about McClure, & you may come home in June expecting to be entirely free from all annoying conversations about him. I shall accept the *inevitable* as the will of God, & bow as I may, though it may be a "thorn in the flesh." I have done all I can to have things according to my desire, as you must admit, & now have nothing more to do or say except to wish you prosperity & happiness. . . . And now, Hattie, I bid you goodbye.

> Believe me to be as ever
> Your affectionate father,
> A. Hurd.

However crabbed, however clear that the Hurd household would welcome Hattie but never McClure, this letter could be construed only as consent. It meant a wedding in early September; it lent, as well, urgency to McClure's affairs, for he was still getting only ten dollars a week. When his dream of an Eclectic Magazine collapsed—he found that G.P. Putnam's Sons were already publishing a monthly Topics of the Time, which was simply his idea under a better name—he concluded that his only course lay in bearding Colonel Pope and getting a raise. Happily, he was handed an unexpected argument when one day, unannounced, into his office walked William Howland, a man about his own age.

Howland was editor and publisher of Outing, a magazine a few months the senior of The Wheelman and appealing to the same, but a rather larger, readership. Howland was having his troubles, too. Outing was neither so large nor so well edited as The Wheelman. Advertising came hard. "Why not," said Howland, "consolidate?" McClure was delighted with the idea, for privately he had long since decided that The Wheelman was an impossible anomaly. But of course a merger was for Pope to approve. And so for a time action on Howland's idea was postponed.

But Howland was persistent. If a swift consolidation could not be arranged, perhaps at least he could pry McClure loose from The Wheelman.

"What," he asked McClure, "would induce you to leave?"

"It would take a pretty good proposition."

"Do you mind," pursued Howland, "telling me what your present salary is?"

But of course McClure had every reason for keeping his salary a pitch-dark secret. "You can guess pretty closely," he said. "I shall be married next month, and able to keep my wife nicely in Cambridge in a beautiful home."

"More than two thousand dollars a year, eh?"

"Well—not quite that much," said McClure calmly, "but I'll be getting that much in another year."

"Will you at least promise to give me first chance, if you're ever in the market for a job?"

McClure temporized with Howland but at once demanded a raise of Pope. He was, he reminded his employer, planning to marry in September. The colonel chose to be whimsical.

"Marry," he inquired, "when you're still so young? You'd better wait a while." He smiled blandly. "Remember your Bible," he added. "Remember Jacob and Rachel."

"I've already waited seven years," McClure answered.

"But Jacob slaved for fourteen years," said Pope triumphantly. "You see? You don't know your Bible."

"Jacob married two sisters," McClure retorted. "I'm marrying only one."

Routed on exegetical grounds, Pope raised McClure's salary to fifteen dollars a week.

Back in Galesburg, Hattie had need for good news. From the day she got home her family was sullen and bitter; all over the town her affairs had set malicious tongues to clacking. When she went to Mrs. Read's for tea, Mrs. Webster, Mrs. Perkins and Mrs. Bangs all hushed significantly upon her arrival, and eyed her speculatively. And presently:

Mrs. Perkins: Are you going back East again?

Hattie: Yes.

Mrs. Webster: And will you be teaching the same subjects at Abbot Academy again next year?

Hattie: No.

Mrs. Read: No? Then what *will* you teach?

Hattie: Could I have some more of your delicious tea, please, Mrs. Read?

Mrs. Read: It's none of my business, of course, but I should so like to know what you are going to teach next year.

Hattie: I have not the slightest objection to telling you, Mrs. Read, that I am going to return to the East, but that I never expect to teach again.

Omnes: Oh? Oh, really? How interesting!

Mrs. Read: Then *what* will you be doing, dear Hattie?

And when she fled home, she would find her father eating his supper, late and alone and very cross.

Hattie: I'm sorry to be late, Pa.

Professor Hurd: *I* know enough to come home when *I* go visiting. Clear away the dishes. Good night.

Hattie: Good night.

When she told her family's friends that she was to be married, they burst into tears. Toward the end of July she wrote to McClure: "Pa has spoken. His word has gone forth. He says you may come twice to the house before we are married, and no more. . . . He says he doesn't want to have things any more unpleasant than they must be, and that if you come oftener than twice he will quarrel with you as sure as fate. He says he only means it for your own good. He spoke of it of his own accord, realizing that it must be definitely settled before you come. . . . At best, my conscious hours are to me so many nightmares."

In Boston, McClure busied himself with finding a house for them to come home to; with buying himself a dress suit ("It makes me look lots taller," he wrote Hattie proudly); with having printed their wedding announcements. But mostly he sorrowed at the way her father was souring her last days in her old home, days that should have been so festive and gay.

"My mother," Hattie wrote him, "would make it all nice for us, Sam, if she only could. You may just believe that wholesale. . . . But there is no use in being angry about anything that my father orders, and that means all that goes on here. He is blinded and hard-tempered. We all just have to endure and forgive. . . . I just give up every plan I make, and submit silently, and go without ever so many things I have earned a right to have. It makes me indignant and wicked. . . . I am all starved out and wearied. . . ."

And, two weeks before their wedding day: "Pa can't *bear* the very idea of seeing you and me together. He knows it would be too much for him, and make him very angry. He wants us to wait till we go away, and the sight will not torment and anger him."

McClure got to Galesburg six days before his wedding day; he was permitted to call at the house only once before he came for the actual ceremony. There were few guests. None of Hattie's classmates was invited, for to invite one was to invite all, and one of these was Joe Gaston, McClure's uncle, whom Professor Hurd refused to allow in the house. Hurd ignored John Phillips, McClure's best man, as he ignored the groom himself. Consistent to the end, he accepted a small piece of his daughter's wedding cake (she had baked it herself) and then withdrew to the farthest corner of the small parlor. Outside in his yard, a considerable company of curious gathered to peer through the windows during the ceremony and the wintry party that followed it. As soon as he decently could, McClure summoned a hack and departed with Hattie for Chicago and a wedding trip through Canada.

Early next morning Professor Hurd went out into his garden, silent and grim, to survey the damage done his flower borders by his uninvited guests of the evening before. He heard a woman's voice: "Well, what about the wedding?" and another woman's shouted reply: "I caught cold standing out there last night, didn't you?" He turned the corner of his house, cold and dignified, to stare into the street. The two neighbor women, abashed, hugged their hands under their aprons and disappeared into their homes.

And Hattie, when she got home to her new house at 22 Wendell Street in Cambridge, found a letter from Angeline Potter. "Cyclones, volcanic eruptions, tidal waves and nuptial waves succeed one another so rapidly that I am completely bewildered," that strong-minded maiden had written, with some trace of discomposure. "If your husband is as persevering and loyal to one vocation as he has been to one woman, success will crown his labors."

Even Miss Potter could learn.

[VI]

At 22 Wendell Street, plump purple grapes were warm and ripe on a vine that climbed over their back verandah; and the course of their days, in a house that was fairly dazzling with autumnal sunshine, was serene and doubly sweet, coming after so many long years of disappointment.

They were very happy and very self-centered. They lived in an academic atmosphere especially congenial to Hattie: her tranquil prospect included attendance at two free courses of lectures at the Institute of Technology, in French and in German literature; Matthew Arnold was coming to lecture at Harvard in the winter; and Edwin Booth was about to perform in a repertory of six of Shakespeare's plays. McClure's work entailed greater responsibility than before, for both his brother Jack and John Phillips had left his staff to attend Harvard; but the challenge delighted him. When Colonel Pope expressed a desire to widen the scope of The Wheelman's interest, McClure's eyes sparkled—this was what he had urged for months. He visibly expanded as though suddenly reflecting a swollen circulation list.

Nor was there any financial pinch. In early October he went to New York and found the city thick with editors who wanted his stuff, free-lance. Kirk Munroe, the editor of Harper's Young People, who as a founder of the League of American Wheelmen was an old friend, filled him chock-a-block with advice and with names of editors. S. S. Conant, the editor of Harper's Weekly, urged him to send some short squibs; the editor of The Modern Age wanted him (or Hattie) as Boston literary correspondent; Art Interchange wanted reviews; so did The Continent—all magazines by now thrice-forgotten but then lively and respected journals.

It was an age of magazines. They sprang up at every hand, on any pretext, for any readership—general magazines, farmers' magazines, women's magazines, church magazines; magazines for literary folk, for scientists, for businessmen, for teachers, for children; magazines tumbling out of the presses like the rats out of the houses of Hamelin: great magazines, small magazines, lean magazines, brawny magazines, grave old plodders, gay young friskers. As against only seven hundred periodicals in 1865, there were more than twelve hundred in 1870, twice as many again by 1880, and by 1885 there would be three thousand, three hundred weekly and monthly journals in the United States. In those benighted days before Progress, marching implacably into the future, would bring cinema, radio, and television, magazines were the chief and best—almost the only—means by which to amuse, entertain, elevate, and instruct. Their editors were, in consequence, insatiably hungry for bright and energetic contributors.

Into these literary rapids McClure plunged as zestfully as a spawning salmon. By November he was earning, in addition to his weekly pittance of fifteen dollars from Colonel Pope, some thirty-five dollars weekly as a free lance. To a young man of modest ambition, it might have seemed that the ultimate goal was well in sight.

But McClure was not so sure. Pope was at last negotiating with Howland for the purchase of Outing. Where there had been two editors-in-chief, there would presently be only one, and who would it be? McClure had long since developed an acute sense of status. "For a young man," he told Hattie, "it is better to be *first*. At present *I* get credit for all that Mr. Pope and my subordinates do, besides what I do myself." And yet, in truth, he didn't care greatly if the top job were not to be offered him. "At best it's hack work," he said. "First class for a person just out of college who has little self-determining energy, but—"

While the negotiations were still in hand, he went to New York, ostensibly to buy some engravings but in fact to sniff out his prospects for a better job. He took Hattie along and she was immensely impressed, most of all with her visit to the offices of The Century. "Such gentlemen! Oh, they treated us royally," she wrote her sister. "You never saw anything like those lovely rooms. And aesthetic furniture!" Presently the publisher, Roswell Smith ("a very solemn, severe old man"), took McClure aside for a lengthy talk. He promised to do his best to find an opening. "I shouldn't think it any robbery," he added, "to steal you from Colonel Pope at your present salary."

When it developed that Howland was to have equal authority with McClure in editorial and business matters, McClure waited only for a word from Roswell Smith. It came promptly: a letter urging him to take a job at the De Vinne printing house, at the time the best in the country. Theodore De Vinne likewise wrote a warm letter, offering him twenty-five dollars a week to start. At the same time Hattie was offered a job at fifteen dollars a week to help prepare the Century Dictionary. To meet the expenses of the move to New York, "you can count on me," Smith wrote McClure, "for any sum you may want up to a thousand dollars."

Everybody was generous, everybody was thoughtful and considerate. The McClures arrived in New York on a packet of the Fall River Line and Hattie's eyes were wide at all the Byzantine splendor. "Just before dawn," she reported, "I sprang up and saw a beautiful sight. We were approaching the Brooklyn bridge, which is lighted with seventy electric lights, and the river was full of great steamers all lighted in the windows and having their red and green lights. It was glorious. Sam said the bridge looked like a rainbow of suns over our heads. Our own steamer, too, was all lighted with little electric lights. There was one in front of our glass door, and inside we had a nice large lamp with a globe. . . ." They arrived on a packet, but more important they arrived on a great wave of mutual esteem and enthusiasm and high hopes. To Hattie, De Vinne was "very kind, and just about the nicest gentleman I ever saw"; he had them to dinner, took them to an art exhibit, found them lodgings, and assured McClure that all would go well at the printing house. Both McClures were delighted, as well, with Hattie's job at The Century offices; indeed, Hattie regarded it as "a perfect holiday." She was to read the works of "the best authors", as she herself chose, and find examples of the uses of words for the great Century Dictionary. In short, a masterful bit of boondoggling. As for McClure, it was evident that the officers of the Century Company were grooming him to become an executive in their nascent book publishing business. De Vinne, who had all The Century's printing business, was quite content to go along with this prospect: McClure was entered on his payroll as an expert printer—which he was not—and, since the wages of an expert printer were then eighteen dollars weekly, De Vinne paid him an additional seven dollars every Saturday night out of his own pocket. Everybody agreed, Hattie wrote, that McClure "had a very rare opportunity."

There was only one flaw. McClure was a wretched employee.

Off the evidence he appears to have been one of the most trying employees in history. Trying to mold McClure into his generation's equivalent of the Organization Man was a hopeless, even ludicrous task. At first he was assigned to the composing room as an unwanted assistant to the foreman. So clearly did he show his detestation of the tedium and the jailhouse hours that he was presently removed to clerk in De Vinne's own office. Here he forgot things, walked around for days with important uncorrected proofs neglected in his pocket and hotly resented being required to cool his heels in the waiting rooms of the rich and important clients to whom he was occasionally dispatched. After less than four months De Vinne, with no doubt a sigh of relief, sent McClure packing off to The Century's offices. "A connection with The Century," McClure wrote later, "was the uttermost limit of my ambition", but nevertheless his stock as an employee did not rise much higher.

The difficulty was that he, who had been an editor-in-chief, was now a very junior editorial assistant and assigned the dull routine of an editorial assistant's work. He was bored and discharged his duties indifferently. "Mr. Smith," he confessed, "was not pleasant to me." Hattie, who had been most happy at her work, shared his office hours only briefly before something happened that was, in her view, "rather awful." Roswell Smith, having noticed that she was pregnant, asked McClure when she expected to bear her baby. His interest was warm and kindly, but in Hattie's circle one was not expected to speak of such matters out loud; when she heard of his question she was mortified. "I asked Sam if he blushed," she wrote her mother, and a week or so later she concluded she had better resign.

They took a cottage in a New Jersey suburb. McClure was given his two weeks' vacation in July so that he might be with her when the baby was born. It was during this period of idleness that he compounded all his felonies as a junior editorial assistant by thinking. In the course of his thinking he came up with ten separate plans—one major and nine minor—for making the Century Company some money. His phrase for them—and it was one that must have grated on the genteel sensibilities not only of Roswell Smith but also of The Century's editor, Richard Watson Gilder—was "schemes to bring in the ducats." To think was of course an insufferable error. All progressive company managements urge their employees to weigh in with suggestions—it is part of the folklore of American business that vice-presidencies are born of bright suggestions—but obviously no true executive wants a very junior assistant to start bombarding him with new ideas. It shakes his sense of the fitness of things. The better the ideas, the less he likes them; he can apprehend them only as unfriendly criticisms of his own ability. A McClure who would sit about doing his decent minimum and decently waiting for the final logic of the actuarial tables to clear the way for his promotion, that was one thing; but a McClure so pestiferous as to suggest better ways of running the business, that was too much.

All innocence, McClure took his ideas, grandly set forth in a sixteen-page prospectus, and laid them on Roswell Smith's desk. An hour passed, and then McClure was summoned. It was an awkward interview, for Smith was in the unhappy position of having to confess he had erred. He didn't think, he said, that McClure would ever get very far working for the Century Company. McClure was not, he took it, "fitted to work to advantage in the offices of a big concern." Better, he felt, that McClure "go out and try to found a little business" of his own. If Smith emphasized the words "try to found" it was not because he doubted McClure's ability—or was it? In any case, McClure's salary would be paid until the first of October—a very generous severance pay. But, no doubt about it, McClure had been fired.

On the commuters' train to East Orange and later, in his cottage, McClure brooded on the dismaying turn of events. Why fired, when his ideas had been so good? They *were* good ideas, weren't they? He turned again to his principal scheme and inspected it narrowly. The more he considered it, the more attractive did it seem.

Back and forth McClure paced in his tiny living room. Upstairs his daughter Eleanor was screaming, now with delight, now from hunger. McClure's classmate Robert Mather had come on a visit and remarked that the infant was a perfect miniature of Professor Hurd. "Except, of course," Mather had added thoughtfully, "that she's a girl." Downstairs McClure walked back and forth, reflecting on his ideas and on his having been fired. Perhaps he was not meant for a journalist. "He has always wanted to preach," Hattie had written to her parents, "and I hope he will be able to realize his desire." Had he, after all, a vocation? He listened more intently than ever for the still, small voice. No! No, his was a good idea—he would prove it—he would show them. He had shown them before, hadn't he? Hadn't he gotten through college? Wasn't he married to Hattie? And so he would take the best of the ideas he had submitted to the Century Company, and he would make it work.

THE SYNDICATE

1884-1893

[1]

McClure's idea was to sell literary material by the most popular writers of the day to the newspapers: to sell a short story for which he had paid, say, one hundred and fifty dollars, to a hundred newspapers at five dollars apiece, and so to make a modest profit. In short, to launch a literary syndicate.

In My Autobiography and again in the entry he prepared for Who's Who in America McClure stated that he invented the newspaper syndicate. This was, shall we say, a fib; moreover, McClure knew it. When he claimed to have originated the service of syndicating features to newspapers he was merely trumpeting his defiance at his competitors, crowing commercial hot air. Such syndicates had been invented twenty times over, and years before he came along. It took no shrewdness to invent the service; any dolt could have done so much. McClure seriously underrated his own contribution. What he did had vastly greater ramifications. He seized upon the primitive notions of others and, what nobody had been able to do before him, made them work successfully for the metropolitan American press. By securely establishing the feature syndicate in the country's biggest newspapers, McClure touched off two revolutions of far-reaching significance. The first changed the character of the American newspaper and the second, even more important, changed the character of American fiction. Neither of these profound changes was brought about overnight, and each required the efforts of an army of men and women to come to fruition; but it was McClure's initial energy that set the forces in motion. The part he played in transforming the American newspaper has been to some extent recognized by historians of journalism. But his part in turning the course of American fiction has gone wholly ignored. Indeed, the root cause of that shift is imperfectly understood; McClure's role, as will be seen, was crucial.

For McClure to refer to his achievement as an invention was in keeping with the spirit of the times. It is customary for literary historians to dismiss the 1870s and 1880s as a gross and swinish period; and assuredly the money power—raw, arrogant, and shamelessly greedy—that seized control of the country following the Civil War and corrupted judiciary and legislature alike did its best to pollute as well the national taste. And yet, with all the vulgarity and opportunism and exploitation, those two decades were pervaded by a restless excitement, a churning sense of something new and vital in the air. The hint of it was in the novel by Mark Twain, The Gilded Age, that had lent its name to the times: "If there be any place and time in the world where and when it seems easy to 'go into something' it is in Broadway on a spring morning. . . . To the young American, here or elsewhere, the paths to fortune are innumerable and all open; there is invitation in the air and success in all his wide horizon." And Walt Whitman confirmed it: "I perceive clearly," he wrote, "that the extreme business energy, and this almost maniacal appetite for wealth prevalent in the United States, are parts of amelioration and progress, indispensably needed to prepare the very results I demand. My theory includes riches, and the getting of riches. . . ."

The laying of the Atlantic cable and the opening of the first transcontinental railroad were still recent events; the dust raised by Darwin and later by Huxley and Tyndall was still far from settling; at every hand, moreover, men were inventing odd and useful things: the typewriter, the fountain pen, the linotype; a way to make paper from wood pulp; the incandescent lamp, the telephone; celluloid and rayon; the steam turbine, manganese steel, the electric trolley car. It almost seemed that if a man wished to look his fellows in the eye he was constrained to invent something. And so McClure "invented" the syndicate.

He came to his inspiration by reading the newspapers and so learning of what others were up to. Early in the summer of 1884, Henry Irving, the celebrated English actor, arrived in New York with a rather less celebrated English novelist, Joseph Hatton, who told a young reporter assigned to interview him that he was meeting the expenses of his trip by writing some American letters home to a syndicate of English newspapers. The reporter, Irving Bacheller, was intrigued by the idea. Hatton suggested that Bacheller undertake to syndicate in like manner a Hatton novel in the American press; he engaged, moreover, to urge other English authors to turn their material over to Bacheller for the same purpose. Bacheller decided it would be worth trying. A few weeks later, here came another English visitor, the Lancashire publisher, William Tillotson, who told American reporters all about his syndicate

of seven newspapers, by then already a dozen years old and regularly serializing the works of the most popular British novelists. And in that same summer, Charles A. Dana, editor of The New York Sun, announced that a syndicate of a half-dozen big American newspapers had been formed to publish
short stories by Bret Harte, Henry James, and William Dean Howells. The
idea was not novel to Dana: he had himself paid the costs of his trip to Europe
in 1848 by arranging with four newspapers to print simultaneously his letters
from abroad.

Despite all this ferment of hopeful activity, when McClure suggested that
The Century organize a similar syndicate Roswell Smith had ample reason
for both rejecting the idea and firing its sponsor. In the American literary world
of 1884 the syndicate had a very bad smell. Nearly every country weekly in
the United States printed some sort of syndicated stuff and it was all uni-
formly dreadful. As early as August, 1865, one Ansel Nash Kellogg had
launched the production of what came to be called first "patent insides" and
later "boiler plate"; by 1871 he was serializing tenth-rate fiction and by 1875
he was circulating his stereoplates to more than one thousand country weeklies. But while Kellogg was getting rich off the profits, the magazine editors
of the time looked down their noses at his operation. In their view it was of
a piece with all that was coarse and common in the age. They were confident,
moreover, that all conscientious writers in the country agreed with them.
What was printed in the magazines was literature; what was printed in the
newspapers was journalism—oil and water; they would never mix.

Additionally, the magazine editors assured themselves, no prudent writer
would ever fall in with a newspaper syndicate scheme, for it was common
knowledge that, thanks to the laxity of the copyright laws, newspaper editors
all over the country cheerfully plundered the best of their rivals' stuff at no
more expense than the cost of scissors and paste. Pay for material written by
someone a hundred or more miles away? Ridiculous.

In short, anyone planning a syndicate was demented. From Galesburg,
where he was on vacation from Harvard, McClure's closest friend, John Phillips, joined the chorus of advice against the enterprise.

> As to the scheme you wrote of—it seems to me too extensive to be
> feasible. Even if the capital &c were secured, I doubt if the best Ameri-
> can writers would agree to put themselves under such bonds for any
> length of time. . . . And then I surmise that many would object to the
> manner of publication—which will be quite indiscriminate. Perhaps
> they would prefer (not speaking of price) to publish once in a choice

journal like Century to a broader circulation through the medium of 2nd & 3rd rate papers. Of course by this the writers would receive larger remuneration for stories, but that is not all they look at.* Another point —would a *large* number of papers . . . go into the plan? I doubt if the number would be large. . . . On the whole it seems to me impracticable because of the extensiveness of the plan—& the consequent difficulty of bringing the many incongruous elements into harmony. Am afraid of trouble in both directions—getting literary men to make contracts for writing, & papers for publishing. . . .

McClure had only his own conviction to sustain him, but it was enough. The more he thought about the syndicate, the more he believed in it. "It became an obsession with me," he said later. "Again I was a man of one idea, as I had been when I was determined to get an education, as I had been when I was determined to get my wife. Everyone with whom I discussed the idea manifested a great indifference." His old friend Frederick Bancroft was hard at work fighting Blaine in the New York headquarters of the Independent Republicans—the Mugwumps. "Let us get together," he urged McClure, "& get up some scheme whereby we can do good service vs. Blaine. . . . Couldn't we work up a literary bureau & furnish short articles to friendly papers? Yours for reform, F.A.B." If ever there was a Republican designed and shaped to become a Mugwump, it was S.S. McClure, and the campaign of 1884—Cleveland against Blaine—was the Mugwumps' proudest hour; but the strokes that tolled from the bell-tower failed to summon him. He was off on other errands.

Early in September, 1884, McClure left for Boston to test his conviction on the writers and newspaper editors he had met when he was editing The Wheelman. "I am real glad for him," Hattie wrote her family, just as though he was off on Century business. "Don't be worried about anything. We'll do very nicely," she wrote to him, but she was anxious.

He was on the wing: to Nahant, to call on Helen Hunt Jackson, whose Ramona had just been published and was selling fast all over the country; to Newburyport, to visit Harriet Prescott Spofford; to South Berwick, Maine, to talk to Sarah Orne Jewett; to Andover, to see Elizabeth Stuart Phelps, whose The Gates Ajar had made her one of the most popular writers in the country. With each interview his enthusiasm for his own scheme grew. All his boundless vitality was concentrated on it, as though he were a missionary

---

*In defense of this curious view, it must be remembered that Phillips had had at the time very little practical experience with writers.

spreading the gospel, and the lady authors watched him, silent, entranced by his shock of fair hair, his bright blue eyes, and his ready, infectious eagerness. They were all his converts.

When he came home it was to announce that he had decided to risk the venture. He had to have a New York address, so they moved back to town, to a sunny four-room apartment where the parlor became his office. After paying twenty-three dollars for the first month's rent, he was almost penniless, but nevertheless his first printed circular presently appeared, to be mailed to newspaper editors all over the country.

No. 114 East 53d Street, New-York, N.Y.
October 4th, 1884

DEAR SIR:

I have made arrangements with a number of our most popular authors, including W. D. Howells, H. C. Bunner, J. S. of Dale, Mrs. Helen Jackson, Mrs. Harriet Prescott Spofford, Dr. William A. Hammond, and over a score of others, to furnish serial and short stories for simultaneous publication in syndicates of leading newspapers.

This method of publication has been employed very successfully in England and France for a long time. . . . There is no reason why American newspapers should not reap great advantages from a similar arrangement.

A dozen, or twenty, or fifty newspapers—selected so as to avoid conflict in circulation—can thus secure a story for a sum which will be very small for each paper, but which will in the aggregate be sufficiently large to secure the best work by the best authors. A small outlay will enable a newspaper to furnish its readers with stories by our most noted writers, which have not been published before, and which will be accessible to its readers in no other periodical. I shall be glad to correspond with you further in regard to this plan, and to furnish definite terms on application.

Very truly yours,
S. S. McCLURE,
(*Late* Editor of The Wheelman.)

It is not easy to imagine a less promising commercial undertaking than the McClure syndicate at its outset. Its manager had less than twenty-five dollars in the bank, no capital to buy the stories he proposed to sell, no name on which to trade, a very slender reputation, precious little familiarity with his clients, and only indifferent experience as judge of his wares. His business was new and strange not only to him but to everybody with whom he proposed to deal; he kept no books, had never even had a bank account before, had no assistant except his wife (who was able to help only part-time), was obliged to attend to every detail himself, yet abhorred the routine of clerical work.

He had commitments from a few papers—The Boston Globe, The New York Commercial Appeal, The Hartford Times, and two or three others—and he blithely assumed other publishers would start a wild scramble to sign up. "Both writers and journals will be so much benefited," Hattie wrote to her mother, "that they can't fail to go into it. The writers *have* gone into it, and he is just writing to papers. He may look for very quick replies." This cheery prediction summed up McClure's attitude: he was euphoric.

But the business very nearly never got off the ground. He had planned to release his first story—"A Daring Fiction," by H. H. Boyesen, to whom he had pledged two hundred and fifty dollars—on November 16. This allowed six weeks from the time he had mailed his first circular to newspaper editors, surely long enough to get contracts and funds from enough papers to clear a pleasant profit. The quick replies were, however, few and discouraging, and in most cases there was no reply at all. What funds came in he was obliged to spend on stamps and envelopes for still more circular letters; Boyesen would have to wait for his pay; McClure and his wife spent all their hours addressing, stuffing, stamping and sealing envelopes. Late in October he sent a letter to scores of writers: "I shall need between 300 and 400 stories during the year, and can profitably use all the stories you will write for the newspaper press. . . . I will meet your views. Please let me know your terms, the number of stories you will write this year (1885), and the probable length of the stories." And another circular went to newspaper editors.

114 E. 53D STREET,
NEW-YORK, OCT. 27TH, 1884

DEAR SIR:

The following well-known authors have either placed manuscripts in my hand or have notified me that stories will be ready for me in a few days:

J. S. OF DALE,	J. T. TROWBRIDGE,
HARRIET P. SPOFFORD,	W. O. STODDARD,
GEORGE PARSONS LATHROP,	DR. W. A. HAMMOND,
MARION HARLAND,	JULIA D. WHITING,
JULIAN HAWTHORNE,	HELEN KENDRICK JOHNSON,

and others.

The following well-known authors have promised to contribute to the series soon:

W. D. Howells,	Helen Jackson (H. H.),
J. Esten Cooke,	Noah Brooks,
Brander Matthews,	Louise Chandler Moulton,
W. H. Bishop,	Sarah Orne Jewett,
E. P. Roe,	Maurice Thompson,
H. H. Boyesen,	and others.

I am in correspondence with other leading writers, and can safely announce that I will be able to furnish stories, either short or serial, from every first-class writer in the United States whose literary engagements will give him time to accept additional commissions from me. The expense will be very small,—from $1.00 to $5.00 per thousand words, according to the price the author receives or the number of papers that take the story.

Over fifty newspapers, including daily papers in nearly all our large cities, and wide-awake country papers, have signified their intention to enter this plan.

Definite terms, giving name of authors, length and character of stories, exclusive territory, price, etc., etc., will be issued to those desiring it about the 5th of November. An early reply will greatly facilitate the work of arranging the syndicates.

Very truly yours,
S. S. McClure

It would have been more accurate to say that "over fifty newspapers" had answered his letters. Only about thirty had agreed to terms; and, while according to these terms McClure was paid or promised two hundred dollars, he had no money to give Boyesen, since all his receipts had been spent on his own expenses. McClure, who had been in transports only four weeks before, was now in despair. He couldn't sit still, couldn't stay in his own apartment. When he learned from each morning's mail that the newspaper publishers were moving with glacial deliberation or not at all, he would plunge out into the city on long, anguished, erratic walks. New York was a city of six-story buildings; great stretches of the upper West Side were unoccupied and Harlem was a country district; the street-lamps were lighted by gas, the street-cars were hauled by horses, the elevated trains were pulled by little steam-engines; and it seemed to McClure, in these fits of despondency, as though this were a finished metropolis in a finished world, where no new idea could ever get a toehold; no chance for change, no room for growth.

The buildings of Columbia College were then near McClure's apartment and once, in his gloom, he walked into the library and took a job sorting and filing newspaper clippings at three dollars and fifty cents a week. Ask him if he still believed in the newspaper syndicate and he would answer, "Yes," passionately, but there were times when he *knew that it could not succeed because too much depended upon it*. Those italics are his, as is the odd statement; both reflect his anguish in late October, 1884, when he considered how Professor Hurd would smile thinly and tell his daughter, "I told you so," and how the editors at The Century would shrug their shoulders and dismiss him from their thoughts.

At length McClure could abide the tension no longer. As ever when he was disheartened, he was compelled to hurry away, anywhere, away from what appeared to be impossibilities. It made sense for him to travel: if he was to convince editors they should buy, he had to meet them face-to-face, impress them with his energy, and infect them with his enthusiasm. And so he began a trip that seemed, at its outset, as risky as a seven-horse parlay.

From a friend on the staff of The Century he borrowed five dollars, which he used to go to Philadelphia. There he sold the Boyesen story to one paper and a story by J. S. of Dale * to another, pocketed forty-five dollars, and proceeded to Baltimore. Here he wrote Hattie a letter.

> My dearest:–
> I got here at eight and went straightway to the newspaper offices. There are five papers here—Sun, American, Herald, News, Telegram. I saw the first two & will see the third before I sleep. The American took Boyesen on consideration. . . . I feel quite hopeful about Baltimore. The election crowds are comparatively quiet here. The American is a Republican paper, & it is guarded by policemen. You know the Boston mob attacked the Journal, a Blaine paper, in Boston last night.
> Phila. was all Blaine last night & perfectly wild, but this morning it cooled down for it appeared that Cleveland stood the best show. Balto is a Cleveland crowd & all are yelling for Blaine. . . .
> I may make over $100 if I have good luck. I shall in all probability have to run three Sunday stories, besides the mid-week story, & if I make $25 on a story, I will thus earn $5,000 a year. . . .
> Dear old love! I hope very eagerly that good success may come. I saw an *elegant* bonnet in the train & I made up my mind that you should have a nice one very soon. . . .

---

* This was the pen name of Frederic J. Stimson, who, a friend at Harvard of John Ames Mitchell, the first publisher of Life, and Edward S. Martin, its first editor, had already made several contributions to that comic weekly. By November, 1884, Life was nearly two years old. Stimson gave up a promising career as a writer of fiction in exchange for a distinguished career as a constitutional lawyer.

I am evidently first in the field & I mean to remain first & last & the only one. I believe I can dispose of all the stories that all the better self-respecting authors can produce.

Good bye, dear love. I'll write you again tomorrow, & *be sure* to ask the postman to bring your mail Sunday morning. He will do it about ten—pshaw—*I'll* be home long before that. I'll be home by 6 a.m.

Be very careful & very good, & *be sure* not to bother about *prices,* nor to make any rash statements to anyone.

Oh! dearest one. May God bless us & bring us together in joy & success.

Your lover
Sam

In Baltimore he pocketed another forty-five dollars; in Washington he did poorly; he hastened to Boston, renewed his contract with Colonel Charles Taylor of The Boston Globe, and, loath to spend an unnecessary cent of his money, got Howland (who was still the editor of Outing) to wangle him a pass to Albany. Because of a faulty railroad connection he had to spend the night in North Adams, a small New England mill town where the only paper was The Hoosac Valley News; but he wasted no time. On November 13 he concluded a contract with the editors of this obscure journal, guaranteeing them exclusive territory for copyrighted stories by the best American novelists at a uniform rate of fifty cents per thousand words. In Albany he did better, signing contracts for five dollars a week.

Back in New York, with cash and contracts in his pocket, he found letters awaiting him. The San Francisco Argonaut and The St. Paul Pioneer Press had joined the syndicate at eight dollars a week. He heaved a great sigh of relief. "I realized," he said later, "that I was started."

At the time, however, this view was optimistic, for he was started only on a long steady decline into a morass of growing debt and a tangle of unforeseen problems. One of these lay in keeping his syndicates clearly defined. The Hartford Times published daily in one area, The Poughkeepsie Eagle in another; but The New England Homestead, a weekly, overlapped them both. How to feed a regular flow of fresh material to all these clients without offending any of them? If a New York paper published a story on Saturday, it was likely to anger the Philadelphia editor who proposed to print the same story on Sunday, and his schedule would in turn upset the editor in Pittsburg * whose chosen day for publishing fiction was Wednesday. Another difficulty

---

* I am observing the orthography of the time. Pittsburg had as yet not insisted upon the terminal aitch.

was mechanical: he was not always able to get the copy for his stories delivered on time. His sanguine practice was to turn the author's manuscript over to one newspaper, giving it free in return for the printing of, say, four dozen sets of galley proofs. But, the linotype being still in its infancy, the paper was likely to run out of the necessary type, might have to wait until the forms for a day's regular publication had been broken, and so would deliver the proofs too late for the mail to the West Coast, ten train-days away from New York. Moreover, despite increasingly strict copyright legislation, McClure got frequent complaints from clients who were paying perhaps twelve dollars a week for his service that their immediate competitors were airily snitching it for free.*

McClure suffered headaches, embarrassments, losses of weekly checks, and even cancellations of contracts for an entire service from each of these bugaboos; but the worst threat to his infant business came from his competition. In the late fall of 1884 Allen Thorndike Rice, the editor of The North American Review, came home from a European trip to announce plans for the syndication of four or five articles a week by "the most famous writers in the world." These were to be non-fiction, and so represented no direct threat to McClure's service; but his friends were apprehensive, and so was he. Sarah Orne Jewett wrote advising him to combine with Rice lest he be wiped out.

McClure responded by planning to expand. There were contracts to be clinched in the Midwest; rather than leave Hattie alone again, he could take her with him to Galesburg; her family would be overjoyed to see the new grandchild. They would have a happy family holiday over Thanksgiving and then come back east. But at the last moment his affairs kept him in New York, so Hattie and the baby went on without him. Distracted by his debts, bedeviled by the threat of his competitors, he followed a few days later, took care of some business in Chicago, and then eagerly hastened to Galesburg for the Thanksgiving reunion at the Hurd house, where he might briefly forget his harassing problems.

But he was reckoning without the implacable Professor Hurd. Mrs. Hurd met McClure at the door. She was, she told him, carrying out her husband's wishes in forbidding him to enter. His wife and his child were in that house, and welcome, but he was to stay outside. He was stunned. "You are to leave

---

* In 1879 a Federal postal appropriation act prohibited the mailing of any publication that violated a copyright. This was well enough intentioned, but it was very feebly enforced by the government. And if someone like McClure cared to defend his copyright, he was in the position of chasing after a thief who had a ten-block lead. Nor did such United States legislation avail in Canada, where McClure had plenty of clients.

at once," Mrs. Hurd told him, "and if you don't Hattie will be sent away too." McClure's restraint was admirable. He thought of how Hattie had yearned to visit her mother and sister; he swallowed his anger and his pride and his humiliation, and he walked away from the house alone.

Back in New York, he threw himself into his work with the renewed energy that follows on such an unpardonable affront. Rice proposed to syndicate articles? So also would he: he would measure his editorial acumen against that of the editor of The North American Review and see if he could not easily do better. He queried some of his newspaper friends: what about a series of short articles by eminent statesmen and public figures? Talcott Williams, then the managing editor of The Philadelphia Press,* wrote him advising that "the way to work that vein will be to watch for highly important subjects and then to secure an important article bearing on the subject. . . . I do not think," he added, clearly with Rice's proposed series in mind, "that articles by important men, in the air so to speak, and divorced from news, will be very salable, but a telegram on the heels of an important event announcing that an important man had something to say about it would almost always bring prompt custom."

Sensible advice; but Hattie still lingered in Galesburg, so McClure, unconsoled, came up with another idea, a series on "Celebrities at Home." "It is a long way better than Rice's [idea]," wrote M. P. Handy, the editor-in-chief of The Philadelphia Daily News. "By all means perfect your scheme and count us in. Meanwhile advise me as to your progress. You are developing a great head for business!"

"My dearest love," McClure wrote to Hattie in mid-December:

> I have broken down a mill-dam & must either utilize the water or be destroyed by it. I am under great pressure on all sides. Competitors on all hands are trying to secure a field which appears to be a veritable gold mine. I *must* keep ahead. I am doing so, but at a terrible expense of strength & toil. Now, if ever, you are indispensable to my worldly success. . . . Every day authors are flocking to our home. I need you badly. I must be away a great deal & you must be here to keep the "office open."
>
> I want you to get home next week. It isn't a matter of choice. It is a matter of the highest importance. I am reaching the limit of my endurance. I need you to share the management of the details. . . .

* Williams capped his long career by becoming the first dean of the School of Journalism at Columbia.

I am receiving proposals of partnership all round—but I have a partner—who fills all my needs. *I shall be so delighted to see you.* Oh, how I *love* my dear, dear wife. Love to your mother & sister & *baby.*

Your loving husband,
SSMcClure.

Rice's articles were to be syndicated beginning with the New Year. Since no very important issues were bobbing up in the stream of news, McClure was obliged to have recourse to a series of articles by Kate Field, a well-known Washington journalist, on Mormonism, a question that was agitating some folk at the time; and these pieces took hold fairly well.* And he sold some letters from London to a few papers. But still Hattie tarried in Galesburg. Her father was delaying her return, she wrote; couldn't his mother or his younger brother Robbie take care of his office business for him?

"My darling, darling," he exploded, just before Christmas:

> I dont want Robbie—or anybody—Mother is too officious. I want *you.* My heart is just breaking this morning. . . . Your people didn't treat me in a manner that would secure much concession from me. I want you & I am awfully, *awfully* disappointed. I can't stand it another week. . . .
> If you havent started & *cant start* I'll come after you. I am glad if they are indignant
> You are *mine* & I am dying for you
>
> > My *own dear* Hattie,
> > Your heart-broken Sam.
>
> Dont come by Lake Shore—real terrible measles in Cleveland.

At length Hattie came home to find that McClure, although he was sinking deeper into debt every week, had nevertheless determined to expand still further. In January, 1885, he announced that in addition to his regular weekly service he would furnish the newspaper press with daily stories written, as usual, "by the most noted writers"; and this ambitious project was launched in March. That month he dropped six hundred dollars further behind and by April the strain of seeing to all the details of a complicated business was beginning to tell. "Between us," he wrote later, "Mrs. McClure and I did every kind of office drudgery, all the things that in an ordinary business there are half a dozen people to do. We did the office boy's work and the clerk's work and the stenographer's work. Our office hours were from eight in the morning

---

* Except with The Salt Lake Daily Tribune, whose editor was disenchanted. In his area, he complained, such a series "was but carrying coals to Newcastle."

to ten o'clock at night." In addition, of course, he was doing a heavy stint as editor and as salesman.

"Dear Mr. McClure," Sarah Orne Jewett wrote him early in May, "believe me, it is the poorest economy to overwork yourself. Cannot you get just the right man to help you & so by and by have a kind of lieutenant who could manage for you?—You will be needing a rest, you know—Don't enlarge too fast—it keeps on always at such a strain, and doesn't not [sic] make sure of a comfortable foundation."

This friendly scolding came too late, for by May McClure was netting one hundred dollars a week. And on June 6 he sat down to pen a stiff note in which, however restrained, the note of decorous jubilation was clearly audible:

> My dear Mrs. Hurd—
>   Hattie thinks that I had better write to you about my business, as I can tell it so much better than she can, & as I have especially good news to tell.
>   The enterprise has been quite successful from the start, but as I had no money to live on, so to begin with I have been very much crippled in many ways. . . . I was in debt before I fairly began. Then failure threatened & to avoid it I had to go to Philadelphia, Balto, Washn, Boston, Albany etc & all that took money. Then I went West & Hattie went West & afterwards I went West again, & then for four weeks in March I lost $125 per week. Now, to show you how much money I have made, I will say that June 1 I was actually ahead in my business $169.00. That is, I have both established the business & have made all expenses & that sum of money. . . .
>   My present contracts will enable me to be ahead by Sept 1 $1000.00, a sum which will enable me to pay all my debts & have several hundred dollars left. I have by no means exhausted the capabilities of the enterprise, & have no doubt but that by Oct 1 I shall be clearing $200.00 per week. I never expected to make much money & I hadn't built any great hopes on the scheme at all, but every one thinks that I have established a business that will give me an independent income & make me rich besides. . . . We have made heavy sacrifices to enable me to be saved from the slavery of being employed by others. . . .
>   I enclose one of my later circulars.
> With much love, your son
SSMcClure

For once he was not overly optimistic. The literary syndicate of metropolitan newspapers was an accomplished—and profitable—fact. In rather less than eight months McClure, singlehanded, had established a newfangled business, unprecedented in its variety and scope, a business for which, more-over, he was conspicuously inexperienced and at which he had made nearly every possible mistake. In volume he had already outstripped his chief competitor, Irving Bacheller; and before the year was out Allen Thorndike Rice's syndicate would gurgle down the drain.

Here, no mistake about it, was a genuine achievement. Yet, while it is clear that McClure deserves full marks for his daring, his pertinacity, his energy, and his editorial mastery, it is likewise clear that these qualities alone—or any others, vested in only one man—could never have turned the trick. He needed the unstinting help of powerful allies. And he found it among the writers. As he said himself of the early days when he was sliding steadily deeper and deeper into debt: "I got along by paying my authors $10 or $20 on account. I paid out a little less than I collected, and my actual working capital was the money I owed authors. I made no secret of this, and the men [and women] who wrote for me were usually willing to wait for their money, as they realized that my syndicate was a new source of revenue which might eventually become very profitable to them."

There is no doubt that the writers who sold their stuff to McClure were willing to take less than their hard-won price and to wait longer than usual to be paid. Another letter from Sarah Orne Jewett, a writer of the first rank, can be offered in evidence. "While I am interested in your success," she wrote McClure late in August, 1885, "and have tried to do all I could to help you, I do not feel as if even in a business way it would be quite right to do this thing again, and if I do any more work for you I must have my regular price and be paid at once. I believe most heartily in enterprise," she went on, as a fond mother might more lightly wield a hairbrush, "but I am always afraid that you are not keeping firm ground under your feet, and that your constant enlargement of your business is only increasing the risk of it and decreasing your own percentage of profit. Oughtn't you to have put a safe and profitable business in good order by this time? or is that what you will have done by the first of October? You see, it troubles your writers and makes them lose a little confidence, and it has already given you a serious pulldown in the way of illness. Don't resent my unasked-for advice for indeed I mean it most kindly, for your sake & your wife's—I am sure she is not like my poor little Hattie of the story!"

And there is no doubt that some writers co-operated with McClure only because of their natural rapacity when tendered the prospect of a spanking new market.

But still, since writers as a class loathe taking less than their usual fee and ordinarily relegate anyone who delays in paying them to the nethermost bowels of hell, some other reason must be sought for the extraordinary measure of cordiality with which they greeted his new enterprise. And this other reason can be found only in the temper of the literary world of the 1880s. It was an unusual microcosm, and so will warrant an interested glance.

The chief patron of the serious writer, as had been the case for a hundred years, was the book publisher. In the post-bellum period he not only printed and sold books; he also, taking his cue from his English counterpart, launched literary reviews in which the fiction of the day could be discussed and promoted. But by the 1880s, while most of these literary reviews were, for one reason or another, in eclipse, there remained The Century, The Atlantic, and Harper's; and these three journals had gradually come to assume an increasingly important—even dominant—position in the literary world. In their pages was fought out the battle of realism versus romanticism; the criticism of new fiction printed here was the most influential; the acceptance of a manuscript by the editors of these magazines was crucial to a literary career. However benign and well-intentioned they might be, however reluctant to exercise their powers, three editors—Richard Watson Gilder of The Century, Henry Mills Alden of Harper's, and Thomas Bailey Aldrich of The Atlantic—were in effect dictators, economic as well as cultural, of the literary world.*

There were several reasons why such a situation was distasteful to serious writers. For one, these editors, like the book publishers, were too much concerned with English writers and not enough with American. (The American writers themselves, it must be admitted, with only a few exceptions wrote their stuff with one apprehensive eye on the English literary canon.) For another, these editors paid poorly. To be sure, by 1884 The Century was paying a William Dean Howells or a Henry James five thousand dollars for the first serial rights to a novel; but even this was a source of irritation to the generality of American writers, for one serialized novel took the place of ten or a dozen short stories, and at one time (in 1885) all the space available for fiction in The Century was given over to three novels running concurrently—Huckleberry

* There were of course other magazines at this time that stood as patron to serious writers. The Nation under E. L. Godkin printed excellent literary reviews. Lippincott's in Philadelphia, The Lakeside Monthly in Chicago, and The Overland Review in San Francisco all opened their pages to writers of merit. The Youth's Companion and, for a still younger constituency, St. Nicholas, Wide Awake, and Harper's Young People printed some stuff by good writers. And there were others. But The Century, Harper's, and The Atlantic held undisputed cultural and economic hegemony.

Finn, The Bostonians, and The Rise of Silas Lapham—which meant that three writers were pocketing what ten or twenty or even thirty might have shared. It can be argued that the choice of these three novels over thirty short stories by writers of dubious distinction has been amply vindicated by history; but it is not an argument that would have, in 1885, persuaded authors with egotism and bills to pay—which is to say, most authors. And such high fees were notable exceptions. But there was another, more heartfelt source of dissatisfaction, and this had to do with the personal predilections of the three editors.

Gilder, Alden, and Aldrich were each exceedingly sweet-natured gentlemen, each cultured and erudite, each dedicated to good taste in literature—and each excessively genteel. Indeed, they constituted a kind of three-headed vestal virgin, blue-stockinged from hip to toe, barring the gate to the temple of literature lest it be defiled by any breath of passion or vigor. Gilder, before he serialized Huckleberry Finn, required Mark Twain to make cuts that resulted, as he wrote a reader, in "the most decided difference" from the book. He went further. He wrote the same reader that "Mr. Clemens has great faults; at times he is inartistically and indefensibly coarse"—and sent a copy of his letter off to Mark Twain. When an English critic referred to America as a nation of prudes, Gilder did not protest but only murmured that "if so, we can only say that this is the price we pay for being, on the whole, the decentest nation on the face of the globe." It is a judgment which, set against the staggering venalities and vulgarities of the age, seems incomprehensible. His Boston compeer, Thomas Bailey Aldrich, was even less sensitive to the literary trade winds. Aldrich, like Gilder, was a poet of enormous refinement; he wrangled bitterly against the trend toward realism and naturalism; it was, he wrote, "a miasmatic breath/Blown from the slums." And Alden of Harper's is remembered because, ten years later, he would gut Hardy's Jude the Obscure and even bowdlerize the sentimental Trilby.

In sum, these three editors, so wholeheartedly in pursuit of the good, the true, and the beautiful, fetched up more often with the conventional, the trivial, and the decorative. In one sense they were not wholly to be blamed, for their constituency of readers demanded little more. In another sense their fault was total, for they failed properly to gauge what was dying and what was surging up to replace the decayed and second-hand.

What was in birth was the writer's awareness that there is more to life than piety, sentimentality, romantic chivalry, and a reward for virtue on the last page. This comprehension had first been evidenced demurely enough in poems and stories that drew on local or regional material; no more was required of the writer than an ear for the rhythms of local speech and an eye on one's neighbors and the way they lived. The resulting literary product had, in the main, gleamed with what William Dean Howells called "the smiling aspects of life that are the more American." So far the editors of The Century, Harper's, and The Atlantic could offer no objection. On the contrary they printed shoals of such stuff, much of it in dialect. They printed James Whitcomb Riley's Hoosier poems, Joel Chandler Harris's Uncle Remus tales, H. C. Bunner's rather superficial sketches of the colorful New York slums, George W. Cable's Creole vignettes, and Sarah Orne Jewett's simple, precise stories of Down East Yankees.

But the ear was getting keener and the eye more observant, and both alike were gradually informed by a more troubled conscience. The fact that Howells had referred to the smiling aspects of American life suggests that he recognized there were some more malign aspects, and indeed there were. The fashionable writers and editors could gather in the amiable clubs they were wont to form during the 1880s; they could, over their friendly pipes, be shocked by Zola's recently formulated theories of fiction, in which he held that life should be documented precisely as it is; they could console themselves with discussions of Brander Matthews's essay on the well-made short story; but outside their club windows workingmen were on strike for the eight-hour day; presently Henry George, the apostle of the Single Tax, would run for mayor of New York City and would very nearly be elected; and in the meantime, at a labor rally in Haymarket Square, a bomb would be exploded amongst some Chicago policemen, and guns would be drawn, and men would die in their own sudden blood. That was in May, 1886, and the fashionable writers and editors exclaimed with dismay, in chorus with most Americans, over the excesses of the anarchist workingman; but still there were some few writers, among them Howells, who sorrowed when four innocent men were hanged for alleged complicity in the Haymarket tragedy, and who read with sober concern the last words of one of the four, Albert Parsons, who cried as the trap was sprung, "O men of America, let the voice of the people be heard. . . ."

In that time of transition there were no writers with either the inclination or the talent to exploit in their stories such complex and violent forces, or even any part of them. Perhaps the closest to filling the bill was Edward Bellamy, who was already at work on his fantasy, Looking Backward; but in 1886 Theodore Dreiser, Stephen Crane, and Frank Norris were youngsters of fifteen or sixteen, and Jack London was only ten.* There were, however, writers disposed to tinker with the new techniques of realism and naturalism, and ready to search the unsmiling aspects of life for their material. When they found the editorial doors of the magazines closed to their contributions, they would likely have shrugged and returned to the old ways—except that the newspaper syndicates had the welcome mat out. No wonder, then, that so many of McClure's contributors were willing to take less than their usual fee, willing even to wait for their money.† What the writers wanted was a sympathetic reading and economic support for material which, in some cases, even they felt was infra dig. Only McClure could meet their needs. With increasing frequency stories of Western farm life, of factory workers, of Pennsylvania coal miners bobbed up in his syndicate service. And so it can be said that McClure helped turn the stream of American creative writing into a new and deeper channel.

At first, however, the stories McClure bought were not very different from those published in the best magazines of the time. We are, indeed, permitted the discreet speculation that at least some of his early stories came from their authors' trunks; that is, that they were efforts previously rejected by a half-dozen magazine editors. Nor can it be claimed that McClure ever made a deliberate search for realistic fiction. His personal preferences were all for romance; in later years he would extravagantly admire Conan Doyle's historical romances and Robert Louis Stevenson's tales of adventure. But he was also a superlative editor and as such he was eager to buy any form of expression so long as he found it well-written and interesting. Interesting! It was his favorite adjective; he should have paid it time-and-a-half; it popped out whenever he got a leg up on something new. And so it was natural that he should greet the first competent efforts at realism with enthusiasm.

---

* Of these, all but Dreiser were first given a national readership by McClure, through either the syndicate or the later magazine.

† Many, but by no means all, were willing to wait. There was, for instance, an extremely fashionable writer named Edgar Fawcett, the author of great masses of stuff now fortunately all forgotten. (His notion of satire was to give the characters of his society novels such names as Lord Slantingforehead and Lord Willowthewisp.) Fawcett, when he was not promptly paid, saw fit to send his valet to McClure's flat to collect. McClure was on the road, selling, and Hattie most earnestly assured the valet that she had no money, but nevertheless back he came for three solid days and sat, waiting.

Helen Hunt Jackson was another popular writer who was early vexed by McClure's inability to pay her fee. She forbade him to use her name in his future circulars to newspaper editors. When he persisted, she retaliated by selling her stuff to Irving Bacheller. McClure was unperturbed. He bought the serial rights to her stories from Bacheller, wrote her telling her what he had done, pointed out that she had lost money in the process, and flabbergasted her by inviting her to write for him a 20,000-word serial at still better money.

Moreover, he needed volume to keep all his syndicates well-fed and contented: a story a week to start, then two a week, then three, and later as
many as eight or ten a week. In order to meet his quota he was obliged to
buy inferior stuff, and he knew it; he was the happier, then, to come upon
the occasional well-wrought realistic story.

And so, by all the gods, were his clients, the newspaper editors. These
worthies suffered much at the hands of the fashionable writers. McClure's
files for the first year of his syndicate service resound with their growls:

The Philadelphia Press: "Harriet Prescott Spofford's story [is not] worth
printing . . . carelessly written . . . improbable. . . . I am very much disappointed." And again: "Prof. Boyesen's story seems to me dull and unin-
teresting."

The St. Paul Pioneer Press: "Some of the daily stories you send out are
fossil chestnuts from the antediluvian strata of literature." And again: "You
have been paying famous writers high prices for their fourth rate work." And
yet again: "At least half of the daily stories you send out are mere rubbish.
. . . I don't think famous names go for much."

The Pittsburg Chronicle Telegraph: "The new authors excite more interest
than the old stand bys. You get more originality with the new writers. . . .
A reader of a *short* story in a daily newspaper cares very little about literary
polish. He only wants to be interested or amused. . . ."

The Newark Evening News: "Please send me a good short story by some
unknown writer. I want one that people who are not 'literary' will appreciate."

During the first year of McClure's syndicate service newspaper editors could
afford to scold, for McClure was selling fiction in a buyer's market. As a syndicate editor he was in a far more difficult position than is his counterpart
today, for at option his clients could reject a story or even cancel an entire
contractual arrangement, and often did just that. He was constantly on his
mettle. He could buy only such manuscripts as, in his judgment, he would be
able to sell to at least twenty reluctant newspaper editors. In consequence,
McClure began to deal more severely with the well-known writers. As early
as September, 1885, he was flatly rejecting stories submitted by even such
popular writers as E. P. Roe,* and demanding changes in the manuscripts of

---

* E. P. Roe is forgotten today, but in the mid-1880s he towered over other American writers,
such as Howells and Henry James, and he left Mark Twain and Herman Melville literally
nowhere. In 1887 The Critic, taking the sales figures of the largest wholesale bookseller in
the country as its gauge, revealed that Roe was by all odds the most popular author in the
country. For every one thousand copies of Roe's books that were sold, only fourteen by
Howells were sold, and only one by Henry James. Neither Mark Twain nor Herman Melville
even appeared on the list.

such fashionable writers as Noah Brooks and Elizabeth Stuart Phelps. Authors tended to be long on description and slow in development; they were stingy with action, dialogue, and suspense: all these habits, in order to forestall the complaints of the new patron, had to be overcome. "Most reluctantly," Miss Phelps wrote McClure, she would adopt his criticism. "I am sorry," wrote Noah Brooks, "the story did not meet your views," but he offered to submit two others.

As to new writers, McClure began to see their manuscripts before they were submitted to the magazines. In the early summer of 1885 a young businessman, Henry Harland, showed three of his stories to E. C. Stedman, the poet who was by day a broker in downtown Manhattan. The stories dealt with life among the Jews on the lower East Side; and Stedman turned them over to McClure, who paced excitedly back and forth in his apartment all night as he read them, gradually realizing that here was the work of a new writer with real talent.* And he sold them with great success.

And so as he bustled about, always bursting with enthusiasm for the stories in his satchel, McClure earned the regard of newspaper editors all over the country. This was as well, for great changes were afoot which would wholly alter his relationship with his clients. To his delight, McClure gradually came to realize that he was the principal merchant in an apparently ever-expanding seller's market.

The changes came in both the quantity and the quality of the newspapers. In 1880 there had been a scant nine hundred daily newspapers in the country, and they circulated in limited fashion. Of the nation's total daily circulation, more than half was printed in six cities—New York, Philadelphia, Chicago, Cleveland, Boston, and San Francisco; New York newspapers alone accounted for almost one-quarter of the daily national press run. But Americans had become dedicated newspaper readers, and so the number of daily papers swelled fantastically with each succeeding year. Slowly at first: in 1884, the year that McClure launched his syndicate service, there were still less than twelve hundred dailies, but in the next decade they were to multiply at the rate of almost a hundred a year.†

---

* Harland, having set out (under the pen name of Sidney Luska) to write in the new mode, thereafter swiftly hauled down the flag. He removed to London a few years later and, with Aubrey Beardsley, launched The Yellow Book, a fin-de-siècle journal that has not been generally praised for its emphasis on realistic writing. Harland's later stories, indeed, may be dismissed (as they have been by time) as graceful but thoroughly decadent examples of the romantic tradition.

† Precise figures are hard to come by, but perhaps the best study is by Alfred M. Lee, in his The Daily Newspaper in America. The peak was reached in 1909, when there were more

These quantitative changes, breeding competition, brought about even more striking qualitative changes. The newspapers of the early 1880s were puny things, running usually to no more than eight pages even in the great cities. They were, by today's standards, oddly barren: aside from advertising they printed only local news, political articles, a smidgeon of foreign news by cable, and a few paragraphs of wit snitched from their rivals' columns. The first primitive comic strips would not appear until 1894. There were no columnists, national or local; no women's features, no puzzle pages, no Sunday supplements, no book reviews, no cooking recipes, no theatrical gossip and of course no chatter from Hollywood; nothing from out-of-town except, as one journalist remarked, the "mere brute fact" syndicated by the Associated Press.

But developments in the technique of making paper out of wood pulp punctured the cost of newsprint. The size of daily editions could be doubled, the size of Sunday editions quadrupled. Every editor faced the same problem: how to fill the new space so as best to discountenance the new competition? And every editor, as he looked up, found McClure coming in at the door, his face alight with apostolic zeal. Book reviews? He would get them. Cooking recipes? He would, if necessary, write them himself—and so he actually did, for a time, under the name of Patience Winthrop. Was Edward Bok planning to syndicate features for a woman's page? He engaged to do the same—better, faster, and more plentifully. The service of short stories was augmented by serialized novels, the occasional letter by series of correspondence, the stray article by regular departments covering science, sports, travel, etiquette, care for babies—whatever was new, whatever was interesting.

And still the genteel magazine editors refused to acknowledge that a revolution was at hand, that all at once the writer had found a new patron. As late as July, 1887, William Rideing, the editor of The Youth's Companion, dismissed the syndicates in a sneering, contemptuous letter addressed to The Critic. "My conclusion," he wrote, "is that so far from being bureaus of employment for authors, they are bureaus of relief for necessitous and

---

than two thousand, six hundred daily newspapers being published in the United States. Thereafter the clammy hand of consolidation began to clutch at the throttle of American journalism. In 1963, there were only one thousand seven hundred and sixty dailies being published, despite the fact that population had nearly doubled since 1909.

But in 1885 (to revert to the time under discussion) an English visitor to the United States was struck by the liveliness of the American press. There was, he noted, one newspaper for every ten thousand inhabitants; this compared to one newspaper for every one hundred and twenty thousand in Great Britain and Ireland.

uncapitalized persons, whose energies are misspent in a hopeless business."

McClure could afford to smile. He was at the time publishing three serials, one by Jules Verne in thirteen newspapers, one by Julian Hawthorne in twenty, and one by E. P. Roe in nineteen. His service, which in November, 1884, had carried only a weekly five thousand words, was in 1887 distributing fifty thousand words a week to well over one hundred newspapers, and he was making contracts for the fall that would increase the service to nearly one hundred thousand words a week.

Talcott Williams, who, as managing editor of The Philadelphia Press, had viewed at close range the changes exploding all about him, would later write, of McClure: "It is not easy to speak without exaggeration, and it is impossible to contemplate without enthusiasm the skill which has secured the confidence of both authors and editors, won the good-will, on the one hand, of the distinguished names of letters of whom we all know, and, on the other, of the thousand men who pass on manuscripts and supplement in our newspapers. . . .

"The creation of a new audience is the most difficult feat known to literature, and the most important. Such work is not often done; when it is done it brings revolution for both writer and reader. . . .

"This revolution, this discovery of a new audience, has multiplied by millions those who read and know the first authors of the day in certain classes of literary work; as the short story, it has doubled and trebled the price before paid, in all it has widened the market of the pen. . . .

"These are great fruits to come from a life of thirty-four years. They have made the spare figure, the gray-blue eyes, the thin, light hair, and the keen, mobile face of the author and inventor of this revolution, known in more newspaper offices and to more authors than any other man in the two centuries in which our letters have known the newspaper."

[II]

Early on a bitter cold morning in February, 1887, a muffled figure hurried down a North River pier and slipped aboard the S.S. Etruria, bound for Queenstown and Liverpool. Hidden inside the scarf and greatcoat was a slender man who had taken the trouble to identify himself, wrongly, as "S. Sidney" in the list of the Etruria's passengers printed that morning in the New York newspapers. But this was no absconding bank cashier, nor yet a transatlantic confidence man weaving dreams of easy pickings at the card tables. This was S. S. McClure, coping with his competition. He had heard that Irving Bacheller, his chief rival, was forming plans for a trip to Europe to get material from English and continental writers for his syndicates; if Bacheller had plans, then McClure had to have passage.

McClure's concern, his cloak-and-dagger hocus-pocus, and his impetuous haste were alike wholly justified. To be sure, he was at the moment on top but, scramble he never so shrewdly, he was finding it as ticklish a task to stick to his odd eminence as it had been to get there. His service regularly offered stories by every popular writer in the country. He had engaged to deliver to his clients that mercurial substance, humor, and had even done so with some limited success.* He had, moreover, undertaken so ambitious a scheme as the publication of the first Sunday supplement. He had announced this project in February, 1886, in a circular sent to a few authors, whom he urged:

> 1. This is not a *proposed* plan. I have made the contracts with the newspapers; I made them less than a month ago.
> 2. The subscription lists of the newspapers taking this service aggregate over 2,000,000 subscribers—a circulation ten times that of the most popular magazine. It will be virtually a weekly magazine, with a circulation to begin with of 2,000,000 copies.
> 3. This service will be published as an integral part of the subscribing newspapers [in over twenty of the larger cities of the United States].
> 4. This is the first enterprise of the kind in the world. Never before has a popular, *comprehensive* magazine service of literature been furnished to a syndicate of newspapers.
> 5. The newspapers have combined to secure the best and most popular literature. Every idea that would be available for a popular magazine will be available for this service.
> 6. Millions of people will be led to appreciate good literature, and the book-buying public will be largely increased.
> 7. This will be a powerful agency in destroying the market for vile literature.

---

* Bill Nye, the foremost humorous paragrapher of the time, was delighted to get McClure's offer to syndicate his stuff. Nye had been vexed to find his output "gobbled up," as he wrote McClure, "by every crossroads paper and 'patent inside' in the country. . . . If all my work could be done for your syndicate and copyrighted . . . I would be protected from the pastepot-and-scissors fiend." Nye agreed "to write exclusively for the syndicate" for sixty dollars a week and a percentage of any increasing business.

Opie Read, who had by 1885 already won some fame as a humorist under the pen name of the Arkansas Traveller, wrote McClure: "I do work for other syndicates but I am free to say that I prefer yours."

And if he failed to perceive that the Sunday supplement of the future would do little to destroy the market for vile literature, the fault was not his.

So far had his business expanded that he was swanking about under a new trade name, The Associated Literary Press, and had taken an office in the Tribune Building down on Newspaper Row, where he kept busy a growing staff of readers and stenographers. He was not yet a Big Business but he was unmistakably on the way. His old friend and preceptor at Knox, Melville Anderson, had written him in mild reproach. "Where," asked Professor Anderson, "is the ardent young philologist and Platonist" who was going in for just enough money? McClure was nettled. "Can you answer," he wrote back, "what is just enough money? Moreover, the work I am engaged in seems to be sufficiently educational."

> I suppose [he went on] I am completely wedded to journalism. People at our age cannot profitably change their occupation. The *cui bono* comes in just here: how to make the modern newspaper a complete and artistic reflex of modern life. My mission is to furnish to the newspapers a service which will give them the results of the intellectual progress of the world. That I must do. That kind of work is needed and no one else seems to take it up.
>
> I appreciate your position that an author must be coffined before he becomes an author to you, but for me an author in that position is nothing at all. It seems to me that the scientific spirit of the times, when applied to literature, means a study of current product. By studying the present you see the animal growing, you see it developing; of course it is unpleasant to place a certain estimate on an author and find that in ten or twelve years he is utterly out of sight. But then you have the fun and excitement of watching the gradual growth and the tendencies of the times. . . .

But while McClure was first and thoroughly enjoying it, he was acutely conscious of his rivals' threats to overthrow him. Late in 1886 he had been dismayed when Bacheller, his principal competitor, had combined with Ansel Nash Kellogg, the boiler-plate king, whose stereotype plates of fiction, farmed out to country weeklies, had already made the word "stereotype" an arrow of opprobrium in the critical quiver. Writers and newspaper editors generally had only contempt for Kellogg's syndicate; but McClure fancied he could see the threat of monopoly, with Bacheller able to offer American writers ever higher fees, thanks to Kellogg's lucrative business.

There seemed only one solution: to insure a steady supply of fiction from the more popular English authors, who in 1887 were accorded more veneration, however ill-deserved, than their American contemporaries. By that time the English writers whose works sold best in America—Dickens, Scott, George Eliot, Thackeray, and Bulwer-Lytton—were all coffined and therefore nothing at all to McClure. But Wilkie Collins was still writing; Ouida was at the height of her meager powers; Thomas Hardy's best books were before him; H. Rider Haggard had just made a great success with King Solomon's Mines, and indeed McClure had a copy of Haggard's latest novel, She, with him aboard the Etruria. There were, as well, American writers living in England: Bret Harte, whose reputation was secure; Henry James, in the full flush of success; and Harold Frederic, barely thirty, hard at work on his first novel, and destined to die before he had realized his promise. Moreover, some weeks before he sailed, McClure had been about, picking the brains of his friends for whatever was new and interesting; Charles de Kay, Richard Watson Gilder's brother-in-law, had told him of a tale of adventure, Kidnapped, that had been published the year before in England, and so the name of Robert Louis Stevenson had been carefully entered in his notebook.*

But before McClure could take off after such prizes, he had had to find someone to mind the store while he was gone. For more than a year he had searched for a trustworthy assistant—someone with patience, a taste for details, and decent editorial sense; someone who would free him to take off wherever and whenever he listed, on whatever capricious errand; someone who would, as well, have faith in his genius for making his caprices pay off. Hattie was no longer a possibility, for in 1886 she had borne a second daughter, Elizabeth,† and her time was now given over to her children. One after another, McClure's younger brothers—first Jack, then Tom, then Robbie—had taken a stab at helping him, but none had filled the bill. And then his old friend and classmate at Knox, John Phillips, appeared in New York.

* No perspicacity was required to "discover" Stevenson at late as 1887. Treasure Island was published in November, 1883, and proved a quick success, at least in England. Months before that, McClure had himself reviewed Stevenson's An Inland Voyage for The Wheelman; he had praised it unstintingly, in language that the publishers might cheerfully have reprinted as their blurb: "Most delightful . . . very pleasant reading, bright, original, and touched here and there with penetrating appreciative humor." The Strange Case of Dr. Jekyll and Mr. Hyde was published in January, 1886, and here too was an overnight success. It was followed in July by Kidnapped, after which there could have been no doubt on either side of the Atlantic as to Stevenson's literary potential.

† "To give you an idea that I am really heavy," Hattie wrote her mother, during her second pregnancy, "I'll tell you that I split the pot de chambre when I sat down on it last night."

Since he had left The Wheelman, Phillips had taken his degree at Harvard and gone on to study for a year at Leipsic. Now home again, Phillips found that the syndicate business he had so gloomily discounted was fairly established; he was about to get married and he needed a job. McClure gladly hired him.

Painstaking, even-tempered, somewhat owlish in appearance with his steel-rimmed glasses and his pensive air, Phillips was precisely what was needed in the home office of the expanding business. McClure, once he was satisfied that Phillips was in quiet command, was ready in February, 1887, to take off for London.

It was a venturesome journey. London was the established and complacent capital of the English-speaking cultural world, ready to deliver McClure a double snub on the grounds of his being an Irish-born American; moreover, his competitive stakes against Bacheller were high. But his confidence had waxed mightily: he was only in a hurry, impatient to get the job done. The Etruria, as though hustled along by his impetuosity, broke the transatlantic record to Queenstown.

March 4th

My dearest Hattie:

This is Friday & tomorrow we reach Queenstown & next morning Liverpool & a special trainload of people has been made up to go right through to London where I will arrive in time for supper, or dinner as these people call it. . . .

You cant imagine how it feels for me to be so long away from news of the world & knowledge of my business.

I have discovered a new salad—celery, lettuce & a few slices of Spanish onion. The result is delicious & I am known among the stewards as the king of salad-makers. . . .

It is only 4.30 & I am *hungry* again. . . .

March 4

My dear John—

. . . My only important piece of advice is to publish the news of my contracts in London—if I succeed—*as soon as possible,* in The Critic & elsewhere, so that Bacheller will not write to them & perhaps make tremendous offers, after they have engaged to me at quite moderate sums, as I hope. . . .

This is an awful isolation. I don't know *anything* about what is going on. . . .

I have acquired a *tremendous* appetite. I could easily handle a whole sirloin steak at the Astor.

Use the cable liberally. I will. Keep things steady, handle every one carefully & according to his weak points. . . .

March 5

My dearest Hattie

I am *very* homesick for you. . . . I want you to REST. . . . I am eager to try my luck on these authors. Read "She." It is a tremendous story & think that I adore & love you more than anyone could adore her. . . . Goodbye sweet love

When he was riding the crest of his enthusiasm, McClure was one of the most effervescent talkers in an age that abounded in men who loved to gab. Words bubbled up in him and boiled over in a froth of ebullience. The effect was irresistible: curmudgeons celebrated for their icy reserve, meeting him for the first time, thawed forthwith. In part, his charm was due to his lack of ceremony. It was not that he chose to ignore the customary social proprieties, but rather that he had never been taught them; he was as straightforward as an exuberant puppy, and like a puppy he was cheerfully unaware of snubs or scowls but simply plunged on, unbridled and gay, unable to sit still, walking excitedly about, jingling the coins in his pocket, his bright blue eyes dancing, his mind darting from one idea to another, his laugh ready and infectious. During his first days in London he was at a peak of such animation.

March 7

My darling Hattie

Today has been a very busy day. I called on several publishers & had a very pleasant time. . . . My main success was this: I find that Bret Harte, H. Rider Haggard, Wilkie Collins & a number of the most famous authors in England do all their business through a gentleman named Mr. [A.P.] Watt. I called on him, found him a most agreeable man & learned *that Tillotson & Son had just bought stories by both Bret Harte & Haggard.* It is now my point to see them & make as favorable terms as possible for the American rights. . . .

I have already forestalled my rival completely. . . .

I am getting very strong, & young & fresh & feel the old boundless vigor in my veins & feel the conscious thrills of perfect life & health, I feel as if difficulties would melt before me. My brain is fresh, so is my body, & I feel able to found a great publishing house. . . .

William Tillotson had been the head of Tillotson & Son since the retirement of his father, fifteen years before; it was he who had first thought to syndicate fiction in his chain of Lancashire newspapers and elsewhere. He was a chunky, bearded man of forty-three, hard-headed, with a reputation for crisp, laconic business dealings; like his brother-in-law, William Lever,* he stood for no nonsense. He liked to strike a bargain in five minutes where another man might take an hour. But McClure had a tale to tell, and he was nine hours in the telling.

March 9

My dear John—

I have accomplished it, & in a far better way than I dreamed of doing. I have nothing to be announced to the American Press. I have much to tell you when I see you. I will give you the mere bones for the present. I found that Tillotson had Harte & Haggard & Collins. How I talked to Tillotson from 3 P.M. to midnight, how I managed the most difficult, intricate, & dreadful negotiation I ever attempted, how I succeeded, absolutely, perfectly, & how Mr. Tillotson & I parted, with the highest admiration & respect for each other & how we engaged in a treaty offensive & defensive to monopolize the syndicate serial service of the world—on the basis, that I pay him $\frac{2}{5}$ of all I get in America for English authors, & he pay me $\frac{3}{5}$ for all he gets in the rest of the world for Am. authors (paying me $4000.00 outright for [Frances Hodgson] Burnett) & how we arranged to have Harte, Haggard, Stevenson, Collins, Burnett, [Charles Egbert] Craddock, [Frank] Stockton, et al.—& all the other points of the most dreadful & most successful negotiation, I will tell fully when I return.

Bacheller is utterly routed & badly beaten

Tillotson will secure all possible serials from all the names worth having in Europe. I will secure all worth having in America.

Success, absolute & cloudless, is ours. I will devote the remainder of my time to securing special features by the most famous living Europeans—send this & all other letters and telegrams to Hattie

Very sincerely yours
SSMcClure

It was characteristic that he should ignore tourist attractions. His attention was engaged by far more interesting considerations.

---

* This was the man who sold enough Sunlight Soap to become Lord Leverhulme; his American company, Lever Brothers, stands solid today as purveyor of both soap and soap-opera.

March 10

My dearest Sweetheart

. . . I am accomplishing a great deal & see a great future before me.

I want to give you a few of the peculiarities of London & England.

1 The breads are splendid, various, healthful & common sense.

2 Waterclosets in trains are closed with a trap just like those in private houses.

3 Few trains are warmed—almost none—people travel 8–10 hrs in damp, cold cars. . . .

4 Hotels have waterclosets & bathrooms on every floor.

5 There is a charge always for attendance 1s. to 1s. 6d.

6 Many of the principal streets are numbered up one side & down the other, consecutive numbers being together.

7 Vegetarian restaurants abound, also Coffee Houses, also wretched coffee.

8 Hotel employees are dressed in the most elaborate & varied costumes.

9 American news is very scarce in London, sometimes only a few lines, & never over $\frac{1}{4}$–$\frac{1}{3}$ column.

10 The English regard the Americans as a very uneducated, pushing, money-grabbing race.

11 You don't have butter at a meal unless you ask for it.

12 They eat only the most rotten cheese, the smell of which is perfectly horrible.

13 When giving directions to a stranger they never say north or south, but right or left.

14 There is a greater regard for privacy here. . . .

Your most loving husband
SSMcClure

McClure was addressing all his letters to 35 Beekman Place. This was the house owned by the father of the young writer, Henry Harland, whose first pseudonymous stories McClure had published through his syndicate. McClure had struck up a warm friendship with young Harland, and this had led to his taking an apartment on the upper two floors of the Harland house. He assumed that Hattie was there now, awaiting his return. But the day after he left for London, Hattie had gone to Galesburg to visit her family, taking her two daughters with her. Only now did he learn of what she had done.

March 11

My darling wife

Your most welcome letter of Tuesday eve, March 1, is just at hand. . . .

You may be sure I was thoroughly astonished to hear of your return home & made very angry by the fact that your father took occasion to write you a good many hard things. When equal success & honor & reputation attend me in England & America I am not in a mood to tolerate such unreasonable, absurd, & unjust treatment.

In short I am very deeply enraged, & I am through bending a single item to *anyone*.

I am real glad you went home. *Your* joy & pleasure & comfort are all I care for. . . . Of course, knowing me as you do, & knowing that my lonesomeness for you affects me like a disease of the mind, you must anticipate that wherever you are on my return to America I will instantly go to you by the most rapid expresses.

This you will regard as absolute, & if your father prefers to have you return *alone* rather than to allow us to meet in Galesburg, I shall deem it only our duty to absolutely hold no further intercourse with him. This absence gives me the terrible experiences of those horrible years, & I wonder how I tolerated such tragic experiences.

I am awfully in love with you & consumed with a kind of restless feverish and awful melancholy that renders my very existence a burden. Your letter was *very* sweet & dear to me. It has helped me all day.

No power under heaven will separate us when it is possible for me to reach you. Nor will any considerations keep me away from you an hour when trains are running.

Kiss my dearest daughters for me & take all my love & adoration for your own sweet self & remember me warmly to your dear mother & sister.

Your loving husband
SSMcClure

"The cable is none too rapid," he wrote her next day. By that time, however, his rage had somewhat dissipated: an angry cable sent the same day as his letter had drawn from her a lenitive if ambiguous cable assuring him that he would be welcome in Galesburg, but not stipulating for how long a time. His plans required of him a swing across the country to San Francisco and Los Angeles, selling his service as he went. With his customary sublime optimism he counted on stopping off for a week's visit in Professor Hurd's house.

March 12

My dear John—

. . . I am anxious about the various schemes, especially about money. I suppose it's *slow*.

However, the *future* is secure. I think we are now in a position to compete with the world. . . .

I have no advice except for you to Push, Think, Decide, & make it hum. . . .

Sincerely
SSMcClure

That night Harold Frederic, who was London correspondent for The New York Times, took him to a special night at the Savage Club. "The Club," McClure wrote Hattie, "is composed of the brightest Journalists, Litterateurs, Artists, Authors, Actors, &c &c, & they have songs, recitations, pantomimes, etc. all by their own members, & mostly by people who are remarkably brilliant." He enjoyed himself hugely, laughed immoderately at the sophomoric proceedings, and returned to his comfortable rooms at the Hotel Métropole, where he was pleased to find a fire burning in the grate. "I like the *hours* these English keep. Why, they take tea at nine, & sleep *late* & take life easy & aren't rushed. I think I'll enjoy being rich."

He met Harold Frederic again for breakfast next day. At this time Frederic had published only his first novel, Seth's Brother's Wife, a book shot through with his detestation of farm life, and one of the earliest sustained efforts at realistic writing by an American. McClure had read it aboard ship and had confided to Hattie that he thought it "truly capital," a judgment made possible solely by virtue of McClure's own vivid memories of how drab is the life of the hind. The two men had, indeed, much in common. They were both country bumpkins who had turned to journalism. Each had been mortally unsure of himself when first he hit the big city. When Frederic was offered the Times post in London he had turned up in the office of E. P. Mitchell, the Sun editor, wearing a long green coat that made him look like a cucumber, to ask Mitchell how he should comport himself aboard a transatlantic liner, and he had scrupulously jotted all Mitchell's paternal advice down in a notebook. But London had been kind to him; he fitted in well. He too was a great talker. The poet Louise Imogen Guiney said of him later: "The quality of his talk was equal to the quantity . . . and that is saying much. He had an off-hand, mock-heroic, chaffing flow of speech. . . . In his indignations, there was a fine Niagara freshet of words."

These two talkers, then, McClure and Frederic, met for breakfast. McClure reported the encounter to Hattie: "We talked a few minutes apparently & it was two o'clock! I then lunched with him & we talked a few minutes & then it was . . . evening." Evidently McClure outtalked the Niagara freshet.

In proof, their marathon gabfest had two results: Frederic undertook to be McClure's European representative; and when, two months later, Frederic wrote his second novel, The Lawton Girl, he gave its hero a boyhood identical with McClure's and even put McClure's own phrases in his hero's mouth.*

"Where is my wandering boy tonight?" sang Hattie, on that same Sunday evening, and as she sang her eyes filled with tears. Where, indeed, was he? She was at the Galesburg Methodist Episcopal Church, attending a temperance meeting and singing gospel hymns, but where was he? The only word she had had from him was his angry cable, to which she had cabled her answer. She was, poor woman, still grist between the millstones, but she liked to think she had perceived a change in her father. "He says," she wrote her husband, "for you to come here to visit me for a day or about that length of time, and says he will consent to your passing the night and eating your meals here, and will conduct himself as usual on the occasion of your visit. He will do that rather than have me return to N.Y. alone with my children to meet you there before you start on your Western trip. . . . It is yielding everything on his part, and I am sure you will appreciate it at its true worth and meaning. The time will soon come, I am very sure, when you can visit here as freely as I. . . ."

McClure found her letter at his office when he landed the following Sunday. (The S.S. Etruria, having broken the eastbound transatlantic record with him aboard in February, broke the westbound record with him aboard in March.) He noted that he was invited to spend "a day or about that length of time" with the Hurds. He dispatched a telegram: "Galesburg Tuesday afternoon. Leave for Pacific Coast about Saturday."

He reached Galesburg Tuesday afternoon. He left for the Pacific Coast on Sunday.

[III]

When the sole owner of a successful, flourishing, worldwide enterprise confesses, after his six most prosperous years, that he has accumulated a net profit of only two thousand, eight hundred dollars, his admission provokes some interest. Since incompetence and fraud are by definition ruled

---

* The passage in question carries over pp. 104–108 of The Lawton Girl. Some of the phrases are remarkably close to those McClure used in "writing" My Autobiography.

out (the enterprise having been successful) the possible conclusions seem to be limited to three:

1. The business is a very odd one indeed;
2. The sole owner is not concerned with making money, or at all events has more exigent matters on his mind;
3. The sole owner has a hole in his pants pocket.

Many of those who were associated with him both at the time and later would have clamored that there was a fourth, and comprehensive, conclusion possible, to wit:

4. The sole owner is S. S. McClure,

but this is arguing in a circle. Certainly McClure was one of the very few men who could have managed a thriving business with such slim pickings; certainly McClure had acquaintances who, in the face of his visible triumphs, nevertheless constantly predicted his imminent bankruptcy—but still the wonder is, Why? How was it possible for a man to become the envy of so many of his contemporaries, to expand his business all over the United States and Canada and into Great Britain, Australia, the West Indies, and India, to come up season after season with the prize literary discoveries—and still have so little to show for it?

The question is more easily asked than answered, nor will McClure himself be found sitting still in one place long enough to work out a coherent explanation. (In the six years from 1887 to 1893 he made eight round trips across the Atlantic, and crisscrossed the United States to call on his clients, the newspaper editors, another eight times.) His trail, however tangled, is easy enough to follow. The difficulty is rather that his activities were so manifold and so bewildering. For every ocean crossing there was a new and stupendous scheme for bringing the world of literature to his feet, for every night on the road a prodigious idea for a story, a serial, a series of serials.

Why were there not more writers in the world, so that his ideas might be seized upon, admired, curled and furbelowed, and so sent forth to instruct and amuse the reading public? He met them all in these six years: Stevenson, Kipling, Conan Doyle, and Meredith; Hardy, Henley, Besant, and Haggard; those of lasting talent and those of inflated; Tennyson and Ouida, Julia Ward Howe and Whitman, Mark Twain and Randolph Churchill, Barrie and Howells; journalists, historians, romancers, and poets; Lafcadio Hearn, Jerome K. Jerome, Arthur Brisbane, Richard Harding Davis, Gertrude

Atherton, and Joel Chandler Harris; a grab-bag of the truly great and the truly pretentious; Henry James and Hamlin Garland; Ruskin, Swinburne, and William Morris; Francis Parkman, Edward Bellamy, Theodore Roosevelt, and John Burroughs; prophets and philosophers; Ned Buntline and Samuel Smiles, Bret Harte and Edmund Gosse, Andrew Lang and Bernard Shaw, Brander Matthews and Arthur Quiller-Couch: McClure met them all and bought from them all (except Bernard Shaw), and yet not all of these together could field, to his satisfaction, all the fungoes he sent arching up against the sky.

So, in retrospect, McClure might have explained the meager rewards his syndicate business brought him. But it may be suggestive, and entertaining as well, to focus on a handful of his salient concerns from 1887 to 1893, and so to form an independent opinion.

Of all those concerns, McClure would himself have insisted that the most important was his friendship with Robert Louis Stevenson. It was a loony relationship, perhaps the looniest in all literary history between an editor and an author. There were only some half-dozen face-to-face encounters over as many months; but in terms of confusion, vexation, heartache, and headache the two men managed to squeeze a lot of mileage out of those six encounters; and when they resorted to correspondence matters got, if possible, even more moonstruck. Emotionally it was all one-way: while McClure idolized Stevenson, Stevenson repaid him chiefly with snobbish condescension and amused contempt. Practically it was likewise one-way: Stevenson profited enormously, both in popularity and in cash, while there are grounds to suspect that McClure actually lost money on his transactions with Stevenson. Yet McClure never faltered either in his affection or in his willingness to gamble on Stevenson's stories. "John," he once told Phillips, "I want the syndicate business to be run exactly as if it were being conducted for the benefit of Robert Louis Stevenson." And so it worked out.

McClure had sought to meet Stevenson in February, 1887; he had written him a letter at Bournemouth, where Stevenson had gone for his health. Characteristically, Stevenson lost the letter and so could not answer it. But early in September a young man looked up McClure at his office in the Tribune Building, introduced himself as Stevenson's stepson, Lloyd Osbourne, and invited McClure to call at the New York hotel where Stevenson was stopping.

Considerable excitement attached to this visit. Stevenson was not yet at the height of his vogue; that would come later, at his death and in the

years that immediately followed, and McClure would have much to do
with his reaching it. Three generations have passed. Today one is able to
conclude that Stevenson wrote two or three poems that will live, two or
three short stories, two or three adventure tales for children. His essays,
once so warmly recommended, go largely ignored. It is hard to recall the
names of his more ambitious novels. But in 1887 he was a literary figure to
reckon with; the crest of the wave was not far off; the spume was, so to
say, already dripping from his long locks of hair.

McClure took his wife with him to the Hotel St. Stephen, where Stevenson lay in bed in the attitude of the Saint-Gaudens medallion, for which he
was then posing. McClure was at once and entirely enchanted. A cynic, of
course, would have it that McClure perceived that Stevenson was money in
the bank; and so, indeed, one or two of Stevenson's intimates interpreted
McClure's impulsive affection. But his emotion was quite genuine. "Stevenson was," he said many years later, "the sort of man who commanded every
kind of affection: admiration for his gifts, delight in his personal charm, and
respect for his uncompromising principles. . . . It was probably this unusual
combination of qualities that made one eager to serve him in every possible
way." While Stevenson's gifts and his personal charm were both beyond
question, as to his principles there may be some doubt; but McClure's
generous estimation of them must be charged to his naïveté, not to any opportunism.

At all events, McClure was more than eager, he was once again enthusiastic. How could he serve Stevenson? He hustled over to Joseph Pulitzer
at the offices of The New York World and, having argued persuasively,
hustled back to tender Pulitzer's offer. Would Stevenson accept ten thousand
dollars a year for a series of short weekly essays? It was a huge sum for
the time: Stevenson, reflecting on his raffish and irresponsible past, when
five English pounds had seemed a fortune, was dazzled. He snatched at it.
But he also mentioned the offer to E. L. Burlingame, editor of Scribner's, who
urged him to repudiate it and instead undertake a dozen monthly essays for
his magazine, at three hundred dollars apiece. Since to a writer twelve labors
at three hundred dollars are infinitely more enticing than fifty at two hundred
dollars, R. L. S. agreed to squirm out, if possible, from under the commitment to McClure and retired to Saranac Lake to have his tuberculosis treated
by Dr. Edward Trudeau. The first encounter, then, netted Stevenson a
lucrative contract and McClure a headache.

Nevertheless McClure, still anxious to please, pursued him. He had heard that Stevenson had written an adventure yarn, The Black Arrow, which had been serialized in an English children's magazine but which was so lightly regarded that it had never been published in book form. Would Stevenson sell him the syndication rights? R. L. S. hesitated. His wife had never liked the story and, he feared, might be reluctant to have it republished under his own name. Pending her decision, he agreed to send to England for copies of the magazine, Henderson's Young Folks. Here, however, was a ready-made occasion for disentangling himself from the Pulitzer offer without offending McClure, who had, after all, made possible the agreement with Burlingame. Stevenson composed a conciliatory letter:

> Dear Mr. McClure,
>   The Black Arrow has come, and I believe I see my way to make something of it for your purpose: I dare not say before January; I think not unlikely by that time. This I hope will please you; though once more, I must beg you to observe that I tie myself to no date; having done that before and lived to repent it too often.
>   On the other hand, I am very sorry, but I must beg off letting you print the essays. I find, if I do so, I shall involve myself in real difficulties with my publishers; and I am sure you will regard this as a sufficient excuse, and pardon me my precipitance at the time and my present forced resiliation. If you are able to announce a story, I think it should console you.
>   Yours very truly,
>   Robert Louis Stevenson

Console him? It galvanized him. Back to Saranac he hurried, to read over the tear-sheets of The Black Arrow. Fond he might be of Stevenson, but now the editor was at work. At length he looked up. "This looks all right," he said, "but just cut the first five chapters." Stevenson agreed quite affably; but McClure wanted more. Surely Stevenson had in mind some future novel? Charles Scribner's Sons would be publishing the book, but what of the serial rights? the syndicate rights? Carried away on the flood of McClure's enthusiasm (or perhaps moved by other considerations), Stevenson agreed. Yes, he planned a sequel to Kidnapped, and he had in mind another novel, too. McClure's eyes glowed.

"How much, Mr. Stevenson," he asked, "do you want for the serial rights to both of these?"

Stevenson replied that the serial rights to the last of his novels had been sold for eight hundred pounds—at the time worth about four thousand dollars. It was clear that he was naming his price.

A shrewd but stupid editor would have forthwith drawn up a letter of agreement on the terms offered. A shrewd but clever editor would have thought to himself, "How easy to keep this writer happy!" and smilingly offered one thousand pounds and struck a friendly bargain. But McClure was McClure, a man moved by the sharp pinch of his own necessity. He retorted:

"I will pay you just twice your sum. I will pay you sixteen hundred pounds."

Was Stevenson elate? Did he caper about, kick his heels together, and kiss McClure on both cheeks? Well, no. He only blushed confusedly, murmured he didn't think any novel of his was worth so much money, and begged time to think it over. He had, after all, only just agreed that Charles Scribner's Sons should have first call on all rights to what he wrote in the future. But on November 1 he sent McClure a brisk letter in which he kicked up his price still higher:

> Dear Mr. McClure,
> The next story I finish of the same character as Kidnapped, I shall place in your hands, as soon as it is done, for American serial publication only, without regard of course to book rights or serial publication elsewhere, for the sum of ten thousand dollars.
>   Yours very truly
>   Robert Louis Stevenson

McClure did not know it at the time—all he had seen were the modest blushes—but in fact Stevenson was already savoring the sweetness of his unexpected offer. Stevenson wrote to his friend Charles Baxter: "I am offered £1600 for the American serial rights on my next story! As you say, times are changed since the Lothian Road. Well, the Lothian Road was grand fun, too; I could take an afternoon of it with great delight. But I'm awfu' grand noo, and long may it last!"

But of course Stevenson had no right to promise McClure the sequel to Kidnapped and so he wrote to Charles Scribner: "Heaven help me, I am under a curse just now. I have played fast and loose with what I said to you, and that, I beg you to believe, in the purest innocence of mind. I told you that you should have the power over all my work in this country; and about a fortnight ago, when M'Clure was here, I calmly signed a bargain for the serial publication of a story. You will scarce believe that I did this in mere oblivion; but I did; and all I can say is that I will do so no more, and ask you to forgive me." Could Louis Dudebat, the artist of Shaw's The Doctor's Dilemma, have written a more convincing letter?

Scribner was disposed to forgive what has charitably been described as Stevenson's oversight and McClure still knew nothing of it, but Stevenson displayed a becoming embarrassment. He wrote to his friend W. E. Henley: "I have had the most deplorable business annoyances too; have been threatened with having to refund money; got over that; and find myself in the worse scrape of being a kind of unintentional swindler." Swindler or no, his interests had been well served: owing to McClure's lavish offer, Burlingame had been obliged to bid the same sixteen hundred pounds for yet another projected novel.

Meanwhile, all unaware, McClure delightedly proclaimed to his clients in a special announcement that "the foremost romancer of today," "the prince of adventurers in adventurous stories," "the most romantic and unmodern character of his time," "the Knight Errant of the Nineteenth Century," had turned over to him the serial rights to his latest work. This was, of course, The Black Arrow, which, in the absence of a strong copyright law, McClure sold as The Outlaws of Tunstall Forest, a subterfuge to circumvent any possible pirates who might otherwise think to buy their own copies of Henderson's Young Folks and print at will. McClure engaged Will Low, Stevenson's close friend from their Barbizon days, to illustrate the serial with line drawings and took off on a trip around the country to make sure the tale would sell.

On his return, McClure called again at Saranac, bringing ice skates with him. It was his plan to skate with Stevenson on a nearby pond, but he found the eminent author a-bubble with—in about equal parts—vexation, amusement, and alarm. When McClure learned the reason, he found it as hard to comprehend as will most of today's readers, familiar as they are with publishers' stratagems for the promotion of their authors' wares. Today the intimate photograph, the chatter of the gossip columnist, the gruesome trespass upon privacy, the outrageously hyperbolic puff—all these are common coin, ignored or at any rate discounted by nine-tenths of the book-buying public. But in 1887 Stevenson, it appears, was appalled by the phrases McClure had used to describe him in his announcement, perturbed by the vivid appearance of the circular (McClure had used red ink as well as black), and aghast at the rodomontades heaped upon him. (These were, by later standards, quite demure.) McClure undertook to explain to Stevenson that at the time many American newspaper editors had to scratch their noodles to recollect who Shakespeare was; to such men Stevenson was a cipher, and a story by a man so-called worth no more than a story by Joe Doakes. As merchant of a strange new commodity—culture—to a bewildered mass audience, McClure was constrained to devise new methods of promotion; his circulars were a first fumbling effort in that direction. Stevenson, an early victim of this inexorable force, could not be expected to take a kindly view of it. Clearly, his view and McClure's could never be composed.

The two men put on skates and went out to the frozen pond.

Back inside the cottage, it was Stevenson's turn to suggest a deal. He handed McClure a story Lloyd Osbourne had written, "The Wrong Box." Stevenson had touched it up; he opined that if it went out under his own by-line as well as Osbourne's it should fetch five thousand dollars. If the naked dishonesty of this proposal occurred to McClure, his affection for Stevenson led him to ignore it. Instead he took the story away with him, read it, and promptly returned it together with a letter strongly urging Stevenson not to put his name to it.* To Stevenson this was lese majesty: his exasperation with McClure began to burn brighter. He sent McClure a curt note giving him to understand that if he transgressed again it would be a serious matter.

But Stevenson was not ready for a ruction. The fact was, he wanted money. He had long been hankering for his own yacht and an ocean cruise; it was only because of this, he told McClure, that he had accepted such high prices for the serial rights to his projected novels. McClure, recalling Stevenson's earlier travel books which he had so much admired, at once suggested that if Stevenson would write a series of letters describing his travels, he would syndicate them for enough money to pay the expenses of the trip.

It is one of the more delectable ironies of their weird relationship that the more mightily McClure strove to make possible Stevenson's dream of a trip to the South Seas, the more vexed Stevenson became with him. McClure dispatched to Saranac a box of books about the South Seas, including a directory of the South Pacific. In mid-March McClure arrived in person,

* McClure felt so strongly on this point that he tried to get others of Stevenson's friends to add pressure. Henry James, for one, thoroughly agreed with McClure. "Ah," James wrote McClure, "if Osbourne would only *always* write 'over his own signature!' & not over Stevenson's."

having in tow Robert Bonner, the publisher of a weekly, The New York Ledger, who was anxious to buy still another Stevenson yarn. But Bonner faded into the background as McClure and Stevenson began to conjure up wondrous fantasies about the South Seas. What enchantments might not emerge from such a trip? Stevenson thought of the immediate sweet surcease he would find on an ocean voyage, but McClure envisioned the trip only as a necessary prelude to a triumphal return, complete with a lecture tour embellished by recordings of "the sounds of the sea and wind, the songs and speech of the natives," and booths outside the lecture halls where copies of In the South Seas would be on sale. "It was all real that night," said McClure later, "and out of that talk came the South Seas cruise."

McClure, having advanced Stevenson some money to buy his yacht, left for Europe with his wife and two children. Stevenson, having reflected on the glum fact that he was now bound to deliver some fifty letters in order to pay for his trip, commenced to brood. Already McClure had begun to take shape in his mind as a character in a story, "my benignant monster," as he would call him. By May, Stevenson had found a yacht for his Pacific cruise, the Casco, at once a symbol of his freedom to sail the ocean and of his obligation to hack out half-a-hundred letters—exquisite agony. All McClure's fault! But what could he do?

Meantime McClure was hip-deep in problems of his own making. Owing to his overzealous espousal of Stevenson's The Outlaws of Tunstall Forest (né The Black Arrow), he had grievously blundered. A word about this bobble may not come amiss.

Despite the appearances, it should not be imagined that Stevenson was McClure's sole concern. Throughout these past six months he had been busy, as well, getting and selling stories by Thomas Hardy and Walter Besant, by Jules Verne and Julian Hawthorne, by Wilkie Collins and Émile Zola; a poem, "The Dying Veteran," by Walt Whitman (for which he paid twenty-five dollars); letters from Newport by Julia Ward Howe; intimate recollections of Lincoln by Colonel Ward Lamon; and a myriad articles on a myriad subjects—by Edward Everett Hale on the tariff, by William Morris on socialism in England, by Hamlin Garland on wheat farming in the Dakotas, by Mrs. Frank Leslie on the wiles and pitfalls of society (her first piece was called "Danger to Rosebuds"), and by James Parton on juvenile delinquency. There were articles on "How to Succeed in Business" by, of all people, Jay Gould; a series on American millionaires and another on the toilers of Europe; articles on exploration and on popular science—a glimpse not only into McClure's far-ranging mind but also into what interested Americans of the late 1880s. Clearly, McClure had had many preoccupations, and Stevenson's story was merely a primary concern. And so, when we learn that he arrived in England and blithely set about selling the yarn to English newspaper editors in flagrant violation of his year-old agreement with the English syndicator, William Tillotson, we may be inclined to forgive him.

Tillotson was, however, by no means so lenient. He summoned McClure to an interview at the National Liberal Club in London, reminded him that the syndication of British novels in Great Britain was, by the terms of their agreement, none of his business, and demanded that he turn over all English proceeds from the Stevenson story and, as well, all the profits he had cleared by syndicating Tillotson material in America. A hard bargain, and one that plucked McClure clean, but he paid up.

McClure was stony broke because of his own excess of enthusiasm on behalf of Stevenson. He thereupon borrowed £100 from Tillotson and left with his wife and children on a holiday jaunt through France and Italy. In Florence, Timothy Cole, the engraver, took them in hand and led them through the Uffizi, the Pitti, the Belle Arti, opening their eyes to a world undreamed of. And, as McClure paced along, staring now and again at the treasures of the Renaissance, did he occasionally reflect that his dealings with Stevenson had thus far cost him sorely? that maybe this beloved author was his bugaboo? that he would be well advised to watch Stevenson carefully, lest the letters from the South Seas turn out to be a crate of lemons? No: on the contrary, he wrote Stevenson from Florence only that all was well; "I am sure," he added, "that 40 or 50 letters will bring you at least $15,000."

Back in London McClure found a letter in which Stevenson accused him of "sharp practice." If one views the McClure-Stevenson relationship purely as high comedy, this letter was, considering its source, perhaps the climax.

Stevenson's charge was trumpery * and should have been consigned, with mirth, to oblivion. What has interest is McClure's reaction. It was pure anguish, spread over eight pages of notepaper. "My intense regret," he wrote in part, "is caused not by any sense of criminality, but by my sorrow

---

* It had two parts: that McClure was selling The Black Arrow in England under the new name, as who would sell cold biscuits on the pretense they were hot; and that a New York journal had advertised a Stevenson story as having been bought for ten thousand dollars. As to the first, Stevenson knew all about the change of title and why; as to the second, even presuming McClure to have been responsible, which he was not, so what?

at giving you annoyance. You suffer equally whether I was guilty or not. My dear Mr. Stevenson, I have greater feeling for you than for any other man alive. Your slightest wish & preference is my law & pleasure." It is a curious spectacle: an editor whose reputation for acuity and foresight was already becoming international, permitting himself so to be bullyragged by an author who had brought him only grief. Yet it is a spectacle that would be reproduced, with a variation only in one of the featured performers, time after time in the years to come.

Since comedy demands that for every climax there be an anticlimax, so on this occasion it fell out that McClure's desolated plea was months in catching up to Stevenson, the great romancer having taken off across America and on to the bosom of the Pacific well ahead of the postal service. McClure had little time to fret about Stevenson's fatuous accusations, however, for he was busy repairing the English business smashed by the dissolution of his partnership with Tillotson. Fortunately he brought to this task his usual enthusiasm; fortunately, as well, he unerringly sought out and formed friendships with the sort of people who could prove valuable to him: Sidney Colvin, who, in addition to his residency at the British Museum as Keeper of Prints and Engravings, was an influential literary broker; Henley; A. P. Watt, the literary agent; William Stead, then editor of The Pall Mall Gazette; James A. Froude, the historian; Henry James; William Archer, the critic; and Edmund Gosse, then winning his reputation as England's chief literary tagtail and tufthunter.

McClure was, by 1888, as fully developed an editor as he would ever be; from here on he would profit only by experience, and that not so often as he might have. A peek at his editorial assets and methods may be useful.

His own apothegms are suggestive. "Good editorial work can only be done out of spontaneous personal interest," he wrote; "it can not be forced. To lose his enthusiasm is the worst thing that can happen to an editor—next to having been born without any." And: "My qualifications for being an editor were that I was open-minded, naturally enthusiastic, and not afraid to experiment with a new man." And again: "I never got ideas sitting still. I never saw so many possibilities for my business or had so many editorial ideas as when I was hurrying about from city to city, talking with editors and newspaper men, [finding] out what people were writing and what people were reading, and in which of the happenings in the world people took the keenest interest." And finally, after many years of reflection and life within the penumbra of the Babbitts: "My definition of an editor is this: One who, by the use of other minds, makes a transcript of our civilization. If he does this successfully, & with true art & sanity, the result of his work will be to aid good causes & to hinder evil causes. . . . It is for the editor to translate this upward march of humanity into the printed word."

But McClure also said, in the twilight of his career: "I may have gained by experience, but much I gained by experience is counterbalanced by what I have lost of instinct."

This was a sound observation. What he meant was that he had grown older and wiser. For, as he understood, the tonic note struck by any great editor is the capacity for being interested. And this capacity demands of its possessor naïveté, even ignorance, together with an insatiable thirst to be informed. When as a child in Ireland he was curious about the Latin words in the priest's prayer book, and when on his first day in America he counted the stars in the flag, he was instinctively involved in the editorial function. There was so much that he didn't know! so much that fascinated him!

Indeed, any editor, to work at his best, must have much of the small boy alive in him, perpetually inquisitive, perpetually fresh-eyed, perpetually naïve, perpetually finding all around him new and wonderful. It is a quality that can make a man a bore to his intellectual superiors, and it was bound to make McClure a puzzle or a figure of fun to many (but not all) of the writers with whom he dealt, since their eyes were fixed on different grails. But the best writers always recognize—as they did with McClure—the editor's precious, if simple-minded, gift; they cherish and protect it even while they permit themselves, every now and again, a private, secret smile.

The point cannot be too much labored, for writers and literary folk generally are prone to confuse the editorial with the critical function. If an editor seem a cut below them in literary spit and polish, if he relish an E. P. Roe or a Gene Stratton-Porter (to confine the examples to those safely dead), then the literary folk grow amused and supercilious, and commence to question the editor's judgment. They want the editor to be a critic; but if, overnight, he were to become one he should forthwith resign, for the two functions are (or should be) quite distinct. The good critic reads discriminatingly, the good editor catholically. The good critic is gourmet, the good editor gourmand. The one sips and considers and touches his lips with double damask, the other gulps and smacks his lips and wipes his mouth with the back of his hand. The one is fastidious, the other voracious. And, most significant difference of all, the editor plunks down his money to back up his judgment, but thus far no critic has appeared who is prepared to do the same.

McClure had little or no critic in him, but he was all editor. He read omnivorously, twenty or thirty newspapers a day, ten or twelve books a week, two or three dozen magazines a month, an itch that amounted to cacoëthes legendi; he read whenever he was alone, on train or ship, while waiting in stations, at night in hotel rooms, while precariously balanced between missions in his New York or London office, and at home until late at night. And he was in the habit of scissoring, from this fantastic budget of reading, a daily sheaf of items that had caught his eye and that, if he had anything to say about it, would be transformed into articles or stories for his insatiable syndicates.

The service reflected its editor; it was as wide as the world in its appeal, and it bubbled over with excitement. A pattern emerges from a study of McClure's syndicate records for this period: he aimed to contrive if possible at least one smash surprise package each month, but as a categorical imperative there had to be an annual blockbuster each November, when his season began again.

The flow of genius proving at first unfortunately fitful, McClure undertook to commission serial fiction. He decided, since Mrs. Humphrey Ward's Robert Elsmere had been such a hit on both sides of the Atlantic, on some novelettes dealing with Bible life. But who to get to write them? Ah, if only Stevenson would write the story of King David as a boy! But he thrust this dream aside and hurried down to Summerville, South Carolina, where Elizabeth Stuart Phelps was holed up for the winter. "To this cottage," she wrote later, "came down one day the indefatigable editor of a New York literary syndicate, to whom distance is a myth, and topography a plaything." McClure proceeded to instruct the author of the best-selling The Gates Ajar that what was wanted was more rapidity of action, more suspense, more frequent climax. "Mr. McClure persuaded us," she noted, and so she and her husband agreed to turn out two stories for his series. For a third, he hustled to England, to tackle Mrs. Humphrey Ward herself. He tracked her down in her country retreat, Borough Farm. "This American, Mr. McClure," she wrote her sister, Mrs. Huxley, "is a wonderful man. He has offered me £1,000 for the serial rights of a story [of twenty thousand words]! Naturally I am not going to do it, but it is amusing."

McClure fumed as he considered how unco-operative writers could be. He had penciled Frances Hodgson Burnett in to do David, but she forsook him; H. Rider Haggard to do Samson, but he insisted on doing Esther, which meant that Margaret Deland was frozen out; at length he was obliged to settle for Georg Ebers, an obscure German, to do Joshua.

Even this mixed success, however, did not entirely alienate him from the notion that good fiction could be ordered by the pound, like mackerel. He set a hack named George Parsons Lathrop to work, in collaboration with Thomas Alva Edison, on a Romance of Electricity. It was announced for March, 1890, actually released in March, 1892, and promptly vanished, despite all McClure's brave hopes, into the Bottomless Pit.

He was driven to other schemes to divert his clients. In the absence of any sensational contributors, he took up slack by announcing notable accessions to his staff. Thus, early in 1889, he engaged Frances Hodgson Burnett to edit his new Youth's Department; indeed, since her reputation was at the time secure, thanks to Little Lord Fauntleroy, he announced her no less than three times, concluding with a tremendous hoopla in November. (She was, despite a handsome salary, only a figurehead.) And thus, that summer, he launched his London office with considerable fanfare. These were the rooms pleasurably recalled by Henry James as "in the heart of Westminster, under the Abbey towers, just within the old archway of that Dean's Yard which makes a kind of provincial backwater, like the corner of a cathedral close, in a roaring 'imperial' neighborhood."

Here, imperially, McClure roared that he had obtained for £150 a poem by Alfred, Lord Tennyson, "written expressly" for his Youth's Department; here he also announced the appointment of Edmund Gosse as general European editor. This notice was significant, for the Canadian-born Gosse was a snob of snobs who had at first snubbed the McClures both as Americans and because of their clothes and their choice of food. (The McClures unselfconsciously bought Jaeger clothing and dined at vegetarian restaurants.) When Gosse deigned to traffic with Americans, it was only with the least incorrect—the editors of The Century, say, whose English editorial representative he had been for some time. Yet McClure charmed Gosse into pliability, and almost without effort. One evening he discovered that Gosse's father, like his own mother, was a religious fanatic and of the same (Plymouth Brethren) stamp. It was a bond, and soon McClure was warmly invited to a higher stratum of English literary society. He made sure, however, that his younger brother Robert was firmly installed as manager of the London office. The space was shared with another American youngster, Wolcott Balestier, and this association would have unexpected consequences.

But it was, after all, with writers and what they wrote that he was best able to impress his clients. In 1890 there were novels by Tolstoy and Meredith and Kipling; in 1891 there were Conan Doyle's Adventures of Sherlock Holmes, letters from Europe by Mark Twain, a novel by Howells, and the first of Stevenson's letters from the South Seas; in 1892 there were Mark Twain's An American Claimant, Stevenson's David Balfour, Arthur Brisbane's first letters from New York, stories by Henry James and Richard Harding Davis, and Randolph Churchill's correspondence from South Africa. Some of these prizes he had commissioned, some he had stumbled upon, some had been recommended by others. For instance, in the spring of 1889 he traveled to St. Andrews, in Scotland, to visit Andrew Lang and sign him up for some stories and articles.* Lang mentioned a new historical novel by a young physician, Conan Doyle, who had already to his credit a shilling shocker called A Study in Scarlet with an intriguing detective-hero named Sherlock Holmes. McClure bought the thriller at a newsstand, read it on his way back to London, and at once caught fire—only to find to his dismay that Doyle's next Holmes tale, The Sign of Four, was already bespoke by Lippincott's. He had to settle for an historical novel, The White Company, and restlessly await the short Adventures of Sherlock Holmes which he ran in his syndicate simultaneously with their publication by The Strand Magazine, beginning in July, 1891.

In December, 1889, McClure was back again in England. Kipling was at that time the man of the hour: literary circles were abuzz with his praises; Gosse had just urged Wolcott Balestier to look him up. McClure lunched with Sidney Colvin at the British Museum on the last day of the year; no one writing at the time, Colvin assured McClure, "has done such hot, human things." McClure wrote that curious name "Rudyard Kipling" in his notebook. When late in March The Times of London accorded Kipling a leading article, he became an assured attraction. McClure introduced him to America in June, 1890, with some verse and some short stories; by September he was able to announce The Light That Failed for November 2, the earliest date for publication of the novel.

---

* Lang wrote to Stevenson a few days later: "I met your Mr. McClure at St. Andrews. He seems to admire you on the *other* side of idolatry. His commercial views of literature seemed amusing, but I believe he keeps a business and a private literary conscience."

Meantime, on New Year's Day, 1890, McClure went down to Box Hill, in Surrey, to spend an evening with Meredith. "When he talked," McClure said later, "the air was full of flaming swords." Meredith read aloud from his most recent novel; he was by that time an aging man, and sick; but McClure was fascinated. Back in London, he advised Burlingame, the editor of Scribner's, to snap up the novel, One of Our Conquerors. When Burlingame hesitated, McClure snatched it for his syndicate.

With every triumph, however, there came a hardship. Considered solely as a bravura editorial performance, McClure's effort throughout these years was impressive, but it buttered few parsnips. He was always on the brink of disaster. "I never received my morning mail," he recalled later, "without a tremble lest some paper had stopped [my service]. It was a business of a most awful sort. . . . Every town I came to was a source of dread, because if this town failed and then that, then this other sum that I had gotten would not count."

The difficulty was with his prices. His annual grosses swelled satisfactorily but so, regrettably, did his expenses. Sometimes, as with Conan Doyle, he could buy cheaply enough. He got The White Company for three hundred and seventy-five dollars and the first twelve Adventures of Sherlock Holmes for about fifty dollars apiece. But in such a case his clients would never have heard of the author; would mutinously mutter and shift uneasily from foot to foot, threatening to cancel; would complain the stories ran too long or were too improbable. Not until after McClure had jammed Sherlock Holmes down their throats for six months did the newspaper editors realize they had bought a share in something immortal.

As for the other authors, McClure paid, in order to get their work, steeper and always steeper prices. No editor was ever so beneficent to authors in general; each time he pranced on a loftier financial mountain peak with a coveted author the echo of his heeltaps could be heard all the way down the slope to where the humblest, most impoverished authors were struggling. And these would then take heart. He chose to pay one thousand dollars apiece for a half-dozen letters from Mark Twain in Europe; ten thousand dollars for William Dean Howells' novel, The Quality of Mercy; twelve thousand for Mark Twain's An American Claimant; and each time he had to scramble swiftly to get his money back.* It was disheartening work. And as for the letters sent from the South Seas by his admired friend, Robert Louis Steven-

* These prices were, of course, only for the syndication rights.

son, they were, as we shall see in a moment, the occasion for his bitterest disappointment of all.

By 1890 one thing was clear to McClure: he would never be able to make a comfortable living by operating his syndicates; he had to branch out. But in what direction? Early in February, Fate brushed him again with her wings.

> Boston, Feb 1, 1890

> My dearest Hattie
>   . . . I have had a most interesting time. I had a wonderful talk with Mr Howells, which I must tell you about. . . . Everything is opening up so that I am fairly bewildered. I have much to tell you that I don't dare trust the written page.
>   Love to you my sweetest darling.

>> Your loving husband
>> SSMcClure

A day or two, and then he was home and had told her all about it; another few days, and she was happily retailing the news to her family in Galesburg.

> My dear Mother & Sister:–
>   . . . On this piece of paper I'm going to write a very important piece of news. Sam hasn't allowed me to mention it before, and it isn't to go beyond our own family. Mr. W.D. Howells wants to start a new magazine of which he will be editor. It is to be on the general plan of the magazine described in "A Hazard of New Fortunes." He told Sam about it some time ago, and asked Sam if he would be its publisher, and told him if he favored the idea to make a plan and make Mr. Howells an offer. Sam had a letter from Mr. H. the other day saying he hoped he would be in Boston soon, so that he might talk it over with him. So Sam went and took me. As it stands now, Sam is going to get the money together, which he expects to have no difficulty in doing, and will make Mr. Howells an offer as editor of the magazine, and probably they will move to N.Y. and the magazine will be started within a year. Sam thinks it a very fine opportunity for him, and I am delighted. I think he is greatly honored to have Mr. Howells think of him and mention such a plan to him. Mr. H. is very kind to Sam personally. Mrs. H. has said to Sam that she wanted to call on me when I am in Boston with him, and this time Mr. Howells asked Sam if I had come, and because Mrs. H. was ill in bed he came to see me himself, and asked us to lunch with them the next day. He is perfectly delightful, gentle and kind in his manner, and very witty, sharp and quick at repartee. I enjoy hearing him and Sam talk, and he seems to like Sam's talk very much. When we went there to lunch I saw Mrs. H. & the daughter. . . . She is a *very*

beautiful girl about twenty years old, grave and serious in her manner. Mrs. H. is an invalid. I liked her and got along with her nicely, but I couldn't help feeling that I had a great deal rather hear Mr. H. talk. She is like a good many of the women he writes about. She has a cousin in Galesburg, Mrs. Davis the dentist's wife, Kittie Davis's mother. One of my wisdom teeth is troubling me badly, and I told Sam I would rather he wouldn't speak of it there. But I went with Miss H. to her room to take off my cloak & bonnet, and Mrs. H. ran after me to tell me what to do for my tooth. Sam had told her about it the first thing. She brought a little phial of oil of cloves, and sent her daughter for wooden tooth-picks to apply it. She couldn't find any tooth-picks, so she whittled out a little bundle of smooth sticks and gave them to me instead. . . .

It is not clear whether Howells broached the idea of a magazine to McClure or (as seems more likely) McClure was romancing Howells. In either event, McClure totted up a characteristically enthusiastic set of figures for income and expenses of the projected magazine, demonstrating to his own satisfaction that he could raise ninety-seven thousand dollars, of which, by the gloomiest prognosis, no more than eighty-six thousand would be required to publish the first twelve issues.

Back in Galesburg, weightier matters were troubling Hattie's family. Rumors had reached their ears that Howells had apostasized from the true faith: was it wise for Sam to be associated with a man who was (if the reports could be credited) no better than an infidel? Moreover, in the recently published A Hazard of New Fortunes the character of Fulkerson seemed obviously drawn from Sam; was it true? Hattie hastened to nail these dastardly assertions:

My dear Sister:–

. . . I've always been intending to speak about Mr. Howells and then forgetting. He told Sam that in Fulkerson he sketched the character of Ralph Keeler, a young man from Indiana, and he gave Sam Keeler's autobiography. He also had Sam's business plans and exploits in mind at the same time. He was brought up a Swedenborgian by his father and mother, and although he has departed widely from their beliefs he is a devout Christian, and leans greatly on the comfort of his religion. . . . He is *not* a Christian Scientist.

With very much love,
Hattie

Her family could have spared themselves their apprehensions, for already the dream of a Howells-McClure magazine was fading, after only a few short weeks. Indeed, any talk of McClure's syndicating a Howells novel was, in April, 1890, still premature.

April 6, 1890

My dear McClure,

I think it will be better to let the matter of the story rest till we see each other again, and the other matter too. I don't see how we could manage both very well; the first would kill off the chances of the second. . . .

Very truly yours,
William Dean Howells

So temporarily the idea of a magazine was shelved. But it is unlikely that McClure more than shrugged a shoulder. For already he was stalking bigger game: his quarry was no less than the entire European reprint market. It was a wondrous fantasy, and all the bright-eyed cooks who had a hand in stirring the broth must be introduced.

There was McClure, who told a friend: "I have organized a company for publishing in Germany to supplant Tauchnitz's library. As we have contracts with nearly all the leading authors for their book rights for the Continent, there won't be any more Baron Tauchnitz. He has made three or four millions of pounds out of his business; hence we are going to get it, as we want to make a few millions." Had McClure in fact organized the company? Perhaps; but at all events there was another, and shadowy, figure dimly discernible just off stage; this was

John W. Lovell, an enterprising pirate who had specialized in the reprint business in the United States at a time when he who respected authors' copyrights was deemed a boob. In 1882 he had launched Lovell's Library (books selling at ten cents apiece) and later Lovell's Popular Library (books at fifty cents apiece) and Lovell's Standard Library (books at one dollar apiece). Lovell was a man of grand and monopolistic bent: it was he who engineered the pool of all the cheap reprint houses in America under the corporate banner of the United States Book Company. (This mighty trust was destined to collapse in the panic of 1893.) McClure was not too happy to associate with such a bloodthirsty buccaneer, but the stakes were temptingly high and besides Lovell had dispatched to London a sharp-eyed and honey-tongued scout. This was

Wolcott Balestier, slender, dark-haired, pallid, intense, and in 1890 still less than thirty years old. Balestier's talent for ensnaring authors and critics amounted to genius. Within a year of his arrival in London from America, in December, 1888, he was an important figure in the town's literary life; Henry James and Edmund Gosse were merely two of his closer friends. He was an exceedingly ambitious young man, but what, precisely, was he ambitious for? Literary fame? Commercial wealth? He never answered the question, and so he never achieved anything but promise in either direction. He had written two inconsequential novels before he came to London; a third was to be published posthumously; but his name is remembered today, if at all, because he collaborated with Kipling on The Naulahka, and because Kipling married his sister Caroline and quarreled with his brother Beatty. By 1890, however, as important to Balestier as his connection with Kipling was his friendship with

William Heinemann, two years younger even than Balestier, who had nevertheless opened a publishing house in two small rooms at 21, Bedford Street, Covent Garden, and started off, improbably, with a smash success by publishing Hall Caine's first novel. Heinemann was also ambitious: he dreamed of an International Library (of reprints, of course) and beguiled Edmund Gosse into becoming its editor.

These four cooks were by no means of one mind as to how to season their broth, but the pot was bubbling from the time McClure opened his London office in space shared by Balestier. McClure mistrusted his co-tenant, and his suspicion was cordially reciprocated. Moreover, McClure was determined to elbow Lovell away from the pot if possible, but since Lovell alone had capital available, this was difficult. Heinemann's connections with the German printers who, it was planned, would manufacture the books made him important.

Robert McClure was slated to be in charge of the Leipsic office, and Phillips to replace him in London. But who, then, would head the New York office? Ah, the frets of empire!

If we steal along Park Row and peer into the city room of The Evening Sun we shall get a glimpse of McClure contending with his cares. Here at a desk sits an elegant young reporter, just now beginning to acquire a lustrous reputation in the metropolis. Presently he will be the most glittering jewel in the diadem of American journalism; his dandified manner, his splendid profile, the air with which he twirls his walking-stick will break hearts from Harlem to the Battery, and even a few west of the Hudson. But at the moment he is only a reporter, hard at work. His name is Richard Harding Davis.

All at once, like a genie out of a wine-jar, there materializes a slender man in his thirties with an egregious blond mustache.

"I am S.S. McClure," says this apparition, presenting his card. "I have sent my London representative to Germany and my New York man to London. Will you take charge of my New York end?"

"Bring your New York representative back and send me to London and I'll consider it. As long as I'm in New York," says Richard Harding Davis loyally, "I won't leave The Evening Sun."

"Edmund Gosse is my London representative; you can have the same work here. Come out and take lunch."

"Thank you, I can't; I'll see you on Tuesday."

"All right, I'll come for you. Think of what I say. I'll make your fortune. You won't have anything to do but ask people to write novels and then edit them. I'll send you abroad later if you don't like New York. Can you write any children's stories for me?"

"No; see you Tuesday."

But on Tuesday, despite McClure's sulphurous offer of seventy-five dollars as a weekly salary, Davis still said no. In his stead, McClure hired another reporter, Walter Dohm, of whom all he could boast in his promotion was that Dohm was "champion amateur middle distance runner of the United States," surely one of the more peculiar recommendations for an office editor.

A hurried trip to England to make sure that all was well with his prospective partnership. "Of course," he wrote his wife, "I don't intend to work with Mr. Lovell's capital, either here or in America. I hope soon to establish an American publishing house of my own." His scheme seemed to be shaping up admirably:

Wednesday, July 30/90

My beloved Hattie—

. . . My business trip has been a most unparalleled success. I have achieved the results I planned for all these years in England & far more. No success has ever so far transcended the original plans in all my experience. Balestier & I are true & faithful allies & we have the world at our feet. Bob goes to Germany. I have arranged with Stanton [Theodore Stanton, an American journalist stationed in Paris] to join us & control France. I shall be able to afford a beautiful home here in Surrey as well as in America. At last I see the legitimate outcome of all these years of effort & planning. Never before have I so longed to serve God & to put my work in harmony with him. I want your loving and angelic help. . . .

Your faithful lover
SSMcClure

All proceeded like clockwork. Phillips was dispatched to London in September and with him went Beatty Balestier, Wolcott's scapegrace younger brother, now also on McClure's expanding payroll. Only one thing was wanting to put the whole imperial scheme into operation, and that was a modest dab of capital from McClure. On this score, however, he was not worried, for with the fall came his annual contract renewals, which meant a part of the necessary capital, if enough newspaper editors proved amenable to his salesmanship. And sure enough:

Kansas City, October 24, 1890

My dearest Hattie

Thus far my trip has been a triumphal march & ovation combined. Success everywhere. The ideas I put forth are sound & salable. We will get rich. . . .

But the biggest chunk of the needed capital was to come from his share of the proceeds from Stevenson's letters from the South Seas. In London Wolcott Balestier was already insisting that McClure had no money, that he would never honor his pledges, that he was untrustworthy, that Balestier and Heinemann should go ahead without him; but McClure was unconcerned. For at last, after more than two years of eager waiting, he had been assured that the first batch of South Seas letters were actually on their way from Samoa.

Although Stevenson was half a world away, McClure's indomitable affection for him had continued to hover at fever height. When his son was born, in November, 1888, McClure had solicited and obtained Stevenson's permission to name the infant Robert Louis Stevenson McClure; a year later a gift for the namesake had arrived from Stevenson, a silver spoon and bowl with "R.L.S.M." engraved on the spoon, and on the bowl the figures of the zodiac and the legend "From Robert Louis Stevenson to Robert Louis McClure." In every month's mail McClure had sent Stevenson a long, chatty letter, full of news and gossip and glowing with friendship. When in 1890 he had a large house built in Bronxville, he wrote Stevenson: "It contains a suite of beautiful rooms which have been furnished especially to entertain Mr. and Mrs. Robert Louis Stevenson whenever their royal highnesses may consent to honor their humble servant." Pending that happy day, McClure shipped to Samoa the new books, subscriptions to magazines, whatever he could think of to keep his friend happy.

But month after month had gone by without a sign of the South Seas correspondence. McClure had contracted to sell them to The New York Sun for ten thousand dollars and to various British journals for another five thousand; time and again he had hopefully announced them as "forthcoming" in his prospectuses; but obviously Stevenson was at work on other projects. When, early in December, 1890, McClure was assured the letters were finally coming, he was delighted. "Of course you know," he wrote Stevenson on December 6, "that your letters coming just now are a source of profit to me which is extremely acceptable at a time when I extended my operations in Germany."

The letters arrived. They arrived, however, not as letters but as a small book of travel—In the South Seas—already printed and bound by Cassell & Company, the English publishers. At that moment McClure realized that his hopes of establishing a publishing house in Germany were dead. Thoughtfully he took the little travel book with him to the offices of The New York Sun.

In vain for him to plead that his old friend Stevenson must have had the book printed solely to insure correct proofs. The editors of The Sun quite correctly objected, as McClure sadly wrote Stevenson, "that the letters did not come as letters are supposed to come. They were not a correspondence from the South Seas, they were not dated and [the editors] contended that in no way did the matter in the first series fulfil the definition of the word 'letter,' as used in newspaper correspondence."

And so once again a Stevenson project had blown up in his face. Instead of happily pocketing The Sun's check, McClure was now forced to peddle the "letters" to a syndicate of newspapers all over the country. And as he glanced through Stevenson's copy, he sensed that this would be no simple task, for the "letters" were incorrigibly dull. It was clear that Stevenson had ground them out as joylessly as if he had been picking oakum in the county calaboose.

"Don't feel bad," he told Hattie. "I don't. I have accepted the situation, and all is love. I have abandoned the German scheme, cabled Phillips to return at once, and shall confine my operations to English-speaking countries for a year or two."

But no hint of reproof or reproach crept into the letter McClure sent Stevenson, in which he explained his enforced change of plans for disposing of the correspondence; on the contrary, he only begged Stevenson to approve his course. "I live," he added in a handwritten postscript, "in fear & trembling of your anger."

In the South Seas began to appear in February, 1891. The correspondence was, McClure would recall later, "a disappointment to newspaper editors";

and this is as close as he was himself ever to come to uttering a harsh word about Stevenson.* But six months later he began to understand why the South Seas correspondence had been so long delayed. For in August, 1891, Scribner's began to serialize The Wrecker, a novel written by Stevenson in collaboration with Lloyd Osbourne, which contained a wicked caricature of McClure named, for the purposes of fiction, Jim Pinkerton.† Now, month after month, McClure had before him the record of what his friend thought of him, should he choose to pick the phrases out:

> ". . . a man of a good stature, a very lively face, cordial, agitated man-
> ners, and a grey eye as active as a fowl's . . . a laugh of boyish delight
> . . . [whose] parents were from the old country. . . .
> ". . . about the age of twelve, he was thrown upon his own resources
> . . . [with] a body of magnanimous and semi-intellectual nonsense,
> which he supposed to be the natural thoughts and to contain the whole
> duty of the born American. To be pure-minded, to be patriotic, to get
> culture and money with both hands and with the same irrational fervour
> —these appeared to be the chief articles of his creed. . . .
> "I was unaware that . . . myself, my person, and my works of art
> [were to be] butchered to make a holiday for the readers of a Sunday
> paper. . . . I was . . . interested, amused, and attracted by him in about
> equal proportions. . . . He was a troublous friend to me, and the trouble
> began early. . . .
> "I had a genuine and lively taste for [him]; I laughed at, I scolded,
> and I loved him. He, upon his side, paid me a kind of dog-like service
> of admiration, gazing at me from afar off as at one who had liberally
> enjoyed those 'advantages' which he envied for himself. He followed

* For McClure, the correspondence hatched only grief. He had undertaken both to syndicate and to act as Stevenson's agent for In the South Seas, paying R.L.S. 75 per cent of the gross proceeds. Charles Baxter, the Scottish lawyer whom Stevenson had, in an act of sublime supererogation, appointed his man of business, and who was never able to grasp the ABC of literary trade practices, considered this agreement to be highway robbery on McClure's part when it was in fact a most generous bargain. "I see that fiend McClure charges a commission of Twenty five per cent," Baxter wrote Stevenson, "that is, £250 for getting £1000—It makes me sick . . . Scratch a Yankee, and out comes a Jew: no wonder he and his wife and the baby are devoted to you all!"

† Lest McClure take offense at the cruel portrait, Stevenson wrote him confessing what he had done, and assuring him that Pinkerton was largely fictional. "I have put you into one of my stories," Stevenson said, as McClure later remembered the letter, "but when a man steals a handkerchief the first thing he does is to remove the name, so I have removed the identifica- tion marks; and as in the novel, 'The Wrecker', where Will H. Low is depicted as Lowden Dodd, you are Jim Pinkerton, but you won't know it." Stevenson may well have sent McClure such a letter (although I have never been able to find it), but certainly he intended his portrait of Pinkerton to stand as his idea of McClure. So much can be easily deduced from his letters to Baxter.

at heel; his laugh was ready chorus. . . . It was in this insidious form that servitude approached me. . . .

" 'The Irrepressible' was what I had called him in hours of bitterness. . . . What mischief was he up to now? . . . my benignant monster. . . .

"My trust in the man was entire and my distrust perfect. I knew he would never mean amiss; but I was convinced he would almost never (in my sense) do aright. . . . He never comprehended in the least the ground of my aversion. . . .

"The Irrepressible, did I say? The Irresistible were nigher truth. . . .

". . . he would come down radiant from a weekly balance-sheet, clap me on the shoulder, declare himself a winner by Gargantuan figures, and prove destitute of a quarter for a drink. . . . 'Into the mill again; all re-invested!'

". . . my bright-eyed friend, pacing the room like a caged lion. . . .

"If there were one thing [he] valued himself upon, it was his honesty; if there were one thing he clung to, it was my good opinion; and when both were involved, . . . the man was on the rack . . . and yet I lived and fattened on these questionable operations. . . ."

Perhaps McClure was telling the truth when he said later he had never read The Wrecker. He may have tried to, but it is, on the whole, a tedious and often preposterous novel, easy to lay aside.

At all events, McClure was back where he had started, sole owner of a business that annually grossed one hundred thousand dollars but was annually in danger of costing rather more than ninety-nine thousand—a reasonable facsimile of a treadmill. How to make more money? By publishing books? To be sure, it seemed easy enough. As he had once pointed out to Stevenson after puzzling over the matter for some time, "The reason why publishers do not get fabulously rich is because they publish so many unsuccessful books." But this observation, while numbing in its simple grasp of the chief problem confronting the book publisher, yet did not go all the way to the solution of his own problem.

Moreover, despite eight years of (barely) profitable operation, his syndicate business was still the butt of sneers by some of the more genteel authors. Ouida, for instance, having failed to sell McClure her most recent romance, filled two columns of The Times of London with a waspish exercise of spite in which she referred to McClure, with her customary extravagance of metaphor, as a pig-dealer, a maggot, and a toadstool. Her effusion was a source

of unmixed delight to McClure,* but at the same time it might be symptomatic. The fact was, prestige attached to the editor of a magazine rather than
to the editor of a syndicate business.

Yet was he not, in effect, already editing a magazine? He sent out thirty
separate articles and stories a week, fully illustrated, aggregating fifty thousand
words—enough to make a fair-sized magazine every week. And, as he leafed
through The Century, Harper's and The Atlantic, it seemed to him that
his articles were at least as interesting as anything printed in those august
pages. He was, indeed, being flooded with unsolicited offers of material that
he would take his oath would make for livelier reading. Here: Joel Chandler
Harris tendering the last of his "Uncle Remus" stories; or here: Professor
John Tyndall suggesting he write his autobiography; or here: a letter from
young Theodore Roosevelt, promising three articles on wild-game hunting
and adding, "You have a right to be proud of the work you put up." And
where was that letter from John Brisben Walker, the editor of The Cosmopolitan? Here: "Will you let me know from time to time of any manuscripts
of stories . . . from twenty to thirty thousand words, by prominent authors"
—a confession, to McClure's way of thinking, that the man didn't know how
to edit his own magazine.

The more he thought about it, the more firmly McClure was convinced
that he could edit a better magazine than any then on the newsstands. It
became a passion with him. "I would rather edit a magazine," he told his
wife, "than be President of the United States a hundred thousand times over."
Early in the summer of 1892 he began once again to devise a definite scheme.
This time, if possible, there would be no partners; but even if there were,
even if he had to depend once again on undependable authors, he would
publish a magazine.

---

* The good lady was vexed, in part, because her vogue had given way to that of Kipling
who, she said, "has neither knowledge of style nor common acquaintance with grammar, and
should be whipped and put in a corner like a naughty child, for his impudence in touching
pen and ink without knowing how to use them."

THE MAGAZINE

❧❧❧❧❧❧❧❧❧❧❧❧❧❧❧❧❧❧❧❧❧❧❧❧❧

1893-1912

[1]

The Golden Age of the American magazine was just dawning when McClure's Magazine was launched; and in that Golden Age, which lasted from 1890 to 1915, McClure's was the most exciting, the liveliest, the best illustrated, the most handsomely dressed, the most interesting, and the most profitable of an abundance of superior magazines. Indeed, for the fifteen years from 1895 to 1910 McClure's was probably the best general magazine ever to be published anywhere. Judged from the standpoint of impact on its times, of the daring and vision of its editorial formula, of the sustained excellence of its editorial matter, McClure's has never had a peer. Just as the generation that straddled the turn of the century could rejoice in a profusion of fine magazines never before or since equaled, so McClure may, on the basis of his product, be confidently set down as the greatest magazine editor this country has yet produced.

Golden Ages, of course, do not just happen along by chance. In this case a complex of factors—technical, economic, cultural, and purely fortuitous—combined to yield a crop of magazines cheap in price, national in circulation, and unprecedented in their influence on the social scene. On each score, McClure's Magazine led the way.

It was evident as early as 1890 that magazines could be cheaper and their illustrations better. By that time, thanks largely to the inventions of Frederic Ives in the laboratories of Cornell University, the process of photoengraving had been developed to the point where the halftone could replace the far more expensive fine-line engraving on wood. Here was a salient economy. It was bad news for artists like Timothy Cole and Joseph Pennell; but it meant that such a magazine as The Century, the publishers of which had spent some five thousand dollars a month on engraving alone, could be more profusely illustrated for less than two thousand dollars a month.

Even more significant, however, was the fact that magazines could now make far more money than had ever been dreamed of before. Advertising revenues, beginning around 1890, commenced to zoom. This phenomenon was a reflection of the remarkable growth of the national wealth. In the last quarter of the nineteenth century the country had been busting its britches along every seam; from 1880 to 1900 the population rose fifty per cent (from about fifty million to about seventy-five million); but the national wealth shot up twice as fast. During the decade 1874–1883 the annual flow of goods to the consumer was worth, on the average, about twelve billion dollars; by 1894–1903 the value had more than doubled, to better than twenty-five billion dollars a year.*

To sell this vast flood of goods, new advertising techniques had to be developed; and the magazine was not merely the best, it was the only national advertising medium. Earlier the manufacturer had been content to leave the advertising of his products to the local retailer, who bought space in the local newspapers; but by the 1890s the manufacturer, hustled along by competition, had been obliged to coin slogans, register trade-marks, buy full pages instead of just a few lines, and hire agents to devise more and ever more alluring sweet talk. Once the advertising agency had been born, complete with its twin sirens, the copywriter and the art director, the golden flow of advertising revenue was assured. From then on, in the ear of the uneasy manufacturer there would ever be a seductive voice guaranteeing higher sales, urging fatter advertising budgets, counseling the purchase of more and yet more space, always inspired by the luster of the advertising agent's fifteen per cent. By 1891 magazines with one hundred pages of advertising were commonplace. A few years later the most successful publications would be selling more than one hundred and fifty pages in every issue, at four hundred dollars or more a page.

Grosses like these meant that the magazine editor was, all at once, the chief patron of writer and illustrator, displacing the book publisher. Where today the ambitious and greedy author writes with one eye on the possibility of his being tapped by a book club, a motion-picture company, or a television network, from 1890 until the War of 1914–1918 his most avid daydream was of selling to the magazines. In the circumstances it is not astonishing that, during this Golden Age, so many new writers made their first appearance and had so much of their best work published in the magazines.

* The figures are approximations of those cited by Simon Kuznets in The National Product Since 1869. They are adjusted to 1929 price levels.

But when S. S. McClure first formulated his plans for a new magazine, he could not possibly have imagined that a Golden Age was at hand. The nation seemed anywhere but at the start of a long march toward prosperity. On the contrary, every sign pointed, as usual, toward turmoil, if not disaster. To be sure, in 1890 the Congress had for the first time spent one billion dollars, and this record sum had seemed to augur a rosy Republican future. The Speaker of the House of Representatives in that Congress was the autocratic Tom Reed of Maine, a mountain of a man who looked like W. C. Fields and who twanged out pithy witticisms in a manner that Fields might have envied. (It was Reed who defined a statesman as a dead politician.) Someone twitted Reed about his billion-dollar Congress. "Yes," he retorted, "but this is a billion-dollar country." All very well; but in 1890 eleven of the country's twelve million families were still living on an average of less than four hundred dollars a year, and the pressures of protest were building up.

The ugly fact was that the country's growing wealth, while undeniable, was divided very unequally. Nor was there any longer an expanding frontier along which the angry pressure might be dissipated. The Superintendent of the Census for 1890 had announced that "the unsettled area has been so broken into by isolated bodies of settlement that there can hardly be said to be a frontier line."

On every hand, as the nation entered the century's last decade, there were warning signals of bad times ahead. The price of corn slid down to ten cents a bushel, the price of cotton to six cents a pound; all over the farm country mortgages were foreclosed. Was it any wonder that Mrs. Mary Lease, the Kansas Pythoness, was cheered when she exhorted the Kansas farmers to "raise less corn and more *Hell*"? In the East, responsible conservatives were shocked. "We don't want any more states," wrote the editor of The New York Evening Post, "until we can civilize Kansas."

As if this handwriting on the wall were not vivid enough, in Homestead, Pennsylvania, the employees of the Carnegie Steel Company went out on strike in July, 1892. Three hundred armed Pinkertons arrived on the scene, killed eleven strikers, and wounded sixty more. The news of this slaughter reached Omaha, where the Populist party was in convention, and it stirred the delegates to a hot fury. They denounced the two major parties as pawns of the capitalist interests and adopted a platform—calling for free silver, a graduated income tax, government ownership of the railroads and telegraphs, protection of trade unions, and direct election of United States Senators— with "cheers and yells which rose like a tornado," according to one reporter, "and raged without cessation for thirty-four minutes, during which women shrieked and wept, men embraced and kissed . . . marched back and forth, and leaped upon tables and chairs in the ecstasy of their delirium."

And on the same day that eight thousand state militiamen marched into Homestead to break the steel strike, there was another bloody pitched battle in the Coeur d'Alene district of Idaho between striking silver miners and imported strikebreakers. Once again troops arrived to smash the strike; but the rancor remained. To cap the calendar of violence, the anarchist Alexander Berkman managed to fire a bullet into a Carnegie steelmaster, Henry Clay Frick.

In the face of all this anxiety and misery, so portentous of an evil future, McClure was undeterred. He had made up his mind to launch a magazine, and launch it he would. Whilst others gabbled about impending revolution and wondered what would the harvest be, McClure was concerned with weightier matters. What should he call his magazine? The New Magazine? The Galaxy? Elysium? He darted over to Europe again, in the summer of 1892, and permitted Edmund Gosse to suggest an odd title. "Why not," said Gosse, "McClure's Magazine?" And so it was decided.

The trip to Europe was to dig up the best available material for the syndicate; meantime Phillips was similarly signing contracts with American authors. Between them McClure and Phillips committed the syndicate for stories and articles that would cost them many times their capital. Offstage the thunder continued to reverberate, presaging financial panic, but McClure was obstinately intent; he ignored the gathering menace.

His plan was to use syndicate profits to meet magazine expenses. These, he estimated, would be minimal, since the fiction would come straight from the files of previously syndicated matter. As for his articles, which had to be timely, he hoped to commission enough for sale through his syndicate to afford him a choice of only the best for the magazine. Earlier in 1892 he had circularized all the ablest American scientists and educators, urging they contribute to a series to be called "The Edge of the Future." The difficulty was that none of these men could write with any lucidity.

So, in the back of his mind, another scheme had been taking shape: to hire writers who could seize hold of new, complex, but interesting scientific ideas, study them down to the bottom, and then put them in readable prose. Curiously, no editor before McClure had thought to do such a simple thing, and, just as curiously, there were not many writers around who were equipped to meet the demand. A few months before, McClure had picked up from

Phillips's desk an article that bore the forbidding title, "The Paving of the Streets of Paris by M. Alphand." Only a compulsive reader would have gone any further, but McClure had read the piece, fascinated, all the way through. It was signed by Ida M. Tarbell. "Who is she?" asked McClure. "No idea," answered Phillips, "but from her handwriting I should guess she's a middle-aged New England schoolmarm." "She can write," McClure said. "I want to get her to do some work for the magazine."

Accordingly, in the summer of 1892, McClure suddenly descended upon Paris, lunched with Will Low, winning his promise to design a cover for the new magazine; looked in on Theodore Stanton at the offices of the Associated Press long enough to forget his hat and umbrella; got Henri Opper, the Paris correspondent of The Times of London, to write an article on "Europe at the Present Moment" for his first number; and, late on his schedule, popped up breathless and bareheaded at the door of Miss Tarbell's Left Bank apartment.

"I've just ten minutes," he announced, watch in hand; "must leave for Switzerland tonight to see Tyndall."

Miss Tarbell, a tall, grave, handsome young woman, invited him in. What she saw, she said later, was "a slender figure . . . a shock of tumbled sandy hair, blue eyes which glowed and sparkled . . . a vibrant, eager, indomitable personality that electrified even the experienced and the cynical." Miss Tarbell was not cynical, but she had had, by 1892, a tolerable amount of experience. She was a daughter of pioneers; a girl who had done so well in school that she had managed to get an education in Allegheny College, one of the very few coeducational schools of the 1870s, where she was the only girl in her class. She had been briefly a schoolteacher in Ohio, and then an editor of The Chautauquan. She had commenced to carve out a career, at a time when not many young women considered such a course to be either suitable or sensible. Suddenly, in 1890, with great pluck she had decided to go to Paris, a woman alone, and seek to earn her living as a free-lance writer. It was her dream to write a biography of Madame Roland, the mildly revolutionary Frenchwoman who had carved out a career a century before. While she was gathering her research, she made her living by writing articles for Scribner's and for McClure's syndicate.

She was maternal, attractive, a few months younger than McClure; he was charmed. As for her, his "utter simplicity, outrightness, his enthusiasm and confidence captivated me." His ten minutes stretched into an hour, two hours, three. As was his custom whenever he found a sympathetic audience, he told her the story of his early struggles, a well-polished routine by now, and one always guaranteed to win admiration. This time it wound up with his assurances of her glowing future as a contributor to his new magazine. He had a swarm of ideas for her to work on: an interview with Pasteur, a piece on the observatory atop Mont Blanc, a report on the Bertillon technique for the identification of criminals which, he would proudly assert later, "virtually started the interest in that system in the United States."

Suddenly he sprang up. "I must go," he said. "Could you lend me two hundred francs? It is too late to get money across town, and I must catch the train to Geneva."

"Certainly," Miss Tarbell said. She had just the sum in her desk, carefully put aside for her summer holiday, and as she went to fetch it she wondered fleetingly if she would ever see it again. But she was so fascinated that it never occurred to her to do anything but give it to him. "I'll never see that money again," she thought. She underestimated him: the same night he wired his brother Robby, in the London office, to send her a check. He knew he would see her soon again.

The company set up to publish the new magazine was nominally capitalized at one hundred thousand dollars, one thousand shares at one hundred dollars apiece, but the actual cash capital amounted to less than fifteen thousand dollars. Phillips had saved forty-five hundred dollars; he got forty-five shares. McClure's brother Robby had some money left him by his half-sister Ella; he bought fifty shares. McClure at first held all the rest. He had only twenty-eight hundred dollars in cash to risk, but he was sole owner of the syndicate and its safe full of literary properties, and this was and would be for more than a year the company's most valuable asset.

McClure was indisputably boss: publisher and editor-in-chief; but while as editor-in-chief he wanted only to concentrate on new ideas, new formats, new features, new writers, as publisher he was vividly aware that the need of the hour was more cash. His trip across the country in the fall of 1892 to sell his wares to newspaper editors was, then, crucial; for on the conjectural profits from those sales his embryonic magazine would flourish or die stillborn.

Nothing in life comes easy. At this moment, while McClure was anxiously speculating as to his chances for lucrative sales, his family fell sick with malaria. (There were four children by now; Mary, the third daughter, had been born unexpectedly early in the summer of 1890, while McClure was in London.) One hot August evening, McClure came home to the new house in Bronxville and, as he paused by the gate, he had a sudden vision of coffins, one after another, being carried out the front door and across the porch. A grisly fantasy; incorrigibly impetuous, he at once arranged for his family to be removed to a temporary home in Bay Shore, on the south side of Long Island. Then, apprehensively, he set out on his cross-country trip.

"Our prospectus pleases," McClure wrote his wife from Chicago, "and only editors are vile"; but the truth was that the times were unpropitious. His clients the newspaper editors listened, he found, with only one ear. They were distracted by politics. President Benjamin Harrison was running against Grover Cleveland again, but especially in the farm states of the Midwest there was an ominous rumble, the deep-throated growl of the Populists flocking to the banner of General James Weaver, and no man dared guess what might happen on election day. From New York, Phillips reported that money was uncomfortably tight; the syndicate was clearing the slimmest of profits.

On his way west, McClure tarried in Davenport, Iowa. Here, six years before, his college friend Albert Brady had founded a daily newspaper, The Davenport Times; and here McClure was all at once assailed by one of his characteristically rash schemes—why not hire Brady as the business manager of the new magazine? Impulsively, he offered Brady a five-year contract at five thousand dollars a year if he would take the job.

It was, on the face of it, a harebrained notion. Brady was only thirty and looked younger; he had had no magazine experience whatever, and indeed his only business experience was limited to a town of some twenty-five thousand souls. Moreover, the sum McClure engaged to pay him in the first year was nearly half the capital the infant company had on hand; to earmark so much for an untried man seemed to guarantee ruin. And yet McClure was never to make a sudden decision that paid off so handsomely. Brady was precisely what McClure needed. Calm where McClure was excitable, quiet and thorough where McClure was impatient, tenacious where McClure was mercurial, Brady had as well that rare gift, the ability to say No to a proposition, however tempting, that undercut his policy.* Fortunately, then, for the future of McClure's Magazine, Brady took the job. While McClure pushed on west, Brady began to grow a beard, against the day

---

* McClure, who trusted hunches implicitly and always preferred the snap decision, was quite likely to say Yes to an attractive proposition. In this connection, a long-time associate said of McClure, as a businessman: "If he had been a woman, he would have been pregnant all the time."

when he would have to feign wiliness and experience amongst the urban rubes of New York City.

On election day McClure was in Los Angeles. The Democrat, Cleveland, won the Presidency, but what was worse was the size of the Populist vote: over the million mark, and more than one voter in every twelve: doleful proof of passion unspent. Surely the anguished Populist outcry for free silver—the symbol of easier money—foreboded more trouble? But McClure had time and energy only for his syndicate sales. From Fort Worth he wrote his wife: "Texas is mine at last. Now the whole country is conquered & I must redouble my efforts in England & Australia." From Memphis: "I am simply scooping in the contracts . . . The new magazine is to be one dollar [a year]! & it will be a howler."

But his brave optimism was counterfeited. For his wife had gone back to Galesburg (where she was to undergo a minor operation) and McClure was in consequence the more restive. He was uncomfortably aware that Professor Hurd still took a bleak view of him. In evidence, there was a recent letter from his notably unreconstructed father-in-law.

> My dear daughter, Hattie:
> . . . I cherish no ill-will towards your husband, but I never looked complacently upon him as your prospective husband & nothing has occurred to make me love him any better since your marriage. I do not wish him to visit me—there would be no comfort in it for either party—& how can I visit at his house under these circumstances? It seems that if you wish ever to see your father again you must visit him at his own house, as you should have done several times since you left home. Your *grandfathers* & *grandmothers* never visited *me* or *your mother—we went to see them.* Can you not do the same? Many a daughter visits her father & mother unaccompanied by her husband—why have you not done so? If you had, it would have been much better for every person interested in the matter. In your letter you impute all the causes of our alienation to me. *I* think that view of the case quite unjust. You know that I loved you dearly when you were at home & was ready to make any sacrifice for you—you well knew also that I did not like your husband—before your marriage, as you may remember, I told you that he would be a barrier between father & daughter—and yet *you* disregarded my wishes & married him. Am I the only cause of the unhappy state of affairs? For my sake, as well as for your sake, I wish that Mr. McClure was pleasing to me, but since he is not why can we not all understand & accept the fact in such a way that father & daughter may cultivate & retain somewhat of the old affection? I have never tried to influence either your mother or sister against your husband—they know I am not pleased with him, &

that is all there is of it—I have always been willing that both of them should visit you whenever it was their wish, & that you with your children should visit us. I have very much desired the latter as I could not visit you. I am very much grieved that I am so blamed by you, perchance also by your sister & mother, for not loving your husband, but I see no way out of the difficulty—I must bear the cross. I am lonely. . . . Oh, well! . . . I myself am fairly well for a man who is getting old, who is already old. . . .

I am affectionately,

Your father,

Albert Hurd.

P.S. I have re-read the above this morning, Wednesday, & can truly say that not one word was written in anger or hatred towards any one. I am deeply grieved about the matter.

Affy., A.H.

Surprisingly, however, the professor now thawed. Perhaps owing to his daughter's visit, he began to inquire in friendly fashion after McClure's business, even suggesting one or two articles on education which he considered might possibly be of interest to newspaper readers.

It was as well. McClure was sufficiently distracted by the pressures of his expanding enterprise. "I am simply crushed with work," he wrote his wife. "Oh! the magazine, the magazine! it means seven years of travail, study, thought & energy. I must read the current newspapers to find out who can best write for me. Then I must read all current magazines & reviews & weeklies & study their pictures. I must invent the men & organize a staff for syndicate & magazine that will surpass anything attempted heretofore & in seven years I want to control a great daily & found the *London Times* of America. So you see I am busy. I study & read all evening. I think & plan & invent. This is 1884 all over again. How I like to invent!"

In Galesburg the surgeon had botched his job of operating on Hattie. Far from the excitement of his affairs, she was first fretful and then pettish; why didn't he write to her every day? He wrote in explanation and apology, but no use: Hattie was nursing her grievance, and she even shared it with her mother, who promptly mailed McClure, anonymously, a slip of paper on which she had copied a quotation from a story in The Century: "If your fiancée smilingly accepts even the best of apologies for the smallest of inattentions, she is beginning to cool; and if you make many of them, you are."

McClure was in a cold rage, tempered by hot flashes of self-pity. His pen sputtered on his notepaper.

January 12, 1893

My dearest Hattie:--

I write to explain exactly how I happened to miss writing you every day. My work has been seeing men to raise money, seeing printers paper-makers &c, & I would be detained far beyond my expectations . . . A business interview where you are the pleader is controlled by the other party . . . Why do you doubt me in any way? Has my life been such that you cant trust in my love & devotion unless you are daily informed? Until I got your letter nothing could have shook my faith in you. Not even the experiences of many years previous to 1883. Now your letter casts a sinister interpretation on the past. Your hand did not copy that item from the *Century*. How changed you are to share with others your feelings! Do you know what *I* should do? I should utterly refuse to hold communication with you or your people. I should take you from your father's house. I should refuse to have any letters from you reach any of the people I employ & pay in our household.

I have slaved for you all. I didn't buy new shoes until my feet were actually exposed to the wet. I am wearing thin underclothing because I don't want to spend any money for myself. But I don't begrudge anything to you or the children. I think only of your interests. All these struggles is to ensure a good income so that the daily burden may be far removed from you. You dont seem to realize the great difficulty of a man without capital earning $10,000 per annum. Many people are trying to get some of this money & they render the struggle harder. I work continually and unstintedly. I have not harbored an unkind thought against you & it hurts me cruelly to think that *you* could write me such words.

Oh Hattie . . . don't needlessly increase the strain which many times reaches the limit of endurance. It is not your fault that I have had so far to climb & so much to accomplish in a short time, it is my misfortune, but don't be unkind to me for it . . .

Hattie, I am a very human, imperfect man. It might be possible to harden me against you so that you would be bruised & hurt. *Dont! dont!* I want to treat you just as tenderly & lovingly as if each year was our last together. This letter represents several moods. But I love & adore you as ever. . . .

Your loving husband,
SSMcClure

But he had no time for such luxuries as anger and self-pity. The syndicate, the new magazine—and he was planning to publish, as well, an American edition of The Idler, a sixpenny magazine edited by two English friends, Jerome K. Jerome and Robert Barr. That, however, was to be incidental; it was McClure's that engrossed him.

The first issue was planned for June, 1893, which meant of course that in January he had already to be planning for midsummer and fall. He knew his magazine would be different, he knew it would be interesting, he was confident it would be better than any other general magazine, but he wanted to make sure that those who paused at newsstands would be staggered by the excellence of his wares. Whose name, amongst the writers, was most magnetic? Robert Louis Stevenson's? Alas, he was once more dragging his feet, refusing to deliver the last chapters of David Balfour and, indeed, eyeing the whole magazine venture very sourly. Kipling was the man; Kipling, who was living in Brattleboro, Vermont. Off McClure sped, to tie up everything Kipling might write in the next dozen years.

"He entered, alight with the notion for a new magazine," Kipling recalled later. "I think the talk lasted some twelve—or it may have been seventeen—hours, before the notion was fully hatched out." Clearly, McClure was still a doughty talker. "I liked and admired McClure more than a little," Kipling added, "for he was one of the few with whom three and a half words serve for a sentence, and as clear and straight as spring water."

But Kipling was not so foolish as to promise all his work to one untested publisher. Nor, while his time ran out, could McClure find any writer of the first rank with a suitable story on hand. To stud the cover of his first issue with celebrated names, he was obliged to invent subterfuges—and while these were to be unexpectedly successful features, in February they were only headaches.

The first was "Real Conversations" (an idea he got by glancing at a copy of Landor's "Imaginary Conversations"), in which well-known writers were to chat with still more eminent personages about their careers, and so two names could be featured on the cover. It was swiftly apparent that this series would require the nicest diplomacy, for what well-known writer did not consider himself an eminent personage, better suited for being interviewed than for menially interviewing? On the other hand, if the writer were not sufficiently well-known, the eminent personage often balked and kicked his heels in the air. Hjalmar Boyesen agreed equably enough to interview William Dean Howells, and Hamlin Garland undertook to interview both Eugene Field and James Whitcomb Riley, since he was in any case anxious to be found in public in their company; but F. Marion Crawford, a best-selling novelist, was by no means happy with the notion of waiting upon Oliver Wendell Holmes. And when McClure, shifting his tactics, suggested that Elizabeth Stuart Phelps interview both Holmes and Professor Henry Drummond on the subject of immortality, Holmes snapped, "I will neither be lured nor McClured into anything of the kind!" In a letter to Miss Phelps, he added, "As for saying anything on these subjects (Time & Eternity) to be *reported,* I would as soon send a piece of my spinal marrow to one of the omnivorous editors." But before long Holmes was both mollified and McClured when Edward Everett Hale pressed the doorbell of his house on Beacon Street to interview him. "Holmes was as good as gold," Hale wrote McClure.

What can be glimpsed here, of course, is an early shoot of that rank, hardy weed of journalism, the personality sketch of a celebrity, the intimate sniffing and prying into the private life of a person with a public name.

Another idea of the same sort, still fresh and vivid in 1893, was to portray a well-known person, from his childhood on, in a series of photographs. Today these pictures seem banal and artificial, remindful of those in the Family Album that used to lie in swollen majesty on the table in the front parlor; most useful, perhaps, as a kind of fever-chart of the changing fashions in whiskers during the last half of the nineteenth century. But they proved a formidably successful feature at the time.

Oddly enough, the series was named by the French writer, Alphonse Daudet. When McClure got back to New York from his visit with Kipling, he found waiting for him a man with an introduction from Will Low, who had designed the cover for the new magazine. This was Auguste F. Jaccaci, Bohemian by birth and bohemian by temperament. "From his talent as an artist & his experience as a businessman," Low had written McClure, "you might find it to your mutual advantage to pull together." Jaccaci was also a man of great charm, lively and gay; he had a wide acquaintance among the young artists in New York. McClure at once hired him as art manager and dispatched him to Paris, among other things to get some photographs of Daudet for the first issue. When the idea was explained to him, Daudet exclaimed, "Véritables documents humains!" And so the feature was called "Human Documents."

Editorial offices for McClure's were found on the third floor of the building at 743 Broadway which was for many years the home of Charles Scribner's Sons. Below them were the offices of Scribner's Magazine, above them those of The Magazine of American History. Here, in the demented whirl that always attends on the birth of a new magazine, a staff was gradually assembled and a first issue published. At the end of May, twenty thousand copies were printed and hopefully distributed. Of these, twelve thousand would, in the sadness of time, be returned,* but long before that unhappy day McClure, as ever zestfully enthusiastic, had taken a train to Chicago to look in on the Columbian Exposition, arrange the details of the Eugene Field–Hamlin Garland interview, address a banquet of Knox College alumni, and peddle some syndicate matter. With the syndicate in mind, he called on the editor of The Chicago Inter-Ocean; presently, whilst he was heatedly gabbling about both syndicate and new magazine, a copy boy entered and handed him a telegram. It was from John Phillips back in New York, urgently requesting that McClure collect from The Inter-Ocean for the previous month's syndicate service. McClure tore it up and went on talking. After a time he casually mentioned that he could use the money owing to him. The editor smiled.

"Money? Oh, no! We can't give you any money. Look out there!"

He pointed to the window, and McClure looked out. Below in the street he saw a great crowd pressing against the doors of a bank. "That," McClure said later, "was the first I saw of the panic of 1893." Manifestly he was the last editor in the United States of America to detect signs of economic distress: here is a wry testimonial to, as it may have been, his single-minded absorption.

In fact, the panic of 1893, which was severe, had begun more than a month before. Between April 1 and October 1, more than eight thousand commercial concerns were to fail, with liabilities of nearly $285,000,000. Banks were to fail, railroads were to go bankrupt, unemployment was to soar, before long whole armies of unemployed were to start marching on Washington. In short, with his usual perspicacity as to business, McClure had launched his venture at precisely the wrong time. From Chicago he wrote his wife:

June 9, 1893

My darling Hattie

We are nearly on the verge of failure. Only by cutting our expenses down by $2000 a month can we survive this disastrous financial panic, which is pulling down strong houses.

I have given orders to cut my salary to $60 a week & to cut all salaries & expenses in like ratio. I cant borrow, & we cant collect money due us. . . . Even the Inter-Ocean has to delay payment & the small papers can hardly pay at all. . . .

---

* Eventually, however, thanks to belated library subscriptions and orders for bound volumes, all but fourteen hundred copies of the first issue would be sold.

I will try to borrow from personal friends enough money to ease up
our home expenses, so that $60 a week from the office will do.

This is the worst year that I can remember. . . .

My darling, darling Hattie, I have the great fight of my life in front
of me. You must not suffer in it.

Your loving husband
SSMcClure

A few days later he had somewhat recovered. He might be entering
upon the fight of his life, but after all was he not an infant Lord of the
Press—with copies of his new magazine gleaming orange on (nearly) every
newsstand? For the first time a note of pomposity crept into his letter to
his wife. "The president & active manager of a great business," he admonished
her, "when on a business trip must necessarily keep himself in instant reach
of the home office." He had taken a deep, self-important breath. "I am trying
to learn how to publish without money," he went on. "It is no light task I
assure you. I feel that we are in a terrible plight & I shall have to manage &
finance as I never did before."

He never wrote a truer word. It may, indeed, be hazarded that no one
ever before or since financed a magazine as McClure now did.

For a magazine to live, obviously it must have paying readers and paying
advertisers, and it must win the one to attract the other. McClure had
originally planned to tempt vast hordes of readers by charging only ten
cents for his magazine. This would have been unprecedented. To be sure,
The Ladies' Home Journal cost only ten cents; but of the general magazines
The Century, Harper's, and The Atlantic cost thirty-five, and Scribner's,
The Cosmopolitan, and Munsey's cost twenty-five. The eventual price of
McClure's, fifteen cents, while startling, did not, however, sell many copies.
Provokingly enough, it seemed that his plan for a cheaper magazine was
going to profit only his competitors: in July the price of The Cosmopolitan
was cut to a bizarre twelve and a half cents; and in October Munsey's, which
had been losing money, was cut to ten cents and its circulation promptly
soared.

Meantime McClure's was netting a microscopic six hundred dollars a
month from circulation, a wretched showing; but the advertising was even
worse, averaging about four hundred a month. It began to look as if McClure
had blundered when he hired so young and inexperienced an advertising
manager. Couldn't Brady sell more than seven or eight pages a month?

The answer to this question was Yes. Brady could easily have doubled, maybe even trebled the number of advertising pages. But to do so would have meant undercutting policy, so he stubbornly refused. Ignoring the ways of other magazines, Brady had worked out a rate-card (one which for the first time listed the price for preferred position) and he meant to stick to it. Advertisers refused to believe him. It was the commonest practice—and especially in the case of a young and struggling magazine—to wink at the announced rates, to offer under-the-table rebates, to give an advertising agent an extra five per cent for an increase in his custom. Brady said No. The agent for Pears' Soap, an important account in those days, very sportingly offered to loan him the full-page electrotype of a Pears' advertisement for use free, pointing out that other advertisers would be impressed. Brady said No. He was offered $600 for a $750 contract, even $700 for a $720 contract. Brady said No. McClure's anguish may be imagined. "It is easier to say Yes than No," Brady insisted, "but No is much safer." And so with each succeeding issue the company's indebtedness grew frighteningly higher.

McClure was frantic. To whom could he turn for help? Not to the bankers; as always in a financial panic, they were so many icicles. Not to his friends the newspaper publishers; on the contrary, with every week the panic wore on these worthies were canceling their contracts for McClure's syndicate service, and so bringing him closer to beggary. Not, indeed, to any of the ordinary sources of credit; they were all frozen for the duration. In his despair he was forced to turn to his own contributors.

Professor Henry Drummond, a Scottish theologian and amateur scientist, had written a piece on evolution—"Where Man Got His Ears"—for the first issue. In June he happened to be in Boston, delivering the Lowell lectures. McClure had scouted Drummond years before when he lectured at Columbia on his studies of the slave trade in Africa, and a friendship had sprung up. McClure had fancied that his own father, had he lived, would have been a man like Drummond. Having convinced himself, then, that he wished only to arrange for further articles, and in any case feeling, as always when he was troubled, the need for travel, McClure went to Boston to call on Drummond. It must have been a tolerably amusing visit.

McClure claimed later that he never mentioned his financial distress, "but we spoke of the panic." Drummond told of how successful his lectures had been, of how he had been obliged by the press of crowds to give each lecture twice and had, in consequence, been paid far more than the usual fee. He asked McClure whether he happened to need any money. McClure, electing to imagine that Drummond meant money for his personal expenses, recoiled from the offer as from a puff-adder. Pursuing his thought, Drummond mentioned that he had been given a check for three thousand dollars by the Lowell Institute and that he could easily endorse it to McClure if, by chance, it might be of any assistance to him in his business. McClure hesitated, as if to consider. Then, with delicate haste, he accepted. Drummond made over the check, taking twenty shares of stock in the magazine and advancing one thousand dollars as a loan. "It seemed curious," McClure said later, "that, when all ordinary springs of money were dry, money should have come from a source that a financier would hardly have thought of." Drummond's check made possible the third and fourth issues.

There next appeared one Edwin C. Martin, who tendered McClure five thousand dollars in return for fifty shares of stock and an agreement to employ him at two thousand a year.

And so the magazine limped along, its circulation gradually inching up over the thirty-thousand mark by December, 1893—for after all it was publishing superior stuff, contributions from Thomas Hardy, Kipling, Walter Besant, and Octave Thanet, a couple of Israel Zangwill's earliest tales of life in the ghetto, and Conan Doyle's memorable "The Adventure of the Final Problem"—and the advertisers and their agents were beginning to believe that young Albert Brady meant what he said; but still the deficit mounted thousands of dollars higher every month. Every night when McClure took up his evening newspaper he turned first to the list of bankrupts, fearful that he might find his own name.

He hustled to Boston to lay his troubles before his former employer, Colonel Pope, and spoke so persuasively that he came away with a check for one thousand dollars to pay for future advertising. Pope also advised him to seek an extension of credit from Tileston & Hollingsworth, from whom he was buying his paper. McClure got his month's credit and once more spoke so persuasively that he managed to sell Amos Hollingsworth one thousand dollars' worth of stock. Back in New York, he wrung a month's credit from his printer, a handsome, bearded man named J. J. Little.

Stopgaps, only stopgaps; the need was more cash. Phillips found another five thousand dollars by getting his father to mortgage his Galesburg home; McClure came into the office one morning in triumph since he had prevailed on his wife's doctor's wife to invest four hundred dollars, and so could meet a payroll two weeks overdue. Any visitor, no matter what his business or the condition of his bankroll, stood in likelihood of being corraled by McClure, marched into his inner office, and bludgeoned into buying some stock. But the price stood steady at one hundred dollars a share; at that price, buyers were scarce.

And writers were constantly buzzing about his head. Was it possible that one of them might be temporarily so flush as to invest a dab of cash? Once he even braced Hamlin Garland, the earnest writer from the Dakotas; but Garland wasn't having any. He was smugly confident that McClure's was going to fold, and he looked down a long nose at its editor, whom he regarded as a journalist indifferent to "literary style," as a businessman catering to "the average reader—or the reader below the average . . . not [to] the cultivated few."

But even such a mean creature has his uses. Garland would write for the magazine, and he would send his friend Stephen Crane down bearing a letter to McClure: "If you have any work for Mr. Crane talk things over with him and for Mercy Sake! Don't keep him *standing* for an hour, as he did before, out in your pen for culprits." Either on that Monday early in January, 1894, or soon after, Crane handed McClure the typescript of The Red Badge of Courage. Here is the moment when, if ever, a tear of compassion must well up for an editor: he holds in his hand a masterpiece, but he is too broke to buy it.*

Not only lack of cash troubled McClure. He was constantly dissatisfied with his magazine. (Of the hundreds of issues he was to edit, he would never find one that completely contented him.) What galled most was that, in theory, he knew that a perfect issue was possible. He could describe his dream fluently to a reporter from The New-York Tribune.† "A magazine," he said, "ought to be a unity. It must represent the ideas and principles of one man or a group of like-minded men; it must have a single purpose all through. Anybody could make a magazine by hiring a competent staff of assistants, buying a certain amount of historical matter, a certain amount of

---

* The moment stretched out over an agonizing nine months, during which McClure constantly temporized, always praying for heaven to shower him with enough cash to justify his buying a story against the future when he owed so much for stories printed in the past. Crane quite naturally found such indecision intolerable. "McClure was a beast about the war story," he wrote Garland, a pungent line that has been delightedly quoted by Crane's biographers, who have not troubled to wonder why McClure found it hard to pay for the story.

In early November, 1894, Crane finally took The Red Badge of Courage to Irving Bacheller, to whose syndicate he sold it for seventy-five dollars. It was later in that same month that McClure's prayers were finally, and tardily, rewarded; at last he was in a position to pay Crane handsomely and often. But Crane never forgave him. To the end he classified McClure amongst the Gadarene swine. Sic semper—or, at any rate, sic saepissime—authors and editors.

† The Tribune reporter called on him in October, 1897, when the success of McClure's was assured. But its editor's ideas were thought out years earlier.

fiction, of descriptive articles of travel, poetry, and so on, and mixing them together in suitable proportions; but it would not make a good magazine, nor would it be likely to be a success, lacking unity, the inspiration and direction from one central head."

McClure's hell was that his associates were always subverting his intentions.

"The magazine must first suit its editor," he told the Tribune reporter, "and then suit the public. When these two things happen in conjunction, it is a success. The ideal magazine would be one in which everything, from cover to cover, should be interesting to every class of readers. It is not enough to provide different kinds of articles to suit different tastes. Things must be written so as to be made attractive to people not ordinarily interested in those subjects."

But whom could McClure trust, to assist in such a trifling task? Not Phillips, although he was the least mistrusted; not his own brothers, Jack, Tom, and Robby, each of whom sat briefly at editorial desks in the office; nor any of the special writers with whom he experimented as briefly.

McClure had a horrible jargon word for what, he insisted, had to be done to make a piece worthy of publication. " 'Magazining,' " he said, "is the term we use to describe the treatment of a topic to make it just right for our use. It is an art in itself. Only the magazine staff knows exactly how an article must be presented to be in line with the general attitude of the publication.* That is the reason why I or some of my assistants always collaborate with the author of a great feature, even going so far as to investigate and study his sources of material, so as to get into the very spirit of the work."

In the spring of 1894 McClure was groping toward an innovation which was to solve at least some of his problems. Up till then non-fiction, like fiction, had been submitted by free-lance writers. McClure was reconciled to an intermittent, partial, unsatisfactory control over his fiction; after all, this was work of the imagination, and it came down to whether he liked it or not. But non-fiction was different. The ideas for articles were usually his; he knew how he wanted them written; surely there was someone, somewhere, who could take his ideas and clothe them in lively, accurate prose, and who would agree to join his staff full-time to do so. Such a writer is commonplace on magazines today, but sixty years ago he was so rare that McClure was never able to make up his mind what title to give him. Associate editor? Staff writer? Staff associate? At any rate, he gradually con-

---

* Or, translated: "Only I know exactly how an article must be presented to be in line with my attitude toward my publication."

vinced himself that the someone he needed was Ida Tarbell. As if to defeat his purpose, she was in Paris. So he set out after her.

And of course he needed money. It was his mad hope that among the authors in England, to whom he owed more than three thousand dollars, he might find one or two softhearted enough to loan him still more. Predictably, every writer in funds promptly scuttled for cover, while those less fortunate hounded McClure wherever he went, peevishly demanding the sums he owed them. One of these, H. J. W. Dam, who was about to be evicted from his flat, actually wept. McClure, much affected, wept with him, but he had no money to pay him. Then, drying his eyes, he hurried off to Paris to hire Miss Tarbell.

This was another in the series of decisions—ascribe them either to dumb luck or to an extraordinary perspicacity—which would turn out exceedingly well. Yet on its face it seemed the goofiest of all. For a publisher plunged deep in debt to hire a relatively untried writer (and a woman, at that) is as though the captain of a sinking ship were all at once to lay about him with an axe. McClure did not have one hundred dollars to pay Dam for an article printed five months before, but he had one hundred and fifty dollars to buy Miss Tarbell's passage back to America. He did not, at the time, even know if his magazine was still being published.

It was, but only just. Circulation was holding steady at about thirty-five thousand; Brady was selling some thirty pages of advertising a month for about fifteen hundred dollars; the deficit on each issue had been reduced to about one thousand dollars. Maybe, it was hoped, by shaving the size of the engravings and by cutting the number of pages, that deficit could be eliminated. Colonel Pope agreed to advance another five thousand against future advertising. Could nothing be done to raise the circulation still further? They had been serializing The Ebb Tide by Robert Louis Stevenson and Lloyd Osbourne, they had printed Kipling's Jungle Tales, their articles on science were distinguished reporting and right on the edge of the future. But Mc-Clure was impatient. Somehow, somewhere, he was missing a trick. Irritably he leafed through the letters on his incredibly messy desk. Here: a letter from Bill Nye suggesting a "Real Conversation" with James Whitcomb Riley; it would be, Nye promised, "a dialogue that would settle a great many national matters that otherwise might remain roiled up for years." No, no; that was not what he was after. A letter from a subscriber in Omaha fluttered to the top. Why not, this man suggested, run some pictures of Napoleon in the series of "Human Documents"?

McClure's eyes glowed.

He knew, of course, that France had in the past two or three years gone through a fervent centennial revival of its days of Napoleonic glory; he knew that Scribner's Magazine had recently published a series of articles on Napoleon; he knew, moreover, that The Century was planning one of its long, turgid, historical series on the same theme; here, he felt instinctively, was a chance to slice all the icing off The Century's cake. If only there were some pictures!

There were. Gardiner Hubbard, the wealthy Boston lawyer whose daughter had married Alexander Graham Bell, had for fourteen years been collecting prints of Napoleon and his intimates; he owned hundreds of engravings. When McClure hustled down to Twin Oaks, Hubbard's comfortable place in Washington, the two men had in a half hour littered all the chairs and tables and couches in two rooms with a pictorial history of the Corsican's career. McClure capered about, ecstatic. This was more than a "Human Document"; this was a series. But there would have to be an accompanying text.

Still caprizant, McClure scurried back to New York and cabled to the English writer Robert Sherard, who had written two or three pieces for the magazine, a commission to write the text that would accompany Hubbard's engravings. That was in July; McClure planned to publish in November, simultaneously with The Century. With commendable dispatch, Sherard got his piece across the ocean in August; but it was woefully anti-Napoleon, totally unsuitable, a classic example, McClure decided, of his need for a staff writer who could properly execute his ideas. He wired Miss Tarbell in Titusville, Pennsylvania, where she was spending a holiday with her family, summoned her to New York, explained the situation to her in three and a half words, and then galloped her down to Washington to introduce her to the Hubbards.

Poor Miss Tarbell was painfully self-conscious, a country mouse all at once transported into the midst of urban splendors; and she was in an agony of apprehension on behalf of McClure. She was so anxious that the Hubbards should like him. But his behavior seemed to her so scandalous, his hair so tousled, his manner so careless of the amenities that she was horrified. To her, Twin Oaks was "the most beautiful home into which I had ever been admitted"; she walked in awe of the butler and the maids. But McClure was characteristically unimpressed, regarded the house as a temporary extension of his editorial office, burst in unannounced whenever it occurred to him, scattered page-proofs and galley-slips over the living-room carpet—in short, caught everyone up on the wave of his enthusiasm. Miss Tarbell actually found it necessary to apologize for him. But Mrs. Hubbard laughed. "That eagerness of his is so beautiful," she said. "I am accustomed to geniuses."

Miss Tarbell found herself a desk in the Library of Congress, tucked up her sleeves, and went to work. In six weeks she had finished the first of what was to be a series of seven articles, each lavishly illustrated with the pictures from Hubbard's collection. Her first piece on Napoleon was published in November, 1894. It sent the circulation up to sixty-five thousand.

Editor McClure was ecstatic, but Publisher McClure was plunged in gloom. It appeared that success had come at last, only to show up hand-in-hand with final failure. For in mid-November a note for five thousand dollars was due, and he was strapped. He had, he told his wife angrily, exhausted every possible resource; there was nothing left.

"Then," she said serenely, "you must pray to God to help you."

He stared at her. At length he said shortly: "*You* pray. You can pray better than I can." Then he left for the office.

On the way he recalled that Conan Doyle, who had been on an American lecture tour, was stopping at the Aldine Club. "I had," he said later, "a feeling of having neglected Doyle." This would never do. He determined to look in at the club on his way to the office. Some idea of McClure's strength as a poker player may be deduced from his own account of his visit.

"In apologizing to him for my seeming indifference to his presence in America," McClure wrote, in his autobiography, "I told him that I had been upset by business anxieties, remarking incidentally that I had to finance the magazine as well as edit it. Conan Doyle then said that he would like to put some money into the business himself, if I needed it; that he believed in the magazine and in me. I lunched with him at the club, and after lunch he walked over to the office with me, and wrote out his check for $5,000, exactly the sum we were owing."

Small wonder that Conan Doyle later was persuaded of the efficacy of extra-sensory perception.

Excerpt from a letter written by Hattie to her mother in Galesburg: "Sam said he couldn't help being surprised, it was such an unthought-of way out of his troubles, and yet from the beginning all his emergencies have been met in just such ways, and always just in time. The Lord is very good!"

With the Lord in his corner, the circulation of McClure's Magazine touched one hundred thousand before he had finished publishing the Tarbell series on Napoleon.

[II]

And now the issue was joined between the Old and the New—between the established, expensive magazines of quality and the cheap, popular magazines. Of the new, McClure's posed the principal threat to the old, for while Munsey's and The Cosmopolitan were both content to seek a readership that was middle-class and middlebrow, McClure's had undertaken to compete directly with The Century, Harper's, Scribner's, and The Atlantic, to beat them in their own bailiwick. His chief weapon, as always, was his enthusiasm.

If one editorial feature had lifted McClure's to a circulation of one hundred thousand, it was the excitement of every issue that kept it there. Albert Shaw, the editor of The Review of Reviews, had said of the first number of McClure's, "It throbs with actuality from beginning to end," and each succeeding number had been charged with the same sense of immediacy, the same zest in whatever was new and interesting. In the first issue, under the title, "The Edge of the Future," McClure had printed interviews with Thomas Edison and Alexander Graham Bell, speculations on inventions warranted to make smooth mankind's path ahead; and nearly every month thereafter, whether with papers on polar exploration or reports on diphtheria antitoxin or accounts of man's effort to fly, McClure had beckoned to his readers to come peer with him over the edge of the future.

His readers were, clearly, exhilarated. But were there to be only one hundred thousand of them? It was not nearly enough. Another editorial feature was needed, another "howler."

McClure bent his brows in thought. At length, even before the last in the series on Napoleon had been published, he summoned Ida Tarbell. "Out with you," he bade her. "Look, see, report." Her subject this time was to be the early years of Abraham Lincoln, and she was to follow his path from Kentucky to Illinois to Washington, talking to those who had known him, reporting their reminiscences, borrowing their dusty daguerreotypes, bringing to life again the man McClure described as "the noblest character of our history" and "the greatest man of the Christian era." (McClure's last anxious admonition to Miss Tarbell was that she should take bed-socks with her. "It gets terribly cold in Kentucky," he said.)

It should be noted that the idea of a series on Lincoln had plunked squashily, like an overripe melon, when first McClure broached it to his associates. Indeed there were sound arguments against it. Presuming that anyone wanted to read about Lincoln (which in 1895 still required proof), The Century had just finished serializing the Nicolay-Hay biography; what could be added to that definitive work? When McClure nevertheless persisted, his friends among the newspaper editors warned that he was making his first big blunder. McClure stuck out his stubborn lower lip. "John," he said to Phillips, "they tell me that only my inexperience as a magazine editor leads me to compete with The Century by running a series on Lincoln. Well, inexperience is a thing that doesn't last. Maybe I'd better use it while I still have it."

Someone asked the editor of The Century, Richard Watson Gilder, what he thought of McClure's. Gilder characterized it in just ten words: "They got a girl to write a Life of Lincoln."

Yet there were signs that Gilder was worried about this bustling newcomer to his placid parish. He ran a note in The Century: "In the present increase of cheap magazines, it is well to remember that . . . they contain hardly half the amount of reading-matter that is found in the thirty-five cent magazines; and that at least one-half of the expense of the latter periodicals is the literary material and art work contained in them and the editorial supervision which provides it. The great features which have made the American magazine famous throughout the world are not possible in these lower-priced periodicals."

McClure laughed and retorted editorially:

> How exceedingly prone are we all to pronounce the new thing impossible! The literature of progress may be summed up in this simple dialogue:
>> *The Old to the New*. Thou art impossible!
>> *The New to the Old*. The future is mine.

In this debate, actions, as usual, carried more weight than words. For his part, McClure announced that he would soon publish more of Kipling's Jungle Stories, Anthony Hope's sequel to The Prisoner of Zenda, and the

last novel written by Robert Louis Stevenson.* At the same time McClure
rammed his argument home by reducing the price of his magazine to ten
cents. This decision had been taken with characteristic haste:

> Cohassett [sic] Sunday May 26/95
>
> My darling Hattie We are making history so fast that I hardly have
> time to report. Friday noon we learned that *Cosmopolitan* would reduce
> to 10 cents with July.
>
> I had tried to persuade our people to reduce this autumn but met with
> strong opposition excepting from Phillips who was undecided. This de-
> cided us, only we *must* get money.
>
> I came to Boston. Colonel Pope was not in town but down here. I saw
> Mrs. Phelps-Ward & planned out some capital autobiographical matter,
> reminiscences of old Andover life, of Holmes, Whittier, Longfellow &
> of the whole Great New England life then took late train here arriving
> at 7.40.
>
> The Colonel was hospitable & splendid & took me in & got me supper
> & listened to our dilemma & instantly offered $5000.00!
>
> He is a great friend. I'll try to get 5000 more in Boston & telegraph the
> boys. We can now safely do the 10 cent act with *our* July number. I feel
> so happy & *free*. You cant get behind ten cents. . . .
>
> We are so involved & living so near the edge of the future that I may
> be a day or two late. . . .
>
> Your loving husband
> SSM

The debate between the Old and the New continued to resound throughout the summer of 1895. It was joined by the venerable Henry C. Bowen,
editor of The Independent, an influential Protestant weekly. Bowen lined up
with the Old. Harper's, The Century, and Scribner's, said he, "will wish to
maintain that higher, purer literary standard which succeeds in securing the
best but not the most numerous readers. . . . They cannot enlarge their constituency beyond the comparatively cultivated class that appreciates them."
Bowen reckoned the "fit audience in an educated country like ours" at less
than half a million families. As for the others, they were useful as members

---

* The news of Stevenson's death on December 3, 1894, had affected McClure powerfully. Will
Low, the artist, wrote to Stevenson's family: "Poor McClure brought me a most lamentable
article which he had written for his magazine, one which was written I know from the bottom
of his heart and which he read to me with the tears streaming down his face and I had to
tell him the best that I could that he must not publish it. . . . His honest emotion blinded
him to the distinctions between what he might say to one of us and that which he might
print for the world." McClure had sailed for Europe a few days later; Phillips had considerably
suppressed the article.

of the militia, or when it came to counting up the population, or as members of the lower schools, "but they are not the ones who delight to seek the instruction they need most."

Once again, McClure tucked up his sleeves. "The editor of McClure's," he wrote, "does not theorize as to the size of this audience. He has edited for a *million families* of readers for ten years, and he knows his audience." And he went on to point out that there was not a single writer published by the Old magazines whose stories or articles had not been gobbled up with relish by these readers whom he knew so well.

There was, however, still nothing very new about the New. The differences were only of degree. McClure dressed his material in sprightlier fashion; his pages were livelier and more readable; he used more and better illustrations; his articles on science were at once more thorough and far more swiftly harnessed to the event. But he was, as yet, breaking no new ground.

The truth was that, lacking capital, McClure lacked daring. Until he could command more circulation and more advertising, and so more money, he was earthbound. He could think only of showing how he could beat his elders on their own ground. In the process a brisk, invigorating breeze sprang up to ruffle the pages of the Old magazines; and a shrewd observer, wetting his finger and holding it up to find out whence this New air, could have traced it only to McClure.

It could scarcely be otherwise, in the face of the dazzling success of McClure's Magazine. Merely the announcement of the series on Lincoln carried a wallop. Away out in Clark, South Dakota, one friend of the magazine went out on the street and, on the strength of the announcement, signed up more than forty subscribers in less than an hour. The series on Lincoln began in November, 1895; with that issue the circulation reached one hundred and ninety thousand; in December it passed two hundred and fifty thousand. Albert Brady, recalling the trials of two years before, smiled with satisfaction. Five times in twelve months he had raised the advertising rates; because he had suspected he would be raising his rates, he had solicited no new contracts. Such a thing had never happened before in the advertising business; nor has it ever happened since.

On a Thursday evening in mid-December McClure, a guest at the American Commerce Banquet, strolled cock-a-hoop into Delmonico's. My, what a throng of financiers and industrialists, of publishers and politicians! Here were Henry Rogers and William Rockefeller, Stuyvesant Fish and John Jacob Astor, Mark Hanna and William G. McAdoo, William Randolph

Hearst and Frank Munsey, du Ponts and Sinclairs and Seligmans, bishops and senators, bankers and generals. At the center of the head table, flanked by notables of crushing respectability, sat (who else?) Chauncey M. Depew.

It was a moment for reflection. McClure might have marveled at how far he had come, in less than thirty years, from that first day in America when the firecrackers had popped and his first lemonade had been cool in his throat. He might have speculated on how one bomb, cunningly exploded amongst all these nabobs, would—who can say?—have spared the Republic much woe or, contrariwise, have toppled it over the brink into desolation. But it is safe to conclude that, as he looked about him at the editors and publishers of all the magazines with which his was then competing, one thought drove all others from his mind, to wit:

There were more pages of advertising in the December issue of McClure's than in a single issue of any other magazine up to that time.

To find himself in funds was for McClure a heady experience. By today's standards, that wealth was modest indeed: since the one hundred and forty-four pages of net advertising in the December issue had been sold at various rates, based on widely various guarantees of circulation, the revenue amounted to only $11,369.34.* But the costs were also modest: paper, presswork, and binding cost two cents a copy less than the wholesale price. McClure and Albert Brady reacted characteristically to this promising situation. As for McClure, schemes to spend money gushed out of him like lava; as for Brady, he sought and won his chief's approval for a plan to shave manufacturing costs still closer, by buying a printing plant and bindery.

Space for the plant—nearly an acre big—was found on the top floor of the Lexington Building, on Lexington Avenue between Twenty-fifth and Twenty-sixth Streets. Down in the bowels of the building, at the time McClure's moved in, was the power plant that pulled the cable for the Lexington Avenue cable cars. The editors and business managers of McClure's had offices looking out on Twenty-fifth Street. On Twenty-sixth Street there was access to a freight elevator so vast that a wagon loaded with drums of paper and drawn by a team of four horses could be lifted, horses and all, up to the presses. There were fourteen presses, two of them rotary, the first ever used for printing magazines. The space was rented and the machinery bought by Oscar Brady, Albert's older brother, who had learned production in Chicago as the publisher of a weekly newspaper.

* In contrast, today it costs more than sixty-six thousand dollars to buy space on just one back cover of Life.

In its time, this plant was a prodigy. Here, one day, came Mark Twain, to watch in silence and perhaps to think of the fortune he had lost on printing presses. As he watched, the paper feeding from a roll shifted in its bed; at once the press stopped and a bell rang, automatically summoning a pressman. "My God," cried Mark Twain. "Can that thing vote, too?"

Here, on another day, came Rudyard Kipling, to be shown around by Bert Mackenzie, the plant supervisor. Mackenzie was distracted briefly by a telephone call; at the same moment a team of horses was driven out onto the floor to deliver a truckload of paper. When Mackenzie turned back, Kipling had disappeared. The only figure to be seen was the wildly gesticulating freight-elevator operator, crying out in alarm and pointing down into the black void, eight floors below. His heart pounding, Mackenzie raced over, not daring to imagine what he would see. Away below, slowly rising, he saw the top of Kipling's intent head and Kipling's hand on the elevator's controls. Another moment, and here was Kipling confronting him. "Fascinating!" said Kipling, and, having thanked the flabbergasted operator, took Mackenzie's arm and moved away, murmuring, "Couldn't resist the chance. Hope you don't mind."

The presses and bindery were of course bought on credit.* When the transaction was completed, the S. S. McClure Company owed two hundred and fifty-seven thousand dollars. Never had McClure been so deep in debt. He sensibly concluded that, if his credit was so good, his magazine was a commercial success and he could begin to behave like a commercially successful publisher. He promptly issued a McClure's Quarterly and commenced to agitate for a British edition of McClure's Magazine. He also launched a McClure's Magazine Bible Club, which published "a superb popular edition of the celebrated self-interpreting Bible." The McClure's Quarterly died after only two issues and a loss of thousands of dollars; his associates managed to restrain him from publishing a British edition of his magazine, so we shall never know how it might have fared; and hundreds of sets of his "Magnificent Art Bible," hopefully projected as a device for increasing subscriptions, mouldered for months in a warehouse before being mercilessly remaindered.

His new wealth was, however, far more important to McClure as editor.

---

* Most of the credit was extended by Tileston and Hollingsworth, the Boston paper manufacturers. These partners never required an audit of McClure's books by certified public accountants; Tileston preferred to make his own audit. Those working in McClure's business offices got accustomed to seeing Tileston sitting on a high stool in the bookkeeping department, getting his facts at first hand, his long gray beard brushing the papers in front of him like a feather duster.

With money jingling in his pockets, he commenced once again to cascade ideas.

Now, so far from having to avoid Stephen Crane, McClure could invite that young man to his office and pepper him with suggestions. How about a series of stories to deal with actual battles of the Civil War? (Phillips later wrung from Crane, if not a series, at least one superb story, "The Little Regiment," based on the battle of Fredericksburg.) But McClure could never let a writer who had caught his fancy work on only one idea at a time. He urged Crane to go to Washington to get material for a novel on politics. (Crane was for a time McClure's guest at the Cosmos Club.) Or how about a story to deal with the New York police? (McClure introduced Crane to the president of the New York Board of Police Commissioners, Theodore Roosevelt, in the hope that some spark would ignite a flame.) Or would Crane prefer to sail for Europe with McClure in April? No? But at all events he must at once undertake a series of short pieces suitable for sale through the syndicate—how about a weekly New York newsletter? This bombardment provoked a number of Crane's better stories, including "Three Miraculous Soldiers," "The Veteran," and "The Bride Comes to Yellow Sky," and a number of articles hacked out for the syndicate, including pieces on opium-smoking, the Broadway cable cars, and New York's bicycle speedway up Riverside Drive. It led to a circular sent out by the syndicate in which McClure proudly asserted that "Mr. Crane has been added to the McClure staff, and his writings will be placed before the public exclusively through the newspapers of the Syndicate and McClure's Magazine." It led, as well, to Crane's last novel, The Third Violet, which was released through the syndicate, preceded by an unblushing circular that described it as dealing with "the seamy side of glorious love."

Now, once again in funds, when McClure spotted an item in his morning newspaper, written with the heavy-handed ridicule which at that time journalists traditionally reserved for subjects they could not understand, he could cable one writer to proceed at once from London to Würzburg, dispatch a second writer to a laboratory at Yale, and so score an important beat by publishing both an interview with Dr. Wilhelm Roentgen and the first comprehensive report (together with sixteen photographs) on the epochal X ray.*

---

* These two articles afford a fair example of the speed with which McClure moved. Roentgen read a paper about his discovery to a group of Würzburg scientists on January 4, 1896; he read it again a few days later in Vienna. The newspapers carried a garbled, jocular version in mid-

Now, instead of filching ideas for features from The Century, McClure could afford to venture a few on his own. He assigned Hamlin Garland to write a life of Grant. He was generous; he put Garland on his payroll and paid his expenses as far as Mexico so that he might search out material for what Garland had persuaded himself would be a "different" biography. McClure was enthusiastic, too. "His Grant will be as great a success as our Lincoln," he assured Phillips. "We will never be able to print enough copies and the magazine will be the only magazine in the world."

Now, too, McClure could consider the possibility that there might be some undiscovered writers of talent, somewhere in the Republic, and announce a short-story contest to smoke them out. Since by this time the circulation of McClure's was flirting with three hundred thousand, he realized that the office would surely be inundated by manuscripts from the hopeful; clearly he would have to engage a trustworthy reader. And now attend: for McClure is about to make another of those wild, instinctive judgments that would pay him dividends for years to come.

A young woman, like him fresh and vigorous, came looking for a job. Her name was Viola Roseboro'. Her hair was auburn, and her bright blue eyes danced about with as lively an interest as his; so also did her bright, quick mind. McClure had known her casually for some time. She was from Tennessee, the daughter of a Congregationalist minister, and for more than ten years she had earned her own living as an actor, as a journalist both in Nashville and in New York, and by selling an occasional story to The Century or The Atlantic. But now she was desperate; she badly wanted a regular job.

By the standards of 1896 she was an advanced woman; McClure must have been secretly scandalized when he first saw her light a cigarette. But by that time it was too late, for they had talked. Talked is perhaps too mild a word. "I have heard George Meredith talk," McClure told an associate later, "and Robert Louis Stevenson. One filled the air with flaming swords, the other was like the play of the aurora borealis. But I can't find any expression to describe that woman's talk. It is too varied."

McClure hired Miss Roseboro' at thirty-five dollars a week. Besides being a champion talker, she proved to be the best manuscript reader of her time.

January. McClure sent H. J. W. Dam to Würzburg to interview Roentgen and sent Cleveland Moffett to check the experiments with Professor Arthur Wright in the Sloane Laboratory at Yale. Meanwhile, pictures were got from Paris, London, and Berlin. The photographs and Dam's article were shipped across the Atlantic in mid-February. The whole, spread across twenty pages, appeared in the April issue—the speed of lightning, in 1896.

And now at last McClure could turn to the project that lay closest to his heart and nurse it with his personal care. This was a life of Jesus.

The cynical, as soon as they got wind of this scheme, put it about that McClure was only baiting his hook for a fatter circulation. When Napoleon has pushed you to one hundred thousand and Lincoln has hauled you to three hundred thousand, they snickered, who is left? You have tried Bismarck.* Who is left to float you up to a celestial five hundred thousand save Jesus? But the whispers were unfair. McClure had a fanatically pious woman for a mother and a fervently religious woman for a wife; upbringing, education, inclination, and natural affection had alike conspired to convince him that it was his moral duty, as editor of a nationally circulated magazine, to print the best life of Christ he could inspire. (And if, in the process, his circulation somehow found its way to five hundred thousand, should he complain?)

For more than a year he had tried to find and inspire the proper writer. Professor Henry Drummond had turned him down; so had the Scottish novelist, S. R. Crockett; Elizabeth Stuart Phelps had pleaded her inadequacy; Hall Caine had wanted too much money. But when he and Hattie visited Glasgow early in 1895, McClure had met Dr. John Watson and at once he knew he had found his man. Hattie had written her mother about that visit. "Scotland is the place for preaching," she wrote. "I never saw so many preachers and heard so much theological talk in my life, or so much fun and story-telling either. . . . The Rev. John Watson (Ian MacLaren) was there. . . . How many Scotch stories they told, and what stories!"

---

* And indeed McClure had tried Bismarck:

> Feb. 18, 1895   Schönhausen
>   a. d. Elbe
>
> My dearest Hattie
>   This is something great! Here I am the guest of Count Bismarck, stayed all night, & have had a most glorious time. He is a capital fellow & his wife is very fine & noble & refined & young & their little 15 month old baby is very sweet & Bismarck all over. Count Bismarck told me that his father, the Prince, had examined my magazine with great interest. The Napoleon pictures were revelations to him. I am to have *everything* in the way of pictures for my Life of Bismarck. . . .
>   Yesterday was my birthday & they toasted my health. Nineteen years ago you wrote in my album "Seest thou a man diligent in his ways" &c. Well we have been diligent.
>   Your loving husband
>   SSMcClure

McClure got everything in the way of pictures but could find no writer capable of supplying him a life of Bismarck that pleased him.

The Reverend Doctor John Watson preached from a pulpit in Glasgow; as Ian MacLaren he continued to preach, but in terms of treacly fiction written in a demotic Scottish to which the burrs clung so thickly as to require a glossary. Nevertheless, a collection of his tales, Beside the Bonnie Brier Bush, had found a vast audience on both sides of the Atlantic. To McClure, a Presbyterian clergyman who was also a best-selling author seemed almost too good to be true. He signed Dr. Watson and at once started worrying about illustrations. In the spring of 1896 he took off on a pilgrimage to Palestine to scout out the possibilities.*

Here goes the happy man who has founded a prosperous enterprise, off on a junket halfway round the world; with him are his wife and his four charming children. His wife is to stay at Beuzeval-Houlgate, a pleasant watering-place on the Channel in Calvados. The children are to go to a local school; soon they will all be able to speak French. Is it not a happy picture?

Well, no. The fact is that McClure is in poor health. He is suffering from insomnia and dyspepsia, those twin bugbears of the man who has worked too long, too hard, and under severe mental strain. As for Hattie, she has not felt well for years; most of the past winter she has been confined to her bed, so sick that even the children have not been allowed in her room. What is the matter? The doctors are not sure. They speak of kidney disease; they mention albuminuria; they suspect even Bright's disease. There is also rheumatism—or is it rheumatoid arthritis? (It is, but the doctors didn't know it in 1896.)

At all events, she is a wretched woman. With S.S. off to Palestine in the solicitous charge of Thomas Cook & Son, she sits alone in her room in the Hôtel Belle-Vue, writing him a letter. "It is very cold," she writes, "and the sea is boiling with a loud sound." Presently she lays the letter aside and takes up her diary:

---

* During McClure's protracted search for the proper biographer of Jesus, Cleveland Moffett, then a frequent contributor to McClure's, claimed he had heard McClure complain that he could find no one to write "a snappy life of Christ." This frail jest enjoyed a wider currency than it deserved. But it was symptomatic: it showed that McClure was now fair game for every wit in the market place. From now on he would acquire nicknames, of which the most popular was simply his initials, S. S. These initials inevitably came to stand, in private talk, for quite improper epithets.

Ridicule seems to be the common lot of successful editor-publishers, condemned as they are to associate with waggish writers. The late Harold Ross comes to mind, and Henry Luce. For their part, the editors help the process along. For example, Kipling once asked McClure if he had read David Harum. "No," McClure retorted. "He's dead."

Tuesday, April 28.

. . . This morning I am feeling still very badly. I do not feel very well able to look after the children, and do all the little purchases for them, and do all the arranging and asking and communicating for them all. As soon as they wish to communicate with anybody, I have to tell them how, and my mind keeps uselessly repeating French sentences when I try to rest. It is because I am weak, I am sure. When my brain is called to an effort, it receives so much of a shock or strain that it cannot shake it off and become quiet again; besides, the effort may be very quickly repeated. I rest momentarily in the Lord, and ask Him for an increase of strength and courage; or I ask at least that moment by moment He will supply me with all I need, and support my fainting spirit. He knows how many and how great are my needs; how I have not a bit of strength or ability to think. . . .

Sunday, May 3.

. . . All day yesterday and to-day I am ill, suffering in body and mind, full of dark, unhappy thoughts. I look for help to see things correctly, to be faithful in doing all as well as I am intended to do, and to overcome temptation. I am deeply distressed that I cannot take a happy [but here she laid her pen down for the day].

May 4, Monday.

. . . Why am I so wretched? I revolt utterly from all this lonely seclusion; and yet I am fit for nothing else. I often feel that unless a change to what is interesting and easy begins for me soon it will be too late for me to enjoy it at all. I am too ill and melancholy to be alone so much. To-day I have not enough physical strength and spirit to turn my thoughts into a new channel. What shall I think of? What shall I look forward to? I want repose in a beautiful home, with somebody to love me and live there with me. I don't want to travel some more, and then wait alone somewhere else.

I haven't even anything to read, beyond the one book I brought [The Life of Our Lord] and which is a great comfort to me. My head aches terribly, and my heart is sore with a longing to weep.

But if Hattie was miserable, at least McClure was able to report, first from Cairo and then from Jerusalem, that he was mending. "God was here as a Man," he wrote, "& I can't get away from that." And again: "This is a beautiful & fascinating country. It beats Harper's pictures." On May 16 he was in Shechem:

My darling Hattie

. . . This is the most delightful experience of my life. . . . Jacob's Well has been recently uncovered. . . . We can now see the actual curb stone. I sat on it. . . . This well is the only spot in all the world where we can feel sure that Christ actually was. You can look at the curb stone & feel that Christ sat there. . . .

He cut short his trip when he learned how wretched she was; he hurried back to Beuzeval to comfort her. But soon he was restless again, left for Paris, got her to join him there, was "blue & desolate" when she decided to rejoin the children, but argued that he needed still more relaxation, and so headed for Switzerland to climb some Alps. After all, was this not the first holiday he had had since his graduation from Knox? The first real holiday, indeed, in all his life? After hiking twenty miles a day, over glaciers and mountains, he assured her that it was all for the best:

Zermatt   July 21

My darling wife—
. . . My head has a new feeling of strength & I have the preliminaries of new invention. The philosophy is this: The brain cells that I think with are now occupied in furnishing nervous energy to my legs. This develops and strengthens them as well as taking them entirely away from their usual work. This strengthening makes my head feel stronger & also improves my thinking faculties. . . .
You must not forget that I am a longheaded, cautious, careful planner & I apply the same principles to this business. . . .
I need strength for we shall have a serious year in America.

Your loving husband
SSMcClure

Fortunately Hattie was once again more cheerful, for her father and her sister were visiting at Beuzeval. Mrs. Hurd's death the year before had worked a change in the professor; he now found it possible to enter his son-in-law's house with good grace.

So the summer of 1896 passed; and so, with minor variations, would pass the summers to come. For rheumatoid arthritis is not necessarily the best companion and helpmeet for a boundless, restless energy.

[III]

The magazine continued to prosper. In a year circulation had more than doubled and income from advertising had nearly tripled. In 1896 the gross revenue was nearly five hundred thousand dollars and the prospects were even rosier. A little expansion seemed to be indicated.

While McClure was in Palestine, his brother Robert, in charge of the London office, had got the serial rights to Kipling's Captains Courageous despite aggressive bidding by The Century; thereupon he had sold the British serial rights to Pearson's Magazine for £1,300, which meant that the cost to McClure's for the American serial rights was a trifling £300. This coup had naturally delighted S.S.; it served as well to remind him that he had sometimes lost a desirable novel to a competitor who was able to buy book rights as well as serial rights. High time, he concluded, to establish his own book-publishing house. Kipling, he knew, was furious with nearly all American book publishers for the way they had pirated his work. McClure was confident he could sign Kipling. And there were others.

But who to get to run the house? Who did he know who was experienced in publishing books? At once he thought of Frank Doubleday.

McClure and Doubleday had been friends for several years; they had visited back and forth; each man, for his own reasons, had always been pleasant with the other. Doubleday had for several years been the business manager of Scribner's Magazine, and he had also managed the subscription book department of Charles Scribner's Sons. At this moment, quite fortuitously, Doubleday had got into a row with the Charles Scribner then regnant and had quit the firm. He discreetly put it about that he proposed to start his own company. When word of his plan reached McClure, S.S. characteristically leaped into action.

Doubleday and his wife came to dinner at McClure's town house in February, 1897; that evening the details were arranged. Doubleday would be a vice-president of the S.S. McClure Company; he would be given thirty shares of stock (nominally worth three thousand dollars, but already worth far more); he would also form a book-publishing house, Doubleday & McClure, of which he would retain fifty-one per cent of the stock and for which he was to raise the capital. This house was to offer a list of books in the fall; if Doubleday did not produce, the arrangement was ended.

Doubleday took office at McClure's in March. The reactions to the event were various, but they were all intense. From Vermont, Kipling, whose works Doubleday had solicited on behalf of Scribner's, wrote a letter.

> Dear Doubleday—
> Yours of the 5th with Tribune scrap in comes. So it's S.S. McClure, is it? I thirst for further particulars; because I have a lively recollection of a winter day in Vermont when *McClure's Magazine* was just being born: and for eight (or eighteen) consecutive hours that cyclone in a frock-coat

whirled round our little shanty explaining, exhorting, . . . and prophe-
sying. He is a great man but he'd kill me in a week with mere surplus
of energy . . .

And at McClure's almost at once there was friction.

What had been a smoothly geared team of three men—McClure, Phillips,
and Albert Brady, close friends since their college days—was now beset by
suspicion and mistrust. When he chose, Doubleday could be an exceedingly
charming man, and in his first weeks at McClure's he was at pains to be
affable and circumspect; but the friendlier his behavior, the greater the suspicion. The resentment was keenest in the business department. "Watch
your step when Doubleday seems to be in a friendly mood," one man told another, "and think fast when he puts his arm around your shoulder and tells
you what a fine fellow you are." *

When Doubleday offered suggestions about advertising policy, Albert
Brady bristled. When Doubleday proposed an editorial feature, Phillips
coolly ignored it. As for McClure, in April he once again took off with his
family for Beuzeval, happily unaware of the storm clouds he had left piling
up behind him.

The cause of all the trouble was, as usual, money—or, more precisely, the
profitable S.S. McClure Company stock. Why should thirty shares have been
conditionally assigned to Doubleday, a newcomer, whilst Brady, the company's secretary, owned only a token one share? When Phillips sent McClure
a tactful complaint, McClure promptly cabled an order to transfer fifty of
his own shares to Brady. "As to Doubleday," McClure wrote Phillips, "in
case he does not earn his salary, it is to stop, you know, this fall. That and the
stock is the price we pay for 49% of the new company. But he must produce
results right along & you must see to it that he is not threshing over old
straw. If he is not our man, we can separate."

This served to mollify Brady, but he remained wary. The air was still
electric with mistrust.

* This is reported by Curtis Brady, in an unpublished reminiscence. Curtis Brady, a younger
brother of Albert, came to work at McClure's as an office boy in November, 1896; twelve years
later he was business manager.

It almost seemed that nepotism was an official policy of employment at McClure's. McClure
himself had hired one brother (Robert) to run his London office and another (Thomas) to
manage his syndicate; the third (John) was for years held in reserve to be general manager
of the proposed English McClure's, which was aborted. A cousin, Harry McClure, joined the
company in 1899. Albert Brady brought Oscar and Curtis to work with him. Phillips had no
brothers, but a cousin Ed worked for a time in the advertising department. (Curtis Brady
had to fire him.)

Doubleday next tendered Phillips and Brady a proposition: if they would persuade McClure to give him more shares in the S.S. McClure Company, he would give them some of his holdings in Doubleday & McClure. Doubleday can have had any of several motives for this offer. He may have been finding it difficult to raise the capital he needed, he may have been trying to drive a wedge between McClure and his associates, he may have wanted to exchange something of speculative value for something of proven value, he may just have been trying to make friends. Phillips and Brady wasted no time in guessing; they at once urged McClure to disgorge a few more shares, perceiving that in this way they would be able to vote their stock in the book company with McClure's, and so control it.

McClure couldn't see it. He just couldn't see it. He was not wearing his publisher's hat at the time, he was wearing his editor's hat; he ignored Phillips's insistent request and instead pelted the New York office with suggestions for editorial features: on Tiffany glass, on color photography, on the revivalist Moody, on Tesla, and on the horseless carriage. "This is the great subject of the future," McClure insisted. "All these subjects," he added, his pen sputtering on his paper, "want to be treated from the standpoint of *human need,* with a creative instinct & some intellectual fire." But he had even more urgent orders.

"*Mahan,*" McClure wrote Phillips in April, "his Nelson is the greatest book of recent years. He must be seen at once & talked to. He is the greatest naval biographer & student of this century & his field is going to become more & more popular. [This was a tolerable example of editorial prescience. The war with Spain, chiefly a naval war, was to start in less than a year.] He lives in N.Y. You & Jaccaci should see him *at once.*

"*Roosevelt.* Seems big from here. Write to him & try to get his naval stuff. "*Mahan & Roosevelt are just our size*"

The magazine was good, yes; it was making money, yes; but its editor felt something was missing. Where was the sense of the present, and the impact on the future? Why was McClure's not better reflecting the world in which it lived? There was another dimension right within his grasp; why had he not seized hold of it?

McClure sensed he was missing a great deal. Bryan's Cross-of-Gold speech, the flood of immigration, the complex question of bimetallism, the legality of a tax on personal income—all these were matters that had provoked the nation into an incredibly savage presidential campaign in 1896, yet scarcely a word about them had appeared in McClure's. Scandalous omission!

And there was more on the horizon: the troubling question of industrial consolidation, of the trusts; the minatory power of organized labor; and, as he fancied, the alarming increase in the rate of crime.*

At all events, if McClure were to capture a vision of the whole Republic, venal and splendid, craven and doughty, genteel and vulgar and fearful, he would have to enlist other minds to spread the vision across the pages of McClure's. Providentially, there were talented young men lined up as though on an assembly line, each bursting with impatience to hear his name called, each bursting with impressions of one or another aspect of the Republic, each superbly equipped to help McClure see America whole.

[IV]

The first to arrive was a plump, pink-cheeked young Kansas newspaper editor, full of fun and friendliness. This was William Allen White of The Emporia Gazette, twenty-eight years old, and by the time he came to the office of McClure's in January, 1897, his name was already known across the land. The summer before, in the midst of the McKinley-Bryan campaign, Will White had written an impulsive, angry, funny editorial which so aptly summed up Republican vexation over the finer frenzies of Bryan's Populist supporters that it had been eagerly reprinted in the big metropolitan newspapers. (Mark Hanna, McKinley's campaign manager, had broadcast it more widely than any other piece of Republican exhortation.)

McClure read the editorial in The New York Sun, and marked the name of the author. A few weeks later, when a Chicago publisher brought out a volume of Will White's short stories, McClure at once got permission to reprint two of them, ordered half a dozen more at five hundred dollars apiece, and invited White to New York.

New York made White's "country eyes bug out with excitement." He was

---

* McClure was concerned about the rate of crime, and of fire, and of disease, from the day he first read more than one newspaper. Newspapers, of course, print reports of local crimes and disasters; there is no surer way to guarantee circulation. It is sufficiently unnerving to read reports of only one city's tragedies; but McClure, who regularly read the newspapers of every large city across the country, was consequently horrified by what seemed to him to be a wave, mounting higher and ever higher, of lawlessness and holocaust and pestilence.

met by McClure, Phillips, Miss Tarbell, and Jaccaci; they were, he was to recall, "gracious beyond words to me . . . cordial to the point of ardent." During White's first half hour in the office, McClure "swamped me with assignments, piled ideas all over me for stories and articles." White swayed as in a high wind, but he kept his balance; he smiled, but turned down all seductive offers that might have kept him in New York.

White assured McClure, however, of his allegiance—more, of his warm friendship. McClure and Phillips he regarded as near neighbors. Weren't they from Galesburg? And hadn't the Hurds known his mother when she was living there years ago? Any chilly formalities melted under the sun of his Kansas affability. From that first day onward he was Will, and they were Sam and John and Ida M. (or, rather, Idarem) and Jac. They assured him that he might call on them whenever he needed help; when later he asked for a loan of five thousand dollars to build his house in Emporia, he got by return mail a draft for six thousand.

The fiction White wrote for McClure's was, regrettably, puerile stuff, both in conception and in subject matter. But before long McClure got White to write some sketches of politicians, and at once matters improved. White knew politics and politicians, and loved to write about them. Three sketches were of Democrats (Grover Cleveland, William Jennings Bryan, and Richard Croker, then the regnant sachem of Tammany Hall) and three were of Republicans (Theodore Roosevelt, Mark Hanna, and Tom Platt, the boss of New York State). With one exception, White portrayed them with a murderous geniality. The exception, of course, was Roosevelt, before whom White genuflected adoringly. As for the others, he puffed up a cloud of impartiality through which, nevertheless, his sturdy Republican bias could easily be descried. And yet the gem of the series was the one on Tom Platt ("a dwarf on stilts . . . a thing to be taken apart without finding a soul, yet shrewd and with almost human intelligence in his limited work"), as deft a job of character assassination as can be easily imagined.*

White's piece on Platt was more than the disembowelment of a boss. It was a blueprint of the ways in which a "hard, impulseless, cunning" man could, by co-operating with the lobbyists of the money power, burrow "silently yet with incalculable power, loosening the soil, sagging foundations,

---

* Platt agreed. Thunder rolled out of him; the earth quaked. He vowed to hurl a thunderbolt in the form of a suit for damages so punitive that never again would a magazine dare to besmirch a good name. McClure waited, hopeful, but the suit was never filed.

changing the aspect of the political landscape, preparing the ground for a harvest whose yield, even whose fruit, no man may dare to guess. . . ."

"If a corporation," White wrote, "or an interested citizen, or business concern has a bill pending before the legislature, it is evident that the person to talk to is the man who controls the party caucus. That man . . . is Platt. But why see Platt without a proper introduction? A good way to get an introduction is through the treasurer of your company, saying that during the last campaign your company contributed so many dollars to the Republican State Central Committee and that the bearer has a little matter before the legislature in which he would be grateful for Senator Platt's assistance. . . . The little matter is attended to, the necessity of an expensive lobby at Albany is avoided, and if the matter is not too palpably culpable, the wishes of the people in the matter have merely an academic interest. . . ."

In short, White's political pieces prefigured much of the muckraking material that was to give McClure's its lasting fame. And such forthright talk about a powerful politician was still exceedingly rare at the time it was published, especially for a general magazine.

Will White's barbs were often impudent, they were sometimes angry, but in those early days they were always aimed at targets a small-town, agrarian audience could hiss with gusto. Eight years after the event White would still characterize the Pullman strike of 1894 as "blatant anarchy" and laud Grover Cleveland for having "quelled the mob" by sending Federal troops into Illinois as strikebreakers. The second young man to heed McClure's summons was, although a year or so younger than White, already far too experienced to make such a provincial blunder. This was Ray Stannard Baker, a reporter for The Chicago Record.

Baker was fresh out of college when he went to work for The Record. He was naïve, earnest, and curious. "Everything I saw interested me," he said later, "and everything that interested me I wrote about—a state of bliss." His assignments gave him an education that no college curriculum could provide. He marched with Coxey's pathetic Commonweal Army from Massillon, Ohio, all the way to Washington. He tagged along after William Stead when that odd British reformer and journalist was pursuing his inquiry into vice in Chicago—a quest that would result in the astonishing book, If Christ Came to Chicago. He covered the Pullman strike and, indeed, narrowly missed being shot by the strikebreaking soldiers in a bloody clash

at Hammond, Indiana. Lesser reporters jeered at Coxey, were cynical about
the vice laid bare by Stead, and were either calloused or cowed by the
broken strike at Pullman; but Baker, a decent, sensitive man, only gained in
compassion. And he kept asking questions. When George M. Pullman said,
"The workers have nothing to do with the amount of wages they shall receive; that is solely the business of the company," Baker asked why. And
when he got no satisfactory answer, he still wondered. He was a good reporter.

His reputation was only local when, early in 1897, he queried McClure's
about a possible article. McClure liked the piece, sent him one hundred and
fifty dollars, "though this is more than we have paid before for similar contributions," and a week later urged that he come to New York to "plan
out a series of articles." Blessed moment for a young writer! Baker confessed to "a glow of exultation."

In New York, Baker found that McClure had gone to Europe, but Phillips was there, and Jaccaci, and Miss Tarbell. "Even with S.S. McClure
absent," Baker recalled, "I was in the most stimulating, yes intoxicating,
editorial atmosphere then existent in America—or anywhere else." A glimpse
of Paradise; after which it was, no doubt, depressing to go back to Chicago.
In the next ten months Baker learned, from a succession of letters from the
patient Phillips, that good writing means painful rewriting. Baker could
easily sell to magazines of established reputation, but the editors of McClure's,
he found, were cantankerous taskmasters. Would he, like so many newspapermen, languish indefinitely on a plateau of mediocrity? And then, in
McClure's for January, 1898, his eye was caught by an editorial note:

> Awaiting the special writer who can prove his right to it, we have,
> indeed, a special standing prize. That is a position on the staff of the
> magazine for any one who can do such work as we are now having done
> by other members of the editorial staff, such as Miss Tarbell and
> H.J.W. Dam.

Baker promptly nominated himself for this prize. Phillips was hesitant,
McClure more sanguine, Baker in a torment of suspense. At length in
February Baker was summoned to New York; he left with precipitate alac-
rity.

In the next few years Baker proved that he had deserved the prize. It
was not easy, especially for a credulous man; for McClure kept him unsettled by promising him tempting promotions—as editor of the syndicate,
as managing editor of the magazine, as editor-in-chief of projected maga-

zines—and each time Baker wished, and therefore believed. (The only one that came through was the one he had not particularly hankered for. He was briefly the editor of the syndicate, and found the task exactly what McClure had said it was—"the hardest editorial desk in New York.") But all the while Baker was turning out articles on a remarkably wide range of subjects—on journalism, astronomy, and chemistry, on the submarine and the automobile, on agriculture, economics, and optics, on paleontology and wireless telegraphy—interspersing this heterogeneity with sketches of Theodore Roosevelt, Admiral Sampson, General Leonard Wood, and J. P. Morgan. Each piece was, moreover, workmanlike. Small wonder that Baker won a reputation as the best journalist in the country.

When Baker joined McClure's in February, 1898, there was a shy, slender, self-conscious man, also in his twenties, who wandered uncertainly about the offices, one day editing syndicate material, the next reading proofs of magazine articles. This man worked only in the mornings, for a wage of twelve dollars and fifty cents a week; in the afternoons he disappeared to his rooms across town, in Chelsea, where it was understood he was writing a novel. He was Frank Norris, from California by way of Harvard and Paris, and he was another who had heeded McClure's call.

The hiring of Norris was typical. Ever the compulsive reader, McClure had scanned the pages of an obscure California weekly, The Wave, and had admired some stories by Norris. Even more he admired Moran of the Lady Letty, Norris's first novel, which was serialized in The Wave. That same February McClure was off to Europe again, but before he left he wrote Norris a warm letter, dangling before him all sorts of rewards if he would accept McClure as his literary godfather. Phillips followed up McClure's letter with a telegram that found Norris in St. Louis; Norris at once came on to New York.

The notion was that Norris would write stories to be published in McClure's and novels to be published by Doubleday & McClure, but almost at once Norris itched to break away. For on February 15 the American battleship Maine, lying in the harbor at Havana, was ripped by an explosion that killed two hundred and sixty-six officers and men. History, Norris was certain, was beckoning to him. Every day for weeks thereafter the copies of Mr. Hearst's Journal and of Mr. Pulitzer's World that were delivered to the editorial offices of McClure's reeked of brimstone; and, as if this were not enough, the very syndicate copy that Norris was charged with editing resounded with cries of "Cuba libre!" To Norris, who believed that the novelist should "deal with elemental forces, motives that stir whole nations," this imperialist clamor was irresistible. And so, when at length President McKinley sent his war message to the Congress, Norris wangled a job as correspondent for the syndicate and hurried south to Tampa.

Norris failed to distinguish himself. He failed even to see the war with any clarity. His report of the surrender of Santiago was jingo enough even for Hearst: "It was war and it was magnificent. . . . Santiago was ours . . . ours, by the . . . Anglo-Saxon blood of us. . . . We rode . . . triumphant, arrogant, conquerors." Only later, and in a private letter, would Norris summon up "a hideous blur of mud and blood" that had "precious little glory" but only "horrors."

He was sick; he went home to San Francisco. When he came back to work in New York in October it was as a reader for the book department. Here his mornings were more serene. But before long he got an idea for a novel—more, for a trilogy—"an idea that's as big as all outdoors." He took it, carefully cupped in his hands, to McClure and Phillips. They caught fire; they agreed he should go west again to gather his material. McClure promised him that his salary, now fifty dollars a week, would be paid on the nail. And so Norris left New York again, to write The Octopus.

The next young writer to help McClure make a transcript of America was preceded by an ecstatic annunciation. The angel of the occasion was Viola Roseboro', who came striding into the office one morning with tears in her eyes, calling out, "Here is a serial sent by God Almighty for McClure's Magazine!" She had in her hand the manuscript of Booth Tarkington's first novel, The Gentleman from Indiana, and from that moment on no discordant note was struck while a young author marched to glory. Especially from Tarkington's viewpoint, every circumstance fell deliciously into place, just as he might have ordered it in his most ravishing daydream.

First, a confirmation, to forestall any doubters. McClure gave the manuscript to Hamlin Garland, to see if his opinion would sustain Miss Roseboro' 's. Garland read it and nodded gravely. "Mr. McClure has given me your manuscript," Garland wrote to Tarkington. "You are a novelist."

Second, a prompt assurance of hard cash. After Garland's letter, the next mail brought Tarkington a business note from McClure: "We accept your manuscript to be published in book form, and we are considering it for serial publication in the magazine, though for this purpose you would have to cut it almost in half. If the idea interests you, perhaps you had better come to New York as soon as you can."

Third, a triumphal reception. To make his subsequent joy more delirious, Tarkington permitted himself some quavers of apprehension, as he sat in the waiting room at McClure's, on a crisp morning in January, 1899. Was it true? Did he dare pinch himself? An office boy appeared, took his card, and disappeared. Despite the weather, Tarkington broke out in a gentle sweat. But there was to be no stain on this wondrous morning. The office boy reappeared and ushered the young writer into Jaccaci's office where, as Tarkington later wrote his family, he was greeted with "a joyous and polite howl." "We haf waited for you!" cried Jaccaci. "So it iss you!" Jaccaci bustled him into McClure's office. McClure bounced out of his chair. "You," said McClure enthusiastically, wringing Tarkington's hand, "you are to be the greatest of the new generation, and we will help you to be!" Tarkington blinked. McClure prattled on gaily, telling him that an Anthony Hope yarn had been postponed to make room for The Gentleman from Indiana. Was it possible? Anthony Hope, whose Rupert of Hentzau had run in McClure's, illustrated by Charles Dana Gibson? Tarkington's cup was overflowing. But there was still more. People pressed into the room—Doubleday, Garland, Miss Tarbell. To her, as he introduced Tarkington, McClure announced: "This is to be the most famous young man in America." When Tarkington was wafted out to lunch at the Holland House with McClure, Jaccaci, and Miss Tarbell, who could blame him, if his feet never quite touched the ground?

At the time, McClure was living in Lawrence, on Long Island. Here Tarkington was invited to stay while he cut his novel into serial-sized helpings. All was fitted for his comfort: a large, pleasant room with a fire blazing merrily, a midnight snack brought him on a tray, a publisher who plied him with succulent temptations. Come to Europe with me this summer! Take a job with me—at seven thousand a year! It was such a pleasure to say no; Tarkington smiled and went off to dinner at the Doubledays, where he would meet and actually be able to talk with Rudyard Kipling. What could touch the joys of the literary life?

Even when his book was published, Tarkington could find nothing to complain about:

Indianapolis, November 2 '99

Dear Mr. McClure:

I don't know about the public's recognizing a good thing, but if "The Gentleman" doesn't sell 1,000,000,000 copies it will not be because it hasn't been advertized in Indianapolis! The "New York Store" ads are relatively small, playing opposite to Uneeda Biscuit, and about the same size, also, the Bowen-Merrill newspaper "notices" could rarely be read across a three-acre lot; they *could* be read across a *two*-acre one. Last night the *News* had a D[oubleday] & Mc[Clure] ad which, if it weren't for the curvature of the earth I would ask you to examine for yourself— an opera-glass from your window would make it plain.

Besides this, our house is a little over a mile from the Bowen-Merrill establishment; well, they have got a sign up, and you will probably think I am not adhering to the plain truth, but the end of it sticks in our kitchen-window. . . .

The point of it is that it isn't fair to the author to give him *no* chance to say that his book would have sold better if it had been better advertized. . . . However, I do not complain—odd as it may seem! . . .

With many thanks for many things

Yours Faithfully
N. B. Tarkington

This continuing love-feast promised much. But unfortunately for Mc-Clure's transcript of American civilization, after The Gentleman from Indiana, which had dealt with politics and the Ku Klux Klan, Tarkington sheered away violently and came up with Monsieur Beaucaire. Fair enough, and McClure was happy to serialize it; but when Tarkington's next effort was Cherry, a piece of fluff, McClure sensibly advised him not to publish it, and Tarkington took it to Harper's.

Who else could help an editor conjure up an interesting and reasonably accurate image of America?

Stephen Crane? After sending the magazine a story based on his experience as a filibuster,* Crane had first gone off to Greece, whence he (or his wife Cora) mailed dispatches to the syndicate about the war between Greece and Turkey, and had next come back to Cuba to report the Spanish-American War—for McClure's, among others. (Frank Norris caught one glimpse of Crane, on a patrol-boat off Cuba, writing something, his desk a suitcase flat on his knees, while cradled between his feet was a bottle from which he occasionally took a nip. Norris was too shy, or too proud, to intro-

---

* It was called "Flanagan" and was published in October, 1897, but has never, so far as I know, been reprinted by any of Crane's anthologists. This is a pity, for the story is alive and gleaming with fresh, tart metaphors. It would seem that "Flanagan" has been overshadowed by "The Open Boat," which is generally conceded to be Crane's finest short story. Both stories were inspired by Crane's filibustering adventure; "Flanagan" tells of what happened before the four men huddled in "The Open Boat."

duce himself.) But then, after writing the first of his Whilomville stories for McClure's, Crane had left for England, where he was to die before his thirtieth birthday.

Hamlin Garland? After quarreling with McClure over his life of Grant (McClure had wanted revisions but Garland, lost in a biographical experiment, had resisted them), Garland had accepted a commission to report the gold strike in the Yukon for both magazine and syndicate. But he and McClure were disenchanted with each other; his contributions grew fewer.

Still, however, the talented young men pressed forward, clamoring for recognition; and some of them cast a long shadow before them into the future.

There was Lincoln Steffens, a cocky little New York journalist. Steffens had been a police reporter for The Commercial Advertiser when Theodore Roosevelt was one of the Board of Police Commissioners. The two had become friendly. In 1898, when Roosevelt was elected governor of New York, Steffens was still on an intimate footing with him, so it was natural for John Phillips to suggest that Steffens write a life of Roosevelt for Doubleday & McClure. The book fell through, but a piece Steffens wrote on Roosevelt for the magazine delighted McClure. "A jim-dandy," he crowed; "a rattling good article. I could read a whole magazine of this kind of material." And before long Steffens would swing closer into the orbit of McClure's.

There was a big-boned, slow-moving youngster from Terre Haute by way of Chicago, who as early as 1897 was hacking out copy for the syndicate. He wrote pieces with such titles as "Palatial Private Street Cars" and "The Dominant Coon Song," and at that time he signed his stuff Theodore Dreisser. But before long he was to drop one ess from his name and start selling short stories to the magazine.

There was W. S. Porter, of 211 East Sixth Street, Austin, Texas, who in November, 1897, hopefully submitted a batch of stories, one of which, "The Miracle of Lava Canyon," was bought by the syndicate. It was the first story by W. S. Porter ever to be sold. "It has," some barely literate thickwit on the staff of the syndicate wrote to Porter, "the combination of humane interest with dramatic incident which in our opinion is the best kind of a story. If you have more like this, we should be glad to read them. . . . The other stories we return herewith. They are not quite available." Despite the invitation, no other stories were ever submitted by W. S. Porter, which was not strange, for he had been jugged in the Federal penitentiary at Columbus, Ohio, for embezzling funds. A year or so later, however, a man called

O. Henry sold *his* first story, "Whistling Dick's Christmas Stocking," to the magazine; it was the first of many by the same author to be printed in McClure's. And by the time inquisitive persons had found out that these two writers were the same man, who cared about the prison term? O. Henry's tales were a sufficient vindication.*

There was Jack London. In 1899, London was only twenty-three, but he was already the battered veteran of a childhood spent earning pennies as a pin boy in bowling alleys and as a janitor in saloons along the California waterfront, and of a young manhood spent as an oyster pirate, a deckhand on a sealing expedition, a coal heaver, and a tramp. The news of the gold strike in the Klondike took him north in 1897, and when he got back to San Francisco he had all the material he needed for rough, raw, red-blooded stories. McClure saw one of them in The Black Cat, a magazine of fiction that specialized in attracting unpublished writers by offering prizes. At once McClure wrote London a letter: "We are greatly interested in you and want you to feel that you have the warmest kind of friends right here in New York. I wish you would look upon us as your literary sponsors hereafter. If you send us everything you write we will use what we can, and what we cannot we will endeavor to dispose of to the best possible advantage. . . ." And later, when London wanted to write a novel but complained that he had no money to venture it, McClure at once wrote: "We will back your novel on your own terms. We will send you a check each month for five months for $100, and if you find that you need $125, why, we will do that. I am confident that you can make a strong novel. At any time when you feel in need of any sort of help, please let us know." With characteristic en-

---

* An immense pother has been raised as to who first discovered O. Henry, quite as though it made any difference. A claim has been staked by the poet Witter Bynner, who worked for five or six years in the editorial department of McClure's, but O. Henry's first stories were published in McClure's while Bynner was still in college. Other literary historians have credited McClure with the discovery, but this is patent nonsense. In fact, McClure did not care much for "Whistling Dick's Christmas Stocking." Late in 1902, when he was in Europe, Viola Roseboro' wrote him that "we have just taken 'A Phonograph and Graft.' It is riotously funny, we all think. . . ." In all likelihood, Miss Roseboro' was the reader who first perceived O. Henry's talent; it was her job to do so, and if she had not she should have been fired. As to W. S. Porter, if the person who discovered him also wrote the letter accepting his story, he (or she) merits scant congratulation.

The syndicate's announcement of "The Miracle of Lava Canyon," incidentally, would seem to have been written by the same nitwit who wrote the letter of acceptance. This was the announcement: "The principal character is a wester sheriff who was believed to be the bravest man in Arazona but was really attacked by the cold chills every time he was called upon to make an arrest. The story tells how he finally became as brave as he was reputed to be, and the share that a certain young woman had in bringing about this change. A well-told and thoroughly American story of western life."

thusiasm, McClure was to offer a job as editor even to London, a young man, inexperienced, angry, alcoholic, and radical. Fortunately for all hands, London declined. But he was moved. "I think," he wrote a friend, "they are the best publishers, or magazine editors, in their personal dealings, that I have run across."

[v]

William Allen White, Ray Stannard Baker, Frank Norris, and Booth Tarkington; Stephen Crane and Hamlin Garland; Lincoln Steffens, Theodore Dreiser, O. Henry, and Jack London—these were among the minds McClure had enlisted in the spring of 1899, and it seems, in retrospect, a fair collection of talent. There were of course others, especially from abroad: since 1897 the syndicate had been prospering, thanks to short stories by H. G. Wells and W. W. Jacobs, and to political correspondence by Sydney Brooks; Bram Stoker's Dracula had appeared in 1898; McClure's alert brother Robert had by the end of that year bought the American rights to Joseph Conrad's The Rescue,* Heart of Darkness, and Lord Jim; and enough Scottish and Irish writers to overstock a feis (S. R. Crockett, Seumas MacManus, James Barrie, Shan Bullock, and Herminie Templeton, to name a few) were publishing through McClure.

The magazine, due to a special war issue in June, 1898, had passed four hundred thousand in circulation, and in every issue carried far more advertising than did any rival.

Doubleday & McClure, after less than two years, was showing handsome profits. Most of the books on the firm's list had been quarried out of the pages of McClure's Magazine; Kipling and Mary E. Wilkins were their best-selling authors; but Doubleday had planted, as well, some sturdy perennials, like Mrs. Rorer's excellent cook book, and a pair of handsomely illustrated books about birds by Neltje Blanchan (who was, in private life, Mrs. Doubleday).

Even the syndicate was grossing a tidy fifty thousand dollars a year.

All this profitable activity was bound to attract attention, but not even McClure, in his most ebullient moment, could have imagined how Olympian

---

* Robert McClure paid £ 250 for the American rights to The Rescue, but there was a hitch. Conrad kept postponing delivery of the manuscript. In fact, he did not finish it until 1920, by which time the syndicate had passed through the hands of three different owners.

was the gaze that was bent upon him and his activity. Nevertheless, the fact was that McClure had aroused the interest of J. Pierpont Morgan himself.

As it happened, Morgan had for some time been investing money in the publishing business, and for the most praiseworthy of reasons. To a banker of Morgan's resources the sum was trifling, but to a publisher it was immense. By February, 1899, it amounted to $2,500,000, and took the form of bonds issued by Harper & Brothers, which reposed in Morgan's bank at the corner of Wall and Broad Streets. The transaction was less a capital investment than a semi-charitable loan.

In 1899 Harper & Brothers was the largest and one of the oldest publishing houses in the country. Besides conducting a substantial book business, the firm published four magazines: Harper's Monthly, Harper's Weekly, Harper's Bazar, and Harper's Round Table. To the casual eye there was no more prosperous publishing house in the country; certainly none was more respected or influential. Actually, however, it was a rickety house, sagging crazily on its foundations, eaten by dry rot. Various Harpers held all but two thousand of the twenty thousand shares of capital stock, worth a nominal $2,000,000; whenever a male Harper attained his majority he was added to the payroll; one such drew a large salary as the company's postmaster, an office of grave and exigent responsibility, requiring that he sort and distribute the incoming mail. Bankruptcy loomed.

If it seem out of character for Morgan to have shoveled good money into a company already exuding a cadaverous odor, there was yet a reason. For Harper & Brothers was at the time the country's biggest publisher of textbooks, and as such was a vital cog in the nation's educational machinery. As Morgan saw it, Harper & Brothers could not be allowed to die, no matter how profound its death-wish.

But as the months passed and the coupons on his bonds remained unclipped, Morgan wearied. A business, even if it is an estimable traffic in textbooks, is still a business, and should be conducted in a businesslike fashion. Morgan summoned certain advisers and deputed them to canvass the publishing field, to determine who was best able to convert his bonds back into money. Their conclusion—and Morgan agreed—was that the best man was McClure.

Morgan's offer of Harper & Brothers, for a proper price, was tendered to McClure in February by William Laffan, publisher of The Sun. McClure listened with pardonable satisfaction. So might a puissant and impatient prince have heard that the venerable king lay ill unto death. (*The New to the Old*: The future is mine!)

After Laffan had left, McClure paced rapidly back and forth in his office in high excitement. He had, God knows, plenty else on his mind to keep him busy. For months he had been planning an encyclopedia that would be to the United States what the Brittanica was to England; it was a ten-year project, and it waited only on the selection of a proper editor. For weeks he had been planning to establish a lecture bureau; the manager was to be William Walker, his wife's cousin. There was the matter of getting Admiral Dewey to hold still while his memoirs were written for him; there was the Marconi scheme; * there was Kipling, lying desperately sick in a New York hotel; there was that new man out in San Francisco, Edwin Markham, who had just written an astonishing poem, "The Man With the Hoe." . . . Wasn't all this enough? Why should he take on, as well, the whole House of Harper?

It may be doubted that these questions even occurred to him. If they did, they were surely flung aside so that he might savor the sweet prestige that would be his, the unexampled triumph. He saw no obstacle, but only gleaming opportunity, with himself the head of the most powerful publishing house in the country; no, in the world. He summoned his associates.

Phillips was impressed and almost as excited as McClure. Brady was impressed but cautious. Where was Doubleday? The jubilant McClure found him immured in a telephone booth that had been recently installed in the office so that long-distance calls might be more easily put through. McClure hammered imperatively on the glass door. Doubleday, who had already dropped ninety cents in the slot so that he might talk to Philadelphia, shushed

---

* McClure proposed, in his report of Marconi's wireless telegraph, to score still another of his impressive beats. In March, 1899, at the request of the French government, Marconi was to attempt the unprecedented feat of sending a wireless message across the English Channel from Dover to Boulogne. To the satisfaction of the French, Marconi succeeded, on the evening of Monday, March 27. Two days later Marconi made his equipment available to McClure's. Cleveland Moffett was at Boulogne; Robert McClure at Dover. Moffett handed the wireless operator a message in simple cipher:

McClure, Dover: Gniteerg morf Ecnarf ot Dnalgne hguorht eht rehte. Moffett.

The Dover operator had no difficulty in receiving this backward message, after which:
Moffett, Boulogne: Your message received. It reads all right. Vive Marconi. McClure.

Marconi, Dover: Hearty congratulations on success of first experiment in sending aerial messages across the English Channel. Also best thanks on behalf of editors McClure's Magazine for assistance in preparation of article. Moffett.

Moffett, Boulogne: The accurate transmission of your message is absolutely convincing. Good-by. McClure.

Moffett's article appeared in the June issue. It was a clean scoop.

him and waved him away. McClure was not to be shushed: he waved his arms, he hammered again, he shouted. Doubleday, cursing the loss of his ninety cents, capitulated. Out he came. He was not in a good humor, and nothing McClure had to tell him put him in a better humor. Why should Doubleday rejoice? It was, after all, not the Doubleday & McClure Company which had been offered this succulent plum; it was the S.S. McClure Company, in which Doubleday was a very minor stockholder. If McClure could successfully engorge Harper & Brothers, what need would he have any more, for the Doubleday & McClure Company? And if there were no need for Doubleday & McClure, what would become of Doubleday?

But it was agreed that the partners should at once enter into negotiations.

Next morning, when an exuberant McClure and a thoughtful Doubleday presented themselves at the sedate iron-fronted building in Franklin Square and made known the reason for their visit, they got a reception at first bewildered, then downright frosty. But there was nothing the Harpers could do. The negotiations began.

A battery of accountants moved in. Attorneys gathered like vultures around carrion, opened their briefcases, and commenced to discourse in their stately jargon. The liabilities of Harper & Brothers made for glum reading. There were:

Bonds held by J. P. Morgan	$2,500,000.	
Bonds held by various others	205,000.	$2,705,000.
Bonds held in treasury of Harper & Bros.		295,000.
Total of all bonds		$3,000,000.
General debt	$2,029,740.	
Mortgage	6,000.	
Current liabilities	64,189.	
Preferred liabilities	165,342.	2,265,271.
Total of all liabilities		$5,265,271.

The negotiators agreed that the $2,265,271 would be funded. So, while the package was wrapped up in dainty paper and tied with a nice red ribbon, inside there was a prior debt of $5,265,271 in nasty red ink—cause for concern.

McClure and his associates undertook to buy sixty-seven and one-half per cent of the capital stock of Harper & Brothers at fifty-two dollars a share.

This put a price-tag of $692,000 on the old house; it was to be paid in ten equal annual installments, with four per cent interest on the unpaid balance. Thus in the first year the purchasers engaged to fork over some $95,000 even before they began to reduce the debt.

The purchase agreement noted that the S. S. McClure Company had, as of March 17, 1899, a total indebtedness of $261,082.59, and further that the company had earned more than $60,000 net in 1897, more than $80,000 net in 1898, and more than $40,000 net in less than three months of 1899; its property and good will were estimated as being worth $1,000,000. A handsome record for a company that had started from scratch less than six years before. It was good enough for the Harpers; it was good enough for Francis Lynde Stetson, Morgan's attorney; and it was good enough for J. P. Morgan himself. But it was not good enough for Albert Brady. That paragon of prudence insisted on the insertion of a brief clause in the article setting forth the terms of payment. At his stipulation, payment was to be "either in cash or by the return and surrender of the stock so purchased at the unrestricted option of the Purchasers." To win the clause cost him something; he was obliged to agree that the rate of interest on unpaid balances during the last five years would be five per cent. But he smiled in his beard: he was not disposed to think the five per cent would ever pose a problem.

Nor, for other reasons, was McClure. "I can't feel anxious to save my neck," he told his wife. His chief concern was the four magazines that he would soon control: what changes would have to be made? what new blood infused?

He contemplated no changes in the editorial policy of Harper's Monthly. Already rumors were inevitably circulating that the veteran editor, Henry Mills Alden, was slated for dismissal; but this was not so; McClure had great respect for Alden. McClure planned to cut the price of the magazine to twenty-five cents (and he did, with the September issue) but that was all—at least for the moment.

The able editor of Harper's Bazar was Margaret Sangster; her job was safe.

The children's magazine, however, Harper's Round Table, was limping along very feebly, affording St. Nicholas meager competition. It wanted a new name, a new approach, certainly a new editor. McClure proposed to assign Ray Stannard Baker to the post. ("S.S. McClure is a publishing genius if there ever was one," Baker wrote his father, with something less than detachment.)

McClure's only headache was Harper's Weekly. Far and away the best of the general, illustrated weekly journals, with a reputation for courage and pugnacity earned during the battle against the Tweed Ring, Harper's Weekly had latterly been edited by Carl Schurz. But Schurz could not stomach the jingo imperialism of the Spanish-American War and its aftermath in the Philippines; he had resigned late in 1898. His successor, John Kendrick Bangs, was a humorist who had done well as an editor of Life but who was out of place editing Harper's Weekly. McClure decided to draft John Finley.

At thirty-five, Finley was already a man of extraordinary parts. He was tall and vigorous, liking nothing better than to go off on a thirty-mile day's walk; he was merry and witty, with a knack for occasional light verse; he was a classical scholar who could talk Latin extempore; as an economist he had collaborated with Richard T. Ely on a book on taxation; he had pioneered in social service. In 1892, when he was twenty-eight, this remarkable young man had become president of Knox and had been celebrated as the youngest college president in the country. From that time his friendship with McClure had grown warmer.* But would he leave the presidency of Knox? To edit Harper's Weekly he most certainly would. He agreed to come east at the end of the academic year.

At which point McClure could take a few moments out to plan his annual European holiday. This year it was to be a triumphal voyage, as befitted a prince on his coronation day. He would be attended by a swarm of relatives and servants: the four children, two of his wife's maiden cousins, and his wife's sister and father; a cook, a maid, a French governess, and a man to care for their bicycles. There were, as well, twenty-one trunks, a dozen bicycles of various types, and uncounted pieces of hand baggage, telescopes,

---

* In 1896 Finley had dashed off a hasty doggerel:

To McClure

With all thy Irish wit, lure on,
With all thy Scottish grit, lure on
From every part of earth the best,
From ancient East, from youngish West,
From Bergen down to Buda-Pesth;
From Alp and Rhine and Adriatic,
From hill and valley Asiatic,
From islands where the birds aquatic
Equip with pens such bards as he
Who sleeps beneath Samoan tree,
O'erlooking that great silent sea.
Lure on, till *all* the best shall be secured,
Till China even shall not be immured;
Till all this whirling sphere shall be
McClured.

and steamer rugs—"enough," McClure said happily, "to almost fill a baggage car in France."

There was one sour note. A few days before they were to sail, his wife was ordered to Johns Hopkins for a hysterectomy. McClure was wretched, but Hattie bid him leave on June 3 without her. He wrote her five times that day, ending with:

Lawrence   Friday evening June 2

My darling wife—

I am almost too nervous to write. I hate awfully to sail without you. At the same time I am imperatively in need of rest. This Harper matter is almost closed. Tomorrow at 9.30 I sign the final documents that conclude the operation. Today I signed notes aggregating $692,000 & tomorrow I sign the deed of trust & get 13,500 shares of their stock, leaving them 6,500 shares. I am writing in your room & it is full of mosquitoes! June is the limit here. . . .

The Harper matter will cause me little trouble. I expect an easy life hereafter, & I shall have much time with you. Ah, my darling, darling wife! How many, many years you have been a sweet joy to me! Your wonderful courage & endurance can now be turned to affirmative ends. I really think you have some special work to do in the world to bring it back to God. . . .

Your loving husband
SSMcClure

And next morning, distractedly:

June 3, 1899

My dear Hattie:

I have just met Mamie and your father and [your cousins]. They seem to be in very good condition.

The baggage is all on the ship; the children I expect every minute. I have to go down town to sign stock certificates, so I shall be busy up to the last moment. But I have hired a carriage and will use it for different purposes this morning. The family will have a little lunch at eleven o'clock at the Holland House, and from there will go on the ship. I shall try to go along with them, but if I cannot I will go somewhere.

I will be jotting down little things to you as I have time.

Later, June 3

My darling wife

Somehow I am happy & content. I feel that you are to be renewed & made perfectly happy & well. I *cant* feel anxiety. . . . You are doing wonderfully. I am closing all my arrangements for Europe & making everything go right. I am thinking of you continually, you sweet dear lady. God bless you, sweetheart!

Your loving husband
SSMcClure

He signed all the papers; he sailed. That day the New York newspapers confirmed the rumors: S. S. McClure had taken control of Harper & Brothers. He was the head of the strongest publishing house in the country, comprising a syndicate service, five magazines, a lecture bureau, and two book companies.

And there, if life were any respecter of literary conventions, we should leave him by ending a chapter on a proper note of climax. But life resists such neat coincidences; and as for climaxes, McClure habitually flung them down and danced on them. So it must be reported that, as soon as his steamer reached Plymouth, McClure put his party in charge of his sister-in-law, disembarked, and went straight to Liverpool where he caught another steamer back to New York. The cable announcing his imminent arrival alarmed his associates in New York: now what had happened? Two things dictated his impetuosity: he wanted to be with Hattie when she sailed for France, and he had been torturing himself with second thoughts about his business affairs.

Phillips, as McClure knew, was not well. He was troubled with what McClure called "a rapid heart," but nevertheless he had undertaken to supervise the Harper company singlehanded. Miss Tarbell had come up from Washington to edit McClure's Magazine in the absence of Phillips and McClure. But Finley would not get to New York until July; and, besides, what of the cherished encyclopedia? How, McClure asked himself, had he dared sail for Europe with his affairs in such a muddle? Another strong executive officer was needed at once, and McClure knew just the man: Walter Hines Page, the able editor of The Atlantic.

There was not much time, for McClure was anxious to get to Beuzeval for a long rest. Besides, New York was in the grip of a heat wave; McClure's secretary, Iola Van Ness, reported that the mercury stood at 106° on the corner of Fifth Avenue and Twenty-third Street. In consequence, McClure's wooing of Page was urgent and ardent. A telegram:

I HAVE GREATLY ENLARGED MY BORDERS. I WANT VERY MUCH TO SEE YOU.

Another telegram:

SHOULD SEE YOU IMMEDIATELY. HAVE BIGGEST THING ON EARTH—SEVERAL, IN
FACT.

A letter:

> I have got the earth with several things thrown in, and am eager to
> see if you don't want one or two kingdoms for yourself. Anyhow, we
> could have an interesting conversation. I have got four or five major-
> generalships to give out and I regard you as the one indispensable man in
> the world for our enterprises at the present time.

This got results. Page wired that he would resign his post as editor of The
Atlantic and come to New York in July. McClure was ecstatic.

> My dear boy:
> Your splendid telegram caused great jubilation in this hot part of the
> earth. We have now the strongest combine of men in the editorial and
> publishing fields in the world. I hope that you will go in with John
> [Phillips] and me into great magazine work for the next few months.
> But the encyclopedia is a worthy work for you. However, as I said, we
> are a band of independent brothers and you can pick out your own
> planets to rule. Oh my dear boy, *we* are the people with the years in front
> of us!
>
> Very sincerely yours,
> S. S. McClure

He sailed for Europe with Hattie on July 8. It never occurred to him to
crow about it, but the debate between the Old and the New was now finally
ended. Of the Old magazines—The Century, The Atlantic, Harper's, and
Scribner's—McClure controlled one and had brought into his camp the
business manager of a second and the editor of a third. "I am feeling first-
rate again," he told Hattie. "I could go off and stay for ten years."

[VI]

All at once, in 1899, the country was rich. It was like a warm sun after a
raw and miserable night. The cheerful signs were at every hand, and McClure
set Ray Stannard Baker to gathering them for an article on "The New
Prosperity": wages up from coast to coast; the number of savings accounts
up, and the number of dollars in the average savings account also up; production of steel and coal and copper and lumber and gold—all away up; annual

exports worth more than two billion dollars for the first time, surpassing even British exports, likewise for the first time; a balance of trade so favorable that in the three years 1897–1899 more than a billion dollars borrowed from European investors was repaid; the price of wheat up from forty-nine cents a bushel in 1894 to eighty-one cents a bushel in 1897, after which there followed in 1897 an enormous crop and in 1898 yet another, the biggest ever to have been harvested.

"And every barn in Kansas and Nebraska has a new coat of paint." After all the bitter hard times and the bitter Populist discontent, here, Baker wrote, was "a picture of improvement and smiling comfort such as no array of figures, however convincing, could produce. The West painted again: how much that means!"

The new prosperity did not, to be sure, bring wealth to all alike. Baker was a watchful reporter and he noted that, during the first seven months of 1899, hundreds of trusts with a gross capital value of more than four billion dollars were incorporated under the benign laws of New Jersey, the cradle of trusts. Nevertheless, the country was on the crest of a surge of prosperity, and, Baker concluded, "all the present indications are for its substantial continuance."

Moreover, the country had emerged from isolation into contention for world power. Whether or not all the people wished it to be so, the swift and successful Spanish-American War had forced the fact. Cuba was a problem, Puerto Rico a responsibility, the Philippines a ferocious headache. The more clearly American citizens came to appreciate the legacy of their victory over Spain, the more determinedly many of them scrambled to be shut of it. Too late: from all sides they were prodded, needled, bamboozled, and exhorted. In Emporia, Kansas, young Will White was already shaping the phrase "manifest destiny" and in Indiana young Albert Beveridge, hot in his campaign for United States Senator, was hollering hosannas for "imperialist destiny." As early as February, 1899, McClure had made it clear where he stood on this grave issue: he had spread across the first two pages of his magazine a poem by Kipling, "The White Man's Burden," which has been much misused to malign its author by those who have never read it.

President McKinley fully comprehended how the United States had been suddenly thrust, front and center, onto the world stage. One warm Sunday evening in September, 1899, he sat relaxed in the Cabinet Room of the Executive Mansion, talking with three young Republican politicians—George Cortelyou, his secretary; Charles Dawes, a close friend whom he had appointed to a post in his administration; and James Boyle, a former secretary whom he had sent to be consul at Liverpool. Boyle, recently home, remarked how much more were Americans now respected overseas, thanks to the Spanish-American War. "Yes," said McKinley; "from the time of the Mexican War up to 1898 we had lived by ourselves in a spirit of isolation." He spoke of the war, and of the role the United States had assumed in the Philippines. "And so it has come to pass," McKinley went on, "that in a few short months we have become a world power; and I know, sitting here in this chair, with what added respect the nations of the world now deal with the United States, and it is vastly different from the conditions I found when I was inaugurated."

Especially for the newspaper readers, the war with Spain had been a splendid little war: four or five glorious victories, with very little American blood shed; four or five gallant heroes—Sampson, Dewey, Schley, Hobson, Roosevelt; four or five rousing songs; and, after ten short weeks, the enemy's total capitulation. In short, just the sort of enterprise to keep the sales of newspapers up during the slack summer season.

More prosperous, more powerful, and more confident in both her new money and her new muscle; such was the state of the Union in 1899.

In that same September of 1899, McClure deemed himself, like the Republic, more prosperous, more powerful, and more confident in the access of his new wealth and influence. But there was a fatal difference. The entire empire McClure had built around the purchase of the House of Harper was about to topple with a crash, and after less than six months. Even to think about it would be, for McClure, to taste the bile of the ox.

McClure had ordered his affairs, as he thought, wisely and prudently. Phillips was running Harper & Brothers; under his supervision Walter Page was in charge of the book publishing department, John Finley was editor of Harper's Weekly, and Henry Mills Alden was editor of Harper's Monthly. Doubleday was in charge of Doubleday & McClure. Miss Tarbell was editor of McClure's Magazine. Albert Brady had a finger on the pursestrings of both the S.S. McClure Company and of Harper & Brothers. But something had gone wrong. McClure could not decide where the difficulty lay. Was it lack of capital? Or was it Doubleday's incessant interference and overmastering ambition? Phillips had no such doubts. Throughout the summer of 1899 he sent reports to McClure in France, complaining of Doubleday's meddlesome, officious ways. McClure studied these reports and at length agreed.

"I made a great blunder in regard to Doubleday," McClure confessed to

Phillips. "He cant help forcing himself into your place & mine & he cant help trying to make himself not only first but the only one. . . . Leaving him out we have a most perfect & harmonious personnel. . . . I really think that he will have to choose once for all whether he will subordinate himself to being one of us or else quit entirely."

Now that McClure thought about it, he found other reasons for suspecting Doubleday. Kipling had recently spent a month visiting Andrew Carnegie: had he gone at Doubleday's request, to raise enough money so that Doubleday might be able to fund the debt of Harper & Brothers, and so quickly take control of the business? "In a certain sense," McClure told Phillips, "I fear [Doubleday]. His sense of fairness could never withstand his temperament. . . . I can see the difficulty in managing affairs so as not to have friction & yet maintain control. However, he's head of D[oubleday] & M[c-Clure] & you are head of H[arper] & B[rothers] & that's the whole situation. . . ."

Unhappily, that was not the whole situation. There was still the burden of reducing the enormous Harper debt. Phillips and Brady had sliced heroic slabs of fat from the Harper operating expenses; if all the men McClure had assembled could only have worked together harmoniously, in a few years they might have been free of the burden and the possessors of an illimitable future. But instead of harmony there was clashing discord; and in the meantime all the revenue from McClure's was being gobbled up to pay off J. P. Morgan's loans.

McClure arrived in New York in October, full of bounce and ready as always to tackle the impossible. His partners sat him down and showed him the implacable figures: from advertising alone McClure's would gross better than four hundred and fifty thousand dollars in 1899; it was their best year ever, up nearly thirty per cent over the year before; yet they would end up in the red, all because of their purchase agreement with Morgan.

It should not be supposed that McClure relinquished his empire without a struggle. He waged what he called "a cruel war" to hang on; the office reverberated with his anguish. Doubleday confided to Kipling his belief that McClure was crazy; Phillips walked up and down the corridors, pale and tense; Miss Tarbell withdrew to a sanitarium at Clifton Springs for a rest-cure. At times McClure protested that he was sick himself. His wife, who had gone straight from the steamer to the Johns Hopkins Hospital where she had been put under the care of the celebrated Dr. William Osler, urged him to join her in Baltimore. "Tell the doctors they must get hold of me as they can," McClure retorted, "and the problem they have to solve will be how to make me well quickly." Then he resumed the battle.

McClure proposed a new company, in which would be merged the S. S. McClure Company and the Doubleday & McClure Company, and which would be capitalized at an additional five hundred thousand dollars. These funds, he argued, would tide them over until they were able to put Harper & Brothers on a firm footing. But Doubleday, who would be a very junior partner in such a new company, rejected the idea. McClure then sought a reduction of the terms in his purchase agreement. This too was rejected. Was there no capitalist who would advance him a sum large enough to fund the Harper debt? If there was, McClure could not sniff him out.

At this moment, as though McClure were not sorely enough beset, here came Frank Munsey, the publisher of Munsey's Magazine, to launch a violent and well-publicized assault on McClure's Magazine. Munsey alleged that McClure's circulation figures were inflated and its dealings with advertisers cunning, secretive, and crooked. What most riled Munsey was that there were two hundred and sixteen pages of advertising in the November issue of McClure's, whilst there were only one hundred and twenty in Munsey's— this, Munsey pouted, despite the fact that his magazine had an average net paid circulation almost twice that of McClure's.

The charges were false and so was the assumption on which they were based. Munsey boasted for his magazine a circulation of more than six hundred thousand, but in fact it was rather less than four hundred thousand. He could juggle figures as he chose, for in those innocent days there was no Audit Bureau of Circulation to check on wish-fulfillments. Munsey's claims of net paid circulation coincided precisely with his press-run. Since he owned his own distributing apparatus—the Red Star News Company—he was spared the necessity of counting the number of copies unsold and returned. All circulation figures for McClure's, on the other hand, were turned over to a certified public accountant, and Albert Brady saw to it that the sworn totals got to the advertisers. At the time (1899), McClure's guaranteed its advertisers a circulation of three hundred and twenty thousand a month, but it gave them, on the average, more than three hundred and sixty thousand, with some issues reaching four hundred thousand. An honest count would have shown that McClure's was neck-and-neck with Munsey's throughout 1899, sometimes pushing slightly ahead. Brady did his best to make such an honest count. He offered Munsey the opportunity to investigate "anything and everything concerning McClure's Magazine," including all matters having to do with circulation and "every advertising contract," Munsey to grant Brady the same convenience. But after Munsey's business manager had made free of the records of McClure's, Brady was denied comparable access to those of Munsey's.

The advertisers and their agents, however, paid no attention to Munsey. The trade magazine Printer's Ink noted that in the years 1895–1899 McClure's "carried the greatest quantity of advertising of any magazine in the world." It was the advertisers' way of expressing their judgment as to both quantity and quality of circulation.

Six months before, McClure would have greeted Munsey's fulminations with glad cries, deriding them for what they were—a sour confession that McClure's was the superior journal. But the fire of his enthusiasm had been damped. Opposed and assailed when he felt he deserved encouragement, he had fallen into a fit of despondency. It was the sort of mood which, years before, would have driven him to run away; even now he itched to book passage for Europe and be quit of all his nagging problems. But for once he couldn't run away; at least, not yet. He was obliged to sit still until he had consented to the cancellation of the agreement to purchase Harper & Brothers. It was a desolate hour; there was another to come.

Two weeks after the Harper purchase had been vacated, Frank Doubleday sent McClure a brief note announcing his decision to dissolve their partnership and revealing that Walter Page would leave with him. McClure was crushed. He had expected Doubleday to leave; he had even anticipated the moment of his departure with a dread that was mixed with pleasure; but the loss of Page hurt badly. Not that McClure set such store in Page's editorial talents; in fact, he had planned only to put Page in charge of the projected encyclopedia. What hurt McClure was, as he told Doubleday, that Page "sort of preferred you to me."

Here was a revealing remark and, as almost always with McClure, it was without guile. It came in the course of a long, rambling, unhappy letter to Doubleday in which McClure spoke of his "sense of loss" and his "bruised feeling." "I have had so many wrenches to my personal feelings," he wrote, "that I have not been able to sleep well, and therefore have not been able to judge well. For the past few nights I have been awake until midnight, and I always awaken at five o'clock and frequently in between." He thanked Doubleday for his "thoughtfulness" and Page for his "unselfishness." "I am sure it is infinitely more important," he added, "that we really remain good friends than that anything else should happen."

Here, once again, McClure showed his curious reaction to a rupture with an admired associate. Where another successful editor-publisher would have snarled his self-sufficiency, declared his contempt, or even sworn his vengeance, McClure was humble, propitiatory, even penitent, as though he had been put on notice and was seeking to make amends.

The fact is that success, however notable, was not enough for McClure. He had prospered by winning a succession of victories over the impossible. His education, his marriage, his syndicate service that had surmounted every adversity, his magazine born during panic and now thriving to the envy of his competitors—this record of achievement was still not enough. There had to be more. The string of triumphs had to be prolonged, whenever possible over the opposition of his advisers, for only so would McClure get what he most needed: a steady supply of affection, admiration, and flattery. The meat on which McClure had fed, that he had grown so great, was praise. When it was withheld, he despaired.

From McClure's point of view, the cancellation of the contract to purchase Harper & Brothers meant that he was a failure. The split with Doubleday proved it: instead of being admired and praised, he was betrayed and deserted. Not only Page was gone; others had deserted him, too—men he had discovered and put on the payroll, men like young Frank Norris. That hurt.

It would have hurt McClure worse if he had seen the letter Norris wrote to Phillips:

The Anglesea. 60. S. Washn. Sq.

January 9
1900

My Dear Mr. Phillips:

I have got to write you about a bad business and I never realized till now how very inadequate mere letter-writing can become. I have got to tell you that which must seem to you most disloyal and ungrateful. But it is only a 'seeming' believe me, and the fact that I have gone with Mr. Doubleday does not mean that I have forgotten or underestimated for one moment all that you have done for me. It has been a miserable business. I must trust to you to try to understand—I mean this severing of one's connections that the split in the firm has involved. . . . I practically owe you everything. . . . You have been the very best friend I've had outside of California. I owe my start to you and whatever measure of success I have achieved so far. . . . The little income I get, I must feel absolutely assured of, and my position with my firm must be distinctly and clearly defined. You see it is not as if I had only myself to think of, and I do feel—and I am sure you agree with me—that my obligations to the girl I am to marry are the ones I must consider the first and the most seriously. I cant afford to take risks and I felt that such would be the case if I stayed with Mr. McClure. It is not that I distrust Mr. McClure in the slightest degree. You know that. But I am afraid that he would forget all about me in one week's time. And what use could I be to him in the management of his magazine or syndicate? He asked me once how I should like to help him sub-edit the magazine, and this very fact I think shows how little he understood what I was fitted for and how out of place I should have been in his business. . . .

Remember [me] very kindly to Mrs. Phillips and to Mr. McClure when you see him and believe me always

Very sincerely yrs,
Frank Norris

But Phillips was of course far too tactful ever to have shown McClure the letter. In the case of Norris, as in many another, McClure proposed and counted on Phillips to dispose.

Around this time McClure sat for a photographer. The pictures show a small, frail man whose fair hair has been impatiently pushed back without the help of comb or brush. The flesh of face and neck is firm but there is a deep, lasting line graved between the eyebrows; there are lined pouches under the eyes; the forehead, too, is lined, even in repose. There is in the expression no bright enthusiasm, no zest; it is wary and apprehensive. The eyes are fearful.

The successful editor-publisher was not yet forty-three.

[VII]

Yet at his worst McClure could function better than could most editors at their best. "I really feel as if I wanted a tremendously long rest," he wrote Miss Tarbell, at her hideaway in Clifton Springs. "For fifteen years now I have done nothing but try to get out schemes for articles, etc., until that nerve is about drummed out." He was about to demonstrate that it was far from being drummed out. But first he had to reorganize his forces. He sent Phillips off to Italy for a two-months' holiday. He summoned Finley from Harper's Weekly and put him to editing McClure's. He found an editor,

Florence Bate, a junior editor, William Morrow, and a salesman, James Corrigan, to manage his new book department, which would be called McClure, Phillips & Company. He persuaded himself that he was well quit of Doubleday and Page. Their departure, he assured Miss Tarbell, had removed "foreign and alien associations, and I am in my soul happier than I have been for years." His spirits began to rise. He still had his projected encyclopedia; there was a new magazine, to be called McClure's Review; and now he conceived another scheme, for a library of universal knowledge, to be written by the greatest authorities in each field. And see here: a letter from Alexander Graham Bell:

> Dear Mr. McClure:—
> . . . We are anxious to give a wider circulation to the National Geographic Magazine, than it has yet received, and if you can give me any hints or suggestions how to accomplish this, they will be gratefully received. . . .

It amounted to a request to take over and publish The National Geographic. Would it be worth the effort? Quite possibly! McClure's spirits rose still further.

But the needs of his own magazine were paramount. McClure had to plan his great features for 1901. The question was not what, but how. There was no doubt in his mind as to what would most concern his readers a year hence. The issues were two: the new accumulation of great wealth, in the proliferating trusts and industrial combinations, and how it was being used or abused; and the gross corruption of government, at every level from precinct to White House. Evidence? It was in every day's newspaper. Only an editor stone-deaf and stone-blind could have ignored it.

The public debate over the trusts had raged for more than a decade, hotter every year. As long ago as February, 1890, McClure had arranged for his syndicate a symposium of opinion under the heading, "After the Trusts— Are They Legal and Who Derives Benefit?" He had got contributions from S. C. G. Dodd, the attorney for the Standard Oil Company; Carnegie; Henry George; John Parsons, the architect of the American Sugar trust; the distinguished lawyer, John R. Dos Passos; and a panel of judges, governors, and congressmen. By 1897 Finley Peter Dunne could have his Mr. Dooley say, "I have seen America spread out from th' Atlantic to th' Pacific, with a branch office iv th' Standard Ile Comp'ny in ivry hamlet." And in September, 1899, the debate had bubbled up so fiercely as to draw hundreds of politicians, professors, labor leaders, and editors to a rancorous four-day convention in Chicago on the uses and abuses of trusts and combinations. William Jennings Bryan was there. His silvery trumpet tones were muted; but when he called for Federal legislation to restrict the trusts if not abolish them, when he cried out, "One of the great purposes of government is to put rings in the noses of hogs!" his followers, who had jammed the Academy of Music to bursting, roared and stamped their feet for more. Not all those at the conference agreed with Bryan. The editor of The Review of Reviews, Albert Shaw, asked rhetorically, "What do I think of the trusts?" And he answered, "What do I think of the celestial system? They are both inevitable." But no matter what his bias toward the trusts, each delegate could agree with Governor Atkinson of West Virginia. "It seems," said Atkinson, "that our country has within the past few years gone trust crazy."

It had; and a week later the governors of a dozen states proved it again by meeting in St. Louis to proclaim their perfervid opposition to the octopus of monopoly capital. None of this clamor had escaped McClure, on the other side of the Atlantic. "The great feature is Trusts," he wrote Phillips from London in mid-September. "*That* will be the great question. . . . That will be the great, red-hot event. And the Magazine that puts the various phases of the subject that people want to be informed about will be bound to have a good circulation."

Back in America, McClure had found nothing to shake his opinion. On the contrary, he found that the easy money of the new prosperity was pouring into Wall Street to finance a speculative binge of unprecedented proportions. More than a million shares a day were being traded, and the talk was of a market in which two or even three million shares might change hands. No week went by without a newspaper story of some gambler who had made a fortune out of Tennessee Coal & Iron, or the Third Avenue Railway, or the Sugar Trust, or a salt trust, or a trust in Havana cigars.

As for corruption, it was everywhere. In New York City, the Lexow investigation of 1894 had been succeeded by the Mazet investigation of 1899; no sooner was one sewer aired out than another, still gamier, was laid bare. Nor could anything be charged against the administration of New York that could not be charged more confidently against the administration of Boston or Philadelphia or Chicago or St. Louis or San Francisco—indeed, against the administration of nearly every city, large and small, throughout the whole, glorious Republic. The scandals reached from the cities to the state capitals and on to Washington. They concerned municipal water sup-

ply and Federal military procurement, public lands and private railroads—
any enterprise where politicians could spy profits.

An editor could choose to ignore these facts. Most editors did.* McClure
did not.

Once McClure had decided to treat these facts, the only problem was one
of method. It was a problem that would occupy his attention for the next
few years, and on his solutions his editorial reputation would chiefly stand.
He began by summoning to his office two young men of exotic background.

The first to arrive was Edwin Lefèvre, a financial reporter for a New York
newspaper, The Commercial Advertiser. Lefèvre's father was English, his
mother Colombian. He was twenty-eight; he was slim; he wore a pince-nez
and a mustache that measured six inches from tip to tip. In his head were
stored a hundred tales of chicanery and double-dealing on the Wall Street
exchange. He had written a story, "The Woman and Her Bonds," which
had arrested McClure's attention. It was a trivial yarn,† but it showed that
Lefèvre knew how to describe the intricacies of the stock market in an
entertaining way. Could he, McClure wondered, be moral and instructive,
as well as entertaining, by telling some of what he knew about the evils
of speculation? Lefèvre needed no encouragement. The stories poured out
of him. They purported to be fiction but they were in fact accurate accounts
of real people engaged in real thefts. Out of respect for the laws of libel,
however, Lefèvre lowered over these realities a very sheer veil. James R.
Keene, a notorious speculator of the time, was transformed into Samuel W.
Sharpe; Jay Gould became John Greener; a youthful buccaneer named Jesse

---

* An honorable exception was the earnest Unitarian, Benjamin Orange Flower, who edited
The Arena. During the 1890s Flower persistently crusaded for reform, but unfortunately his
magazine was not only tendentious, it was also dull.

† It is worth the time to summarize the plot, for a story goes with it.

A busy broker, to help the widow of an old friend, advises her to buy some municipal bonds.
When she agrees, he buys them at 96, assuring her that they will advance to 110. They drop
to 93. She is aghast—if only she had her money back! The broker promptly repays her full
investment and orders the bonds transferred to his own account, thereby taking a loss of
$3,000. The bonds go back up to 96; the widow returns, demanding that they be sold to her
again at 93, and is vexed when the broker refuses. When the bonds have reached 104, she
is back again, furious, to insist that he buy them for her at 96. He did once before; why can't
he do so again? When he protests, she angrily announces that she will see her lawyer, that
she will sue.

When McClure first read this story, he was dubious. Who would believe that even the silliest
of women would react so? He took the story home and asked Hattie to read it. She read it
through with mounting indignation. At the end, she was in a high temper. "Why," she cried,
"what a dreadful man!"

McClure at once bought the story.

Livermore was renamed Larry Livingstone; the infamous Whisky Ring masqueraded as the Turpentine Trust. No special knowledge was required to recognize any of Lefèvre's characters; in Wall Street especially they were all at once identified; copies of McClure's were pounced upon as soon as they were delivered to the newsstands and delightedly passed from hand to hand. Only once did Lefèvre depart from reality, and that was when he unwisely essayed a prediction. In January, 1901, when a three-million-share day was a common occurrence, he wrote: "The most prosperous period in the industrial and commercial history of the United States begot an epidemic of speculative madness such as was never before known, and probably never again will be." Only once were Lefèvre and McClure's threatened with legal action, and that was when a newcomer to Wall Street considered that he had been grievously libeled by a story about a broker who went bankrupt after speculating with his clients' money. But the suit was abandoned when the man learned that there were several oldtimers who all had good reason to believe that it was they who had been libeled.

Lefèvre's Wall Street stories were to be a striking feature of McClure's during 1901, but even more startling were the handful of articles written by the second young man summoned to McClure's office. This was Josiah Frank Willard, who had much in common with McClure. Like McClure, he had been fatherless from the age of nine; like McClure, he came from a family of strong evangelical persuasion (Willard's family were Disciples of Christ, and his aunt, Frances Willard, who had recently died, had been nationally celebrated as the leading gadfly of the Women's Christian Temperance Union); like McClure, he had been an incorrigibly impulsive boy, running away from home again and again. Willard was twelve years younger than McClure, but the two could have exchanged stories of tramps down the same country roads and rides hitched on the same freight-cars, for Willard's boyhood, like McClure's, had been spent in the Midwest. Willard, however, had become a professional tramp: he had bummed his way not only all over the United States but all over England and Europe as well, even pushing as far east as Russia, where he had sought out and talked with Tolstoy.

In the course of this anomalous career, Willard had found acceptance in two quite different worlds: the literary world of London, where he had formed friendships with Arthur Symons, Ernest Dowson, and others; and the grubby underworld of thieves, pickpockets, confidence men, and their doxies. In order to move smoothly from one world to the other, he had adopted a pair of pseudonyms. To his family he was Frank Willard; as a writer he chose the name Josiah Flynt; in the underworld his monicker was Cigarette. Indeed, he smoked constantly; he also drank heavily; he was also addicted to drugs. Just now, however, he was seriously trying to write.

All this McClure knew. He had bought some of Willard's sketches of tramp life a year before and published them through his syndicate. He had commissioned Willard to collaborate with a rather precious young man named Alfred Hodder on some underworld stories, a few of which he had just bought to run in the magazine. He was not entirely satisfied with these stories. They were written in an arch and roguish style (was this Hodder's fault?); they were encumbered with slang (like "bloke" and "by Jove") that rang false. But the moral they pointed—that the thieves and the police of the big cities were closely and systematically allied—was it true? Willard insisted that it was. Could he document it further? Would he undertake a programmatic investigation of underworld conditions in a half-dozen American cities, devoting one article to each? Tracing the connection, wherever possible, between those who give and those who take bribes? Linking crime with law enforcement?

Willard—or rather, Flynt—or rather, Cigarette—would. He left the office and joined the throngs hurrying along Lexington Avenue. When he returned some months later, he had the material for a sensational series, "In the World of Graft," which ran in McClure's under a menacing headpiece engraved by Frederic Dorr Steele. There was a prefatory editorial note:

> . . . These studies were made, not to gratify an idle curiosity, but in the hope that they will aid the movement now in progress to better the government of our cities. . . . It is a mere coincidence that these articles are published just as Chicago and New York are arousing to the need of reform. . . .

There followed revelations which, since they were the first of their kind ever to be published in a reputable magazine of wide circulation, were stunning. The prose was lean and brisk; the tone was indisputably knowing; the impact on the cities whose affairs were ventilated was impressive.

Chicago, it appeared, was an "honest" city; that is, the thieves and grafters knew exactly where they stood. Willard's conservative estimate was that Chicago harbored a standing army of fifty thousand known thieves who operated night and day amongst the city's total population of one million, seven hundred thousand. He named two dozen burglars, robbers, and pickpockets protected by the Chicago police and offered to supply the addresses of each. He cited specific instances of police protection. His closing sentence was magnificently cynical. "When the present administration finishes its operations in the city," he wrote, "it is the opinion of the Under World that a reform administration will be necessary, in order to save something for the next City Hall clique to spend."

New York, Willard reported, was a "dishonest" city, which meant simply that the Tammany Hall authorities who ran the city's affairs were hypocritical, professing to be rigorous enforcers of the law but in fact accepting bribes at every compelled opportunity. Willard toured New York with an affable thief who identified a half-dozen saloons as the most popular hangouts for thieves. As for the crusade against vice in New York, Willard was skeptical. "The present excitement in the city concerning corrupt policemen, gambling dens, and disorderly houses is simply a passing manifestation of public curiosity," he wrote. "The citizens will get tired before long of the chatter about crime and vice, and the town will then settle back into its customary indifference to such matters."

Willard characterized Boston as a "plain-clothes man's town," by which he meant that the amateur sleuths of the Watch and Ward Society were so exasperatingly diligent that an honest cop could buy a drink after hours only if he were in uniform.

Willard's articles stung both reformers and police into action. Even before his series was finished, the word went out that the New York police had threatened him with reprisals; the chief of the detective bureau blustered that "Flynt" would be given the third degree. But Willard could afford to ignore the threats: Cigarette had disappeared; Flynt appeared only as a by-line on the articles and books written for McClure's and McClure, Phillips; and Willard was hard at work where no fly-cop was likely to find him.

Both these series—Lefèvre's and Willard's—dealt with material so novel that the writers had to instruct their readers in what were virtually new languages. The jargon of the stock market was still so strange to the generality of readers that Lefèvre felt it necessary to put quotation marks around such terms as deal, tape, go short, odd lots, corner, break (in the market), and tip. The argot of the underworld was of course even more unfamiliar; Willard had to translate such words as hangout, mouthpiece (which at the time, however, meant informer, not lawyer), mob, pinch (for arrest), pull (for influence), squeal, speakeasy, fix (for bribe), and mugged (for photo-

Young Sam McClure, immigrant. He was then about thirteen. This picture is from a daguerreotype.

S. S. McClure at the time he graduated from Knox College.

Harriet Hurd, as she appeared a few days before she was married to McClure.

BELOW, LEFT, Hattie McClure, around the turn of the century. BELOW, RIGHT, is her father, Professor Albert Hurd.

The cottage at Drumaglea, in County Antrim, where McClure lived as a child. Here, on a sentimental return, he stands in the doorway.

The year is 1900, and McClure is at Aix-les-Bains for his health.

Frank N. Doubleday started as a book publisher in association with McClure.

TOP, Albert Brady and BELOW, John Phillips: McClure's classmates at Knox and his closest associates on his magazine.

Viola Roseboro' was far and away the best of her time at recognizing literary talent in an unknown writer.

Miss Roseboro's discoveries included (ABOVE) Booth Tark-ington and O. Henry. McClure himself sought out Jack London (RIGHT) and Frank Norris (BELOW) after seeing their earlier work in obscure magazines published on the West Coast.

In 1887 McClure and his wife called on Robert Louis Stevenson at the New York hotel where he was staying. This drawing by Frederick Dorr Steele was used to illustrate McClure's autobiography, when it was published serially in McClure's Magazine.

McClure and Phillips sit for a photograph in their office. S. S. himself scrawled a caption for this picture: "After the Battle—1895." The battle had been to establish McClure's Magazine. By the end of 1895 McClure's was carrying more advertising than any other magazine.

In 1924 McClure lunched with three of his old associates, and later they strolled into a park to have their picture taken together. From the left: Willa Cather, Ida Tarbell, and Will Irwin.

In the summer of 1903, McClure went abroad with a party that included Florence Wilkinson, Cale Young Rice, and Alice Hegan Rice.

Back from a walk in the snow. The winter of 1898-1899 was a severe one, in Lawrence, Long Island.

In 1917, McClure was a roving correspondent in China. When floods destroyed railroad bridges, travel was precarious. He rode ten miles perched in this way on the engine.

graphed). He even had to define the word "graft"; it had not before been used in a respectable publication. Indeed, the very word "underworld" was first given its criminal connotation by Willard.

But the novelty of the two series must not obscure their significance. They broke ground for the brilliant journalism that led to so many reforms. They were the first examples of what Theodore Roosevelt would later demean with his glib epithet, muckraking.

To McClure, however, dispirited and weary in December, 1899, Willard's articles and Lefèvre's stories were only a pair of potentially exciting editorial features. He fretted. There was still the matter of the trusts. How to handle it? He was stumped. He was inclined to think that Ray Baker was the staff writer to tackle it; but how? He gloomed. Was the magazine to have no truly great feature in 1901? He had dispatched a letter to Mark Twain in London, urgently requesting stories, articles, a serialized novel, whatever Mark Twain might have on hand. To no avail. He despaired.

And then, like the answer to a prayer, there came a coded cable from his brother Robert in London: Kipling had just finished a new novel; what was he authorized to offer? It was the excuse McClure had been waiting for. He left for Europe the next day.

As soon as McClure took a turn around the deck, sniffing the salt air, as always his spirits soared. Why should he care that the Harper sale had fallen through? He would invent and publish his own new magazines. Why should he care that Doubleday and Page had left him? The only decent titles on the Doubleday, Page list would be books that he, McClure, had invented. He would get the serial rights to this new Kipling novel and if Doubleday wanted the book rights he would pay through the nose for them. *Aha!* Another turn around the deck. And while he was in London, he would look in on Clemens and arrange to have all Mark Twain's new books published by the McClure, Phillips Company. Why not? Indeed, why should he not take over *all* Mark Twain's books, old *and* new? And, now that he thought of it—

He walked faster, his mind racing.

Why not a new magazine, to be edited by Mark Twain?

Now *there* was an idea!

In his excitement, McClure all but forgot about Kipling's new novel. (It was Kim.) At the first opportunity he hurried to Knightsbridge, where Clemens was living, to press his suit. Clemens, who had been having troubles with his writing, was unexpectedly cordial. McClure, who had been merely hopeful, grew suddenly ecstatic. It was as though the floods clapped their hands and the hills were joyful together. McClure spouted assurances sweeter also than honey and the honeycomb. To wit: a straight twenty per cent royalty on all books published under the McClure, Phillips imprint, beginning with the first copy; one hundred and fifty dollars per thousand words for any and all sketches and stories, long or short; and, for editing the projected magazine, ten per cent of the stock for the first year's service and a second ten per cent for the next two years. McClure walked blithely to his London office and dictated a letter in which he counted up Clemens's profits for him. "It would," he wrote, "be a very moderate estimation that this twenty per cent would earn twenty thousand dollars a year after three or four years and certainly after the fifth year. . . . I want your interest in it to be of such a nature that you will be risking nothing whatever and that you will simply have a certainty. It cost me $300,000 to found McClure's Magazine but this past year it earned $150,000 and it will probably never earn less.* . . . I want it so there will be no risk on your part, nothing to cause you an anxious moment at any time. . . ." Lest Clemens still hesitate, McClure added a postscript in his own bold hand: "Of course I will guarantee profits of $5000 a year for five years."

Then he went off to lunch at the Savoy with Anthony Hope Hawkins. "This is a *black* time for you to be in London," said Hawkins, his mind on the Boer War. Black? To McClure it seemed quite rosy. At any moment, he was confident, he would find himself the publisher of a second magazine, guaranteed successful by virtue of its being edited by the most celebrated literary figure of the day. He would not be distracted by mournful talk about the plight of besieged Ladysmith. His concern was for Clemens: might he be having mournful second thoughts about the amount of time required to edit a magazine? Clemens had to be reassured on this point. There were other matters to attend to. What to call the new magazine? And he would need new printing presses; he should get back to New York at once; the Teutonic was sailing from Liverpool tomorrow; he should book passage. He made his excuses to Hawkins and hurried to his office in Norfolk Street.

"The editor-in-chief business I know down to the ground," he wrote

---

* Here McClure's natural buoyancy led him to a trifling exaggeration. In fact, the magazine had earned about one hundred and twenty-five thousand dollars in 1899, but the cost of the abortive effort to buy Harper & Brothers had landed the magazine nearly seventeen thousand dollars in the red. Editorial expenses were thereafter so generous that the magazine would never earn more than one hundred and twenty-seven thousand dollars in a year.

Clemens. "There will, under no circumstances, be anything in the relationship that will cause you the least anxiety or loss of freedom." Nor was there much work involved. "I should imagine that in the course of a month you might have as much reading as would make an ordinary book—that is to say a day's reading—at the outside two days' reading." Of course, there might be some need for correspondence. "I should imagine that in the course of a month you would wish to write at least a dozen letters. If it occurred to you to have a series of important papers or an article by Governor Roosevelt, you might drop him a note, this in addition to a letter from me, going more into detail. If you wish to have a contribution from Admiral Dewey or Lord Kitchener or Kruger your name would go much further than mine in getting them to contribute." As for being tied down to an office in New York, the notion was laughable. "As editor-in-chief of McClure's Magazine I have been absent from New York considerably more than half of the time during the past four years. I should imagine in your case that it would make little difference where your residence was." But even if Clemens should choose to disappear, he could still delegate editorial responsibility to William Dean Howells "or someone in whom you have great confidence."

In short, Clemens was to be a figurehead. Indeed, McClure almost said as much: "One of your greatest services to the Magazine will be simply the fact that you are the editor-in-chief. You will thereby attract to you a great deal of s[up]port on account of your personality." To this extraordinary proposition, Clemens replied that in all likelihood he would accept.

Here was a splendid confluence: two men with large, loose desires; the one bent on selling dreams, the other uncritically disposed to buy them; each naïvely dazzled by dollar-signs; each supremely capable of self-illusion. In a narrow sense, it is a pity that their dreams were censored: together McClure and Clemens could surely have made a remarkable magazine. But each, for good or evil, had his tutelary daemon. In New York, Henry H. Rogers, a guiding spirit of the Standard Oil Company, was reading Clemens's reports of his negotiations with McClure and ruefully wagging his head. And John Phillips, home from his holiday in Italy, was for quite different reasons quite as rueful, as he read McClure's accounts of his European triumph.

McClure, unaware, sailed on the Teutonic, and visions of a magazine edited by Mark Twain danced in his head. Before leaving Liverpool he had been handed a wire from his brother Robert. Charles Scribner, he was informed, had topped his bid of fifteen thousand dollars for the American serial rights to Kim by offering sixteen thousand. McClure waved his hand impatiently, as who would shoo away a fly, and sent a telegram to London authorizing his brother to buy Kim for twenty-five thousand. *That* should stop the auction. (It did.)

McClure now christened his new toy The American Magazine and began to devote all his energies to it. He would get Finley Peter Dunne to write one of his "Mr. Dooley" pieces for every issue; he would talk to Governor Roosevelt about a series of articles to have the general title, "The American"; he would order some more stories from that young man, Jack London; he couldn't wait to get started.

But at about the same time McClure was hustling happily down the gangplank in New York, in an office a few blocks away Henry Rogers was dictating a cool letter to Clemens. "If the scheme is to be just as you express it," he was saying, "I believe it would be well for you to make an arrangement with McClure, but—" There were so many buts. "I would not advise your spending that twenty thousand dollars that he thinks you will get at the end of the third year," Rogers told Clemens. "I know you have a lot of sporting blood in your veins, and so suggest that you sell that twenty thousand at a discount of twenty-five or fifty per cent, if you can find a purchaser on the spot. Joking aside, I think it would be a nice business for you. . . . I am sure you would make a success of it . . . but . . ."

And when McClure got to *his* office, his partner John Phillips greeted him warmly, bided his time, and then began to ask questions in his patient, earnest way. Who was to edit The American? Why, Clemens, of course— with some help from McClure. And who was to help Clemens to edit The American the way he, Phillips, helped McClure to edit McClure's? The question mark hung in the air for some days, nagging and reproachful. At length, by the end of February, McClure was ready to write Clemens a sensible letter. "The controlling editors of a magazine," McClure confessed, "have to be at least a considerable part of the year in intimate physical contact with the magazine." He went on with a technical discussion of the different qualities of paper to be used; the requirements that each quality of paper imposed on illustrators and therefore on the dates for closing of forms; the need for having all editorial matter ready for printing before the advertising matter arrived at the press room; the difficulty of selecting editorial matter so as to achieve a proper balance between fiction, biographical articles, scientific articles, and timely political articles; the ever-pressing obligation to change the make-up of the magazine "at the last moment for causes beyond our control"; the slippery way a magazine has of growing under its editor's hand, influencing, lending its weight, with luck sometimes achieving timeliness, ever demanding a certain variety. "If," wrote McClure, warming to his task, "if the editor is responsive and clear-headed, keen-sighted, has good literary judgment, good instincts for human interest, keeps himself fairly in touch with the human race (I use the word *race* in both senses of the term), he will produce a magazine with a soul—which is McClure's Magazine—as distinguished from a magazine that is made up—which we will say is Munsey's Magazine." It was as though Phillips were there at his elbow, prodding him. "When I come to think the matter over," McClure went on, "there is practically no instance where the editors-in-chief of a magazine are out of practically physical contact with their business."

That did it. McClure was still irrepressibly sanguine. "Subject, then, to all of these limitations and principles," he urged Clemens hopefully, "we can work together in making up the greatest magazine the world has ever seen." Too late; the dream had slipped away; and try as he might, McClure would never recover it. Clemens, counseled by Rogers, withdrew his approval of the scheme. Once again McClure's enthusiasm had been crushed. Predictably, he fell sick. From the Johns Hopkins Hospital he penciled a letter to Hattie at their home in Lawrence, on Long Island:

Mar 12

My dearest wife—

I am a miserable wreck. for 96 hours I have suffered terribly from grip last night being the worst.

I have reason to hope that I am improving, at least my temperature is better this morning. . . . I sleep little and have no appetite. . . . I have three doctors prescribing for me & several nurses (I am the only man in this part of the world)

Miss Tarbell was in Balto & has now gone to Washn. She called on me & cheered me a little. She is getting hold of a great series of articles on Secret History of the U. S. Steel will make a great feature. My love and thanks to the children for writing. . . . This grip has been terrible on you.

Your loving husband
SSM

He was sicker than he knew; sicker, indeed, than his three doctors realized. What did they know, in 1900, of what ailed him? They prescribed a long rest-cure, together with a milk-and-cream cure. He was to leave at once for Europe; he was not to return for at least a year. By the end of

March, with infinite effort, his party had pulled itself together—S.S. and his wife, their four children, two trained nurses—and they were off to Aix-les-Bains. At the last moment, the children had gone on strike. Why were they forever being dragged off to Europe? Why, when they had just made friends with other children, were they to be torn away? McClure had to agree. The accusations were true. Who, he asked them, were their most particular friends? There was a shrill, angry tumult. At length two names emerged: a girl's, Eleanor Hinman, and a boy's, Jack Greene. McClure got on the phone to their parents. And so the party of eight became a party of ten.

From Aix the party removed to Divonne-les-Bains, for McClure was fretful. His nurses also grew restive. Throughout July and August, however, McClure was strangely passive. But he itched to see the September issue. Towing a nurse behind him, he suddenly took off for Paris to buy a copy of his magazine. The lead article was by Samuel Hopkins Adams. It dealt with the training of lions, tigers, and other great cats and it was illustrated by Charles R. Knight. It was, McClure concluded sourly, the only readable feature in the entire magazine. He dispatched an angry snarl of a letter to Phillips: what was Phillips trying to do, pull down by its foundations an entire structure which he, McClure, had struggled over several years to erect? He poured into his letter all the angry disappointment he had suffered over the cancelled contract to buy Harper & Brothers and all his frustration over the cancelled agreement with Clemens. He ordered Phillips to hire Samuel Hopkins Adams as the new editor of the McClure Syndicate; he cursed Phillips and reviled him as the worst enemy of the S. S. McClure Company. Then, still storming, McClure took off for Italy with his children.

Along the way, he was assailed by remorse. How could he have written so to his best friend? He resolved to make amends.

Florence, October 30

My dear, dear John

I am in bed again. My trip to Paris was fatal & I can only get on sound ground by taking a rest-cure again. I do not understand my Paris letter. I feel utterly different in all respects. I am simply heart-broken to have caused you such grief.

My dear John, in some respects my case is pitiable. I am by no means as strong as when I left home. A walk of a few blocks tires me terribly. Riding in a cab tires me. I cannot see any of the beautiful things here. No place, or prospect, or plan interests me. At the same time I have a healthy, lusty body. I seem to have lost something. I am a mere animal. I seem to have lost morally and physically.

As for you, dont I know what a terrible self-sacrificing life you have lead. I must not write, as I must rest. My poor friend, how I have hurt you. *I do not understand it.*

I have become half hopeless & half comatose. Perhaps that is how one is built up. We are going to Rome when I can move. But that doesnt interest me. When I get rested I become very restless, but no place I plan to go interests me for many hours. No *plan* interests me long. I am waiting & hoping. The rest-cure has left a lot to be done. Perhaps my condition is normal & this is the way one gets over brain exhaustion.

I have realized increasingly the last year or two that my judgement was becoming more & more faulty, in both small & large matters. yet you have never even hinted a complaint.

You are the most wonderful friend & comrade a man ever had. Destroy the Paris letter. It was the expression of jangled nerves & a crazy brain. I seem to be deprived of even my old strength & mind, while I am getting renewed. I sometimes think that it is like taking off a leaky roof before putting on a new one. for a while the condition is worse than ever.

I feel hopelessly sad to have caused you such terrible & useless pain. I really ought to have died some time ago.

I often fear that I will never be a strong man again. My condition puzzles me more & more. I look well. I am about 20 pounds heavier. I have a splendid appetite & digestion & yet my strength & nerves are the lowest of my life

How can it be accounted for. I sometimes feel that I am withering, or something terrible has happened to me. Then I hope that *this* is being a vegetable & that in this condition I am making real progress.

I have no desire to go back. I have no pleasure here & I have no desire to go anywhere or do anything. So, as I have a pain in the old place, in the small of my back & feel tired easily, I have gone to bed again & I dont mind that much either.

In my mad scramble which in one way or another seems to have existed all my life, I have sacrificed much that is most important in life. I have dragged you all through terrible difficulties & now what of it? I seem even to have lost my faith in God. I have lost clearness not only of mental but of moral vision. I was happy during the early summer, because I thought I was on the sure road to renewed health, but I see now that even if there is a road, it is a very long & tedious one.

. . . I would give anything if I hadnt added to my crimes that letter from Paris. I wish you would remember the good things about me & forget all the bad.   Yours with life-long love
                                          SSMcClure

One scant year before, he had counted himself the most fortunate and successful of men.

[VIII]

In November, 1900, the McClure family (attended now by a tutor for the children as well as by the two nurses) sailed from Italy to Egypt. In Cairo, S. S. regained some of his old gusto. He hired a king-sized dahabeah, the Safa, and outfitted her for a journey up the Nile to Aswan; he bought sixty books dealing with the customs, the religions, and the history of Egypt and set them on shelves in the Safa's saloon; he engaged a dragoman; restively he awaited the guests who were to join his party.

Albert Brady, whose health had been poor for some months, had hoped to come along. Brady was in Naples with his wife and a physician; at the last moment he sent a telegram regretting that he was too sick to travel. But John Nicolay and his daughter Helen arrived (Nicolay was the journalist who had collaborated with John Hay on a lengthy biography of Lincoln), and after a round of parties for some United States Army officers stationed at Cairo, McClure gave orders to set sail.

The wind was contrary. When after three days they were still lying idle at their mooring, McClure hired a tug to tow them at least as far as Sakkara. Day after day dragged by, breathless and still, while McClure grew ever more fretful. Sometimes the crew would haul the Safa along by her anchor-chains; sometimes they would inch her forward by punting. McClure constantly paced the deck. It was insupportable: he could get off and walk to Aswan faster than this. He took to measuring the Safa's leisurely progress against the pace of donkeys strolling along the river's bank. An entry in Hattie's diary for December 15:

> . . . We set sail early but there was no wind for a time. Finally we started with a very light wind, the men punting. A dahabeah appeared following us, & Sam told the reis [the Safa's skipper] he would shoot him if he let it pass us. We kept ahead nicely with a better wind. . . .

Five days later, S.S. could stand it no longer. He was, Hattie wrote in her diary, "exceedingly nervous." In two weeks the Safa had come one hundred and twenty-five miles upstream; it was not enough. S.S. headed back for Cairo and a new start on his rest-cure. By Christmas Eve, the Safa had reached El Minya, which was, Hattie reported, "exceedingly dirty." The older children, Eleanor and Bessie, sixteen and fourteen, had commenced to fidget; the younger children, Robbie and Mary, twelve and ten, were still enchanted by the taste and smell of the couscous prepared for the crew to eat, by the thin, mournful music the crew made when they sang together, by the sight of the huge moon perched on the Safa's sail at night, by the donkeys and camels and sphinxes and sand, by the wizardry of heiroglyphics, by the dry, hot air and the cool, brown Nile.

Another few days and S.S. abruptly reappeared aboard the Safa, his face drawn and tired. He brought bad news. Albert Brady had died in Rome, on the day before Christmas, at thirty-eight. No one had worked harder for McClure's Magazine, no one had done more to make it a commercially profitable venture. McClure was the best judge of how sorely Brady would be missed.

As abruptly as he had come, S.S. left the Safa again, this time taking Hattie with him and appointing the nurse, Miss Bean, to care for the children. Miss Bean took a severe view of McClure's extravagant behavior. "The only way to keep his mind quiet," she commented, in a letter to her family in Baltimore, "is to keep his body quiet, and take all his playthings away from him." While this observation may have been accurate diagnosis, as a course of therapy it failed. For it left unanswered the question as to how his playthings could be taken away from him—or better, how he could be kept away from his playthings.

McClure was at Aswan to greet the Safa when she arrived at the end of January. He managed to stay aboard during the swift return trip downstream to Cairo. He bid the Nicolays farewell. He dispatched the tutor to Palestine for a holiday. He convoyed his family back to France. But then there was no holding him. He sailed for New York in early April. He had been away one year to the day.

[IX]

McClure landed without his customary enthusiasm. At the office, he listened with indifference to an account of his affairs. Samuel Hopkins Adams had for the past six months been editing the syndicate service. Good. Albert Brady's older brother Oscar was now charged with the company's business management, whilst his younger brother Curtis had confidently assumed responsibility for the advertising department. Good. As he could see from the circulation figures, Kim was a successful serial, and that was good; but on the other hand Phillips had seen fit to reject Jack London's first novel, and that was too bad. The presses were busy: as McClure had recommended, the company had undertaken to publish The National Geographic Magazine, and at Phillips's suggestion they were also publishing Popular Science Monthly. Good. "Business matters here are in good shape," McClure wrote his wife.

But what were they to do for 1902? What would be their great features? Nobody seemed to know. Phillips had no ideas; Miss Tarbell had none; Ray Baker had gone off on a jaunt to Tucson and on to Los Angeles; and S.S., to whom ideas had always come in such wild torrents, was bewildered and exhausted.

Two days after he had landed in New York, he left for Baltimore and for the next three days he tossed and fidgeted in a bed at Johns Hopkins Hospital. "The doctors say I shall have to stay abroad at least a year and perhaps longer," he wrote his wife. Miserable physicians! Was there no elixir they could concoct to revive his enthusiasm?

Back again in New York, he had a lengthy talk with Miss Tarbell. The great issue, he was still convinced, was the phenomenon of the trusts; but how to tackle it? Miss Tarbell had given up the idea of a series on the United States Steel Corporation; she hadn't been able to work it out. McClure was disappointed; he urged her to try again. Or if not steel, then which other trust? They had before them a letter suggesting a study of the Sugar Trust. The suggestion was reinforced with some persuasive arguments: the way the Sugar Trust had influenced tariff legislation, the power of its lobby in Washington, the violent fluctuations of its stock on the exchange (rigged by whom? to whose profit?), its effect on the price paid by a housewife for a pound of sugar. Good stuff, and yet—sugar seemed so trivial, compared with steel. Maybe Miss Tarbell should turn the whole scheme over to Baker; maybe he could come up with a fresh approach; what was he up to, anyway, out in California? A letter from Baker had, indeed, arrived at the office only that morning; he wanted to write an article on the discovery of oil in California.

Oil?

McClure couldn't see it. Miss Tarbell couldn't see it. No: the story they wanted was the story of how business and industry were consolidating to control the country's rich natural resources. And the Steel Trust appealed to them both as the likeliest subject. After all, hadn't J. P. Morgan announced the formation of the United States Steel Corporation only six weeks before?

The answer they were looking for loomed so big before them that it seems incomprehensible that neither of them could see it. If they wanted a trust to dissect, why not the mother of trusts, the model, the inspirer of them all—the Standard Oil Company? Moreover, Miss Tarbell was uniquely equipped to write a history of the Standard Oil Company; so much so, indeed, that one could believe that Fate had once again decided to intervene in McClure's destiny by plunking Miss Tarbell down in the right place at the right moment to undertake a preordained task. She had been born and raised in the heart of the Pennsylvania oil fields; her home was only a few miles from the spot where the world's first oil well was drilled; her father had been intimately involved in the early development of the oil industry; she had personally known most of the men who fought the trust in its early years; she had seen with her own eyes the growth of its terrifying power; the hatred and the fear it had bred in the community had moved her so deeply that she had even thought for a time of writing a novel about it; she had eagerly read Henry D. Lloyd's brilliant account of the trust, Wealth Against Commonwealth; her brother Will was an executive in one of the few oil companies that had managed to stay independent of the trust. Here was a story she could write straight out of her guts, but in April, 1901, when she and McClure puzzled over the problem of how to write about the trusts, she couldn't see it.

And so McClure went back to Europe with the question of the great feature for 1902 still up in the air. And presently Miss Tarbell sat down at her typewriter to write to Baker.

April 29, 1901

Dear Mr. Baker:

Forgive me for having delayed so long to answer the suggestions in your letter of April 17. . . . You speak of something on the part the discovery of oil is playing in California. I shy a little at the subject. I do not see how it could be made a McClure article. Unquestionably, we ought to do something the coming year on the great industrial developements [sic] of the country, but it seems clear to me that we must . . . find a new plan of attacking it—something that will . . . make clear the great principles by which industrial leaders are combining and controlling these resources. . . . What I am struggling with is, as I say, a new plan of attack: how can it be done, so as to give a big idea of what is really going on, in an entirely fresh and novel way? We have succeeded in handling one side of the municipal question freshly through Josiah Flynt's investigations. Those Wall Street stories of Lefevre's attack the evils of stock broking in an excellent form. Have you any ideas on the industrial situation? Could we do it by telling the life history of, say a great coal collier; a great steel plant; showing its small beginning as an individual enterprise, its growth, its forced alliance to get transportation, its combination with other colliers to defend its rights, and so on, until it is finally absorbed into a great Trust . . . ?

I wish you would think of all this, and see if you cannot give us some suggestions. When Mr. McClure was here, he told me he thought this was the only side of present day interests that we did not seem to be grappling with properly in the magazine. It ought to be one of our great features for next year, and it seems to me that you are as well adapted to make suggestions on this as anybody: think it over, won't you? . . .

Very sincerely yours,
Ida M. Tarbell

But Baker responded only with trivial ideas about irrigation, and mud volcanoes, and salt mines. The question of the trusts remained in abeyance.

At this time, Miss Tarbell was running the editorial desk.

They were always casual about titles on McClure's (so long as everybody remembered that S.S. was the Chief) and this post was treated most indifferently of all. Many men and a few women sat at the editorial desk, sometimes grandly styled managing editor, sometimes meanly deprecated as desk editor.* It was a post with little authority, although S.S. would often try to make it seem as if whoever filled it could make the lightning to flash and the heavens to rumble. The duties of the desk editor were clear enough: to handle the routine editorial correspondence, dispose of would-be contributors who insisted on calling in person, and be sufficiently alert to recognize any obvious talent that drifted past; to maintain liaison with the London office; and to keep S.S. (and any other editor who happened to be out-of-town) abreast of features and fiction scheduled for future publication. A bright desk editor soon learned that he could easily dump most of this work into Bert Boyden's lap. Boyden was a cheerful, likeable youngster who had come straight from Harvard to the art department. McClure had been favorably impressed by his knack for keeping everybody happy and had made him the editorial production manager; Boyden had entirely justified McClure's confidence.

---

* Samuel Hopkins Adams once suggested to Will Irwin that they give a party and invite to it all the men and women who had been desk editor at McClure's. Irwin shook his head. "We'd have to hire Madison Square Garden," he said.

Broadly speaking, however, the abler the man, the briefer his tenure as desk editor. John Finley, for example, stayed only a few months before accepting Woodrow Wilson's offer of a chair as professor of government at Princeton. After him others had come and gone, and now Miss Tarbell was filling in temporarily. Someone would have to be found at once; Miss Tarbell was too valuable to waste on the editorial desk.

Phillips had for some time had his eye on Lincoln Steffens. Steffens had left The Evening Post to become city editor of The Commercial Advertiser, he had written five or six articles for McClure's and a few for other magazines, he had acquired a slender reputation. He was about thirty-five, talented and thoroughly aware of it; a banty rooster of a man, who wore a pince-nez, a mustache, and a Vandyke beard. He had a quick, coruscating wit and a quick, calculating eye on the main chance. Phillips considered at length and then wrote Steffens a brisk letter offering him a job as managing editor at ninety dollars a week. "We want you as soon as you can possibly arrange to come," said Phillips, "the sooner the better; in one week rather than two."

Steffens accepted the offer but insisted on first taking a long vacation. It was then May: he would come to work in October. So Ray Baker obligingly came east to manage the editorial desk until Steffens should be ready to take over.*

Steffens spent his summer at Fourth Lake in the Adirondacks. He was there when the crazed anarchist Leon Csolgosz fired two mortal bullets into William McKinley's stomach. The Vice-President, Theodore Roosevelt, was vacationing in the Adirondacks, too; when he bustled first on foot, then by horse-and-wagon, and finally by special train to take his oath of office in Buffalo, he sent out ripples of excitement all around him. It was clear even to a dullard that something new and exhilarating was in the air, and Steffens was no dullard. Within the week he bobbed up at the office of McClure's, ready to go to work.

At last Miss Tarbell had stopped wrestling with the inevitable. She had resolved to attempt a history of the Standard Oil Company. Late in September, 1901, she and Phillips agreed she should sail for Europe to get McClure's approval for a series of three or four articles.

McClure, the world's most impatient patient, was in Vevey, Switzerland,

---

* Steffens wanted the long summer because he hankered to write a novel. Baker, when he agreed to be desk editor pro tem, reluctantly put aside the dream of his own novel. Neither of these superlative journalists, despite his intermittent efforts, ever completed his novel.

irritably submitting to a rest-cure.* He regarded Miss Tarbell's visit as a godsend and promptly swept her and Hattie off to Lucerne, and then to the Italian lakes, and then to Milan. Should they go on to Greece? "I want a good time!" McClure cried. But he decided he needed more rest, more cure, and so they came to Salsomaggiore, where he could lie now in mud, now in steam, and sip foul mineral waters, and chat with Cecil Rhodes and the like.

Here S.S. gave his enthusiastic blessing to Miss Tarbell's Standard Oil project. But there were, he also insisted, many other things that were being ignored. Santos-Dumont had flown his dirigible around the Eiffel Tower; Marconi had an incredible new scheme for telegraphing a wireless signal across the Atlantic; there was the story of that unfortunate American missionary, Ellen Stone, who had been kidnaped by bandits and was being held for ransom in the wilds of Macedonia. He would attend personally to one or another or all of these world-shaking events and he would arrive in New York around Thanksgiving.

He did. He found the office comfortable and serene. In no time he had it spinning. He summoned the entire editorial staff and scolded them individually and severally. He sent Ray Baker scooting up to Newfoundland to find out what Marconi was up to, and whether the inventor had actually received any wireless signals from England. Looking about him, he noticed Lincoln Steffens and demanded to know what he was doing. Steffens, he was told, was the new managing editor, being trained to assume responsibility for what went on in the New York office. S.S. was aghast. "At a desk?" he demanded. He turned to Steffens. "Get out of the office," he ordered. "Go to Washington, Newfoundland, California, Europe. Meet people, find out what's going on, and write yourself."

By now he had rattled most of the staff. They spread before him the newspaper advertisements for their Christmas book list. They set great store by these ads; Phillips, Jaccaci, Boyden, and William Morrow had all worked on them. S.S. surveyed them with distaste, shook his head, and ordered

* One of his nurses, Mary Cloud Bean, wrote her mother on October 4: "Of course as he gets better, it is all the more difficult for him not to work, or to keep him away from America. He certainly is not sufficiently improved to go back, and he is in anything but a good state anyway. He had got Mrs. McClure in a most frightful condition of fatigue . . . and . . . he would have got the children and me into a state but little better if he had remained here. . . . He has at last concluded that the children are better off without his constant presence. . . . I feel sorry for Mrs. McClure every day that I live, and of course I feel intensely sorry for Mr. McClure himself. Whether he will ever permit himself any calm of existence is very much to be doubted. . . . The difficulty is to get him to rest. Two days in any place is long enough for him, he says, and it is true. He was constantly in a state of unrest here, except one day when he staid in bed on milk diet. . . ."

Samuel Hopkins Adams brought from the syndicate and placed in charge of all future book advertising.

What was most exasperating about the rumpus McClure raised was that he was right. Steffens *was* woefully miscast as a desk editor; Adams *could* write better advertising copy. And as for Baker, shivering in the raw midwinter fog that cloaked the Newfoundland coast, he found to his delight that he was the only reporter on hand to witness the unqualified success of the first transatlantic wireless transmission. McClure had enabled him to score a clean beat. Other editors may have known what Marconi hoped to accomplish, but they had refused to believe he might succeed.

A few days later McClure visited Alexander Graham Bell's house in Washington on one of the famous Wednesday evenings when a distinguished company would gather for stimulating conversation. The talk turned to Marconi's outrageous claims of success. Someone remarked that Edison was skeptical. The head of the U.S. Weather Bureau also scoffed. "It is impossible," he told McClure. "Nothing goes one foot over the ocean." McClure smiled. He had seen a preliminary report sent by Baker.

McClure was beginning to feel his oats again. Back in New York for a small staff meeting, he leveled a finger at Sam Adams. "Sam," he said, "I want you to outline a plan of the way this magazine ought to be run and bring it in tomorrow morning. I'm looking for a new managing editor." Jaccaci, who was a good friend of Adams and indeed shared an apartment with him, jumped to his feet, sputtering. "Sam Adams," he exploded, "iss abssolutely incompetent to do this job!" So was touched off an epic spat. Voices gradually whined up to the decibel level of fire-sirens. Only Adams sat silent and amused. Miss Roseboro' burst into tears and fled. The howls mounted higher. Fists were hammered down on desks. Unforgiveable words passed. Feet were stamped. Finally doors slammed.

And now the entire staff was trembling. Mary Bisland, a tall, handsome lady from New Orleans who edited the syndicate's Woman's Page, was so agitated that she dashed off a letter to Miss Tarbell in Pennsylvania: ". . . very serious condition of affairs here. I fancied there might be a possibility you would think it well to come on for a day or two. The fat is finally in the fire. J[accaci] has at last overstepped the bounds, there was a terrible scene today & Mrs McClure tells me this afternoon that S.S. has fully made up his mind to end the connection. . . . Mr. Phillips . . . has been ill with a very severe cold that he tells me settled on the top of his lungs . . . & he came in looking deathly ill & wretched enough to wring your heart. . . . This miserable affair . . . How it will end heaven alone knows but it is bound to bring suffering all around. Mrs McClure says she & her husband feel that the break must be final, that after all J[accaci] said this morning there could be no healing of the breach. . . . I do believe you might be an angel of peace. . . ."

Miss Tarbell, happily at home with her family, fetched a deep sigh. It was only four days till Christmas and she had looked forward to a pleasant holiday, peaceful and blessed with good will. She sighed again and took a train to New York. When she got there, she found, of course, that they were all astonished to see her, that everybody loved everybody, and that everybody was anxious that she have a merry Christmas. She ground her teeth and went back to Titusville.

McClure, having provoked an immense rowdydow and satisfactorily churned up everybody's juices, sailed for Europe on the last day of the year.

[x]

A month later McClure turned up in Salonika. "I am very proud," Hattie wrote him from Switzerland, "that you have really gone like a belted knight of old, to rescue a fair one from a robber's den."

After having suffered at a succession of dreadful Balkan hostelries that were as guilty of bedbugs as they were innocent of plumbing, McClure didn't feel much like a belted knight. Nor was he particularly anxious to rescue the fair one, but only to secure the exclusive story of her adventures for McClure's if she should ever contrive to be rescued, an eventuality which, by February, 1902, seemed more and more unlikely.

The fair one in question was Miss Ellen Stone, an American missionary who, along with a young Bulgarian missionary, Mme. Katerina Tsilka, had been kidnapped by Macedonian brigands in September, 1901, and held for ransom. The two women were still captive somewhere on the southern slopes of the wild, snow-covered Rhodope Mountains, on what was then the Turkish-Bulgarian border. The news of their capture had scandalized the Christian world. Two weak, helpless women—two virtuous, God-fearing females—at the mercy of a gang of fierce desperadoes! What unnameable indelicacies must have been their daily fare! Newspaper editors had licked their lips and assigned to the story whichever of the rewrite men had the readiest command of suggestive adjectives.

The brigands, reasoning that since Miss Stone was an American her father must therefore be a millionaire, had put on her head a price of £25,000 Turk —rather more than one hundred thousand dollars. Unquestionably they would have settled for a tiny fraction of this sum had it not been for the brouhaha in the American press. Various newspapers launched campaigns of popular subscription; before long, in Sunday schools all over the United States, children were dutifully handing over their pennies; by January, 1902, the impressive sum of seventy-two thousand, five hundred dollars had been raised, converted to gold, and shipped east to Salonika.

All that money affected the Turkish police as catnip would a cat. They considered it a point of personal and national honor that the ransom not reach the brigands until as many Turkish officials as possible had sliced a tithe off the top. This circumstance hideously complicated the task of Miss Stone's would-be rescuers: their chief problem was now to keep the gold from being highjacked by the forces of law and order before it could be handed over to the kidnapers.

Meantime the brigands were surely repenting the day they had carried Miss Stone away. She had proved to be a notably fractious prisoner. There was nothing weak or helpless about her. She was a woman of heft and vigor; twenty years of missionary work in these parts had given her a granite jaw, a cold eye, and an expression that brooked no nonsense. She had also her own brand of logic: when her captors warned her not to try to escape, she contemptuously retorted that, since they had stolen her God-given freedom, it was their duty to restore it, and she would not help them to do so by so much as lifting a finger. Throughout her captivity she ordered her captors about briskly, scolded them on theological matters, occasionally reduced them to tears, and even got the more impressionable of their number to swear off smoking tobacco. They were a band of credulous, incompetent, timorous males who obviously yearned to be rid of her as quickly as possible.

McClure knew nothing of this. He had arrived at Salonika on January thirtieth and had at once set about organizing an expedition into the mountains to snatch Miss Stone back to civilization. Dissuaded from this gallant, if demented, scheme, he had fumed and fussed from Salonika all the way to Constantinople and back again. Wherever he went he was followed by Turkish police, secret service agents, and spies, in and out of uniform; his mail was opened. He was not amused. He wanted action. As a feature, the story of Miss Stone's life among brigands was worth only so much of his time; she should have been released within a week of his arrival in Macedonia.

At length he strode irritably into a telegraph office and dispatched a cable to President Roosevelt:

HAVE MADE THOROUGH PERSONAL EXAMINATION STONE MATTER. HER RELEASE IMPOSSIBLE AS TURKISH MILITARY OFFICIALS PERSIST IN MASSING TROOPS VICINITY ATTEMPTED NEGOTIATIONS DESTROYING VALUE SULTAN'S IRADE. THESE TACTICS SHOULD BE MET WITH WARSHIPS IN SALONICA. S.S. MCCLURE MCCLURE'S MAGAZINE

After that, it followed as the night the day that McClure was intercepted on the street by a Turkish officer and ordered to come to police headquarters. This seeming to him an irregular request, McClure shrugged and headed for his hotel. When the officer attempted force, McClure dug in his heels. Other soldiers moved in; a great crowd gathered. Happily, the American consul chanced to be passing by and he intervened. There was a heated bilingual exchange, after which the Turkish officer tendered a smooth apology: it was all a misunderstanding; the chief of police merely wished to have the pleasure of meeting the distinguished American visitor.

Before McClure could get into more serious trouble, word came that Miss Stone had actually been released and was even then on her way by train to Salonika. McClure rushed off to greet her, outdistancing all competition, and signed her up for what, he was confident, would be a spectacular feature in the magazine.

It was not. Despite Ray Baker's valiant efforts to transform opéra bouffe into Grand Guignolism, Miss Stone's story was a dud. But it served, nevertheless, a salutary purpose: it restored McClure's self-esteem. He had made a long journey into a strange land; surrounded by enemies, he had overcome them all; at length he had fought a mighty battle against the dragon of his competition and had snatched from its fiery jaws the prize. "This has been a terrible pull & last week was a terrible week," he wrote Hattie on March third. "The most difficult contract I ever made. *But I won* against the world." Perhaps, after all, he *was* a belted knight.

[XI]

When McClure got to New York he found that Phillips was thoroughly exhausted and sent him away for a long holiday. As soon as he was gone, McClure sat down and scrawled a hasty note of appreciation of all Phillips had done in the two years past, while McClure had been so much away. He scribbled his initials at the end of the note and then turned the page and added: "I give & I want a great deal of affection from all of you." Then once again he began to turn the office upside down, shaking the staff out of its shoes.

Bert Boyden, for one, was seriously annoyed at what seemed to him to be McClure's inexcusably meddlesome behavior. He sent off a letter of complaint to Miss Tarbell in Cleveland, where she was engaged in the exasperating work of tracing the devious development of the Standard Oil Company. Miss Tarbell sensed how angry Boyden was with McClure. Maternally she both soothed and scolded him:

Dear Mr. Boyden:—
. . . Things will come out all right. The General may stir up things and interfere with general comfort but he puts the health of life into the work at the same time. And there's nobody else who can to the same degree. When he's fussing & fretting & bothering you keep your eyes open, something is weak or wrong. He feels it and the rest of us are too much occupied with our little daily tasks to be conscious that there is a weakness. . . . Never forget that it was he & nobody else who has created that place. You must learn to believe in him & *use* him if you are going to be happy there. He is a very extraordinary creature, you can't put him into a machine and make him run smoothly with the other wheels and things. We don't need him there. Able methodical people grow on every bush but genius comes once in a generation and if you ever get in its vicinity thank the Lord & *stick*. You probably will be laid up now and then in a sanatarium recovering from the effort to follow him but that's a small matter if you really get into touch finally with that wonderful brain. . .
Above all, don't worry. What you are going through now we've all been through steadily ever since I came into the office. If there was nothing in all this but the annoyance and uncertainty & confusion—that is if there were no results—then we might rebel, but there are always results—vital ones. The big things which the magazine has done have always come about through these upheavals. Try not to mind! . . . The great schemes, the daring moves in that business have always been Mr McC's. They will continue to be. His one hundredth idea is a stroke of genius. Be on hand to grasp that one hundredth idea! . . .

Faithfully yours
Ida M. Tarbell

April 26

This upheaval was the genuine article, with department heads whirling apprehensively about as in a game of musical chairs. The head of the London office was summoned home to take charge of the book business; the editor of the syndicate's Woman's Page was dispatched to London in his place; nobody was safe. McClure, reviving an old grievance, now decided that Jaccaci must go.* He also concluded that Baker should become editor-in-chief and urged him most earnestly to accept. "You can always call upon me for advice," he assured Baker, "and upon all of us, but mainly upon me, and in the conduct of the magazine you will be responsible to the American people first of all, and to me only." Baker reserved his decision.

What was so wrong, to have precipitated all this fussing and fretting? Quite simply, the magazine. In S.S.'s absence, it had not only lost its vitality, it had also lost some fifty thousand subscribers. He got all the editors together and launched into a long, rambling lecture, as mercurial as a passage of free association from a patient lying on a psychoanalyst's couch.

"The editors of McClure's Magazine," he began, "should attempt to do something on every great event that happens that is great, such as McKinley's death, et cetera, that is of interest because it has happened. To produce a great deal each month of the proper material the men who do these great things must be met, seen, and talked with, no matter what they do, and these editors must learn by observation what is well done." At this point his editors could have been forgiven for thinking that perhaps McClure felt they should have published an article in praise of the anarchist Leon Csolgosz, but it developed that what McClure meant was that they were publishing nothing timely, nothing that reflected what people were concerned about.

"I am going to try the experiment of shifting this editorial work on the staff of McClure's Magazine and see the result. It will be a different magazine, because every man makes a different magazine; it is simply judging men and women and seeing what should go in. I read the papers and when I find anything interesting cut it out." Now from one pocket after another he pulled forth enough clippings to cram a wastebasket. "For example I see this announcement in the newspapers of wonderful etchings . . . arrange to have them reproduced in the magazine . . . go and find out at the Grolier Club . . . perhaps nothing comes of it but perhaps something does. . . .

"Lord Kelvin in Rochester; he is one of the greatest scientists living . . . people have forgotten how much the present conditions in the world are due

---

* S.S. invented a number of reasons for firing Jaccaci, charging him with lack of judgment, lack of originality, and so on; but the real reason he confided to Hattie: "I do not like the way he keeps a diary of all I say to him in our personal relations." It is a pity that diary has not survived. It might have been a comic classic.

to his inventions. . . . Take Pupin who made the invention for telephoning to San Francisco. . . . This Harper advertisement is not very good, we can do better, but there are ideas there. . . . Here are a lot of men, the Columbia strong men, there are a lot of things to be had from those chaps, how they got strong. That is worth investigating. . . . Look it up sometime, every one of these ideas leads somewhere."

He brushed the clippings aside and said something startling: "The proper policy of doing business is never to originate if you can imitate. It is my policy. I let Munsey demonstrate the success of the ten-cent magazine in two ways, getting circulation and getting advertising, before putting the magazine down to ten cents. I am so conservative I am rarely willing to perform experiments myself. To Mr. Munsey's boldness is due the success of the ten-cent magazine largely.*

"I mean to add to the size of the magazine," McClure said, a few minutes later. "I wish I were in form to talk about the beauty of the cover, human interest, inside grasp on vital movements of the times, but I cannot today. . . . This I have to let go, I cannot do it.

"There are two elements required in editing this magazine, one the proper brain and the other the proper environment. Get something out of everything, look everywhere for stuff, every man you meet is an original source of information. Now, the editor of this magazine has to read daily newspapers in different parts of the country. I read four hours a day during all those years of my editing. . . .

"Half of the stuff in McClure's is stuff that comes without work. There are three or four high-salaried members on the staff and we are short of articles. I don't understand it.

"My present plan is to found another magazine so as to have something for you all to do."

He nodded. The meeting broke up. Bert Boyden left with the others, no doubt wondering where was that one hundredth idea.

It came. There were, as McClure had said, three high-salaried staff writers, yet the magazine was short of articles. He considered, but only very briefly.

Miss Tarbell, as he knew, was hard at work on her history of the Standard Oil Company and had been ever since the previous October. (Indeed, McClure had been instrumental in supplying her with an unexpected and most

---

* How Munsey would have appreciated this tribute, had McClure ever made it public! But of course McClure did not. As for origination *vs.* imitation, it is clear that McClure never himself realized when he was original and when he was imitative.

authoritative source of information. Soon after the projected series was announced in the issue of November, 1901, McClure had run across Mark Twain, who asked him whether Miss Tarbell, in gathering her research, would care to talk to his good friend Henry H. Rogers. Since Rogers was one of the chief executives of Standard Oil, Miss Tarbell had of course grabbed at the chance.) McClure was eagerly looking forward to reading the first three of her articles, which were, she had told him, nearly finished.*

Baker, as S.S. knew, had been industriously at work not only writing articles for McClure's under his own by-line but also doctoring the account of Miss Stone's adventures amongst the brigands.

But what in thunder had Lincoln Steffens been doing? (In fact, although McClure had no way of knowing it, Steffens had been seriously planning to chuck his job on McClure's either to buy and run a small Connecticut weekly newspaper or to have another stab at writing his novel.) It was clear that Steffens was not earning his salary at a desk in New York. Already McClure had once bid him get out, travel, look around, meet people, listen, learn. Now more firmly he issued the same orders, but this time he accompanied them with "that one hundredth idea." He instructed Steffens to scout the possibilities for a series of articles on state and municipal governments. It was in McClure's mind that William Allen White might write some of the articles; maybe Steffens might write some, too; but there was plenty of material for a series; McClure was sure of it; he had newspaper clippings in his pockets to prove it. Miss Tarbell agreed with him: she had learned enough about Cleveland, while researching her Standard Oil series, to be sure that there was an article in the reform mayor, Tom Johnson.

A reform mayor? Steffens sniffed. His heart wasn't in the assignment. But he permitted himself to be thrust out upon the road to fame.

At last McClure's two pet projects—the trusts and the iniquity of municipal government—were in capable, if reluctant, hands. As for the third of his high-salaried staff writers, McClure was still hopeful Baker would be editor-

---

* Later both McClure and Miss Tarbell exaggerated the length of time she spent in preparing her History of the Standard Oil Company. In his autobiography, McClure claimed that she "spent nearly three years on this work before the first chapter of it was printed." Miss Tarbell, in her autobiography, wrote: "I had been at work a year gathering and sifting materials before the series was announced." These errors have been, if anything, compounded by the historians of the period.

This is what happened: Miss Tarbell sketched out a tentative outline for a series of three articles early in October, 1901; the series was at once announced in the issue of November, 1901; she had finished a draft of the first three articles by May 26, 1902; the first article was published in the issue of November, 1902.

in-chief. Perversely, Baker would not. He went west in July and before long he was absorbed in another attempt at writing a novel.

Fortunately Baker was more journalist than novelist. He had the journalist's dream of The Great American Novel. It was to illumine all the murky forces in American life which he had himself witnessed in opposition: Debs and Pullman, Coxey's Army of the unemployed and the new prosperity of 1900, the invisible government of capital and the record floods of immigrants that were being channeled into reservoirs of exploited labor. When his work on the novel began to falter, when he found that even a close reading of Sidney Webb's Industrial Democracy gave him no hint as to how a man feels when he is out on strike, Baker showed that he was an instinctive journalist. He laid down his pencil and took a train to Wilkes-Barre, where the hard-coal miners had been on strike for nearly five months, so that he might gather material for his novel at first hand.

Here, forsaking his novel, Baker turned again to McClure's Magazine like a filing to a magnet. For McClure was also in Wilkes-Barre.

Now S.S. had encouraged Baker to work on his novel—had insisted on paying him half his salary while he was doing so, had assured him that it would be a great success, and had even talked of selling a hundred thousand copies of it. But McClure was in Wilkes-Barre to chase down an idea that had interested him; in no time he had infected Baker with his enthusiasm.

The coal strike was about to be settled and even the manner of its settlement was a sign of the changing times. Earlier Presidents would have called out the army and driven the miners back into their pits at bayonet's point. But Roosevelt unprecedentedly stepped into the dispute and, bespeaking the rights and interests of the public, forced the owners and miners to submit their quarrel to arbitration. It was a long time since a President had not instinctively backed the business community.

Interesting; but something else had brought McClure here. There were seven thousand miners who had refused to go on strike and another ten thousand strikebreakers who had been brought into the area. Leaving aside the strikebreakers, what about the non-strikers? The press had been filled with lurid stories about their stormy life: their houses had allegedly been stoned and sometimes burned; allegedly many of them had been attacked, some seriously injured, and a few killed. The operators had naturally accused the union of these crimes; spokesmen for the union had hotly denied the charges and attributed all violence to "the coal and iron police . . . mostly city thugs with orders to shoot and kill." Where was the truth? And—no matter who was right—what had made seven thousand miners decide to stick to their jobs, no matter what the danger to themselves and their families? In 1902, these questions were still as sticky as fresh paint. In his room in the Hotel Stirling, McClure put the questions to Baker and, to his delight, Baker undertook to answer them.

In mid-November Baker's article reached the New York office. It was a dispassionate indictment of the lawlessness of a few members of the United Mine Workers. "This article," McClure wrote Baker, in congratulation, "will undoubtedly be the most important publication of this winter."

Meanwhile, Steffens's article on the corruption of municipal government in Minneapolis had likewise arrived in New York. "You have made a marvelous success," McClure wrote Steffens. "I think [your article] will probably arouse more attention than any article we have published for a long time, although we are going to get a hummer from Baker on the coal mines."

As for Miss Tarbell, her third article on the Standard Oil Company was already at hand. McClure scarcely needed to write her a letter of praise; he had already shown what he thought of her series by giving her a substantial block of S.S. McClure Company stock.

Here they were, then: three long, vivid, arresting, carefully documented articles, each probing deep into a sore in the American body social and politic. McClure could take deep satisfaction in them. They were the culmination of his editorial schemes; what he had been groping for in 1899 and 1900 was coming alive under his hand. He would publish all three articles in the issue of January, 1903. A lesser editor might have hesitated. Wasn't it poor policy to print three such contentious papers—arraignments of industry, labor, and government—all in one issue? McClure never hesitated. Each article interested him intensely: that was all that mattered.

But he was aware that he was making an extraordinary decision. He recognized that he had to show his readers he knew what he was doing. He wrote a special editorial, perhaps the most important ever to be published in an American magazine. "Concerning Three Articles in this Number of McClure's," he called it, "and a Coincidence that May Set Us Thinking":

How many of those who have read through this number of the magazine noticed that it contains three articles on one subject? We did not plan it so; it is a coincidence that the January McCLURE's is such an arraignment of American character as should make every one of us stop and think. How many noticed that?

The leading article, "The Shame of Minneapolis," might have been called "The American Contempt of Law." That title could well have served for the current chapter of Miss Tarbell's History of Standard Oil. And it would have fitted perfectly Mr. Baker's "The Right to Work." All together, these articles come pretty near showing how universal is this dangerous trait of ours. Miss Tarbell has our capitalists conspiring among themselves, deliberately, shrewdly, upon legal advice, to break the law so far as it restrained them, and to misuse it to restrain others who were in their way. Mr. Baker shows labor, the ancient enemy of capital, and the chief complainant of the trusts' unlawful acts, itself committing and excusing crimes. And in "The Shame of Minneapolis" we see the administration of a city employing criminals to commit crimes for the profit of the elected officials, while the citizens—Americans of good stock and more than average culture, and honest, healthy Scandinavians—stood by complacent and not alarmed.

Capitalists, workingmen, politicians, citizens—all breaking the law, or letting it be broken. Who is left to uphold it? The lawyers? Some of the best lawyers in this country are hired, not to go into court to defend cases, but to advise corporations and business firms how they can get around the law without too great a risk of punishment. The judges? Too many of them so respect the laws that for some "error" or quibble they restore to office and liberty men convicted on evidence overwhelmingly convincing to common sense. The churches? We know of one, an ancient and wealthy establishment,* which had to be compelled by a Tammany hold-over health officer to put its tenements in sanitary condition. The colleges? They do not understand.

There is no one left; none but all of us. Capital is learning (with indignation at labor's unlawful acts) that its rival's contempt for law is a menace to property. Labor has shrieked the belief that the illegal power of capital is a menace to the worker. These two are drawing together. Last November when a strike was threatened by the yardmen on all the railroads centering in Chicago, the men got together and settled by raising wages, and raising freight-rates too. They made the public pay. We all are doing our worst and making the public pay. The public is the people. We forget that we all are the

* This was Trinity Church in Manhattan.

people; that while each of us in his group can shove off on the rest the bill of to-day, the debt is only postponed; the rest are passing it on back to us. We have to pay in the end, every one of us. And in the end the sum total of the debt will be our liberty.

This editorial was a flaring balefire, rallying progressives and reformers all across the country. Its impact was felt first on the newsstands. The January number was sold out. At one stroke McClure's Magazine had recouped all its lost circulation. "The greatest success we have ever had," McClure wrote exultantly to Baker. "Your articles have been more important than anything appearing in any other magazine," he told Steffens. "Your articles are the great magazine feature of recent years," he wrote Miss Tarbell.

Other magazine editors, after their first shock of astonishment, hastily gobbled down the McClure formula. For some it meant an overhaul of format, even sometimes a change of title; but the direction in which they had to go was clear enough, and McClure had pointed the way. Collier's, Leslie's, The Cosmopolitan, Success, Everybody's, Pearson's, Hampton's—one after another they acquired new editors or owners, one after another they embraced the new journalism of exposure. Even The Ladies' Home Journal had a genteel fling at it.

The muckraking era had begun.

Was it, as McClure had insisted, just a coincidence? He wrote: "We did not plan it so"; and subsequent historians have agreed that the origins of the muckraking movement were largely accidental.* Conceivably they might be considered accidental if Steffens, Baker, and Tarbell had all been free-lance writers who, working independently of an editor and of each other, had simply happened to simultaneously submit their pieces to a receptive editor. But, as we have seen, they were staff writers directed and supervised at every step by an editor who knew precisely what he wanted, who regarded them, indeed, as extensions of his own intelligence. The only thing McClure didn't know about their work—for he generously afforded them every latitude to study their subjects thoroughly—was when they would have their articles ready. In that sense only was there any "accident" about the origins of muckraking in the issue of McClure's Magazine for January, 1903. McClure himself, when he wrote, "We did not plan it so," was disingenuous. He had begun planning it two or three years before.

* See, for example, Richard Hofstadter, The Age of Reform, pp. 191–194.

There was, however, one genuine coincidence, totally unforeseen by Mc-Clure or by anybody else. In the same January number that launched the muckraking movement there appeared a poem, no doubt inserted as leaven for the richly documented contemporary history that surrounded it. "A Boy's Point of View," it was called, and since it was mercifully brief it can be quoted in full:

> Sometimes the road to Sunday School
>   Drags out so hot and dreary,
> But that same road to go trout-fishing,
>   It springs along so cheery.
>
> I get so tired running errands
>   I'd almost like to drop;
> But when I'm playing hare-and-hounds
>   I never want to stop.

It is hard to conceive of a clumsier banality. What could have possessed the editor who bought it? And how, having bought it, could he ever have steeled himself to print it? Did it have some mysterious appeal vouchsafed only to the editor and not to his common readers? Indeed, it did. Its powerful charm, for McClure, lay in its tall, young, comely, dark-haired authoress, Miss Florence Wilkinson, and the magic she worked on McClure would play its own modest, mysterious part in the unfolding drama of the muckraking movement.

[XII]

It is a day in March, and Theodore Roosevelt is striding back and forth in his office in the White House, dictating a confidential letter to his Secretary of War, William Howard Taft.

> . . . I do not at all like the social conditions at present [the President dictates]. The dull, purblind folly of the very rich men; their greed and arrogance, and the way in which they have unduly prospered by the help of the ablest lawyers, and too often through the weakness or shortsightedness of the judges or by their unfortunate possession of meticulous minds; these facts, and the corruption in business and politics, have tended to

produce a very unhealthy condition of excitement and irritation in the popular mind. . . .

So far he might have been dictating with a copy of McClure's Magazine in his hand, opened to the page on which had appeared the editorial of January, 1903. But suddenly the President's mind swoops away on a bewildering tangent, intuitive as usual but this time loonier than usual:

> . . . which shows itself in part in the enormous increase in the social-istic propaganda. Nothing effective, because nothing at once honest and intelligent, is being done to combat the great amount of evil which, mixed with a little good, a little truth, is contained in the outpourings of the *Cosmopolitan,* of *McClure's,* of *Collier's,* of Tom Lawson, of David Graham Phillips, of Upton Sinclair. Some of these are socialists; some of them merely lurid sensationalists; but they are all building up a revolutionary feeling which will most probably take the form of a political campaign. . . .

This letter, written on March 15, 1906, signified Roosevelt's abrupt dis-enchantment with the very magazines which had helped to make possible nearly every positive achievement of his administration in domestic affairs. So far his ingratitude was private and confidential, but two days later Roosevelt attacked his bewildered allies again—ambiguously, to be sure—at a dinner of the Gridiron Club. But speeches at the Gridiron Club traditionally go unreported, and the President was determined to show his temper and gouge and bite in public. He got his chance when he was asked to speak at the laying of the cornerstone of the office building of the House of Representatives.

There were, the President said on this occasion, tendencies toward evil abroad in the land, and, as he spoke, he swung his arm in a wide gesture over the heads of the assembled Senators. He was rewarded with a roar of unsolicited laughter in which, after a moment, he boyishly joined. Then he grew more serious.

"In Bunyan's Pilgrim's Progress," he said, "you may recall the description of the Man with the Muck-Rake, the man who could look no way but downward, with the muck-rake in his hands; who was offered a celestial crown for his muck-rake, but who would neither look up nor regard the crown he was offered, but continued to rake to himself the filth of the floor." This figure, Roosevelt went on, typified those writers who ignored what was lofty and concentrated only on what was "vile and debasing," and he assailed them as "potent forces for evil" in society.

Roosevelt had, of course, got it all wrong. In Bunyan's parable, muck is a symbol of money and the Man with the Muck-Rake symbolizes those most criticized by the literature of exposure, those whom Roosevelt himself would later call "the malefactors of great wealth." Moreover, since Roosevelt prided himself on his wide reading, it can be presumed that he misinterpreted Bunyan's parable deliberately.

At all events, the epithet was delightedly picked up by those newspapers which had customarily defended the malefactors of great wealth. Muckrakers! The word was derisively nailed into headlines all across the country. Roosevelt had, however, been so ambiguous in his speech that the question at once arose: Whom had he meant to pillory? To Baker he denied that he had meant Baker. To Steffens he denied that he had meant Steffens. To David Graham Phillips he is said to have denied that he had meant David Graham Phillips. Others may have asked him if he meant them, and if they did in all likelihood he also denied that he meant them. But, as his letter to Taft shows, he meant all of them.

In short, in this episode the President, who always postured so self-righteously, is revealed as mendacious, hypocritical, equivocal, and dishonorable; in short, as a politician. One is reminded of the gashes H. L. Mencken made with his scalpel when he performed an autopsy upon Roosevelt: "No man, facing Roosevelt in the heat of controversy, ever actually got a square deal. He took extravagant advantages; he played to the worst idiocies of the mob; he hit below the belt almost habitually."

But leaving aside the question of his intended target, there are even more perplexing questions posed by Roosevelt's Man with the Muck-Rake speech. What was his motive in attacking his most effective allies? What had they done? Was there truly a danger of revolution in the apparently tranquil United States of 1906? Was there any truth to the charges Roosevelt had leveled against the journalists who wrote the literature of exposure? In his first message to Congress in December, 1901, Roosevelt had guardedly discussed the "abuses connected with the accumulation of great fortunes," yet against these he had balanced the "incidental benefits [conferred] upon others." He had indicted the business world for "crimes of cunning" and at the same time scolded labor for its "crimes of violence." "Publicity," he had said then, "is the only sure remedy which we can now invoke." Publicity he had been given, and in full measure; almost all that publicity had been calculated to inflate the President's rubbery self-esteem. Why then was he disenchanted?

To answer these questions will require a glance at a report on the State of the Union, as submitted by the muckrakers, from the fall of 1902 until the spring of 1906.

[XIII]

The best-grounded, most careful, most substantial, and most devastating contribution made by the muckrakers to the general enlightenment was by Miss Tarbell. Her History of the Standard Oil Company, at first planned as a series of three articles and extended to six on the basis of her preliminary research, reached a total of nineteen before she was done. Few if any serials in American magazine history have had so great an impact on their period.

At the time she was writing, Standard Oil enjoyed almost a complete monopoly. The company refined nearly eighty-five per cent of the country's crude oil, most of which was still produced in the Oil Regions of Pennsylvania; it owned nearly all the forty thousand miles of pipe lines and carried through them virtually all the crude oil produced; it manufactured more than eighty-six per cent of the country's illuminating oil;* its control over the price of all types of oil was absolute. This monopoly, so cordially detested at the time, so respectfully admired in retrospect, was the more remarkable because the wells it owned produced less than two per cent of the total. Standard Oil's strangle hold had been applied at the expense of the producers; it was maintained at the expense of the consumers. Most remarkable of all, John D. Rockefeller and his associates had constructed their monopoly in less than twenty years. It was the story of this commercial exploit that Miss Tarbell had undertaken to tell.

She set out to write a balanced study, to be neither apologist nor critic but only dispassionate historian. She conscientiously sought out those Standard Oil officials who would talk to her—notably Henry Rogers, the suave and courtly chairman of the company's manufacturing committee, and Henry Flagler, who had been one of Rockefeller's earliest partners—to check the accuracy of her material and to solicit the company's point of view. She used terms of the highest praise for the company's "perfection of organization" and for the "ability and daring," the "extraordinary intelligence and lucidity," and the "indefatigable energy" of its officers. It was, she wrote, "the most perfect business machine ever devised."

* In 1900, oil still lighted more American lamps than did electricity.

But in the course of her thorough, painstaking inquiry, Miss Tarbell was bound to form a bias. It was inescapable. Each fact she found—each affidavit, each of the many legislative investigations into the burgeoning monopoly, each of the many judicial proceedings mounted against it—served to deepen her cold contempt for the Standard's "illegal and iniquitous" policies, for its "huge bulk, blackened by commercial sin," for its "contemptuous indifference to fair play," for the "greed [and] unscrupulousness" of its officers. It was the logic of those facts that set her against the Standard and ranged her on the side of the independent producers.

To dig up the facts was not easy, for Rockefeller and his associates had been at pains to conceal their methods. Secrecy was second nature to the officials of Standard Oil. But Miss Tarbell found a valuable research assistant, John Siddall, a short, plump, excitable youngster who was anti-Standard by background, by temperament, and by conviction. Siddall had been born and raised in the bitterly anti-Standard Oil Regions, and when Miss Tarbell hired him he already had the crusader's zeal, for he had served as secretary of the Board of Education in Mayor Tom Johnson's reform administration of Cleveland. At Miss Tarbell's request, Siddall went on the payroll of McClure's and was later put to work as a desk editor in New York.

To put the facts together Miss Tarbell had to pick her way through a swamp of suspicion and mistrust and fear. Her friends in the Oil Regions tried to dissuade her: thereabouts the Standard loomed ugly and menacing; it was reputed ready to resort to any brutality against those who criticized it. Even her father advised her to abandon her project. "They will ruin the magazine," he warned her. When she tried to interview men on the lower echelons of the Standard, she found herself confronting the prototypes of the Organization Man. "The trust man must be a discreet man," she commented, with icy disdain. "He cannot afford to hold opinions, or at least express opinions, which will conflict with the policy of the trust. He cannot afford to support candidates who are not friendly to trusts. His only safety is silence in public matters. Can we afford to close so many mouths?" On the other hand, merely her willingness to talk to Standard Oil executives gave the independent producers the shakes. They were convinced she meant to whitewash Rockefeller and his ruthless methods. Even Henry Demarest Lloyd grew suspicious of her. Lloyd, whose brilliant polemic, Wealth Against Commonwealth, had so effectively stigmatized the oil trust, at first engaged to help in her research; but when he heard that she was meeting with Henry Rogers he did his considerable best to keep the independent producers from talking to her. Later, when her articles began to appear, Lloyd had a change of heart. "I want to congratulate you on the extraordinarily interesting and effective work that you are doing in McClure's," he wrote her in April, 1903. "When you get through with 'Johnnie',* I don't think there will be very much left of him except something resembling one of his own grease spots."

By that time, without ever having raised her voice, Miss Tarbell had told the story of the conspiracy hatched in the State of Pennsylvania and chartered under the bland title of the South Improvement Company. Ninety-five per cent of the stock in this concern was held by five oil-refining companies; the largest single block, thirty-six per cent, was held by officials of Standard Oil. During the winter of 1871–72 the South Improvement Company, with Rockefeller playing a leading role, made secret and illegal contracts with three railroad systems—the Pennsylvania, the New York Central, and the Erie—under which the railroads agreed to grant juicy rebates on every shipment of oil by the five refiners. To be specific: Standard Oil, the only Cleveland refinery in the conspiracy, would be charged forty cents a barrel for crude oil, while the twenty-six other Cleveland refineries which were the Standard's competitors would be required to pay eighty cents a barrel. This was raw enough, but the conspirators went further. The South Improvement Company would be paid, as well, what was called a drawback; that is to say, Standard Oil would not only get a forty-cent rebate, it would also be paid forty cents out of every eighty cents paid by its twenty-six competitors to ship crude oil to Cleveland. (It's pleasant when you can force your competitors to pay for all your shipping costs.) And still the conspirators were not satisfied. In addition, the railroads agreed to furnish the South Improvement Company with full waybills of all petroleum shipped, thereby giving complete information about all competitive business. A magnificent scheme; but it never got off the ground, for the secret was inadvertently let slip in the Oil Regions, touching off such a mammoth squawk by the producers that the South Improvement Company had to be hastily shelved. Rockefeller, however, could not have cared less: for weeks, using his contract with the railroads as a club, he had been busily convincing his Cleveland competitors that they must sell out to him or be wiped out. By March, 1872, twenty-one of his twenty-six competitors had sold him their refineries—on his terms. The cat, having gobbled up most of the mice, was purring and licking his whiskers.

Month after month Miss Tarbell's history was studded with such evidence of dishonesty and her readers followed her with the absorption they would

* That is, John D. Rockefeller.

ordinarily have accorded the most suspenseful detective story. The historical account of a business enterprise? Rather it was a revelation of an invisible government; and since that government's policies vitally affected every citizen it is no wonder that Miss Tarbell held her readers' attention. It was common knowledge that somehow the Standard Oil Company had elbowed its way to a position of almost invincible power in national affairs; but here were the facts, vivid and implacable. Miss Tarbell offered nothing else; she let her readers draw their own conclusions. So monstrous were the Standard's profits that perforce its tentacles had reached out to control banks, railroads, insurance companies, state legislatures, United States Senators. Given those facts, what could Miss Tarbell's readers conclude about Standard Oil? Rockefeller, as its principal officer, was transformed in the public mind into an ogre obsessed by money; his piety was transformed into hypocrisy, his skill into wiliness, his prudence into miserly greed, his superlative business achievements into naked evil.

Month after month Miss Tarbell's reputation grew. "The way you are generally esteemed and reverenced pleases me tremendously," McClure wrote her. "You are today the most generally famous woman in America. You have achieved a great distinction. People universally speak of you with such a reverence that I am getting sort of afraid of you."

When she was done, Miss Tarbell had drawn a formidable indictment. She had shown that almost every step the Standard Oil Company had taken toward trust and monopoly had necessarily trampled a competitor to death, and had been accompanied by fraud, deceit, special privilege, gross illegality, bribery, coercion, corruption, intimidation, espionage, or outright terror.

Was she accurate? Writing nearly forty years after her, and with all the Rockefeller papers having been made available to him, Allan Nevins said: "Much of her indictment of Standard methods was absolutely irrefutable."

That Miss Tarbell's History of the Standard Oil Company—published as a book in the fall of 1904—hurt the colossus badly there can be no doubt. Her indictment became a text alike for sermons and for newspaper editorials. Her work, said The New York World, "gives us the same insight into the nature of trusts in general that the medical student gains of cancers from a scientific description of a typical case." The company made no direct answer to her accusations—"Not a word," said Rockefeller; "not a word about that misguided woman!"—and indirectly the only response was that the company footed the bill for a wholesale distribution of the two or three adverse criticisms given the book. These featured sophomoric lapses into bad taste, such as references to Miss Tarbell as Miss Tarbarrel; and for a time her mail was swollen with letters from indignant professors, librarians, and clergymen who resented having been put on the Standard Oil's free-list.

But there is a better way of assessing the impact of her History. While there is no need to urge that post hoc, ergo propter hoc, nevertheless the calendar is suggestive.

The first part of Miss Tarbell's series began in McClure's in November, 1902. The second part, which dealt with almost contemporaneous history, ran from December, 1903, to October, 1904. Beginning in 1905, Herbert S. Hadley, the attorney-general of Missouri elected on a reform ticket headed by Governor Joseph Folk, collected information which led to a suit filed on March 29, 1906, charging a combination to fix prices and throttle competition. On May 2, 1906, the Federal Bureau of Corporations released a report charging Standard Oil with having wangled secret rebates on oil shipments by the railroads. The United States Attorney-General, Charles Bonaparte, on November 18, 1906, began prosecution of the Standard Oil Company of New Jersey under the Sherman Anti-Trust Act. Also in November, 1906, the Standard Oil Company of Indiana was prosecuted for violation of the Elkins Act, which forbade rebates. On August 3, 1907, Federal Judge Kenesaw Mountain Landis fined the Standard Oil Company of Indiana twenty-nine million, two hundred and forty thousand dollars, a judgment which was later set aside. (President Roosevelt publicly gnashed his teeth.) But on November 20, 1909, a Federal Circuit Court sustained the government in its anti-trust suit against Standard of New Jersey, and on May 5, 1911, the Supreme Court affirmed the judgment and ordered the dissolution of the monopoly. Where once there had been one huge combination, now, at least in theory, there were to be thirty-eight competitive rivals.

But only in theory. In fact, of course, the thirty-eight companies, despite the fact that they had no officers or directors in common, managed miraculously to parcel out territories and to function in smooth and friendly fashion with each other. Nevertheless, there was a difference. The monopoly had been shaken; its competitors before long had a fighting chance. The dissolution ordered by the Supreme Court was more than a token.

Finley Peter Dunne's Mr. Dooley once remarked that the Supreme Court "follows th' iliction returns." It is not too much to suggest that Miss Tarbell's History of the Standard Oil Company heated the national fever against the monopoly so hot that the Supreme Court had no difficulty in reading the thermometer.

[XIV]

If Miss Tarbell's was the most substantial contribution by the muckrakers, Lincoln Steffens's series on corruption in government was easily the most provocative. He sniffed about in only a half-dozen cities and a half-dozen states, but the clouds of dust he raised set citizens to sneezing all over the landscape. Grand juries launched investigations into the malodorous affairs of cities he had never visited, political bosses everywhere walked more warily, and in at least three states reform administrations were elected—all as a direct result of what he wrote for McClure's. Coast to coast his readers, horrified yet fascinated, called for more. They pressed him to come inspect their own cities, which, they promised him, he would find more scandalous than any he had ever visited. They were inflamed with a severe epidemic of American boosterism, only in reverse.

Steffens, as he overheard men discussing his articles in the dining-cars of trains and the lobbies of hotels, preened himself like a cockatoo. He was almost as much a celebrity as Miss Tarbell. But back in New York, in the judgment of his editor, there was a salient difference between the Tarbell series and the Steffens series. McClure trusted Miss Tarbell utterly; he gave her a free hand. As to Steffens, however, he had the gravest misgivings; the friction between editor and writer sent out a steady shower of sparks.

The trouble lay in Steffens's particular bias. He was convinced that what ailed American politics, from hamlet to national capital, was the American businessman, grasping for profits, corrupt and corrupting; and he spread this conviction as thick as peanut butter over everything he wrote. Thirty years later, when he came to write his autobiography, Steffens would portray himself as a pilgrim wandering wide-eyed through a wilderness of evil, anxious only to keep an open mind, and gradually formulating a theory as to the origin of the evil. This account, while charming, was purest poppycock. What theories Steffens had about American politics were formulated and fixed in his mind months before he came to work for McClure's. When Steffens gathered his articles on municipal corruption into a book, The Shame of the Cities, he took the occasion to write an introduction in which he professed to sum up what he had learned from his investigations. His main conclusion was that the businessman bribed boodlers in St. Louis, defended grafters in Minneapolis, sponsored corruption in Pittsburg, shared with the bosses in Philadelphia, deplored reform in Chicago, and undermined good government in New York. In short, the businessman was the chief source of corruption.

> The business man [Steffens wrote in this introduction] has failed in politics as he has in citizenship. Why?
>
> Because politics is business. That's what's the matter with it. That's what's the matter with everything,—art, literature, religion, journalism, law, medicine,—they're all business, and all—as you see them. Make politics a sport, as they do in England, or a profession, as they do in Germany, and we'll have—well, something else than we have now,—if we want it, which is another question. But don't try to reform politics with the banker, the lawyer, and the dry-goods merchant, for these are business men. . . .

The passage quoted (and a great deal more in the same vein) did not, however, appear for the first time in the preface to The Shame of the Cities. Steffens wrote it first for an article published in Ainslee's Magazine for October, 1901, an article which stands as a kind of bare-bones prospectus for his later series in McClure's. For Ainslee's, Steffens anatomized municipal corruption, but only in general terms: he named few names and gave no details; his tone was cynical, even contemptuous. The American political system, he wrote,

> is the result of the commercial development of the country. The votes which the founders of the republic threw around broadcast, one to each man, are not worth much singly; all together, they are of immense value. Like wheat or junk, they are useless in "the piece"; in quantity, they are marketable at high prices. . . . As time wore on and we all became merchants . . . the ruling power of the votes was left around loose, piled into heaps here and there by old party organizations and prejudices, but free to any man who cared to go about like the junkman and take them away. . . .

When he came to write for McClure's, however, Steffens was obliged to take a different tack. McClure insisted on the specific fact; he distrusted the contentious generality. Within the limits of the libel laws, he wanted corrupt officials and boodlers named, and their crimes itemized. McClure demanded, moreover, a moral tone. He had a positive, puritanical, Scotch-Irish itch: he wanted to arouse the citizens of dishonest communities, to so shame them with the facts about their cities that they would unite in righteous wrath and sweep all their crooked officials away to the pokey. Steffens, whose cast of mind was at once tolerant and rebellious, found this reformist approach irksome and dubious.

His first article—originally assigned to a local reporter but substantially rewritten by Steffens—was a lucid and sprightly demonstration of how venality had overwhelmed St. Louis; it made a national figure of Joseph Folk, the uncommonly conscientious young circuit attorney who had undertaken to scrub St. Louis clean. Steffens, with his wicked gift for plucking the colorful and the characteristic out of a cesspool, neatly epitomized St. Louis when he described how "a practical joker nearly emptied [the chamber of the city council] by tipping a boy to rush into a session and call out, 'Mister, your saloon is on fire.'" Steffens kept his focus on the bribers and the bribed; on the merchants and financiers on the one hand and the municipal assemblymen on the other. According to a grand jury report, those assemblymen were truly inspiring guardians of the commonweal. "In some," the grand jurors concluded, "no trace of mentality or morality could be found; in others, a low order of training appeared, united with base cunning, groveling instincts, and sordid desires."

As this first article went to press, Steffens belatedly waxed enthusiastic over the series. He even suggested a subject for a second article; he proposed, of all places, Paterson, New Jersey. But McClure, once again suddenly home from Europe, peremptorily dismissed the Patersons. He pulled from his suitcase a great bundle of newspaper clippings about Minneapolis, the harvest of a summer's reading. Here was the second article; all Steffens had to do was piece together these reports of a grand jury's investigation. McClure had a title, "The Shame of Minneapolis"; and he had, as well, a reason for the title. If these articles on municipal corruption were to accomplish any positive good, they had to be aimed straight at the civic pride of an apparently shameless citizenry. In this connection, McClure scolded Steffens about the St. Louis article. His focus had been wrong. Instead of aiming at the crooks, Steffens should have aimed at those who, by voting wrong or not voting at all, permitted the crooks to seize and wield power. Too late now; but once Steffens had properly reported on Minneapolis, he would have to go back to St. Louis and tell the story again, this time from the proper point of view.

Steffens did more in Minneapolis than simply take the published facts about corruption and string them together like so many dime-store pearls. In Minneapolis a knave called Albert Alonzo Ames had got himself elected mayor and had appointed his equally knavish brother Fred to be chief of police. This pair had declared open house in Minneapolis for confidence men, gamblers, pickpockets, second-story men, and swindlers generally. There ensued a predictable saturnalia. One hundred and seven policemen were dismissed from a force of two hundred and twenty-five; those spared by the axe thereafter planned and protected several lucrative crimes, including the burglary of the Pabst Brewing Company. Steffens not only traced the connections between vice and police, police and politicians, he also laid hands upon and had photographed a ledger in which was set forth, in coarse detail, the terms of the payoff by criminals to police and politicians. Until Steffens had it photographed for the readers of McClure's, no one save the members of a grand jury had ever laid eyes on this sinful evidence.

McClure was jubilant. At one bound he attained the summit of his esteem for Steffens. Thereafter, however, it would all be downhill. There was difficulty over the second article on St. Louis; McClure felt it necessary to lecture Steffens on how to organize his piece, going so far as to hold up Alexander Dumas as a model when it came to such matters as climax and emphasis. There then arose the question as to which city's infamy should be next described. Steffens urged Pittsburg. McClure considered that Pittsburg would be anticlimactic; instead he suggested that Steffens go next to Philadelphia and then abroad, to report to Americans how much better their European cousins ordered their municipal affairs. Steffens won the argument and proceeded to Pittsburg. McClure had a first draft of his article in hand on March 20, 1903. From Chicago he dictated a letter to Phillips, back in New York:

> My dear John;
> I have been thinking seriously of the attitude Steffens always takes in regard to the people, and I not only feel that he is wrong in his attitude, but that such an attitude is discouraging and calculated to lessen the value of the article. I think it is a mistake to call a man a coward who refuses to take such a stand as will render him liable to serious injury, false imprisonment, and so on. . . . For this reason and for other reasons I wish to go over the Pittsburg article very carefully before it is published, and I also want to go over these matters again with Steffens. I think that the article to begin with should be free from bias, just the same as a news article in a newspaper,* or Miss Tarbell's Story of the Standard Oil. . . . In the case of Pittsburg, and in the case of Rhode Island, likewise of St. Louis, it is evident from what we know that the people are tied hand and foot by certain laws, made in many cases by the state legislatures. The

* !

Standard Oil Company was able to have its way in spite of the utmost fighting, largely because the fighting was not as well managed as the Standard Oil fight was managed. This is no reason for calling the men cowards who were despoiled and beaten.

In any event, the editorial policy of the magazine belongs to you and me. This is just as true of the editorial policy of articles as it would be of editorials themselves. Steffens is not getting at the cause of the trouble by attributing it to cowardice on the part of the people, and therefore his articles will fail to help. The real cause of the trouble lies beyond them, in the passage of laws that render the people helpless. Steffens has a notion that the business man is a coward, and that the business man is to blame for political corruption, and he makes every fact bend to this notion. Now, he must disabuse himself of any predilections in the matter and write up things as he finds them.* So I telegraphed you this afternoon to postpone the article. . . . I should like to have proof of the Steffens article sent to me at San Francisco. . . .

This letter is not to go to Mr. Steffens, and in fact you need not file it. It is rather for your own guidance. You can convey to him the same ideas in different language. . . .

Very sincerely yours,
SSMcClure

Phillips edited Steffens's article on Pittsburg heavily, in accordance with McClure's instructions.

From Pittsburg Steffens went on to Philadelphia, "corrupt and contented," where, as he noted sardonically, the boodlers whimsically divided their graft "in unison with the ancient chime of Independence Hall." From Philadelphia Steffens turned to Chicago, which was then in the throes of a brief, spasmodic reform movement, and which afforded a perfect illustration of the advice he had first ventured in his article for Ainslee's: "Let reformers aim to be bosses. . . . Why shouldn't our ambitious youth aim to be boss? . . . [But] he won't succeed unless he attends, while he fights for the ideal, to the complicated business that is at the bottom of politics everywhere." In Chicago the reformer-boss was a young lawyer, Walter Fisher, later Secretary of the Interior for President Taft, who, as Steffens related, "produced reform politicians working for the reform of the city with the methods of

---

* Compare this with the statement by Steffens (The Autobiography of Lincoln Steffens, p. 375) reporting a conversation with McClure that allegedly took place in the fall of 1902: "I argued with Mr. McClure that it would heighten the interest in the articles we were planning to start out with blank minds and search like detectives for the keys to the mystery, the clews to the truth. He would not have it so." It can be noted that the statement by McClure was made at the time; the statement by Steffens was recollected, if that is the word, nearly thirty years later.

politics." Finally, in an article timed to influence an election, Steffens returned to New York. The aim was to help re-elect Seth Low as mayor;
Steffens's piece, which was palpably campaign literature, was also the weak-
est of his articles. It fizzled; so did Low.

This setback did not, however, deter McClure. He had already resolved
to throw his magazine's considerable influence back of reform and back of
honest politicians, if any.

"I believe," he told Steffens, "we can do more toward making a President
of the United States than any other twenty organs."

Steffens feared that the magazine's power might be abused.

"You can trust absolutely to me," McClure assured him. "I think I may
safely claim to be a man without self-consciousness, and all my life I have
in editorial matters acted instinctively. I shall not burden my mind with
studying out what policy to pursue. I will do the right thing each time that
the question arises, and feel the utmost confidence in my editorial judgment and instincts. I do not believe that I will go wrong."

Steffens was not so sure. He urged a careful study of—

"It would be impossible," McClure insisted, "for me to make any kind of
careful studying how I would do this or that. I have never done such things,
and I remember in talking to Mahan during the Spanish-American War,
when he was member of a small board that directed the movements of the
vessels in the Atlantic under Sampson, that he never took any time at all
to make decisions, and I think you will find as a rule that men competent
to conduct large enterprises make important decisions in just that way. We
won't make any blunders."

In the face of such superb self-confidence, even the self-confident Steffens
must have acknowledged that he had met his master.

"I think," McClure told him later, "we have entered upon the greatest
campaign that any periodical has ever undertaken. I think it will develop
into both a political and business field that we hardly now suspect. It may
be the route by which I shall get to a daily newspaper. I cannot tell. The
only thing is just to keep right on in the work we are doing, and be guided
by the advance as we rise."

They would begin with Folk—Joseph Folk of Missouri—and they would
waft him to political pinnacles undreamed of.

"I wish you would tell Folk from me," McClure instructed Steffens, "that
he is the candidate of McClure's Magazine at the present moment for Presi-

dent in 1908. Many years ago Mr. Laffan * said about Roosevelt if he kept his nose clean he would be President of the United States. I say the same about Mr. Folk, but he wants to lay mighty low, just do his day's work."

For Folk, the stepping-stone to the White House was to be the governor's mansion in Jefferson City; and so, to help him along his way, Steffens traveled again to St. Louis to write another article, this time about the state, not the city. Steffens was delighted with the assignment. He hankered to show how the seeds of corruption sprouted and spread from city to state capital, from state capital to Washington.

It was McClure who named the new Steffens series: "Enemies of the Republic." Steffens suggested that the phrase might be attributed to Folk, as part of the magazine's effort to build Folk's reputation. This was going too far. "It would be a great mistake," McClure retorted. "Whatever the magazine can do that will increase its influence and power it must do, and the invention of that phrase I count as a most important thing. Always remember," he cautioned Steffens, "that I am not simply an editor, but that I have a feeling of jealousy for McClure's Magazine very much like what the lioness has for her cubs."

In the months he had been running Steffens's muckraking articles, Mc-Clure had changed his mind about their author. He had not come to trust Steffens as much as he trusted Miss Tarbell, nor even so much as he trusted Baker; but he was obliged to admit that Steffens's bias against the business-man was rooted in solid fact. Corruption, McClure was now ready to ac-knowledge, came not only from those who bribed police to break the laws —the saloonkeepers, say, and the entrepreneurs of organized vice; it came also from those who bribed legislators to rewrite the laws—the supposedly respectable financiers, bankers, merchants, and industrialists. It was a bitter pill, this new knowledge; but McClure manfully gulped it down.

Steffens had changed, too. The cynical tone was gone; he now wrote with the urgency and zeal and moral indignation of a crusading reformer. Under each rock he had lifted he had found something that crawled and scuttled back into hiding; he had known beforehand it would be there; but now he wrote with a sense of shock, as though he had astonished himself at how loathsome that something was, and how myriad.

President Roosevelt had read Steffens's early articles, too; and while they may not have contributed to his education they may well have perturbed

* William M. Laffan was publisher of The New York Sun.

him. Two of the cities Steffens had roasted—Pittsburg and Philadelphia—were at the time Republican strongholds; in Minneapolis the rascally Ames had run both as Democrat and Republican; but in the Democratic cities—Chicago and St. Louis—Steffens had been able to report efforts by Democratic politicians to halt the corruption, and even in the case of Folk to introduce a man of presidential timber. Roosevelt invited McClure and Steffens to the White House in October, 1903. Whatever the President's secret calculations may have been, over the dinner-table he proposed a series of articles that would tell the stirring tale of how he, Roosevelt, was pluckily battling the contrary dragons of capital and labor. With mounting excitement the three men canvassed the idea until long after midnight; the President agreed to make available the necessary letters and documents; it would be the sensation of 1904. A couple of weeks later, however, McClure reluctantly vetoed the suggestion. It was more important that Steffens resume his series on corruption in government.

In truth, McClure was more than ever appalled by misgovernment—by the depravity of politics and politicians, by their inefficiency and wastefuness, by their criminality. He had always worried about the rate of crime in the United States; now he concluded he had found the reason for it. It was politics. The boss, the ring, the combine, the machine—call it what you will, it was the method by which saloonkeepers and their like came to rule vast cities. Why did they go into politics? For the purpose of breaking laws. What could logically be expected as a result? Disfranchisement of honest voters, lawlessness, a criminal and degraded police force; violence, robbery, murder; in short, a carnival of crime.

In January, 1904, McClure went to Brooklyn to debate before the Twentieth Century Club the role of the machine in American politics. For the occasion his opponent was the Hon. T. L. Woodruff, a manufacturer of typewriters who had served a term as lieutenant-governor of New York. The audience was large, enthusiastic, and eager to laugh at each of McClure's sallies. "There is no city in the United States," he told them, "where the government is honestly administered." He pulled from his pockets clippings from newspapers and read them to prove his point. "Now, this is the most unusual and extraordinary condition of affairs . . . unparalleled in human history. . . . This is the condition that the political machine has brought about in the United States. . . ." The Hon. Mr. Woodruff was so ill-advised as to claim there was nothing unique about the rate of crime in the United States. "There is," Woodruff said, "more crime in London per capita than in New York or Chicago." Moreover, he pleaded, American cities were relatively young, growing, dynamic; it was to be expected that there might be more violence in them. McClure deluged him with statistics. There were, he insisted, more American citizens murdered in a year than there were soldiers lost by Great Britain in the Boer War. The United States a young and growing country? But so was Canada; yet north of the border the homicide rate was less than one-tenth that of the United States. As for London having less crime than New York or Chicago, "Mr. Woodruff," McClure cried, exultantly, "you've run up against the wrong man this time." He pulled from his pockets more scribbled notes and, after examining them, announced: "London averages about twenty-four murders a year, with a population of six million. Last year Chicago had one hundred and fifty-six murders, with a population of two million." His audience applauded. "I am going to reflect over these things," said McClure, "and put them into a magazine article."

It was as well that McClure reflected on these things, for two weeks later Steffens submitted his article on Missouri, the first in the series of "Enemies of the Republic," and it was a bear-cat. In this piece he coined a lasting epithet for the politics of special privilege—"the System"—and he defined it, described in outraged detail how it worked, and summoned the citizenry everywhere to destroy it. It was, he wrote, "a system, a regularly established custom of the country, by which our political leaders are hired, by bribery, by the license to loot, and by quiet moral support, to conduct the government of city, state, and nation, not for the common good, but for the special interests of private business." Under this System the legislature of Missouri had been converted into so many mercenaries; a lieutenant-governor had resigned after confessing that he had taken bribes, and a United States Senator had been implicated. And who were the corrupters? The leading businessmen of Missouri, of course; chief among them a Colonel William Phelps, an official of the Missouri Pacific Railroad. Phelps had been intimate for a time with the United States Senator, the Hon. William Stone, but the two men quarreled. Stone called Phelps a lobbyist. (At the time the term had derogatory connotations.) "Oh," Phelps retorted, "we both suck eggs, Stone and I, but Stone, he hides the shells." Businessmen from outside the state were involved as well, officers of at least three concerns engaged in commerce from coast to coast—the American Sugar Refining Company, the American Book Company, and the Royal Baking Powder Company. The easiest corporate trail to follow back to the moment of corruption was that of the Royal Baking Powder Company, and Steffens followed it with spirit. He showed how the company's agents had bought and paid for a law that put its competitors out of business by stigmatizing the competitive product as poisonous because it contained alum. (The Royal Baking Powder Company had for years been manufacturing, under another name, a baking powder that contained alum.) Steffens even included an incisive sketch of the Royal's unfortunate president, William Ziegler.

The article was freighted with a certain concern for McClure. For one thing, Ziegler's Royal Baking Powder Company was a preferred advertiser which had been buying space on the back cover of McClure's Magazine for the past several months. More important, however, was the way in which Steffens had slashed away at all businessmen and clangorously called for an end to their System. As publisher, McClure was quite prepared to ignore the yawps of a single advertiser. (In fact, the Royal Baking Powder Company continued to buy space on the back cover of McClure's until April, 1906.) But when it came to a condemnation of the entire business community, McClure was, as editor, intransigent. He decreed that the facts must speak for themselves: they wrote their own editorial better than Steffens could. An instinctive conservative and an honest editor, McClure refused to condemn capitalism on account of a few rapacious capitalists.

This was the last time McClure would quarrel with Steffens face-to-face over one of his articles. Late in May, 1904, McClure relinquished active control of the magazine and withdrew to Europe. It was officially put about that McClure was once again in poor health. And so he was, in a way.

Steffens went on to Illinois to resume his study of how representative democracy had been transformed into an oligarchy representative of special interests. Here he lambasted the Republican state leadership for having connived to secure for the traction brigand, Charles T. Yerkes, a fifty-year monopoly over Chicago's street railways. Steffens drew scornful attention to the fact that one of these Republican plunderers, thoroughly discredited and retired from public life by an aroused electorate, had at once been appointed to a cushy sinecure, lucrative and influential, by the self-righteous Roosevelt, no less.

This must have sufficiently vexed the President, but what Steffens reported from Wisconsin made Roosevelt downright cross. For if in Missouri Steffens had found a man—Folk—who might conceivably become a threat for the presidency, in Wisconsin Steffens wholeheartedly supported a man— La Follette—who was already a definite threat to Roosevelt's leadership of the insurgent, progressive forces within the Republican party. La Follette had not only talked political decency and representative government, he had fought for his beliefs and acted upon them. Like Roosevelt, he had proclaimed that he "would favor equal and exact justice to each individual and to every interest, yielding neither to clamor on the one hand, nor being swerved from the straight course by any interest upon the other"; but, unlike Roosevelt, La Follette had lived up to his pledge. He had, to hear Steffens tell it, trounced the System. He had battled and vanquished not only the Democrats but also the old-line Republican regulars—the so-called Stalwarts, led by Henry C. Payne and John C. Spooner. And who was Payne? He was Roosevelt's Postmaster-General. And who was Spooner? He was a United States Senator, one of Roosevelt's trusted lieutenants, whose seat in the Senate, Steffens reported, had been bought for him from the Wisconsin legislature by two Republican businessmen for fifty-two thousand dollars. Roosevelt, when he read the article, sputtered with indignation. "This attack on [Payne] in McClure's Magazine by Steffens," Roosevelt wrote to his friend Henry Cabot Lodge, "was, I think, the immediate cause of breaking him down; and I am convinced that it is an infamously false attack."

Infamously false? This was just more Rooseveltian rhetoric. The attack on Payne was, at all events, accurate enough to discourage any suits for libel. Meantime Steffens had gone on to Rhode Island, which was at the time the personal fief of Nelson W. Aldrich, a United States Senator who was variously known as "the power behind the power behind the throne" and "the boss of the United States"—all this by virtue of his being chairman of the Senate's steering committee, a small junta that maintained a hammerlock on all legislative proposals, permitting only those to be enacted into law which would keep the System purring contentedly. Aldrich was, moreover, the father-in-law of young John D. Rockefeller, Jr., a circumstance that made him, in the public view, an ogre only a trifle less intolerable than John D. Rockefeller himself.

In his exile at Divonne-les-Bains, McClure read the first draft of Steffens's piece on Rhode Island and exploded in a letter to Phillips.

Oct 15 [1904]

My dear John
1st Steffens
    . . . Aldrich article is wrongly constructed & poorly worked out. It has so many faults that I cannot take them up. . . . [It should be] a study of Aldrich. How he secures power in R.I. how he then robs his state & then

how he works for Rockefeller & others in the Senate. . . . Steffens articles must never be rushed I was amazed & frightened that after our experience with [the articles on Illinois and Wisconsin], it was proposed to rush this in

I dont want any of his articles printed until I am perfectly satisfied. His articles are far & away the most terrible stuff we can handle. The material is necessarily full of dynamite & you know I have a kind of general fund of knowledge about the United States. Furthermore they should be read by different experienced editors, merely to get other points of view. There is simply a waste of time in having them "overhauled by all of us" in the office, & a confusion. You & I & Miss Tarbell & on important articles a few outsiders of great experience & wisdom.

SSM

The piece was revised as McClure had directed. Aldrich emerged as a pirate who had made his fortune in traction by ramming unconscionable laws (including a "perpetual franchise") through a servile Rhode Island legislature. When Aldrich needed money for an election campaign, he raised it in masterful fashion. As chairman of the Senate's finance committee, he wangled revisions of the tariff law worth three million dollars a year to the Sugar Trust—and then blandly pocketed contributions from the Sugar Trust toward his re-election. In this way he levied a tiny tax on every sugar-eating citizen of the United States and used the proceeds so that he might repeat the process at his leisure. Nothing was more useful than money in a Rhode Island election: virtually all the voters were quite frankly and openly for sale. Some came cheap, costing only a handful of cigars; some were dear— these were the higher-class citizens—and charged as much as thirty dollars a head. Victory in a general election went always to the long purse; that is, the Republican purse.

From Rhode Island, Steffens turned to New Jersey, which he described as "A Traitor State," a state so venal that, as it was said in a prefatory editorial note, "here we have found ourselves at times off soundings and the leadsman has reported no bottom" to the depths of commercial corruption. New Jersey merited these extraordinary charges; she had won them by accommodating her laws to fit whatever was desired by the financier, the industrialist, the big businessman. Had the Federal government and twenty-two states passed anti-trust laws? New Jersey announced to capitalists everywhere, as Steffens said: "Come to us. We'll let you do anything. You needn't stay here. Pay us for them, and we'll give you letters of marque to sail out into other states and do business as you please. The other states have made your business a crime; we'll license you to break their laws. We'll sell out the whole

United States to you, and cheap; and our courts are 'safe' and our legislature is 'liberal,' and our location is convenient." So many corporations accepted this cheery invitation that the state's revenue from the modest incorporation fee and annual franchise tax was well over two million dollars a year. When the Sugar Trust, incorporated in New Jersey, was threatened with an investigation in New York, its officers had only to load its books in a boat and hustle them over to New Jersey, where the amiable legislature promptly passed a law which said, "No action or proceeding shall be maintained in any court in this State against any stockholder, officer, or director of any domestic [New Jersey] corporation for the purpose of enforcing any personal liability . . . whether penal or contractual, if created by the statutes or laws of any other State." In short, break the laws of another state and you may come to New Jersey and be made innocent again. New Jersey, as Steffens wrote, was in the business of selling not only indulgences but also absolution. The Democrats had initiated the policy that sheltered the trusts; the Republicans perfected it. Matters got so bad that in 1904 the Republican mayor of Jersey City appealed to the Republican governor about the Republican legislature: ". . . The interests of the people are being betrayed. . . . This is a condition of affairs which is essentially corrupt, and which, if unchecked, means the virtual control of our State and our party by corporations. . . ."

The subject for the last article in Steffens's series was Ohio, another bastion of Republicanism. Steffens told of Mark Hanna (dead by that time) and how he boodled his way to political power, to the point where he could nominate a President; how he bribed his way to the United States Senate; and how he made common cause with George Cox, the massive, coarse saloonkeeper who was Republican boss of Cincinnati. It was a murderous portrait, Steffens's sketch of Hanna; nor was he any kinder to the Hon. Joseph B. Foraker, the Republican senior Senator from Ohio who betrayed the people's trust by accepting bribes from the Cincinnati traction company and the Standard Oil Company.

Steffens's method of studying Ohio was to counterpose Cincinnati, bossed by Cox, against Cleveland, led by the reform mayor, Tom Johnson. Cox was "boss of the worst-governed city in the United States," Johnson "the best mayor of the best-governed city in the United States." And Steffens closed with a set of ringing antitheses:

> The forces of evil, beaten in the city, hold the state. The forces of good, winning in Cleveland, fighting in Toledo, hopeful in Cincinnati, to hold

their own, must carry Ohio. Ohio—the whole state—has to make the choice, the choice we all have to make: Cleveland or Cincinnati. . . . It is the square deal, or bribes and brickbats; . . . Tom Johnson or George Cox, all over the United States.

Not, on the face of it, a funny paragraph; but Steffens himself was surely aware of the sardonic humor with which he had loaded it. For he had aligned Cleveland and Tom Johnson with the square deal, a slogan of course identified with President Roosevelt.* To range Roosevelt on the same side with Tom Johnson, however, was low comedy—and Steffens must have known it. In private, Roosevelt called Johnson a "ruffian"; he had never forgotten that Johnson was campaign manager for Henry George, the single-taxer, when George ran for mayor of New York and very nearly won. How could Roosevelt forget such a thing? He had himself run a poor third in that same election. Yet in the name of representative government Steffens, like a puppeteer, had plunked Roosevelt down alongside Johnson and, so to say, wound the President's arm around the ruffianly single-taxer's shoulders. How Roosevelt must have scowled when he read that paragraph!

One way and another, the two series of articles Steffens wrote for McClure's were remarkably influential. Incontestably they helped to sway elections. Steffens's article on Missouri helped Joseph Folk to win the Democratic nomination for governor and pushed him to victory at the polls. (As has already been noted, it was Folk's attorney-general who led off the prosecutions against the Standard Oil Company.) Steffens's article on Wisconsin was crucial to La Follette's successful campaign for re-election as governor. Indeed, immediately after his re-election La Follette wrote Steffens: "No one will ever measure up the full value of your share in this immediate result. It is very great. [Your article] was like the decision of a court of last resort." After the off-year election of 1905, when in state after state and city after city the boodlers and the grafters were routed, Steffens's mail was heavy with congratulations. There was a telegram from Cleveland:

OHIO RECOGNIZES YOUR MESSAGE, CINCINNATI RESPONDS TO IT, CLEVELAND VINDICATES IT, WE ALL APPRECIATE IT.

* What about that phrase, "the square deal"? In January, 1905, Steffens confided to Ray Stannard Baker that it was he, Steffens, who had coined the phrase and turned it into a slogan for the President; Roosevelt stole phrases from him right and left, Steffens assured Baker. We may assume that Steffens truly believed this yarn, for he repeated it circumstantially in his Autobiography. (In fact, Roosevelt used the phrase at least as early as August, 1901, long before the time Steffens claimed to have suggested it to him.)

And this was signed by Cleveland's mayor, Tom Johnson, and two of his ablest assistants, Newton D. Baker and Frederic C. Howe. There was also a letter from a relatively obscure professor of law at Columbia University: "I think you more than any other one man may take credit for the result of the elections wherever 'boss or no boss rule' was the issue. . . . I want to congratulate you on it." This letter was signed by Harlan F. Stone.

More than any other man? The same mail brought a letter to S.S. McClure: "To you, more than to any one individual, belongs much of the credit for this week's rout of the grafters. You were one of the first to grasp the real significance of the evil and to inaugurate its comprehensive exposure. . . ." But this letter scarcely counts, for after all it was written by Herbert Myrick, publisher of Good Housekeeping, and Farm and Home; and it is natural to expect one publisher to congratulate another.

And yet it may be helpful to consider the publisher's point of view. Latter-day students of the period are disposed to credit Steffens with enterprise and courage in writing his articles for McClure's.* Curiously, however, these students never reflect on the courage required of a publisher to print the articles. What Steffens had to say about the System was scarcely calculated to endear McClure's Magazine to the business community of its time. Advertising revenue, in those days, accounted for about two-thirds of a magazine's gross receipts. What matter how high circulation soared, if advertisers withheld their support? But there is no evidence that McClure ever tried to blunt the edge of Steffens's charges, nor that he concerned himself with anything save how well-written, how accurate, and how interesting were the articles he was to publish. Was this bravery? or foolhardiness? McClure would have answered that it was simply good editing.

This is not to disparage Steffens. Indeed, the effect of his articles is not to be measured by the results of a handful of elections won or lost by politicians thrice-forgotten. The final effect, one may venture, was far more pervasive. Steffens and his predecessor, Josiah Flynt, together with their several imitators of the muckraking period, taught the nation a salutary lesson: that a police force, so far from being an agency of law and order, is in fact too often a pack of armed knaves whose hands reach under the table for every kind of graft from one to one thousand dollars. This knowledge was to serve the citizenry well during the national scourge of Prohibition. All by himself Steffens essayed to teach the nation a second lesson, but

---

* See, for example, Louis Joughin's introduction to The Shame of the Cities, reprinted by Hill and Wang, New York, 1957.

this one has proved harder to learn. It is that there is no essential difference between one gang of politicians and another. For his time, Steffens taught the lesson well. It would appear that the lecture needs to be delivered as forcefully for each succeeding generation.

[xv]

The third of McClure's muckrakers, Ray Stannard Baker, enjoyed to an extraordinary degree President Roosevelt's confidence.

One day in October, 1905, McClure was prowling through the editorial offices, momentarily at a loose end. He looked into Bert Boyden's room and paused to chat. On Boyden's desk lay a big square envelope addressed to Baker; it was marked as having come from the White House. McClure picked it up and hefted it curiously. Boyden, alarmed, reached out to take it back, but S.S. brushed him off. "That's all right, Boyden," he said confidently. "I happen to know what this is. Baker sent proofs of his first article on the railroads to the President, for his comments. Let's see what Teddy had to say."

Boyden was in an agony of apprehension. "I don't think, sir, that—"

But S.S. was already slitting the envelope. Sure enough, it contained galley slips. The type-face, however, was unfamiliar.

"Why," said S.S. with quickened interest, "this isn't Baker's article after all! This is an advance proof of the President's Message to Congress!"

Boyden all but wrung his hands.

McClure sat down, settled into a comfortable position, and commenced to read. Boyden paced anxiously back and forth. He knew how erratic his chief was, how impulsive and capricious—what might he not do with this important state paper? Boyden's glance fell on the note from Roosevelt to Baker which had accompanied the galley slips; one phrase leaped out at him: "Of course I must ask you to keep it strictly confidential. . . ." Boyden winced. He had steeled himself to swear his chief to secrecy when McClure suddenly pitched the galley slips back on the desk. He wagged his head in disgust. "Boyden," he said, *"we* would *never* print *that!"* And to Boyden's vast relief he bounced out of the room.

Baker had won the President's admiration by the nature of his assignments and by the way in which he had discharged them. He began by writing about organized labor, ferreting out evidence of trade-union excesses in Chicago, New York, and San Francisco; later he reported and essayed to analyze the causes of a shocking increase in the number of lynchings; still later he turned to the railroads and, in a notable series, showed why the railroad magnates were the best-hated men in America. Superficially, Baker would seem to have been short-changed: Miss Tarbell had one theme, the trust; Steffens played variations on one theme, corruption in government; but here was Baker, apparently obliged to hop about from one subject to another like a flea in a kennel. Like the others, however, Baker had only one theme—that of lawlessness. Miss Tarbell, Steffens, Baker—each of them had for a compass the editorial McClure had written for the issue of January, 1903, and none of them ever strayed far off the point he had ordered them to hold. But the particular aspects of lawlessness that concerned Baker were just those that most agitated Roosevelt. And, to Roosevelt's delight, Baker was the sort of fair-minded journalist who could see both sides of a question. Indeed, Baker was so fair-minded that he could, while deprecating the rope-end result, even sympathize with both parties to a lynching-bee.

Baker was, moreover, backed up by his editor. When McClure withdrew to Europe in 1904 for personal reasons, he dispatched to Miss Tarbell some urgent instructions:

> June 22, 1904, Divonne-les-Bains
>
> My dear Miss Tarbell
>
> The struggle for the possession of absolute power which you find in your work among capitalists & Steffens finds among politicians & Baker finds among labor unions, is the age-long struggle & human freedom has been won only by continual and tremendous effort.*
>
> I hope that Baker will get the fundamental concept in his head. What all three of you want is law-abiding-ness as opposed to lawlessness. . . . The central idea of [Baker's] work is human freedom. Freedom—for the laborer and for mankind—involves the labor union & *the non-union laborer*. No body of men can be allowed absolute power, yet employers would have absolute power if there were no unions & unions on the other hand would have absolute power if there were no non-union laborers. Therefore the Open Shop is the central idea. The magazine believes in Unions, Trusts, large aggregations of laborers & of capital, but the tyranny & power of large aggregations must be checked by the free laborer & the free merchant. Elaborate the idea. . . . It is not advisory it is mandatory. I am right & I want this policy pursued. . . . Oh! I wish I were well!
>
> SSMcClure

---

* We must be charitable. As we will presently discover, McClure's mind was agitated by the tenderest of emotions and so at this time he could express himself only in regrettable banalities.

As an expression of economic theory, this had all the profundity of a dictum uttered by Theodore Roosevelt himself; indeed, McClure may well have picked it up in conversation with the President. As editorial counsel, however, it was wholly superfluous. Baker had already long since concluded that the closed shop was pernicious; indeed, he seemed often to suggest that unions were themselves a threat to the general welfare. The difficulty, as Baker saw it, lay in the firm contracts negotiated by strong unions and strong employers' associations. To be sure, the union members got their higher wages ("Many a teamster in Chicago," Baker reported with dismay, "now earns as much as $25 or $30 a week in winter weather"), but their employers simply raised the price of the commodity or the service and so passed the bill along to the public. Baker fancied he perceived here a conspiracy; legal, to be sure, but still a conspiracy. The public had wanted industrial peace and they had got it; now Baker was consternated to find that they also had got to pay for it.

But in Baker's view the true portent of doom was the situation in San Francisco. When he visited that lovely city late in 1903 he found there had been no strikes in the two years previous. Why? "The ancient master, the employer, has been hopelessly defeated and unionism reigns supreme." Wages were up so high that Baker hesitated to report his findings lest he be not believed. "Plasterers [are] paid eight dollars a day and lathers ten dollars a day for eight hours' work. The minimum wage of bricklayers is six dollars a day, of carpenters four dollars, of tilelayers five dollars, of hodcarriers—who are practically unskilled workmen—three dollars and a half." But—and here Baker wagged his head in perplexity—living was nevertheless cheaper in San Francisco than in any other big city in the country. If he had stopped there, Baker might have been forced to the distasteful conclusion that unions were, just possibly, of benefit to the community. So he hastened on, to reveal that the unions had entered upon such "extraordinary" activities as politics and that, even more appalling, an establishment might be picketed if its owner employed non-union workers.

In short, Baker's articles about the nascent organization of labor were naïve and shallow. Their only interest is that they spotlight the moment of our industrial growth when the wage-price spiral began climbing up, and that they show that sixty years of industrial history have taught precious little to employers, union leaders, politicians, or the general public.

When Baker turned to the problem of lynching, he showed himself to be even more naïve and shallow. He examined in detail the lynchings of three Negroes in the South and of one Negro in the North; he concluded that there was nothing special in the crime; it was merely another "symptom of lawlessness, of the failure of justice, of political corruption." Baker's failure to perceive that lynching is a crime of particular horror tainted his articles with a negative bigotry, and that was bad enough; but he was also capable of positive bigotry. "Nearly all the crimes committed by negroes," he wrote, "are marked with almost animal-like ferocity," and again, a Negro killer was a "black, stolid savage" who fled in "an animal-like panic." When the white man, heretofore "warm-hearted, home-loving," and God-fearing, undertakes to avenge a crime allegedly committed by the Negro, he "becomes as savage as the negro." Baker suggested that the Negro's crimes should be excused because "The negro does not reason," he is merely "imitative" of the white man. As for the remedy? "We, the people, are the government," Baker wrote; "we execute the law, and if we are too bad or too lazy to do our work properly, let us in all honesty take the blame—and not shoulder it on the irresponsible negro." This blandly exclusive view would seem to fall somewhat short of the democratic ideal.

Late in 1904, however, when Baker was assigned to dig into the way in which the railroads conducted their business, he found himself on surer ground. His six-part series, The Railroads on Trial, was a triumph of absorbing, sober, analytical journalism.

Once again it was McClure who was responsible for the assignment. When he was exiled to Europe like a naughty boy by his associates in June, 1904, S.S. had been ordered to rest and recuperate his energy, and most especially his moral energy, and he had addressed himself with diligence to this laudable goal. But his temperament, never suited to relaxation, betrayed him. He fretted. As he studied the successive numbers of his own magazine and those of his competitors he convinced himself that the longer he stayed abroad the worse grew his magazine and the better all others.

There was some evidence on which to base this shaky conclusion. For more than a year McClure's had dominated the magazine field, thanks to its carefully planned, carefully documented attacks on commercial and political corruption; but now other editors were exploiting his editorial acumen and mounting their own campaigns. Some of them McClure had himself assisted. For example, when Edward Bok of The Ladies' Home Journal planned a crusade against the manufacturers of patent medicines, he asked McClure to suggest a writer who was capable of conducting a patient, thorough, accurate investigation, since McClure had the reputation of being able to find such rare birds. McClure proposed Mark Sullivan, then a young-ster fresh out of Harvard Law School, who had attracted S.S.'s attention by writing an anonymous article for The Atlantic Monthly on politics in Penn-sylvania; and Bok had reason to be grateful, for Sullivan did a difficult job uncommonly well.

But other editors had come up with other features that McClure felt should properly have been published in McClure's. Here was young Ellery Sedgwick of Leslie's Magazine yapping at the railroads on account of their appalling record of accidents.* Here, even worse, was John O'Hara Cosgrave of Everybody's Magazine running sensational tales by Thomas Lawson of precisely how Wall Street had picked the pockets of trusting investors. Lawson, himself a somewhat gamy financial promoter, had teamed with Henry H. Rogers and other Standard Oil executives to rig a corner in cop-per; when he was double-crossed by his associates, Lawson had vengefully engaged to tell an insider's story of their duplicities, sparing no reputation including his own. McClure was irritated to find such an account appearing in Everybody's, and when he heard that Everybody's circulation was soaring up past that of McClure's, he booked passage on the next boat back to the United States.

For McClure to assign Baker, in November, 1904, to investigate the rail-roads involved no particular perspicacity; as it happened, however, the as-signment could not have been more shrewdly timed. Public dissatisfaction with the railroads had been building up a head of steam for more than a quarter-century; but gradually the public mood had changed until, late in 1904, it was one of bitter, explosive resentment. The change derived from the nature of the antagonist.

Railroads are, of course, common carriers. Having been chartered as such by the states, the railroads were—at least in theory—required to put a reasonable price on a given service and thereafter to charge every customer the same price for that service without discrimination. But the men who controlled the railroads conspicuously flouted these modest obligations. They fixed their rates, and especially their freight rates, quite arbitrarily and with

---

* Sedgwick angrily called the United States "The Land of Disasters," and the statistics bore him out. Ten thousand persons died in railroad accidents every year; another eighty thousand were seriously injured. Nor for some time did the railroads improve their standards of safety. In June, 1905, the Pennsylvania Railroad announced "the fastest train in the world," eighteen hours between New York and Chicago; four days later the eastbound train was wrecked. To meet the Pennsylvania's boast, the New York Central scheduled its Twentieth Century Limited; three days later a wreck on the Central snuffed out nineteen lives.

no apparent reference to logic or common sense. In the absence of any government regulation whatever, they simply charged as much as the traffic would bear. As a matter of course, the rates were infamously discriminatory, favoring the big shipper as against the small and the city as against the farm. By 1887 the pressure for governmental regulation of railroad rates was so insistent that the Congress was forced to enact a law establishing an Interstate Commerce Commission. This Commission was supposed to regulate rates and decree equity. For public consumption, all hands raised three cheers: once again democracy had been vindicated.

Then the railroad lawyers crept in. One by one the powers and functions of the Commission were scrutinized by the courts; one by one the powers were emasculated, the functions abolished. In 1897, only ten years after the I.C.C. had been created, the commissioners stated in their annual report: "Under the law as now interpreted, there is today and there can be no effective regulation of interstate carriers."

William Allen White, his tongue well in his cheek, was prepared to explain how this had come about. "It was," he wrote, "just as easy to see the railroad's side as it was to see the other side, so the mass of Federal decisions for years favored the railroads."

Commissioner Charles A. Prouty, by virtue of his sweaty, impotent engagement in the battle, was unable to achieve such an ironic detachment. "The railroads own many of our courts and other public bodies," Prouty told a Chicago newspaperman, late in 1904. "Not because they have of necessity bought them by the expenditure of money; they have a different way of doing things. They see to it that the right men, the men of friendly inclinations, are elected. If the Interstate Commerce Commission were worth buying, the railroads would try to buy it," the commissioner added sardonically. "The only reason they have not tried to purchase the Commission is that this body is valueless in its ability to correct railroad abuses."

McClure knew all this in a vague, general way, just as he knew that the railroads had for years handed out passes for free rides to politicians, newspaper editors, and anybody else whose friendship for the railroads might prove valuable. What now aroused his interest was the drumfire of opposition to the railroads that was rattling out on every hand. In Wisconsin, Governor La Follette had launched a well-publicized investigation of railroad income; as soon as his sleuths moved in, illegal payments of rebates by the railroads to their wealthier customers mysteriously dwindled. Since 1904 was an election year, Roosevelt had been out on the hustings, brandishing his fist and mouthing anti-railroad threats. Nor was the I.C.C. wholly ineffectual: hearings had been held in Chicago in June and again in October, 1904, to find out just how much the big butchers paid to ship their meat about the country; there was still another hearing in Denver, at which the cattlemen complained the butchers were unfairly influencing the rates for the shipment of cattle. Meantime the butchers—Armour, Swift, Morris, and others—who had entered into a combination known as the Beef Trust, were being pestered by still another Federal agency, the Bureau of Corporations, and the word was they might be indicted under the Sherman Anti-Trust Act.

In short, there was a mishmash of charge and counter-charge, precisely the kind of muddle into which McClure delighted to dispatch one of his writers, with orders that he should emerge with the truth.

Was it true that a mere ten men controlled the transportation system of the entire nation? Had these men conspired with certain individual shippers like Armour and Rockefeller so as to assist them in organizing their trusts? Had they, by bribery of various kinds, corrupted elections and prostituted legislators? Had they systematically conspired to break the laws of various states by discriminating in their rates on behalf of a favored few? Should Federal laws be drafted to outlaw inequities and encourage free competition?

For their part, the men who controlled the railroads insisted that such questions were raised only by radical agitators, that there was no need for any Federal legislation, and that any change would only bring disaster upon the country.

Where was the truth? McClure took Baker to Washington in December, 1904; they talked with Roosevelt at length. Baker agreed that he would try to dig out, if not the truth, at least some facts. So long as he dug for McClure's, he knew, he would be able to dig patiently and thoroughly. Almost a year would pass before his first article would be published.

By that time the Beef Trust was a notorious stink in the public nostrils. Three other journalists—Charles Edward Russell, Upton Sinclair, and Samuel Merwin—came by different paths to Packingtown in Chicago, were for different reasons outraged, and in different ways proceeded to horrify the reading public. They divided their labor as featly as if they had been slicing up the carcass of one of Armour's steers.

Russell was a good foot-in-the-door reporter who had worked first for Pulitzer as city editor of The New York World and later for Hearst as city editor of The Chicago American, but had retired to tinker with a theory which held that poetry and music were one art, not two, and which called for close study of the amphibrachic foot. He was suddenly wrenched from these cloistered pursuits when, almost by accident, he wandered in to listen to the testimony at the I.C.C. hearings in Chicago in October, 1904. Here the big Chicago butchers were being vengefully assailed by nearly every witness. Now Russell, better than most Chicago newspapermen, had measured the power of the Beef Trust. Not long before, when Chicago's water supply was running dry, he had assigned one of his reporters to dig up the streets, and he had proved that the meatpackers were stealing millions of gallons of water from the city. Yet what had happened? Precisely nothing. Russell was, in consequence, reluctant to get into a quarrel with such all-powerful opponents. Nevertheless, he was so shocked to hear how the Beef Trust had impoverished farmers and cattlemen alike that he engaged to write some articles for Everybody's Magazine. His series, "The Greatest Trust in the World," which began in February, 1905, focused on the economics of Pack-ingtown, on the multiplicity of ways in which a processor can fleece both producer and consumer. He reserved his greatest relish for a sprightly ex-position of how the meatpackers were responsible for the high price of food at a time when crops were plentiful. The packers responded by hiring private detectives to sniff about Russell's private life in the hope of turning up something scandalous they could use against him. (They found nothing.)

Upton Sinclair was an earnest, sensitive, impassioned young Socialist. When the stockyard workers went on strike in September, 1904, in protest against the vile conditions of their work and the even more hideous con-ditions of their life, Sinclair encouraged them with a message written for The Appeal to Reason, a Socialist weekly newspaper. The editor of this journal, a Populist named Julius Augustus Wayland, offered Sinclair five hundred dollars to write a novel about the stockyard workers. Sinclair lived for seven weeks back-of-the-yards, savoring the stink of the Beef Trust, a stink compounded of glue, guts, cruelty, and slaughter. It was, as he wrote later, "a strange, pungent odor . . . that you caught in whiffs; you could literally taste it, as well as smell it—you could take hold of it, almost, and examine it at your leisure. . . . It was an elemental odor, raw and crude; it was rich, almost rancid, sensual, and strong." Adjective for adjective, it was a stink to match the meat factories from which it came, and with this stink still clutching at his throat Sinclair wrote his most celebrated novel, The Jungle; and now he was no longer merely earnest, he was embattled.

He was most concerned with the plight of the workers—men, women, and even young children—who lived in squalor, were brutalized by their jobs, and were victimized at every turn by some money-hungry individual or corrupt institution of the society in which they lived. The Jungle was serialized in The Appeal to Reason, where it reached more than two hundred and fifty thousand readers. But as yet The Jungle was only a time-bomb. The fuse had been fired; the mechanism was ticking ominously; but not until it was published as a book would The Jungle explode and shock the nation into angry action.

Merwin, the third of the crusading journalists to visit Packingtown, was a novelist and short-story writer. Like Josiah Frank Willard, he was a nephew of Frances Willard (reform seems to have raged through that family like chicken-pox), but there the similarity ends, for Merwin was a round, jolly, gregarious man. For a time he worked for McClure as an editor in the book department. He quit when he was tendered a job as contributing editor of Success, a curious magazine that began as an organ of uplift and inspiration but around 1904 was remodeled into a kind of carbon-copy of McClure's. Merwin's series on the meatpackers stressed what would most alarm the housewife, to wit, the accusations that some of the meat processed in Packingtown was dirty, unsanitary, and came from diseased animals—and, moreover, that such meat was processed and sold quite deliberately.

Russell, then, accused the Beef Trust of cheating both producers and consumers; Sinclair arraigned the Beef Trust for oppressing its employees; Merwin indicted the Beef Trust for knowingly selling impure food. It remained for Baker to show, in six fact-packed articles, that the Beef Trust could never have come into existence had it not been for the men who controlled the railroads. J. Ogden Armour could have been forgiven for suspecting that the whole thing smacked of collusion.

In the fight for legislation to control railroad rates, there was never any doubt about the close collaboration of Roosevelt and Baker. The President kept Baker informed of his plans; he sought and accepted Baker's advice on the kind of law that should be drafted.* For their part, Baker's editors saw to it that his articles would be timed to appear when they would have the greatest possible impact on the Congress and on those who could bring pressure to bear on the Congress.

In his first piece, which was published in November, 1905, shortly before

---

* Baker wrote a modest account of his part in the passage of the Hepburn Act in his autobiography, American Chronicle, pp. 190–200.

the Congress convened, Baker jabbed at the maddening absurdities of the freight-rates charged by the railroads. To ship grain east from Omaha cost eleven and one-half cents a hundredweight; yet from Iowa, a couple of hundred miles closer to the eastern market, it cost as much as eighteen cents on the same railroad. Why? The Denver merchant had to pay more than twice as much for a shipment of goods from Boston as did the merchant in San Francisco, a thousand miles and two mountain ranges further west. Why? It cost no more to ship butter to New York City from Iowa than to ship it from a dairy in upper New York State. Why? A wire-fence factory in Hutchinson, Minnesota, had to be plucked up bodily and moved to Minneapolis. Why? In every case, the answer was the same: favoritism. The railroads favored one community over another, one commodity over another, and, what was least defensible, one shipper over another. Most favored of all were the most powerful: the men who had organized the trusts: Rockefeller in oil, Carnegie and later Morgan in steel, Armour in beef, Havemeyer in sugar, and the others. All these, as Baker reported, "used their immense shipments as a bludgeon to drive the railroad men to terms." It made no difference that such inequities were prohibited by the common law; in the absence of statutory law the railroad men scrambled to break promises, to conspire secretly and illegally, to comply with the wishes of their richest shippers—"all the features," as Baker reported with asperity, "of intense competition." Nor did he neglect to point out who paid for these evils in the end. "When the big shipper gets a low rate on oil or steel or beef," he wrote, "the small shippers and consumers who pay the small freights have to make it up. If oil is carried at cost, or below, by the railroads, as it often has been, then other patrons of the road must pay enough more to yield the great profits which the railroads earn. Therefore, you and I who buy food, shoes, hats, houses—against every item of which there stands a freight charge—have paid part toward the enormous fortunes of the trust promoters."

When the Fifty-ninth Congress assembled in December, they heard Roosevelt's message (to which Baker had contributed his ideas) asking for "some scheme to secure to . . . the government supervision and regulation of the rates charged by the railroads." By then the congressmen could also read Baker's second article, which dealt with the rebates paid by the railroads to favored customers.

Now the Congress had many times been assured that there was no such animal as a rebate. Following the scandal over rebates paid to the Standard

Oil Company, the Congress had itself outlawed the rebate in February, 1903, by passing the Elkins Act. Since that time an harmonious chorus had sweetly proclaimed that rebates, being criminal, were no longer imaginable. Quite recently a committee of the Senate had questioned the presidents of various railroads on the matter:

"Does your company pay rebates?"
"No, sir; rebates have disappeared."
"How about discriminations?"
"Discriminations are unknown, sir."

All well and good; but now here came Baker in McClure's Magazine, which had a circulation of more than four hundred thousand, to nail these statements as mendacious or, at the very least, as disingenuous. Baker agreed that rebates were criminal. "They are conspiracies to rob," he wrote, "as much so as if the general freight agent [of a railroad and his favored] shipper got together and agreed to hold up another shipper in the night and steal his pocket-book." But had the rebate disappeared? Baker cited data from Governor La Follette's investigation in Wisconsin to show that, in the first eight months after the Elkins Act became law, rebates paid by only *one* railroad in that *one* state averaged forty-four thousand six hundred and twenty-five dollars a month. (These payments dropped to six hundred and sixty-six dollars a month when La Follette's investigation began.) How enormous must have been the criminality of *all* railroads in *all* states Baker discreetly left to the reader's imagination.

Baker also touched on a few of the devices used to evade the Elkins Act: the sums entered on a railroad's books as chargeable to "the encouragement of new industries," some of which infant enterprises were more than thirty years old; the huge sums paid to a traffic agent, which he then split with the favored customer; the intentionally defective tariff rate calling for payment of "33 cents," later corrected for all ordinary customers to read "38 cents"; and so on. One Wisconsin concern, the Northern Grain Company, had won a monopoly in the grain-elevator business, thanks to rebates amounting to more than one hundred and fifty thousand dollars in five years. Much of this illicit income resulted from the fact that the company's entire sales force traveled about on passes—for free—while their competitors were obliged to pay full fares.*

---

* By a winsome coincidence, two weeks after this issue of McClure's reached the newsstands, the Pennsylvania, the New York Central, and one or two other railroads announced that they

Baker had now laid his foundation: the rates charged were capricious and were formulated by favoritism; rebates from those rates were granted to those who were strong enough or sly enough to demand them. It was time to single out the shipper who had profited most from these illegal practices. This was Armour & Company, the biggest of the Chicago butchers, a concern which had bought a full page to advertise its products in McClure's Magazine in every issue since the eleventh, back in April, 1894.

Armour had raised to a peak of piratical perfection the device of the private car, by which is meant any car operated but not owned by a railroad. In 1906 more than three hundred private freight-car companies owned one hundred and thirty thousand such cars, especially designed for all kinds of shipments—tank-cars for oil, coal-cars, stock-cars for cattle, refrigerator-cars for meat and fruit and vegetables, cars for beer and breakfast foods, for furniture and farm machinery, for lumber and lard, for eggs and stone, and for dozens of other commodities. (Since advertisements of their owners' wares were painted on the sides of these cars, the train of 1906 was, in Baker's apt phrase, "a flying bill-board.") But Armour was easily the largest single owner of private cars. Armour controlled a dozen or more private-car lines; of refrigerator-cars alone it owned more than fourteen thousand. Inasmuch as the railroads had rarely bothered to buy their own refrigerator-cars, they were obliged to lease them from Armour—for a rental of one cent a mile.

All this rolling-stock enabled Armour & Company to do an enormous freight business. Armour cars hauled cattle, grain, fruit, and meat products; Armour's weekly freight-bill for meat products alone was two hundred thousand dollars. Quite naturally, each of the twenty-some railroads running out of Chicago would do almost anything to get this business; quite naturally, in the circumstances, Armour could dictate terms at will.

Rebates? Armour could even force a railroad to sign contracts guaranteeing payment of rebates. Paul Morton, a vice-president of the Santa Fe, told the I.C.C. he had made such a contract, and added:

"Yes, sir; it is an illegal contract. It was illegal when we made it, and we knew that." *

Special handling? Trains hauling Armour's private cars had top priority; it was not unusual for a dispatcher to shunt a passenger train and let Ameri-

---

would issue no more free passes after January 1, 1906. The railroad pass was outlawed by Federal statute in June, 1906.

* Paul Morton was later appointed Secretary of the Navy by Roosevelt.

can citizens fume on a siding while an Armour meat train went highballing past. As a result, Armour realized an annual *net* profit of more than three million dollars just from the mileage fees the company was paid by the railroads.

Rates? In October, 1905, railroad presidents had one after another admitted to the I.C.C. that the packers dictated the rate for shipment of their own products.

But let the I.C.C. or even the Congress inquire how come and George Robbins, the president of Armour's private-car companies, would refuse to produce records or answer questions. "We deny that we are common carriers," said Robbins blandly, "or that we are engaged in interstate commerce."

Baker summed up the matter in one question: "Shall the railroad rate be fixed by Armour and the railroad men, both greedily interested parties who are mulcting the public, or shall it be fixed by the government?"

This third Baker article was an arsenal of arguments for the debate just beginning in Congress. A few days after it was published, Representative William P. Hepburn of Iowa introduced the railroad-rate bill that Roosevelt had asked for. The Hepburn bill extended the definition of transportation to include private-car lines, terminal railroads, and pipe-lines for oil; it empowered the I.C.C. to prescribe and regulate railroad bookkeeping and accounting practices; it forbade free passes; most important, it authorized the I.C.C. to fix a reasonable maximum rate. The bill passed the House by a vote of three hundred and forty-six to seven, but only after it had been amended to give the I.C.C. the absolute right to fix a definite rate—an even more drastic provision. (This was one of the changes that Baker had urged upon Roosevelt.) The bill then went to the Senate, where it was expected to die of asphyxiation. Senators, after all, were neither elected by nor responsive to the needs of the people.*

Meanwhile, Baker's article had had a few repercussions. Upton Sinclair, who would have been satisfied with nothing short of nationalization of the railroads, wrote to Baker: "You can beat even the rest of the folks on McClure's for getting together facts minus conclusions." McClure would have been tickled to read that note, for he had always held that conclusions should be drawn by the readers, but S. S. had something else on his mind. On

---

* The Seventeenth Amendment, calling for direct popular election of Senators, was not adopted until 1913. Before that they were elected by the state legislatures, a method that afforded an unexampled opportunity for plunder, boodle and graft. The Seventeenth Amendment was a dividend accruing to the efforts of the muckrakers.

January 19 he wrote to Baker: "I learned today that there is a very strong possibility of J. Ogden Armour suing us for some of our statements in the January number. It shows these fellows are touched. That makes me feel like going on stronger and deeper and taking up matters more thoroughly in regard to the Beef Trust, and of course we want to be very, very sure of our position. I hope that nothing will happen to hinder you in your work. Of course, we are quite ready and eager to publish the truth about any question and if we have made mistakes to rectify them. . . ." Five days later, S.S. had decided that, on the whole, the Beef Trust exasperated him. Damn their impudence for so much as talking about suing McClure's! "If they should sue us," he wrote Baker, "my notion is to have [Mark] Sullivan and Sam[uel Hopkins] Adams, probably, and you take up the whole Beef Trust question, and mass together all the material possible. . . ."

Baker resumed his assault on Armour & Company in the February number of McClure's, showing how it was extending its grasp beyond butchered animals and dressed meat to fruit and vegetables, and describing how Armour controlled to the point of monopoly the price of California oranges, Georgia peaches, North Carolina strawberries, melons from Indiana and Illinois, and vegetables from Arkansas and Missouri. Baker reported how the president of the Armour Car Lines, called to testify at a Senate hearing, had been asked: "What [rail]roads, then, reaching the South Atlantic states, the fruit regions, are exempt from the exclusive contracts with your company?" "Broadly speaking, none of them," Robbins had answered. "We handle all that business."

Once again there were repercussions. A man named Zuckerman, who had been confidential secretary to old P.D. Armour, the ruffian who founded the Beef Trust, let Baker know that he had shorthand notes of many letters dictated by Armour. Would Baker care to see the transcripts—for a price? This news sent McClure into transports of joy. Miss Tarbell, when she was writing her History of the Standard Oil Company, had been blessed with the same good luck: an office boy had sent her some torn scraps salvaged from a waste-basket which, when put together, formed irrevocable proof of Standard Oil's fraudulence. Baker should at once send to see whether the Zuckerman letters were worth buying.

February 20, 1906

My dear Baker:—

I regard those letters in relation to Armour—that is, the ones in the hands of Zuckerman—as of the very highest importance. I hope that you

will get them into the April number or into your own article on Armour.
I am sailing today. I shall be back in three or four weeks.

Very truly yours,
SSMcClure

After McClure had left the office, the desk editor, John Siddall, scrawled
an additional note to Baker:

> . . . Armour & Co have just cancelled their "ad" contract. To be ac-
> curate—C.P. Brady cancelled it because Armour's "ad" representative
> very evidently wanted it cancelled.

With S.S. in Europe, his associates decided that to use the Zuckerman letters would be dirty pool. (It seems a curious decision: they had had no such
compunctions about the documents sent them by the office boy at the Standard Oil Company; on the contrary, Miss Tarbell had been lavish in her
praise of the boy's honest conscience.) At all events, even if the letters had
been bought and published, they would in all likelihood have been ignored.
For suddenly the Beef Trust had come under attack from another quarter,
and such was the hullabaloo that even the debate over the Hepburn bill
was for a time forgotten.

The sensation of the hour was Sinclair's novel, The Jungle, now published
as a book and now eagerly being read all over the country. Sinclair was
himself somewhat disconcerted by the swift celebrity of his novel. He made
a wry comment: "I aimed at the public's heart and by accident I hit it in
the stomach." It was true: Sinclair had been aroused by the lot of the
workers, but while his readers couldn't have cared less about the workers,
they cared passionately about the product. And according to Sinclair, the
Beef Trust's product left something to be desired. Pork was quite possibly
tubercular; lard was made from hogs that had died of cholera; potted chicken
was in fact "tripe, the fat of pork, beef suet, hearts of beef, and waste-ends
of veal"; what was sold as lamb or mutton was in fact goat; the meat that
was to be canned was scraped off a filthy floor; as for the hams, "a man
could run his hands over these piles of meat and sweep off handfuls of the
dried dung of rats"; the rats being a constant nuisance, poisoned bread was
set out for them, "and then rats, bread, and meat would go into the hoppers
together" to make sausage; occasionally an unfortunate workman would
tumble into a vat, to be overlooked for days, till all but his bones "had gone
out to the world as Durham's Pure Leaf Lard."

Well!

The Jungle was an instantaneous best seller, both here and abroad, and its effect on its readers was powerful. As Finley Peter Dunne's Mr. Dooley groaned:

> Dear, oh dear, I haven't been able to eat annything more nourishin' thin a cucumber in a week. . . . How did it all come about? A young fellow wrote a book. Th' divvle take him f'r writin' it. Hogan says it's a grand book. It's wan iv th' gr-reatest books he iver r-read. It almost made him commit suicide. The hero got a fancy job poling food products out iv a catch-basin, an' was promoted to scrapin' pure leaf lard off th' flure iv th' glue facthry. . . . Ye'll see be this that 'tis a sweetly sintimintal little volume, to be r-read durin' Lent. I see be th' publishers' announcements that 'tis th' gr-reatest lithry hog-killin' in a peryod iv gin'ral lithry culture. If ye want to rayjooce ye'er butcher's bills, buy The Jungle. . . .

The tide of public anxiety and anger now reached to Washington and began lapping at the portico of the White House. The President was obliged to do something. He directed the Secretary of Agriculture to investigate affairs in Packingtown; before long, when he found Sinclair's allegations were backed up by three articles to be published in The World's Work, a magazine owned by Doubleday, Page & Company, the President sighed and appointed an independent commission to probe into Packingtown even more forthrightly.

As it happened, the indignant clamor touched off by publication of The Jungle aroused the aggrieved partisans of still another public issue and incited them to redouble their efforts. These were the advocates of a Pure Food and Drug Law.

The fight for pure food, unadulterated food, food that had not been treated with noxious chemical preservatives, dyes, and deodorants, food that was food and not a dubious, short-weight, prettified and packaged substitute, had been waged for two decades or more, since the time the first processor poked his commercial wedge between farmer and eater. The most intransigent fighter for pure food was Doctor Harvey W. Wiley, the chief chemist of the Department of Agriculture, a crusader by temperament and a proselytizer by conviction. In the course of his campaign, he had enlisted the powerful support of the National Consumers' League and the General Federation of Women's Clubs—in short, he had waked that sleeping giantess, the housewife.

The trouble with food in the early years of the century was that the processors could find chemists who were not so scrupulous as Wiley. Such chemists could take what was stale and rancid, even what was downright rotten, and trick it out so that it could be sold to an innocent customer as fresh and wholesome. The unwary customer would of course be buying a great many things he never bargained for. One indignant analyst reported that, by eating a typical and likely diet, "the unconscious and unwitting patient gets forty doses of chemicals and colors a day" along with his food.*

More and more citizens began to reflect that, if they were to be fed formaldehyde and borax with their milk, saltpeter with their corned beef and cabbage, alum with their bread, coal-tar dye and sulphurous acid with their butter, methyl alcohol with their lemon ice cream, and charcoal, bark, slate, and date-pits with their coffee, they would at least like to know about it first.

As with food, so with medicine. There was no restriction on the sale of a medicine containing cocaine, opium, or such opiates as morphine and laudanum, and no law required a bottle to be labeled so that the purchaser might know what he was buying. In the circumstances, aches and pains could and did lead to drug addiction, and the patent-medicine manufacturer had a guaranteed sale in a predictably expanding market. No wonder the traffic was immense; no wonder sales amounted, in 1900, to nearly sixty million dollars in old-fashioned money; no wonder that here and there a baby died.

Patent medicines were, moreover, advertised as cures for everything from abscesses, acidosis, and acne to yaws, yellow fever and herpes zoster. And they were advertised everywhere. There was no escaping the testimonial letters. No business bought more space in magazines and newspapers. Does your baby cry? Feed it Mrs. Winslow's Soothing Syrup—so long as you don't know that the syrup contains morphine, why should you fret? New York debutantes are never without their Pe-ru-na to "safeguard against catarrhal ills"—why should you be? And why should you care that Pe-ru-na is only a slug of eighty-proof alcohol to which has been added a pleasantly medicinal flavoring?

Since the patent-medicine harpies claimed most often to be able to "cure" dysmenorrhea, it was logical that the campaign against them should have been launched by Edward Bok of The Ladies' Home Journal. Bok began

* Mark Sullivan, who was himself honorably involved in the fight, devoted Chapter 27 of his *Our Times*, Volume II, to a most diverting account of The Crusade for Pure Food.

with a stupid blunder: he charged that a certain patent medicine was sixteen per cent morphine. He was wrong; he was sued for libel; and so, as has already been noted, he belatedly took McClure's advice and hired Mark Sullivan to make a proper investigation. Before long Sullivan turned up some damning facts. He showed that the patent-medicine manufacturers had managed to get the publishers of thousands of newspapers to sign advertising contracts into which two remarkable clauses had been inserted. The first clause read:

> It is hereby agreed that should your state, or the United States government, pass any law that would interfere with or restrict the sale of proprietary medicines, this contract shall become void.

In the event this clause did not sufficiently alert a newspaper editor to oppose any bill regulating patent medicines, the second clause surely would:

> It is agreed that the advertiser may cancel this contract . . . in case any matter . . . detrimental to the advertiser's interests is permitted to appear in the reading columns or elsewhere in the paper.

All this Sullivan tucked into a long article that showed how cravenly the newspapers had lobbied on behalf of patent medicines in Washington and in every state legislature. The piece was too long for The Ladies' Home Journal, but Bok wanted to get it printed, so he showed it to Norman Hapgood, the editor of Collier's. Hapgood was very favorably impressed. He bought the article and he sought, as well, to hire its author, for he perceived that here were the possibilities for an extended crusade. But Sullivan had to turn the offer down. Unhappily he confessed that he had just gone to work for McClure's; he felt that he should at least finish what he had already been assigned to do before he quit. Hapgood agreed.

Relations between Collier's and McClure's, however, were on the friendliest possible footing. Since the one was a weekly and the other a monthly, their publishers did not consider that they were competitors; indeed, at this time they even shared the expenses of a London office. There were other ways in which McClure and young Robert Collier could scratch each other's back. Collier had under exclusive contract at least two illustrators—Jessie Willcox Smith and Maxfield Parrish—whose drawings McClure coveted. For his part, McClure had trained a staff of journalists to write the kind of careful, documented, yet lively prose that Norman Hapgood knew would be needed for any series on the evils of patent medicines. As it might be between the New York Yankees and the Los Angeles Dodgers, a trade was arranged. All at once drawings by Smith and Parrish began appearing in McClure's. And Samuel Hopkins Adams went on Collier's payroll to write his devastating series, The Great American Fraud, in which he carved the patent-medicine manufacturers to bits.

Adams series, which began in October, 1905, had an impressive impact. The reform he urged was modest and reasonable to a fault: it was merely that the label on the bottle should truthfully describe the contents. The patent-medicine fakers howled.

And now Roosevelt, badgered on the one hand by the pure-food partisans and chivvied on the other by the foes of poisonous patent medicines, was forced to bestir himself. The master of hammer-and-tongs political invective inserted into his message to Congress three bald, bare, blank sentences.

> I recommend that a law be enacted to regulate interstate commerce in misbranded and adulterated foods, drinks, and drugs. Such law would protect legitimate manufacture and commerce, and would tend to secure the health and welfare of the consuming public. Traffic in foodstuffs which have been debased or adulterated so as to injure health or to deceive purchasers should be forbidden.

A few days later, in response to this pallid invitation, Senator Weldon B. Heyburn of Idaho reintroduced his Pure Food bill as he had done for three years past, but without any hope that any action would be taken on it. The House had twice approved it; but in the Senate, dominated by Republican spokesmen for the trusts and utterly controlled by Nelson Aldrich (who was, among many other things, a wholesale grocer), the bill had never even been permitted to come to a vote. Surely it would be suffocated again.

But Norman Hapgood of Collier's had determined otherwise; he kept on printing Adams's trenchant articles. And Edward Bok had determined otherwise; in the February issue of The Ladies' Home Journal he printed a copy of the Heyburn bill and urged his readers to bring pressure directly on their congressmen in both Houses. And all at once here, discreetly entering the lists without benefit of fanfare, came the American Medical Association.

In 1906 the members of the medical profession may not have known much, speaking relatively, about therapeutics, but they needed lessons from no man in economics. They took a lively interest in the sixty million dollars that was annually spent on phony patent medicines; that handsome sum, they felt, were far more wisely spent on doctor's bills. Doctor Charles A. L.

Reed, the chairman of the A.M.A.'s legislative council, spoke forcefully to Senator Aldrich, and in back of him, as he spoke, loomed the shadow of one hundred and thirty-five thousand physicians firmly organized into two thousand county medical associations and each in daily contact with a dozen or more patients. This pressure, coupled with that of the popular magazines, was enough. Aldrich buckled. Late in February the bill passed the Senate and was sent to the House.

In the House the bill was received tenderly and tucked away in committee. Those interested were assured that the bill was far too controversial to be permitted on the floor of the House. Lobbyists for the Wholesale Liquor Dealers' Association, for the Proprietary Association, and for the wholesale grocers and food processors smiled, shook hands all around, and left Washington for their homes.

And then, in their tens of thousands, those who had read The Jungle began to kick up a fuss. As Senator Albert Beveridge would later recall, "Public feeling had become intense."

President Roosevelt's temper was frayed by now and wearing dangerously thin. Whatever he did or told somebody else to do he deemed to be sound and prudent, whether he had assumed the posture of statesman, politician, national scold, literary critic, hunter of the lesser fauna, football fan, or birdwatcher. But when others essayed something without first consulting him and winning his approval, the result was likely to be of dubious value. All these articles in the popular magazines were a case in point.

The articles were accurate enough. What Miss Tarbell had reported about the Oil Trust, what Steffens had reported about graft in politics, what Russell had reported about the Beef Trust, what Baker was reporting about the railroads, what Adams and Sullivan had reported about the patent-medicine manufacturers—it was all true, too true. Even what Sinclair had written about Packingtown: he had chosen to write it as fiction, but Roosevelt's own special investigators had already told him enough to convince him that the allegations in The Jungle were, if anything, understated.

The articles were well enough written. If Roosevelt had any doubts on that score, here was the March 22 issue of The Independent, a respected and conservative weekly magazine, in which a critic hailed the literature of exposure as art. This literature, he wrote, "has taken the tale of facts from the year books and the official reports, from the statutes and the decisions, and from unwilling witnesses before investigating committees, and has wrought them into narratives that stir the blood. Its writers have seen in the dead materials that which only the imaginative insight ever sees—their significance, their relation to life, their potential striking force."

In short, these articles constituted a devastating report on the State of the Union, so graphic and so telling that they had wrested from the President his political leadership. He was no longer summoning, he was being dragged. This was what Roosevelt found intolerable in the literature of exposure. In March, 1906, the only important questions remaining before the Fifty-ninth Congress were: When would they pass the Railroad Rate bill, the Pure Food and Drug bill, and a Meat Inspection amendment, and in what form? For pass them they must. That verdict had already been reached by the people, led not so much by the President as by the popular magazines.

Also in March, as if to twist the knife in the wound, there began to appear in The Cosmopolitan a series of articles by David Graham Phillips entitled "The Treason of the Senate." Phillips attacked, one after another, the Senators who were blocking the bills that Roosevelt had professed he advocated, thereby robbing Roosevelt of all his future political thunder. Could a politician be worse served? To make matters worse, if possible, The Cosmopolitan had not long before become the property of the publisher whom Roosevelt most detested—William Randolph Hearst.

As soon thereafter as he decently could, Roosevelt lashed out at what he called the muckrakers, without regard for his former allies.

On June 20 President Roosevelt signed the Pure Food and Drug Act. On June 30 he signed the Meat Inspection amendment and the Railroad Rate Act. "Yes, it has been a great session," he wrote to a friend three days later, in a letter in which he used the pronoun "I" ten times in ten sentences. Walter Hines Page, the editor of The World's Work, agreed. It was, he said, "the most loquacious, one of the most industrious, and at times one of the most exciting sessions of recent years. A stimulating breeze was blowing over the national government all through the session."

The stimulating breeze was puffed up by the muckrakers.

[XVI]

At the outset of the muckraking period, McClure was forty-five years old and once again there was a spark in his eye and a snap to his step. He was his old ebullient self.

The muckraking articles in McClure's, absorbing as they were for contemporary readers and as they have proved to be for historians, did not
wholly preoccupy their volatile editor. As has already been noted, S.S. was
delighted at the way those articles were received, but they were only a part
of what he was after. To make a good magazine, there were many other
parts he had to assemble. In 1903, however, he was once again able to tackle
the task with zest.

The historians would have it that S.S. was delighted because the muckraking articles had sent the circulation of McClure's "mounting rapidly,"
because "muckraking . . . was the most successful of the circulation-building
devices" he could use, because the articles "made McClure's circulation
soar." * There is one difficulty with this otherwise reasonable hypothesis:
the circulation of McClure's did not mount rapidly, neither did it soar.
Here are the figures for average net monthly circulation:

1898	349,623
1899	361,912
1900	364,674
1901	360,259
1902	364,629
1903	371,398
1904	369,677
1905	375,000
1906	414,000

It is clear that the articles by Miss Tarbell, Steffens, and Baker had no
sensational effect on circulation. The magazine had done well during the
Spanish-American War; in 1901, with McClure in Europe much of the
time, it had suffered; the muckraking articles began to appear regularly in
1903, but circulation was actually down in 1904; the gains in the next two

* These brief quotations are, in order, from Harold U. Faulkner, The Quest for Social Justice,
p. 113; Richard Hofstadter, The Age of Reform, p. 191; and Arthur and Lila Weinberg, The
Muckrakers, p. 2. The myth that the muckraking articles were like a shot of adrenalin to
the circulation of McClure's is one of the most persistent in the literature dealing with muckraking.

The most profitable year for McClure's was 1900. (At the end of that year, Albert Brady
died.) Throughout this period, McClure's income from advertising was more than that of
any other magazine, but circulation lagged behind Munsey's and even Everybody's.

years must be chiefly attributed to an intensive (and expensive) drive for subscriptions amongst rural readers. Such a campaign was, indeed, long overdue; until 1906, the peak year for subscriptions was 1900. The fact that circulation was not soaring evidently vexed McClure and his associates, for after 1904 they no longer released sworn circulation figures which had been attested by a certified public accountant. In an advertisement they claimed an average monthly circulation for 1906 of 457,000, and they may have told the truth, but the editors of Ayer's Directory sliced their claim.

No, it was not money that made McClure go. "I cannot think he ever gave money a thought," said Curtis Brady, the advertising manager of Mc-Clure's, "except that more income would make it possible for him to spend more money for features and fiction for the magazine." What had revived S.S.'s spirits was that once again he was busy, and important, and admired. This was the tonic he had needed, the elixir his doctors had been unable to prescribe. He had just moved his family into a big handsome house at Ardsley, overlooking the Hudson River, a house originally built by Cyrus Field, the man responsible for the first transatlantic cable. He had moved the offices of the magazine to more commodious quarters at 44–60 East Twenty-third Street, just south of Madison Square. Rumor said that he was planning a new magazine, a weekly. When he walked into the Holland House or the Waldorf-Astoria for lunch, people turned to watch him and the pretty young woman on his arm. Who was she? Florence Wilkinson? Or some other aspiring young writer? Whoever she was, she would be eyed enviously. McClure had a genius for discovering talent! Not an author but wanted to have his stuff published in McClure's. The President himself had read the issue of January, 1903, sent a flattering comment, and invited Mc-Clure to the White House. Once again life was an exhilarating experience, and forgotten was the little boy who, in his bitter loneliness, had cried himself to sleep in his corner of a cellar back in Valparaiso, thirty-five years before.

The question now was what other parts could McClure find to fit together, to make a good magazine? What else, besides corruption, was on the public mind?

For one thing, there was what had come to be called, by 1902 or 1903, the Negro problem. Theodore Roosevelt had invited the sedative Negro educator, Booker T. Washington, to lunch at the White House, and this mild gesture had provoked pathological hysteria below the Mason-Dixon line, with Senator Benjamin R. (Pitchfork Ben) Tillman of South Carolina strutting forward, front and center stage, in the role of Grand Exalted Hobgoblin. "Entertaining that nigger" would, Tillman croaked, "necessitate our killing a thousand niggers in the South before they will learn their place again." McClure, noting the frenzy, contrived a national debate. He got Carl Schurz to write a paper, "Can the South Solve Its Negro Problem?" To answer, he got Thomas Nelson Page to write three papers entitled "The Negro: The Southerner's Problem." Schurz spoke with authority, for he had been directed by President Andrew Johnson to study the condition of the Negro in five states of the Deep South in the years just after the Civil War, and he had thereafter been concerned, as an intransigent democrat, with the condition of the Negro in every state. He appealed, as have so many ever since, to the "enlightened and high-minded men and women" of the South to "reach the only solution that will stand in accord with the fundamental principles of democratic government," a solution based on "the slow process of propitiating public sentiment" rather than on legislation. Page, the son of a slave-owning Virginia family and a novelist of a certain reputation, was totally unreconstructed. There had been, he insisted, no Negro problem before, during, or even for a few years after the Civil War; whatever problem existed had been incited by Northerners and could be solved only by Southerners.

It seems incredible, but this debate, which was launched in the pages of McClure's in January, 1904, marked the first open discussion of the Negro problem in any national forum for more than a generation. "McClure," as Louis Filler wrote, "opened the liberal and even the conservative organs" to a rational inquiry into the problem. "The demand for information was, in fact, so stimulated," Professor Filler added, "that almost every periodical was constrained to admit to its pages articles on the Negro." * (It was in response to this demand that McClure dispatched Ray Stannard Baker to the South, to report the facts of a lynching.)

Provocative ideas were necessary, but even more S.S. wanted to find young writers with fresh ways of looking at the world around them. In December, 1902, he was handed a manuscript that described, without a single lapse into sentimentality, the cheerless life of the New York children who sold newspapers. It appeared that these young toughs ate little, seldom, and irregularly; knew tuberculosis more intimately than any doctor; slept in doorways; added to their meager incomes by running errands for pimps and prostitutes; were paid for these services not in cash but in kind, as a result of which they contracted syphilis and gonorrhea; froze when the temperature dropped

* Filler's book, Crusaders for American Liberalism (Harcourt, Brace; 1939), is the most extensive and in many ways the most trustworthy study of the muckraking movement.

and starved when they could sell few papers; were nurtured in hardship and matured in crime; in short, were being superbly trained as troops for the gang wars of the Prohibition era. The article, which was in effect a refreshing critique of Horatio Alger's entire oeuvre, had been written by the son of a well-to-do Chicago family who, upon graduation from Princeton, had gone to work for a settlement house in the lower East Side of New York. Obviously he knew his subject inside-out. His name was Ernest Poole, and the manuscript was his first professional attempt to dress his convictions in prose. McClure, having read the article rapidly, at once wrote to Poole in Chicago, where he had gone for Christmas, enclosing a check (which made, Poole said later, a pleasant Christmas present) and inviting him to return to New York to discuss changes. Poole found that all references to venereal disease had been cut from his piece. He protested. The fact that children were being so infected would have, he pointed out, a powerful impact in the campaign against child labor. "All right," McClure retorted. "Now I'll tell you what I'll do. Imagine yourself in a room with six grown-ups and six little girls. Tell this part of your story so that the grown-ups will get it, but the six little girls will not, and then I'll print it." A euphemism was invented, and the article was published in April, 1903—marking the second time that a magazine of national circulation had spoken out against child labor. (The first, also in McClure's, was a piece on the children who worked in the coal mines; it was published in February, 1903.)

There were other young writers whose work first appeared in McClure's: Rex Beach, Arthur Train, James Hopper, Inez Haynes Gillmore, and others; and, just to prove that if you print the work of enough new writers you will sooner or later come up with a first-rate talent, there was Willa Cather.

Miss Cather was then twenty-seven years old, living in Pittsburg with friends, earning a living as a school-teacher. She must have been pleasantly stirred to have McClure come bouncing in upon the tranquil round of her days. He stayed for dinner. As was his wont, he did most of the talking, an exhilarating account of affairs in the great world outside, studded with the names of well-known literary figures; a coruscating monologue that caught his listeners up and tossed them around like leaves in a whirlwind. She had some poems to show him, and some stories; she brought them out hesitantly. He took them all away with him. He would publish a volume of the poems and another of the stories. A few of the stories he would also publish in the magazine. She would, he vowed, hear from him again, and soon.

But for the moment it was enough for McClure that he was once again busy doing what he loved to do, successful at his job, and admired by those who surrounded him.

Alice Hegan Rice admired him. For a young writer, Mrs. Rice was singularly fortunate, in the spring of 1903: not just one but two of her novels, Mrs. Wiggs of the Cabbage Patch and Lovey Mary, were simultaneously on the best-seller lists; she was, moreover, a recent and happy bride. Her husband, Cale Young Rice, wrote high-minded verse dramas destined, alas, for only the most exiguous of sales. Late in May this couple traveled from Louisville to New York on a belated honeymoon. McClure and Phillips took them to lunch.

It appeared that Rice was looking for a publisher. McClure promptly undertook to sponsor his latest poetic play (while Phillips, no doubt, was doing some mental arithmetic, in red ink). It appeared, further, that neither of the Rices had an English publisher. McClure found this incredible. Only one solution—they must come with him to Europe—leaving the next day—arrange to get them a stateroom at once—the Alps! Far better than New York for a honeymoon—he would take them on a walking tour—Miss Tarbell was coming, too—meantime, he would find them an English publisher—no arguments—they could buy any clothes they needed when they got there —hang the expenses—he would take care of that, too—just leave everything to him.

And so, before they could catch their breath, the Rices found themselves on a steamer bound for Europe. Also on board were Hattie and S.S. and their son Robbie, then a boy of fifteen; in the party, as well, was Florence Wilkinson, the tall, handsome, dark-haired young woman whose poems McClure had published in his magazine. Alice Hegan Rice later recalled "starry nights on the boat deck when we lay in steamer chairs and listened by the hour to Mr. McClure's fascinating reminiscences. . . . He held us enthralled." Hattie was in poor health and stayed much in her stateroom; but Miss Wilkinson lay in one of those steamer chairs, her dark eyes fixed on McClure.*

Hattie went on to shop in Paris; the rest of the party stopped first in

* The quotation is from Mrs. Rice's memoir, The Inky Way. Even as a bride on her honeymoon, Mrs. Rice remained a professional writer: she used S.S.'s stories of his boyhood in Ireland and his early struggles in America as the basis for her next novel, Sandy, which was a best seller in 1905.

London. Here Cale Rice was deeply vexed: he had wanted to travel economically, but he found that McClure had reserved for them the costliest suite at the most fashionable hotel. His anger turned to perplexity when he was presented with his first bill. It was for less than £1 a day. McClure, he learned, had instructed the hotel manager that the Rices were "distinguished young authors" who were to be given the best for nothing.

Having found the Rices an English publisher, and having helped Miss Wilkinson peddle some of her poems and stories to an English editor, McClure whisked his party off to Divonne-les-Bains, near Geneva, where they were to be Hattie's guests for two or three weeks. Late in July McClure took the Rices and Miss Wilkinson to Chamonix. Their rooms at the Hôtel de Paris had been arranged according to his wishes: the Rices on the second floor, looking out on Mont Blanc, and Miss Wilkinson and he on the third floor, in single rooms also looking out on Mont Blanc. To see the sun rise on Mont Blanc was one of McClure's special pleasures.

Now Miss Wilkinson made her farewells and went south to Italy. At Zermatt, the town under the Matterhorn, the others were to meet Miss Tarbell; thus reconstituted, the quartet commenced an erratic tour through the Alps: to Luzern, to Zurich, to Chur, to Davos Platz and San Moritz, part of the way by train, part by boat, and part on foot. If night caught them on the road, S.S. would confidently bustle up to a house, bargain for a night's lodging, jolly the hausfrau into letting him take over in the kitchen, and cook a supper for everybody in sight. "He went through life like a tornado, carrying everything in his wake," Mrs. Rice recalled later. In San Moritz, on a sunny August afternoon, S.S. stood watching the throngs of fashionable strollers. Behind him a mountain slope; before him a lake. All at once he seized Rice's arm. "Come on, Cale," he cried; "let's climb up that hill and roll down!" And while Miss Tarbell and Mrs. Rice watched, with expressions in which amusement, dismay, and disapproval were nicely mixed, the two men clambered up and then came careening down the hillside, scandalizing the bourgeois, and fetching up almost under the wheels of the passing carriages.

What was it about him? Was it only an unquenchable exuberance that made everything he did seem a little bit bigger than life-size? Or was there some flaw, some excess that might give cause for alarm? Miss Tarbell, for one, was beginning to wonder how far his eccentricities could be excused on the grounds of the genius which she ungrudgingly accorded him.

Miss Tarbell sailed home with the McClures. The twentieth anniversary of their wedding fell while they were at sea. To mark the occasion S.S. presented Hattie with a magnificent marquise ring in which had been set three large diamonds and eighteen smaller ones. The captain sent to their table (at breakfast, indeed) a cake decorated with flags and surrounded by twenty candles; Hattie was quite pleasantly flustered.

For some time S.S. had been dreaming of an article to deal with the (as he believed) rapid and alarming increase of violent lawlessness, and especially murder, in the United States. He saw it as the capstone of the magazine's campaign against commercial and political corruption; constantly he urged his associates to help him by gathering the facts. His associates, except for Baker, disparaged the idea. There were no facts, they argued, no reliable statistics but only conjectures. But S.S. stubbornly persisted.

In October, 1903, when S.S. mentioned this pet project of his at the White House, Roosevelt was delighted. Here was a scheme the President could back forthrightly: he stood foursquare against murder in whatever shape, form, or guise. S.S. needed no further encouragement.*

The other dream that McClure cherished, of course, was to publish a weekly magazine. Every other director of the S.S. McClure Company—Phillips, Oscar and Curtis Brady, and Robert McClure—was opposed to such a venture. Where was the money to come from? S.S. retorted that he had found money in 1893 during a panic; now, in prosperous times, money was simply begging to be invested. Late in October S.S. hired two promising young Illinois journalists to draw up plans for the new magazine. Phillips was irritated, but he kept his own counsel.

In November, announcing that he meant to gather his own statistics on crime in various European countries, S.S. sailed for England. A night with Kipling, a lunch with Conan Doyle, another with Joseph Conrad and Ford Madox Hueffer, and then S.S. left for a swing around the continent—Berlin, Geneva, Paris. Three weeks later he returned to London with few facts about European crime. "My work," he wrote to Phillips, "was extremely interesting but most discouraging." He had spent a week at Nice, he added, recovering from a cold. Perhaps he had. But as Phillips knew, Florence

---

* Pursuant to McClure's request, Roosevelt later sent Baker some statistics on homicides in the District of Columbia. Boyden, the desk editor, scoffed. "Your friend, Teddy, is hopeless," he wrote Baker. "What does he want to be fooling around with this thing for?" Steffens was even more scornful. "There are no murders down in the District of Columbia," he insisted; "they are too busy stealing to stop for such a trifle as murder."

Wilkinson was still in Europe. Like Miss Tarbell before him, Phillips began to wonder about his old friend.

McClure arrived in New York shortly before Christmas. On Sunday evening, the second day after Christmas, the whole family gathered in the parlor to hear S.S. read some of Miss Wilkinson's wretched poetry.

In January, 1904, McClure spent a considerable time collating his figures on the national crime-wave. This was the month in which he debated the question as to whether political machines were good or evil, with the Hon. T.L. Woodruff, before the Twentieth Century Club.

In February S.S. paid a visit to the White House on behalf of the Periodical Publishers' Association. The officials of this sodality, which had been incorporated less than a year before, planned for April what they confidently termed their First Annual Dinner; they desired the President's presence at their beano, and to McClure fell the task of roping him. He enjoyed the mission as he enjoyed nearly all of what he was doing in those days: it was part of being busy, important, and admired.

Meanwhile Hattie's health had not improved. There had been a visit to Johns Hopkins Hospital; during some weeks at home in Ardsley she had for days at a time kept to her bed. Late in February S.S.'s grim-visaged mother arrived for an extended stay, and before long this suggested to Hattie that she would be happier in Galesburg.

Miss Tarbell was also a regular guest at Ardsley, occupying a suite that had been especially provided for her. This was at McClure's behest. He had written to Hattie: "In buying things for Miss Tarbell's room I want you to know that I told her that *you* were planning to make her a nice home there. Miss Tarbell did us great service the last 2 or 3 years when Jac[caci] was planning to be the whole thing & Mr Phillips was blind. In case of my death she would be your mainstay as Mr Phillips doesnt realize other peoples unreliability & I shall be away a lot next year & you will enjoy having her out."

At all events, thanks to her residence at Ardsley Miss Tarbell could keep an eye on S.S. and on his comings and goings. She did not care a snap about his habits, morals, or suspected extramarital lapses (except for the fact that she was quite fond of Hattie), but she had the liveliest concern for his reputation as editor and chief figurehead of McClure's Magazine. On that score she was appalled by what she considered his insane imprudence. Just now, as a result of its exposure of the sins besetting the Republic, the magazine was approaching the zenith of its influence over national affairs. She and her associates had invested much energy and emotion in their work, and so had McClure; they believed in it passionately, and so did McClure. What then possessed him, that he could so jeopardize it?

Had he written any letters to some young lady friend, letters that might clinch his folly? If so, what if they were to fall into the hands of the odious Colonel William D'Alton Mann, editor of that ineffable weekly scandal-sheet, Town Topics? Even worse, what if they were to fall into the hands of some aggrieved politician, or, worst of all, into the hands of Henry Rogers, her old friend at Standard Oil? Miss Tarbell feared the worst.

Early in April McClure left for a holiday in the Appalachian Mountains of Virginia. Saturday was April Fool's Day. He wrote his devoted, trustful wife from Covington:

> My darling Hattie
>   I am fooling around this mountain country trying to imagine it is the Alps. . . . I hope you are all having a good time.
> My warmest love,
Your lover.

Next day, from Clifton Forge, he wrote:

> My darling Hattie
>   I am having a restful time. I'll walk around this country & feel free. Much love to you & content
> Your lover husband
SSM

Was he alone in that mountainous country, having a restful time and feeling free? In New York, Phillips and Miss Tarbell wondered.

On April seventh, the periodical publishers held their dinner and S.S. sat at the head table together with the President, Secretary Taft, the ambassadors from France and Germany, a couple of Senators, and a half-dozen assorted nabobs. It was a stag affair. Everyone from the staff of McClure's Magazine was there, everyone but the most celebrated of the staff. "It is the first time since I came into the office that the fact of petticoats has stood in my way," Miss Tarbell told Baker, "and I am half inclined to resent it."

All those on the dais had been scheduled to speak, but the hour grew late and S.S. was not called upon. He wrote his wife: "People in general seemed to be very much disappointed, and I suppose I came out with more honor than if I had spoken." Later he wrote: "I have decided to withdraw from active work for a year or two & complete my cure." Independently of him, Phillips and Miss Tarbell had reached the same decision. Their only question was how they were to tell him. And then, quite inadvertently, Witter Bynner gave them their chance.

Bynner, after graduation from Harvard in 1902, had been hired on the recommendation of William Morrow as an office boy in the editorial department at ten dollars a week.* After a time he was given the job of screening manuscripts for Miss Roseboro'; not long afterward he was given charge of the magazine's poetry. Here he was left pretty much on his own. He printed A.E. Housman, Louise Imogen Guiney, William Butler Yeats. On behalf of only one contributor did S.S. intercede to impose his own judgment: this was Florence Wilkinson. In May, S.S. bought one of her poems; he wrote a note of acceptance, called Bynner, and instructed him to deliver it together with a box of flowers. On his return, Bynner was summoned to a staff meeting in Miss Tarbell's office and accused of complicity in an amorous intrigue and, further, of treacherous behavior toward Mrs. McClure.

Bynner was outraged and incredulous. To those present—Phillips, Miss Tarbell, Boyden—he protested. Later Miss Tarbell and Phillips met privily with McClure, and Bynner got a glimpse of S.S. being scolded like a naughty child who sits, meek and penitent, promising to be good in the future.

Hattie now arrived in New York, sad and reproachful. Late in May she and S.S. left, just the two of them, for Europe.

But the unhappy McClure *had* written letters, and it fell to Phillips to recover them. For a shy and retiring man, it was an exceedingly distasteful task; but Phillips traveled to where Miss Wilkinson was staying, in the Finger Lakes district of New York, and made his supplication: she was to write no further to McClure, and she was to return to him all his letters. Miss Wilkinson promised Phillips every consideration of his request. Early in June she wrote him, assuring him that any letters to McClure would in future be sent in care of Mrs. McClure.

---

* At McClure's even the office boys attained to a certain bizarre distinction. Bynner's successor was a pudgy boy called Gene Byrnes, who subsequently created Reg'lar Fellers, for some years a popular comic-strip. After Byrnes came a dreamy youngster of uncertain habits called Jimmy Shields, who would sometimes disappear for hours when dispatched on an important errand, later explaining simply that he had been "sitting on the curbstone, writing poems"; all his life he persisted in writing poems, but under the influence of the Irish renaissance he changed his name to Shaemas O'Sheel.

Phillips was stupended. He wrote to Miss Tarbell: "Is there an epidemic of lunacy? or moon blight? My small nephew used the word 'bughouse' this morning. It expresses my feelings."

Miss Tarbell replied:

My Dear Mr Phillips:—The Lord help us! *I'm* too small for this! There is nothing for us, I should say, but to keep a "stern and unrelenting" front. Evidently Mrs McC is not to be counted on for that. Letters under her convoy! He can persuade her to *anything* and if in the end we see a *ménage à trois,* I shall not be greatly surprised. But that wouldn't last. He would soon want another! He's a Mormon, an uncivilized, unmoral, untutored natural man with enough canniness to keep himself out of jails and asylums. He is not to be trusted and I rather think our only hope is in Miss Wilkinson. Would it not be wise to put his condition still more forcibly to her—to tell her of the other affairs, to make her feel that far from her being the first and only one, there have been others, several of them—and the only reason they have not gone so far is that the other women have refused to travel and sky-lark with him. Why he told me himself, not a month before the break-up, that it would have probably been the same with any woman that he cared for *"if she had been as yielding as Miss W."* It may be cruel to tell her this but we seem to be the only ones to use the knife and somebody must do it. If you wish it and Miss W. will consent, I will go and see her and make an appeal for courage etc. I fear I would be hard with her. I do not mind her romantic vein so much as I do the *graft.* I lost all my respect for her when I saw her wheedling money out of the Gen'l.* I am not hard on those who love in defiance of law—on the contrary—if it is a genuine thing. But this thing was too trivial and calculating to arouse sympathy at the start. But I will honestly try to put that out of my mind and help the girl if she will let me. I have had no answer yet to the letter sent last week. It is quite natural she should feel resentment towards me but if it can be brought about it would be better for me to go . . . than for you. . . . This is, of course, the most vital thing we have on hand and our inexperience in dealing with lunatics makes extra attention necessary!

Faithfully yours
Ida M. Tarbell

McClure had appointed talented women to positions of importance in his organization at a time when women found it difficult to pursue a career and, if they married, impossible to maintain one. Now, in his time of trouble, he was surrounded by spinsters. Now his chickens were coming home to

* One of S.S.'s office nicknames was The General.

roost. Miss Mary Bisland, the cool, starchy woman who never took off her gray suede gloves or her hat in the office, who wore stiff corsets and never relaxed, was now in charge of the London office. Miss Tarbell confided in Miss Bisland, alerting her that the McClures were about to arrive, and why. Miss Bisland answered Miss Tarbell, avidly and at length:

London, July 7th 1904

My dear,

. . . Imagine my surprise on meeting them at the Bedford hotel to have Mrs McClure pour out the odious story in all its base & squalid details. . . . She told me he was already tired of her & was using every artifice to persuade her to return to New York, while swearing that he was having no communications with his light o' love. I knew he was constantly sending letters & cables. Never was I more unhappy & disgusted & moreover never did I see such moral degeneracy as in him. He even looks quite different & one of the worst signs to my eyes was that he wanted to talk of the subject constantly, to laugh & make jests over what seemed to me a black tragedy. Do you know I cant help wondering whether a nature can suffer such a moral sickness at his age & then recover. . . . Your sister says when he came to see her in Paris last winter when in the midst of his pollution that the man's face was absolutely bloated & disfigured with vice, & to show you what a state of mind his was in Paris, he told me that of course he had not told his wife all the truth as she would not be able to stand it, but he & that female beast took an apartment & lived together in it. On top of that he absolutely had the effrontery to tell me there had been no actual moral wrong!!! I told him in the plainest English I could command that his Wilkinson woman was no better than an alley cat, I believed her to be at the service of any man who wanted her, & furthermore I would not sit & listen to such stupid lies. He assured me Mr Phillips believed him pure!!! Good Lord!! His poor wife does swallow his falsehoods & he chuckled in telling me of the way she believed him. You remember I prophesied just what would happen, & now I must tell you I firmly believe he has become a hopeless sort of degenerate. His very genius is against him. He is both wretched & restless away from Miss Wilkinson, he has not the very vaguest idea of giving her up. I could see that in a dozen ways. His wife bores him so insupportably that at times he broke out while we were in Paris, said he preferred her (Miss W.) as the lowest street walker to any other woman in the world & longed passionately to see her. I suppose you know by this time that he sails for New York in September. This is because Mrs. McC. will not leave him over here & he is resolved to get back to his Florence. Now what earthly future is there for that miserable family? He never even speaks of his children, grew impatient if I mentioned the magazine or business & wanted to talk of nothing but his relations with Miss Wilkinson. I fear some vigorous measures will have to be used before the end is reached. Mrs McClure said to me that she felt Mr Phillips was inclined to minimize the gravity of the situation, & there was too much of a disposition to laugh the thing off & treat her husband like a naughty child. If he does misbehave again, he will find her a pretty stern judge I'm thinking. . . . I do so wish I could see you & talk to you for letters at the best are inadequate vehicles, & I am so fearful this affair may yet bring great disgrace upon our firm. Mr Mc-Clure said no one had used such language to him as I had, but pshaw! it was breath wasted, & to save my life I dont see how he is to be controlled hereafter. . . . I do feel so much more might be done if Mrs McClure really knew the true state. She has lived all her life in a world of illusion, has shunned the truth & does not realize in the least the needs of her husband, who like nearly all men of his gifts is more or less of a sensualist, & is going to gratify that side of his nature at all costs. No one knows all this better than you & I, & it does seem to me either S.S.['s] brothers or Mr Phillips should face the situation & provide for it. I am so distressed over this mania that has possessed Mr McClure. . . . I shall keep you informed of what is happening over here & with much love am affectionately yours

Mary Bisland

The juiciest parts of this letter Miss Tarbell faithfully sent on to Phillips. Meantime McClure, who was in Divonne with his wife, was once again in possession of the letters he had written to Miss Wilkinson. "I've done some squirming & squealing," he wrote Phillips, "but I'm all right." Later he added: "I've been an awful fool. My desires & my duties again jump together."

"I am very tired," he told his wife one morning. "I dreamt last night I was sleeping *under* the mattress with a couple on the mattress, so you can imagine my sense of weariness." (A man could display to his wife an innocent and charming lack of self-consciousness, in those happy days before Freud.) Then he said: "I feel that I have touched bottom at last in every way, and from now on will go upward."

The fact that he was both in disgrace and in Switzerland did not deter him from trying to run his business and assailing those who were, as he considered, running it into the ground. Cabled instructions arrived daily in New York, to be followed by angry, abusive letters. As has already been noted, he was upset by Steffens's articles; he was also enraged by some unfortunate advertisements of the magazine that appeared in the newspapers;

finally, he had some outrageously expensive ideas for the book company.

Phillips retorted mildly enough in June ("I am worried and puzzled"), more firmly in July ("I am unalterably opposed . . . to any new scheme requiring new investment. . . . Your overdrafts [amount] in a year & a half to fully $30,000. . . . I beg of you Sam for the sake of your family & your friends . . . trust in and believe me"), and reproachfully in August ("No man ever had more devoted aides & friends"); but the essential element of the relationship between McClure and Phillips, their interdependence and their mutual confidence, had been severely strained.

Late in July McClure began to urge Hattie to go back to New York and protect his interests by working in the office. She wrote to Phillips, asking his advice. "I feel that it would goad him into violent madness," she told Phillips, "if I were not kind & gentle in my acquiescence with this plan." At length she decided to go home; but every day on her way she wrote him a lengthy letter filled with expressions of the tenderest love. In England she spent a night with Frances Hodgson Burnett at Maytham Hall, the house Mrs. Burnett had taken in Kent. There was moonlight, and Mrs. Burnett and Mrs. McClure strolled back and forth across the terrace, talking about McClure. Hattie said: "Of all my children, he is the youngest, my most cherished babe. I carry him everywhere with me in my heart. He is the heart of my heart."

Hattie arrived in New York early in September, 1904, and S.S., characteristically impatient, found his loneliness intolerable and hurried after her a few days later. Miss Tarbell wrote:

Dear Mr. Phillips:—They caught me! I was just leaving for my train when a message from Ardsley informed me that Mr McC was here and I was to meet them at the office! Mrs McC is radiant and full of confidence. He has persuaded her he never saw Miss Wherry but three times in Geneva and that all of the suspicion about her is of Miss W[ilkinson]'s creation, a work of jealousy and spite.* (I did not suggest that we had seen Miss Wherry's letter telling of his project to study and travel with her!) Of course he has come home to put Mrs McC. and the rest of us off the scent. Perhaps, to see Florence. Partly, too, he has come to make a new effort at decency! He talked finely this morning

* Edith Wherry, an American at this time in her early twenties, had spent most of her childhood in China, where her father was a missionary. Returning to the United States when she was fifteen, she had studied for a time at Wellesley, had written some poems, one or two of which were published in The Century, and had gone to live in Europe in 1903. She yearned to write and, indeed, later found a publisher for a couple of novels. McClure never printed anything she wrote.

of his own condition, and assured me he was a changed man! But while he talked his mind was by jerks on something else. He is not changed. He is still the same canny, scheming, unstable soul—now at the height of aspiration and ambition and now in the mire. I don't see what he is up to here precisely and I haven't energy left to care. But it's something. You and I must keep our minds clear on one point. He is not changed. But I don't think we can do anything more. It will be the best thing in the world for him to let him wrestle here with the business. Make him feel the responsibility & you & Mrs P. go off and get some fun—go where he can't reach you. You need it. The future here depends on your sanity—and strength. If you thought it wise, you might write Mr Boyden a line cautioning him to be gentle and appreciative with both Mr & Mrs McC. for she's coming in! Is to have a desk in his room. Bert will fret, I fear, and do harm but a word from you will help him.   It was curious to see how disappointed he was not to have you here to say something he had evidently thought out coming over to say to both of us and he couldn't say it all to me. He went to pieces—that is, his bluff did & he was very humble.

I feel more hope now than last night. There is enough of good in this return to overbalance the subterfuge, I think. . . .

Faithfully yours
Ida M. Tarbell

In this whole affair, it is clear that Phillips believed McClure had acted like a consummate noodle. Phillips was right. No proof is required, the proposition being self-evident. But Miss Tarbell and Miss Bisland went further. They believed that McClure had flouted the Seventh Commandment, not once, but persistently. They may have been right; but it is always difficult to establish satisfactory proof of such flagrancies, short of sworn confessions from the two parties involved, which in this instance are lacking. The affair would be trivial beyond endurance except that it was to have repercussions of some importance. And so it may be profitable to poke about for a moment in this rich compost of emotion, assumption, suspicion, and vindictive incrimination.

To begin with, there is the savagery with which both Miss Tarbell and Miss Bisland tore into McClure. In the face of their extraordinary vehemence, one is invited to wonder. When Miss Bisland speaks of female beasts and alley cats, when Miss Tarbell urges that she must use the knife to help the girl, when they smack their lips over lunacy, moral degeneracy, and faces bloated with vice, are they, perhaps, permitting their perception to be stained by the palest green of envy? What does Miss Bisland mean when she charges McClure with being a sensualist and adds, to Miss Tarbell: "No one knows all this better than you & I"? McClure told Miss Bisland, so she says, that he and Miss Wilkinson shared an apartment in Paris but that nothing immoral took place there. Miss Bisland eagerly believed the first part of this confession but derisively rejected the second. Why? McClure, as should be obvious by now, was capable of anything: the unlikelier the behavior, the likelier he would engage upon it. Admittedly it is not probable, but it is at least possible that an Ulster Irishman of strong Protestant persuasion might talk himself into an amorous situation as an incompetent handyman paints himself into a corner, yet thereafter shrink shyly from an ultimate commitment as from eternal hellfire. Phillips granted such a possibility. Miss Tarbell and Miss Bisland, however, both rejected it.

The ladies may have been right. But each made at least one egregious blunder about McClure. Miss Bisland suggested he was no longer interested in his magazine or his business. He was. Miss Tarbell insisted he had not changed. He had. Indeed, he was always as changeable as the weather.

On his arrival in New York in September, 1904, McClure called together the editorial staff and the advertising staff of all his enterprises and blistered their ears for forty minutes by the clock. He had been dismayed by some advertisements of the magazine that boasted of its achievements as a vehicle of reform. Advertisements, he argued, should convey "as truthful an impression as possible of the goods to be sold" and should therefore be written by the editors and by nobody else. "There is no other way of doing it," he said.

> I am going to give you [he went on] the fundamental principle of the editing of McClure's Magazine.
> McClure's Magazine practically and in a certain sense is the work of my brain. In editing McClure's Magazine I do the thing that is really in me, just precisely as a painter does; the painting is not painted for sale but to express his notion. McClure's Magazine is edited by me and my associates not to be sold, primarily, but to express our notion. The moment we set out to make a magazine with reference to selling it, that moment we mar our work and produce something different. The moment we print an article for any other motive than the idea of McClure's Magazine, we mar our work. The moment we print an article in McClure's for the sake of doing good or furthering a cause or any other purpose than to make the most interesting magazine possible, we mar our work. . . . Now, this is the ABC of art, fundamental creation in every form of activity, creative activity, it is not a new truth. The creative work must be done for its own sake and no other.
> . . . It is one of the incidents of [muckraking] articles like ours to

draw the people's attention to the thought that we are performing a certain mission and in fact make ourselves feel the same thing. That is a thing to keep in the bottom of our minds and not allow it to seriously influence our work; if we do, it will have the same effect upon us that popularity has upon the actor or actress who feels that he or she must live up to it; it brings in an element of self-consciousness that takes a very great talent to stop it from marring our work to a certain extent. That is the last thing to mention out loud. Let other people mention it. Let makers of the magazine stick to their business, which is publishing interesting reading. If we ever try to edit the magazine in any other way, we fail that much of perfect art, which is the thing that every creative mind seeks to attain. . . .

Granted his syntax was occasionally deplorable, what McClure had to say made good sense. (And it should, as well, dispose of the notion that he edited with one ear attuned to the ringing of the cash register.) This was hardly the counsel of a "canny, scheming, unstable soul" but rather of an instinctive and talented editor.

S.S. had finished his article on lawlessness in the United States, which was to be published in the December issue. It consisted largely of clippings taken from various newspapers and purported to show there had been an appalling increase in crime, due to the corruption of local government and the depravity of local police; these sins were in turn charged to the oligarchy then being charted in detail by Steffens. The evidence adduced was a compilation by The Chicago Tribune of murders and homicides from 1881 to 1903, and if these data were to be trusted the United States was indeed a charnel house. There had been, according to the figures, almost nine thousand murders and homicides in 1903, a rate of slaughter nearly five times that of 1881.* But close scrutiny of The Tribune's tabulation shows a very shaky statistical edifice, suggesting that the newspaper characterized as murder or homicide every American death that did not take place in bed and even a few (Cause of Murder: Jealousy) that did. The Tribune's total comprised all deaths by violence reported in the newspapers of the various states and territories. McClure, in short, believed everything he read in the newspapers.

Giving spur to his unbridled hobbyhorse, S.S. galloped off into some splendid extravagances. He had dubbed the oligarchy Enemies of the Republic; now he proclaimed they were worse: "They are enemies of the hu-

* By contrast, the Uniform Crime Reports of the F.B.I. currently list about the same number of murders and non-negligent manslaughters in a population more than twice that of 1903.

man race. They are destroyers of a people. *They are murderers of a civilization.*"

"There are men," he concluded, "and groups of men in every community who realize these truths and who are at work, sometimes winning success like Folk of Missouri, sometimes working half a life-time with discouragement like Blankenburgh and others in Philadelphia, sometimes making slow and sure progress—which will be crowned with brilliant success—like the Municipal Voters' League in Chicago.

"These and thousands of others are the pioneers of a new righteousness which shall become a new passion—*the Love of Country*. We shall see that new passion develop in the American people until we have obedience to the law, *because it is the law,* and the will of the state will be sufficient. And the briber, and the grafter, and the traitor who steals from his neighbors and pollutes the law will be unable to endure the scorn of his fellows."

This fine flight of romanticism makes it clear that as a writer McClure could not obey his own editorial precepts. But the article was scheduled for publication.

With Phillips, S.S. examined the financial health of his corporate empire. It was a dispiriting task. The magazine was not doing so well as might have been expected. The book company, which was being run by his brother Robbie, was actually losing money. Worst of all was the syndicate.

Twenty months before, the S.S. McClure Company had sold the syndicate to S.S.'s brother Tom for about fifty-six thousand dollars. At the time, S.S. had told Tom that he was being given the greatest chance ever offered any man. It was the kind of monitory remark likely to sour even a purely commercial transaction; but in this case the sale was also familial, and so it was apprehended by Tom as a challenge and a taunt.

At all events, Tom McClure had not been a particularly good president and general manager of the syndicate. His payments against the purchase price had not been regularly forthcoming. For this delinquency he was not wholly to blame: he had taken control of the syndicate precisely at the time when four-color comic supplements were coming into vogue, and they were not only expensive but exceedingly uncertain of acceptance. Luck played the greatest part in the popularity of the early comic-strips, and Tom McClure's luck was ragged. But Phillips and Oscar Brady, pressed by the narrowing margin of the magazine's profits, cared nothing about luck. They were interested only in results. Tom McClure was not their brother; in the circumstances, he found himself their adversary.

S.S., himself jumpy and irritable in the atmosphere of suspicion about his private life, was informed by Phillips and Brady that his brother Tom had made a hash of the syndicate. S.S. wired Tom, then out west on syndicate business, to come to New York at once. The next morning Tom arrived at his office, consulted with his associates on the syndicate, concluded that the supplement should be canceled, sent telegrams to that effect to all his principal clients, and went uptown to the offices of the magazine to meet with his brother. He suspected something was up, and Phillips at once confirmed his misgivings. *"We'*re taking over the syndicate business," Phillips told him, "and *we'*ll run it and finance it, and when everything is in proper shape, *we* will give you just what *we* think is right."

Tom McClure was stunned. S.S. instructed him to sign over all his rights in the syndicate. In return he was promised a transfusion of new capital and the chance to buy the syndicate again within three years. Tom studied his older brother for a long moment. Then he signed.

[XVII]

S.S. and Hattie sailed for Europe the next day. He had been instructed to pursue his various cures—his rest-cure, his milk-cure, and a special dietetic cure, urged upon him by some imaginative quack, which called for broiled squab twice a day. On this regimen he remained tractable for some six weeks. Then, as has been noted earlier, he began to fret over the meteoric rise of Everybody's Magazine and, as it seemed to him, the simultaneous decline of McClure's. He announced that he was a new man, ready to come home again. Kipling wrote him: "What a bird of flight and passage you are! You might have winged your way down here [to Bateman's Burwash, in Sussex] for a night and told us the news. . . . There didn't appear to be anything wrong with the old McClure but I shall wait for the appearance of the new one with deep interest. . . ."

In New York again, McClure called once again upon his editorial imagination, brought Ray Stannard Baker to the White House in Washington, and devised the plans for Baker's series, The Railroads on Trial.

By the end of the year, S.S. professed himself once again exhausted. Hattie was at Ardsley, patient and contained. On New Year's Eve S.S. sailed for Europe alone, "a very tired and dispirited man," as he wrote his wife. He added: "I could not have endured another week of it." He was, he said, wracked with pains: "The last few days it seemed as if my nerves were poisoned. . . . My abdomen seems more tired than I have ever felt it. . . . My head beats with impatience when I lie [down]. . . . The pain in the bones of the skull seems better. . . . When I begin to sleep I shall take a good rest. . . . I am sad to be away from you. . . ."

He had told Hattie he meant to visit his family in the north of Ireland, but once aboard ship he had changed his mind. Instead he would go to the south of England; no, rather to Spain; no, to the Italian Riviera. Was this the new McClure? It seemed suspiciously like the old one.

For so many years Hattie had dreamed only of a pleasant home and a life of even tenor. Now once again all was disrupted. She had to dispose of the house at Ardsley, store the furniture, sell the horses, pay the servants off, make sure the children were safe either at college or at boarding-school, and once again take off after her husband. In January she joined him in Berlin. She brought imperative instructions from his physician: S.S. was to come with her to Nervi, on the Riviera, where he was to spend several quiet, restful months.

S.S. scarcely heard what she said. Hadn't she read the papers? About what was happening in Russia? The riots, the massacres, the general strike, the threatened revolution? It was the biggest thing to have happened in years! He was leaving at once. She must come with him. He begged her to come with him.

Hattie set her jaw and shook her head. She was going to Nervi, she said, and she would wait for him to join her there. They parted, she with a very heavy heart.

Hattie was convinced that S.S. was still involved in his amorous intrigues. From Nervi she wrote a long, anguished letter to Phillips: should she not perhaps have her husband committed to an asylum? There seemed to her no other way of controlling him.

Like Miss Tarbell and Miss Bisland before her, however, Hattie had now erred about McClure. He was no longer the lovesick swain. He was once again quite simply the journalist sniffing out a story and having the time of his life. He got to Russia ten days after the infamous "Bloody Sunday," when hundreds of unarmed persons, seeking only to present a petition to their Czar, were shot down outside the Winter Palace.

Hôtel d'Angleterre
St. Pétersbourg.   Friday evening
                                                    Feb 3 [1905]
My beloved wife
    . . . I am very well & life here is simple safe & comfortable & I am
learning a lot. . . . I am out a great deal & sleep well & eat tremendously.
I havent been so busy & absorbed since I was a boy. . . . The people
here are generally wrong. It is very difficult to get at the truth. . . .
The stories you hear are various, contradictory & curious.
    I am trying to collect eye-witness accounts. The whole problem is
easy to understand. Boodle—Tammany boodle & a few other things. . . .
This morning I went over to the Winter Palace & rang the doorbell &
sent in my card to the Princess Orbelini. She was in & received me &
eagerly inquired for you & the children. . . . My beloved! I pray God
to make you happy & contented. I am very sorry you did not come. . . .
                                                    Your loving husband

                                Monday Feb 6
My darling & Beloved Wife
    I am getting very lonesome. It is too utterly bad that you are not
here. . . . The situation is the most interesting possible. . . . This whole
govt. reminds me of the condition of Harper & Bros. . . . Goodbye my
love & lover & resting-place & heaven on earth
    How good you have been for all these wonderful years!

                                Tuesday Feb 7
My precious Hattie:
    . . . I am living in a kind of dream. Days pass full of new things. To-
day for example I am to hunt up that famous Russian correspondent
Dravchenko [?] whose stuff was so good. He is just back. The War
[with Japan] is already decided. Russia is licked & she will have a great
change in govt. I never was in such an interesting place. . . . I am living
in a daze of the most extraordinary contradictions of all sorts. Thats why
I am dazed. . . .
    I am so happy in the thought of you, dearest & best & truest & gentlest
                            good night Beloved

                                Wed P.M.
My darling & beloved wife
    . . . I saw Datchenko [?], that famous Russian correspondent whose
stuff I so admired last year. . . . I have engaged three or four articles
that ought to be good. . . .
                        Good night my darling!

Thursday

My darling Wife
. . . I have secured an unpublished prison story of Gorki which I may be able to use
All love, dearest & best of all the world!

Friday night

I am just off to Moscow. dined last night with Smiths to meet Count Rostoff Private Secretary to the Empress
Awfully busy today Will write from Moscow. ALL LOVE
Your lover & lover always

Moscow Feb 11
My Beloved Wife—
This is the farthest limit of my journey. . . . I am the guest of the American consul. I visited the Kremlin & travelled through the streets & saw the city very fully. These Russian cities are not particularly imposing.

Russia is on the eve of tremendous changes & perhaps of a bloody revolution. I have read the first chapter of a tremendous historical romance & am obliged to quit. The next months & years here will duplicate the most fascinating & most terrible pages of human history. Russia is intrinsically the most interesting country in the world at the present time. Its customs & conditions of life are those of 1 or 2 centuries ago, & the changes to take place will be as fascinating as French history

I cannot bear to leave but I must quit & take my long rest

I saw the Grand Duchess, wife of Sergius sister of the empress oldest daughter of the Princess Alice granddaughter of the Queen *

She is greatly beloved here & actively at work in superintending the preparation of huge quantities of materials for the wounded. She discovered that the goods were stolen & straw & stones packed in their place. She wept & brought about complete reform. They need a lot of good English blood here.

. . . Yesterday there was slight renewal of disturbances in St. P[etersburg] extensive strikes, & threats of uprisings & tomorrow may be very interesting. The great body of the Russian people are against the War. I believe peace is near. I saw several bodies of recruits training today & yesterday in St. P. I saw movements of troops to suppress disorders in St P.

This is the most interesting country I was ever in. . . . They are the most credulous people in the world.

I can hardly bear to quit. . . . This country reminds me of Egypt in

* By way of interpolating commas, what S.S. meant was that he had met a lady who was a sister-in-law of the Czarina and a granddaughter of Queen Victoria.

some ways. All English & American people know each other. It is like living in a very small village . . .

Your devoted husband

On his return to St. Petersburg five days later, S.S. found letters from his wife in which she accused him of romping around Russia with his paramour.

[February 16]

My darling wife—
    I am back from Moscow & starting home. I shall rest in Vienna, stopping a little in Warsaw, but shall get home *sure* by Saturday night. I could just as easily have some wrong person here as I could in Cairo or on the Nile. All the world would know it.
    Especially Mrs Smith. I want only you here. . . .
    I love you & think of all your dear goodness, especially these last weeks. How happy we shall be.

Your devoted husband
SSM

In the lobby of the Hôtel d'Angleterre, S.S. came upon Ernest Poole, who had also been attracted to Russia by the rumors of revolution. (The expenses of Poole's trip had been shared by McClure's and The Outlook.) S.S. asked Poole to come upstairs with him while he packed to go home. "Don't believe what the Reds will tell you," he advised Poole. "This whole situation is quieting down. To bring off this revolution of theirs is going to take ten years at least." His crystal ball was working tolerably well: it took twelve years.

On the same day that McClure left St. Petersburg, bound for Warsaw, Vienna, and Nervi, the Grand Duke Sergius, husband of the lady S.S. had met in Moscow, was blown to bits by an assassin's bomb; it was the first in a series of interesting events that were to justify what S.S. had predicted for that interesting country. Also on that same day Phillips, back in New York, dictated two irritable letters, one to Hattie and one to S.S.; it was as though he too were tossing a couple of bombs. To Hattie he wrote a tart note, ending: "I hope you are well. Sometimes of late, after being hammered day in and day out, I wish that Mrs. Phillips and I might flee to the Riviera or any remote and agreeable spot." With S.S. he was even crisper. He poured scorn over all the ideas S.S. had suggested for magazine articles (some of which seem quite sensible in retrospect); he gloomed over the magazine's financial condition, warning of the possibility that its price might have to be raised to fifteen cents; and he was caustic on the score of the trip to Russia, which had so delighted McClure. "At first it seems all right," he wrote, "the excitement and interest and all that; but I don't believe you can stand it, and I really believe that unless you take seriously all that all the doctors have said, advised and urged—and they pretty much agree—there will be greater remorse and regret than could possibly be occasioned by your having given up the Russian expedition. You have a tough job and no temporary refreshment or improvement ought to satisfy you. That is where the danger lies."

The doctors involved were a posse of specialists who had been assembled by the eminent Doctor Thomas Browne of the Johns Hopkins School of Medicine. Doctor Browne voiced their unanimous disapproval of the Russian trip. He scolded McClure severely by cable and letter: "You promised me that nothing would make you change your plans regarding the long, quiet months in Algiers, Italy, or Switzerland alone with Mrs. McClure—and I want you to keep that promise to the letter."

But after a couple of weeks on the Riviera it was obvious to McClure that what he needed was a different doctor, a different diagnosis, a different treatment. He found what he wanted in Lausanne. Here a Doctor Vittoz told him (and a Doctor Schofield of London agreed) that he would never get well without work, and that he could not begin too soon. It was precisely what he had wanted to hear. At once he began to agitate to get back to New York.

Hattie held him in Divonne for a time. Ostensibly he was resting, still a patient; but in reality he was impatiently chafing. He kept firing ideas at the New York office. To Miss Tarbell he suggested a series of articles on the United States Senate since the Spanish-American War. But Miss Tarbell was by that time ready to shrug off whatever McClure recommended. The suggestion was ignored.*

McClure and his wife landed in New York early in June, 1905. Miss Tarbell was on hand to greet them. Presently she wrote:

> My Dear Mr Phillips,
>   Mr McClure arrived yesterday as you know. I had a long talk with him and it left me with an impression of his condition more sinister

---

* This is a pity. Miss Tarbell would have gathered her facts carefully; she would have founded what she wrote on sound historical evidence; she could have drawn a damning indictment. In the event, the idea was exploited by Hearst in The Cosmopolitan. In the hands of David Graham Phillips, it became a polemic and subsequently sparked President Roosevelt's attack on the Man with the Muck-Rake.

and painful than I can express. I doubt if he is going to be hard to deal
with in the business, except now and then. I doubt that he will be ob-
stinate—I don't know really what I do fear. I am only sure of this—that
he needs us more than he ever has and that we must not both be away
from here [the New York office] for any length of time while he is at
home. He must be watched and dealt with at the same time very gently.
. . . If you could be here the first of the week to talk with him and get
an impression I should be very glad. I really think it is important. . . .

Mr Boyden lunched with him today and said this afternoon "That
man was never so bad off as he is now."

You know how I hate to write this. It seems a cruelty. Still you ought
to know. I have a feeling that the whole affair is going to take on a new
form and that we are both going to feel its tragic proportions so deeply
that we wont mind the irritations and perhaps there will be fewer of
them really. At all events we've got to forget ourselves utterly. His
malady is reaching too serious a phase for us to think of anything but
guarding him.   Of course Mrs McClure is stone blind and deaf
and dumb. She makes me wild.

Get as much sunshine and fresh air as you can. You'll need them!

Faithfully yours
Ida M. Tarbell

[XVIII]

When McClure landed, he was once again all editor. Where, he demanded
when he got to the office, were the great features for the future? Some time
before, Phillips and Miss Tarbell had persuaded Carl Schurz to write his
memoirs; they were to be published, beginning in November; Miss Tarbell
was already at work editing them, as she had earlier edited Charles Dana's
reminiscences. Good, but something timelier was needed. The editorial staff
had been scratching its collective head for weeks without starting a single
idea. McClure read through one day's crop of New York newspapers and
pounced upon the feature he wanted as a terrier pounces upon a rat. It was
the story of the commerce in life insurance.

What? Life insurance, that sacred solace of the widow and orphan? Life
insurance, that holy exercise in the mysteries of mathematics? Just so: for
it was becoming clear that the mammoths of the life-insurance business—
the Equitable Life Assurance Society, the Mutual Life Insurance Company
of New York, the New York Life Insurance Company, and the Prudential
Insurance Company—were thieves as deep-dyed as any railroad or oil

refinery. Indeed, their wrongs were the wickeder because of the sanctimonious cloak of service they had drawn over their operations.

There were as yet no facts on the record. The celebrated investigation by a joint committee of the Senate and Assembly of the State of New York into the malodorous affairs of the life-insurance companies would not begin for another three months. But already there was a whisper of huge political slush funds, of scandalous retainers passed to United States Senators, of vast sums used to corrupt the press—all of it levied from citizens who imagined, in their innocence, that their money was being wisely invested and would be spent only to protect their loved ones from penury.

McClure assigned Steffens to dig out the facts and write a series on life insurance.

Phillips and Oscar Brady now snared S.S. in mid-flight and brought him down to earth to break some surprising news. While he was in Europe, they had decided to build a plant for the printing and production of the magazine and of the McClure, Phillips & Company books as well. Thirty thousand square feet of real estate had already been bought in Long Island City, just across the Queensborough Bridge from Manhattan; all the buildings on this plot of land had been razed; plans for a three-story structure of reinforced concrete had been drawn and approved; the Long Island Rail Road had agreed to put in a siding; a quarter of a million dollars had been earmarked for the project. Now that S.S. had come home, Phillips and Brady considered that he should know about the new plant and give it his blessing.

A quarter of a million dollars! McClure was indeed surprised. But there is no evidence that he disapproved of the project, at least at this time. As it happened, he had some private plans of his own, plans for a new magazine; and so, probably, he consented to the Long Island City plant quite cheerfully.

In any event, McClure begrudged any time taken to fuss over his problems as publisher. He wanted to be an editor again. The details of business management were delegated to those who liked that sort of thing. As for him, it was more important that he take a swing around the country and find out what people were thinking. Impulsive as ever, he hurried out of the office and disappeared into the hinterland.

Miss Tarbell, watching him go, concluded that he was off to meet his ladylove. Miss Tarbell's manner toward him had changed, and he knew it. In the course of his swing through the Midwest, he sent her a brief note, sad and humble. "I have always cared for you in a special manner," he wrote, "as much as a man can care for a woman without loving her."

S.S. had been gone two weeks when Hattie came to the office to seek Miss Tarbell's advice. She brought with her a typescript entitled "The Shame of S.S. McClure, Illustrated by Letters and Original Documents." The author of this remarkable essay was Edith Wherry, who argued that it should be published in McClure's Magazine, along with other "important revelations."

Miss Tarbell's reaction may be imagined. At last it had come: what she had long dreaded, indeed had always known was bound to happen: the threat of public disclosures, a nasty scandal, the end of all their brave efforts. Harsh retribution; but perhaps only just, considering how grievous the moral sin. Well, what was to be done? She and Hattie agreed that S.S. undoubtedly was in Chicago with Miss Wilkinson, that Miss Wherry's threats proved she and Miss Wilkinson were quarreling over their claims to his favors, and that he should be summoned home at once. Hattie dispatched an imperative telegram.

Once again the ladies were wrong. For, when Hattie got home, she was astonished to find a letter from Miss Wilkinson awaiting her. It appeared that Miss Wilkinson, so far from reveling in illicit pleasures with S.S. in Chicago, was lying sick abed in her apartment on Eleventh Street in Manhattan. She had written to ask the McClures to pay her a visit.

Hattie conferred with Miss Tarbell again. Miss Tarbell advised Hattie to write Miss Wilkinson that there could be no further communications between them. Hattie complied.

But the next day S.S. came bouncing back from Chicago, and prudence was upended. Hattie met him at the station and forthwith he hustled her down to Eleventh Street for a confrontation—what in the theater is known as the obligatory scene. One result of their talk was that Miss Wherry's sensational exposure, "The Shame of S.S. McClure," was somehow quietly suppressed. Later S.S. and Hattie lunched with Miss Tarbell at the Waldorf. Miss Tarbell, alert and suspicious, was obliged to conclude that S.S. was no longer interested in philandering. The affair with Miss Wilkinson, if it had ever been an affair, was forgotten. S.S. dismissed it. He refused to discuss it. He turned the talk to the woes of the life-insurance companies. Back in her office, Miss Tarbell wrote to Bert Boyden, who was on holiday in Europe. "She [Miss Wilkinson] has become simply impossible & fancy. Too exacting & unreasonable for even the General who is in a wild state of excitement over insurance etc & who has done some really wonderful work—if we can only carry it out. I believe he's tired of the girl. . . ."

To say S.S. was tired of the girl was a fuzzy formulation. She had simply ceased to exist for him, crowded out of the sphere of his interests by Governor

Folk, whom he had visited out west; by William Allen White, who had been his host for a week or so; by the Senate ("I still think that an article or two on great thieves who became Senators will be a good thing"); by Ray Stannard Baker's series on the railroads, then in preparation; and by the Peace Conference at Portsmouth, New Hampshire, arranged by President Roosevelt to settle the war between Russia and Japan.

S.S. hustled to Portsmouth to scout the Peace Conference personally and then hustled back to grant an interview to a reporter from The Philadelphia North American. This interview (which the newspaper played big, running it in the right-hand column of the front page, under a three-column head) was notable for some uncommonly blunt talk about sacred cows. "These men in politics [said S.S. in bold-faced type] have aimed to get money by sneak thievery, by doing it in such a manner that they cannot be punished. They are sneak thieves, and that form of thievery has never been able to get sympathy. That is why the American people give sympathy to a train robber who risks his liberty and life rather than to a boodler like Rockefeller, who risks nothing out of which perjury will not help him, and still goes on stealing. . . . They are to be compared with men who wilfully poison the source of streams that a whole neighborhood uses for drinking water."

Hattie urged him to take it easy, to move slower. "You dare not get so tired," she told him. "I must live my life as well as I can with my nature," he answered. He was argued into taking a brief holiday at the sanitarium in Clifton Springs, New York. After two days he snarled, "It is the deadliest and dullest place I ever saw. The massage is absurd, and the turkish baths I could get at home." Another two days, and he rebelled. "I cant stand this. I grow tired, indigestive &c. I MUST WORK."

Back again in his office, McClure managed to impress even Bert Boyden. "He's a living fire for sure," Boyden told Miss Tarbell, "and it's certainly a great thing for the magazine to have him here." S.S. was at that time engrossed in editing the first of Baker's articles on the railroads, and an electrical charge leaped the gap between Baker's mind and his:

Sept. 27, 1905

My dear Baker:—
I have been thinking that an awfully good series [of] articles or rather an awfully good lot of illustrations would be the six or eight men who dominate the railroads and the banks and trust companies and coal mines, and so on; then give each of them a half-page. Below each one give photographs of their political and railroad and banking satellites. Or give each

of them a page and then give pages of small portraits of their satellites. For example, give a two page collection of pictures to the Senate; give smaller pictures of men like Ripley,* and so on. Make it so that men like Ryan † would come in somewhere. Such a collection of photographs, aggregating perhaps a hundred, giving the rulers and sub-rulers of the United States would be a stunning thing! It would take us some time to get the material but I wish you would bear this scheme in mind and collect the material as quickly as possible.

Very truly yours,
SSMcClure

This scheme was ignored by S.S.'s associates. It was apparently classified among those ninety-nine-ideas-in-a-hundred that they later praised Phillips for pigeonholing.

McClure was as yet not aware of it, but he was no longer master in his own house. Nominally he was editor-in-chief, he owned a majority of the shares of stock in the parent company, in theory he could command as he chose, but in fact to get something done required a nod from Phillips.

A bit of madness and a bit of magic are needed to make any magazine, each number different from every other yet somehow similar, each number necessarily flawed yet charged with as much hope as though it were a new-born babe. But in the editorial offices of McClure's, in the last months of 1905, there was more than a touch of madness. The captain strode the bridge of his ship, confidently barking orders; his crew, grinning behind their hands, sprang to their tasks only when, from over the captain's shoulder, the first mate gave a wink. It was not quite mutiny. It was worse. It was farce, streaked with cruelty.

And McClure chose this of all times to decide to publish a new monthly magazine.

[XIX]

There was a fateful inevitability about everything that happened at McClure's in the weeks that followed. Reason had fled; events were controlled

---

* Professor William Z. Ripley of Harvard was an academic expert on the railroads who had described the rate structure as "a house of cards."

† Thomas Fortune Ryan, a successful Wall Street speculator, had recently paid James Hazen Hyde a reported two million five hundred thousand dollars for five hundred and two shares in the Equitable Life Assurance Society. The purchase gave Ryan control of the Equitable and its estimated five hundred million dollars' worth of assets.

by temperament and by loyalties that were sometimes twisted beyond recognition. Phillips, for example, was loyal to McClure, thoroughly honest, and incapable of subterfuge or betrayal. But he was under constant pressure from Miss Tarbell and Boyden, who were loyal only to him. Siddall's loyalty lay with Miss Tarbell; where she led, he followed, unquestioning. Baker, who was at this time preoccupied with his series, The Railroads on Trial, seems to have been largely unaware of the pressures building up in the editorial department; when the issue was drawn, his loyalty would lie with the majority. Steffens very sensibly reserved his loyalty to himself, untainted; he stood ready to hop at any moment in any direction that made sense for him. (Just now Steffens was sore at McClure; after nearly five months of hard work on the life-insurance assignment, he had been told by McClure— and Phillips agreed—that he had written nothing worth printing. McClure had hired Burton J. Hendrick, a young reporter from The New York Evening Post, to tell the story of life insurance accurately and with narrative power. Steffens was sulking.)

McClure was unaware of—or indifferent to—these contrary tensions. He could scarcely have imagined his associates would rejoice over his scheme for a new magazine; after all, in the past ten years they had blocked a half-dozen of his variations on the theme. But this time he thought it would be different. This time, by anticipating their objections, he would prove they had been wrong. Perhaps the most touching—or demented—aspect of the venture was that S.S. apparently believed his associates would, in the face of his demonstration, apologize for their past lack of vision and gratefully wring his hand.

Late in November, 1905, S.S. wrote in confidence to Miss Tarbell, telling of his "little scheme." He enclosed a prospectus. He asked her not to tell Phillips of his plan; he preferred to iron out every wrinkle first; but as for the financial details he assured her that he would have two hundred thousand dollars pledged within a week.

A prospectus is like a dream. It rarely makes sense, it rarely coincides with reality, it never predicts with accuracy, and it resists criticism. The Universal Magazine (which is what McClure first called his dream) might have been a howling success; we will never know. Its format was to have been that of The Saturday Evening Post. It was to have run to sixty-four pages, of which forty were to have been editorial and twenty-four advertising. It was to have cost five cents a copy or, by subscription, fifty cents a year. McClure planned to print it on cheap paper, using for illustrations mainly pen-and-ink drawings. ("The half-tone engraving," he commented, "does not go with type.") He estimated the manufacturing cost of The Universal Magazine at less than three cents a copy. He proposed to spend one hundred thousand dollars a year to promote its sale. At a circulation of one million, he estimated a net income of five hundred and twenty-four thousand dollars. But he envisioned a far greater circulation. Why not three million? In which event, the annual net income would be nearly two million dollars. Yet to float this magnificent dreamboat only five hundred thousand dollars of capital would be required. "I believe," McClure concluded, "that this has in it the germ of the greatest periodical ever published in America."

As she studied these figures, Miss Tarbell must have felt the need to pinch herself. Could anybody take such a prospectus seriously? A day or two later, McClure assured her he had already raised a quarter of a million. The new magazine, he added, would not be inimical to corporations but would be "eager to do them absolute justice." And now Miss Tarbell took alarm. Who were his backers? And what were their motives?

Her misgivings were the keener because she was at the time working on the draft of an editorial for McClure's that discussed how the great corporations systematically manufactured public opinion by deceitfully manipulating the press. The evidence was at every hand. Item: The legislative investigation of the life-insurance companies was now nearly complete, and the diligent counsel to the investigating committee, Charles Evans Hughes, had shown that the Mutual Life Insurance Company regularly paid press agents at the rate of a dollar a line for every so-called news item they were able to sell to reputable newspapers; the newspapers charged up to five dollars a line to print this stuff as though it were news. In this way, prejudiced accounts of the investigation itself had been merchandised to newspapers all over the country. (There was no reason to suppose that the Mutual was the only insurance company given to such practices.) Item: Ray Stannard Baker was even then writing a piece for his series on the railroads, in which he would show how artful was the firm of press agents employed by an association of railroad companies. To cite just one example, the newspapers of Nebraska, in the week ending June 5, 1905, had printed two hundred and twelve columns of matter unfavorable to the railroads, and only two columns favorable; but eleven weeks later, after a careful campaign of pressure, suasion, and threats by advertisers, a survey showed two hundred and two columns favorable to the railroads, and only four unfavorable. Item: Mark Sullivan's recent articles in Collier's had proved how the patent-medicine manufacturers

used the sugar of advertising contracts to persuade newspaper publishers
to kill any editorial or news item inimical to the patent-medicine business.
Item: In the spring of 1905, the Standard Oil Company had been caught
paying publishers of small Kansas newspapers as much as one thousand
dollars to print Standard propaganda as if it were straight news. Moreover,
it was common knowledge that the Standard had subsidized a respected
periodical, Gunton's Magazine, to the tune of twenty-five thousand dollars
a year. Gunton's had suffered, so said the editorial in McClure's, "the intellectual dry-rot which overtakes most subsidized concerns"; it had died
earlier that same year.

Was this the fate in store for McClure's? Were S.S.'s backers pledging a
quarter of a million for a new magazine so they could worm their way
into control of McClure's and then throttle it?

The wondrous fact about S.S.'s backers and advisers in his new scheme
was that they could be comfortably fitted into either of two contradictory
classifications. Anyone who chose to denounce them as sinister plotters against
McClure, McClure's, and all crusading journalism could find much circum-
stantial evidence to support his charge. Contrariwise, it was possible to recognize his backers as his lifelong friends and simple admirers of his editorial
genius.

His chief adviser, for example, was president of one railroad company
and a director of thirty others. As if this were not bad enough, he was also
an officer of the Mercantile Trust Company, an institution that had acquired
a certain notoriety during the investigation of the life-insurance companies.
The Mutual Life Insurance Company, the New York Life Insurance Company, and the Equitable Life Assurance Society had, according to Charles
Evans Hughes, "divided the country . . . so as to avoid a waste of effort,
each looking after legislation in its chosen district, and bearing its appropriate
part of the total expense." Each spent substantial sums for politicking,
lobbying, bribery of legislators, and political espionage; each needed a device
to cloak its activities. The Equitable's device was to keep an account with
its subsidiary, the Mercantile Trust Company, "to facilitate disbursements
which would not bear disclosure." In the Mercantile Trust, in short, was
hidden some of the grease that kept the System functioning smoothly—the
System, that secret and intricate webwork by which finance capital subverted
and controlled politics—the System, precisely what McClure's had been ex-
posing during the past three years.

And who was the rascally officer of the Mercantile Trust who was Mc-

Clure's chief adviser? He was Robert Mather, McClure's classmate at Knox College and his old friend.

Another of McClure's advisers was Edgar Bancroft, likewise a railroad lawyer and a bank director, likewise a Knox graduate and an old friend.

Most of the money pledged to McClure was to come from Victor Lawson, another suspicious character, who was publisher of The Chicago Daily News. Lawson had been one of the first clients of McClure's syndicate; he had known and done business with McClure for twenty years.

Steffens and Miss Tarbell both chose to believe that Mather and the others were unscrupulous knaves who had involved McClure in something that "was not quite right." Phillips, who knew Mather and Bancroft quite as well as did McClure, reserved judgment as to their motives and concentrated on McClure. He knew his partner even better. He had every reason to suspect that S.S.'s health was precarious. He urged S.S. to slow down, to take it easy. And he made clear his resolute opposition to any new magazine.

S.S.'s "little scheme" was growing fast. The new magazine had a new name: McClure's Journal. The magazine was still the nub of the matter, but he now unveiled four subsidiary enterprises that had beguiled his imagination: a People's University, which would furnish a curriculum by the correspondence plan and which would also publish textbooks; a Universal Library, to publish classics not protected by copyright; a People's Life Insurance Company, by means of which S.S. hoped to revive the old ideals of honest, fair, economical life insurance; and a People's Bank, to do a general banking business.

To the angry young men in the editorial offices of McClure's, no further proof was required that their Chief had at last gone off his rocker. The wits got to work at his expense. At first their jokes were intramural, but no cruel joke is ever kept private. And so, in the bars and clubs frequented by journalists, the story grew of how McClure, megalomaniacal, was planning a vast publishing Trust, to be financed by a McClure Life Insurance Company and a McClure Bank, and to include in time a McClure Ideal Settlement complete with McClure Mansions and a McClure Foundation for Benevolent Social Betterment.*

---

* These malicious tales inevitably crept into print and so, thanks to the tyranny of type, became the so-called research for so-called history. See, for example, Frank Luther Mott's A History of American Magazines, Volume IV, pp. 599–600. For an exaggerated example, see Ladies, Gentlemen and Editors, by Walter Davenport and James Derieux, pp. 254–256.

As usual with McClure, the truth was bizarre enough to make fictions unnecessary. Why should he plan a new monthly magazine to compete with his own successful property? Why should he plan a new company to publish textbooks when he was already majority share-holder in McClure, Phillips & Company, successful publishers of books? He had shown time and again that he had no particular itch for money; and even if he had belatedly developed some such pruritic symptom, to compete with himself was scarcely the way to get rich. When he wrote to those (like Sir Arthur Conan Doyle) who owned shares in the S.S. McClure Company, urging them to buy shares in his new enterprise, he utterly ignored the bank, insurance company, university, and universal library, focusing all his attention on the proposed McClure's Journal.

On the face of it, McClure's Journal seemed an impossible venture. The only answer to the enigma of McClure seems to be that he believed he had risen to the top by succeeding at impossible ventures; he had once again got his Irish up; the more resolutely Phillips opposed him, the more stubbornly he was determined to prove that once again he could prevail over long odds.

Gently and firmly and perseveringly, Phillips opposed him. McClure retorted by hiring Howard Pyle, the celebrated illustrator, to be art manager of McClure's Journal at what was then the remarkable salary of eighteen thousand dollars a year. He also organized a corporation, called McClure's Journal Company, capitalized at two million five hundred thousand dollars, of which one million eight hundred thousand was to be in common stock and seven hundred thousand in preferred stock.

The news of this development came when Phillips and Miss Tarbell were on holiday with William Allen White in Arizona. Miss Tarbell wrote to Boyden:

El Tovar, Grand Canyon, Arizona

My Dear Bert:—We have just come up 4500 feet on mule-back from the bottom of the canyon. We have been gone two days. It has been a glorious trip. After my little climb up Mont Blanc this is quite the biggest thing I ever attempted. It would be all very fine if it were not for the diabolic condition in N.Y. These letters [from McClure, forwarded by Boyden] make me furious. If anything could prove the General's inability to found & carry out a new business it is this. The vital points he does not touch. The use of the name McClure [on the new magazine] is all wrong—out of the question, as I see it. This system of securing the consent of everybody by means of gifts of sweets [shares of stock in the new company] is humbug. I won't touch it and more if he goes on insisting on using the name McC[lure] He can take my S.S. McC[lure] stock   You see I am not fit to write him. Mr P[hillips] as usual is an angel & has written him a beautiful letter which *ought* to show him what an inferior creature [he] is but which probably he will consider as someway a consent to his scheme.

You insist on his coming out here. I have just [wired] you a message saying it would kill us. . . . We should simply go mad with him banging away in the face of Nature. . . . Don't let him commit himself any more than possible and urge him to wait until Mr P[hillips]'s return. I am sure it can be fixed right then—if not we *can* secede

Affectionately
Ida M. Tarbell

Still unaware of the mutinous pressures building up in his own office, Mc-Clure sailed for Europe late in February. In his absence, Miss Tarbell and Boyden maintained their leverage on Phillips. During this painful time, a letter arrived for Phillips from William Allen White.

The Emporia Gazette

Emporia, Kansas, Mar 17 1906

My Dear John:

. . . I suppose it is hell in the office. I know it must be. I only wish I could help out, but probably I'd ball it up if I tried. Yet if you can see any place where I could help, let me know and I'll do anything or go any place to help. I most earnestly hope that you will hang on until your eye-brows pull out. For there must be over the country a lot of fellows like me who would not know where to go or what to do without you. . .

. . . Got a new story the other day about a man—cowboy, been riding hard all day in the cold wind and struck town and went to the barber shop to get fixed up. It was warm and the barber's hands were soft and the perfume smelled good, and after telling the barber he wanted everything in the shop the cowboy went to sleep. At last the barber shook the cowboy and said "Next." The man looked up sleepily and said "Gimme hair cut." And the barber replied "I did." "All right, gimme shampoo," said the man as he started back to snooze. "Done that too." "Well, shine 'em up." "You've got 'er!" returned the barber. "Zasso? Well, gimme hair-singe!" "She's all scorched," replied the barber. "All right, put on a sea-foam," sighed the weary man as he took in a deep breath. "But I did that half an hour ago," insisted the barber. "Good boy," replied the cowboy as he sank back into the small of his back and closed his eyes in ecstasy. "Now pull a tooth."

Now what I was comin' at in a round about way John is this—dont you get out of your chair in McClures until Sam has pulled a tooth!

With affectionate regards
W.A.White

McClure was home again a week later, and by that time Phillips had made up his mind. "It was a momentous decision for a man of forty-five to make," Phillips wrote, many years later.* "The impelling reasons were personal, almost spiritual. . . . Bitter personal antagonism did not arise and the material points involved were, no doubt, capable of adjustment in a worldly sense, but I felt that I could not submit to being wrenched into courses and proposed undertakings that would arouse inner dissension with no prospect of peace. As soon as the decision was made, there was a great calm, a serene contentment. . . ."

"It's been a wild day," Boyden wrote to Baker at the end of that day of decision, and he was more nearly right. Bitter personal antagonism was tangible enough to be cut up in chunks. McClure said later he sensed "a malignant wave of hysteria" as soon as he walked into the office.

Phillips and Miss Tarbell cornered McClure in his room and closed the door. The three were closeted together for hours. In the corridor outside, Steffens and Boyden and Siddall tiptoed back and forth, pausing to listen to the crescendo and diminuendo beyond the door. Inside, Phillips pounded away at three points: how much McClure had been in Europe in the past few years, how McClure's Magazine had grown beyond the capability of any one man to administer it properly, how urgent was the need to democratize control of the magazine.

At first McClure was bewildered. Gradually, from things that were said, he began to comprehend that Phillips must have been rehearsing his argument for weeks, perhaps for months; Miss Tarbell, he now realized, must have been harboring these ideas for years. The belated insight was shattering.

He protested. Democratization? What did they mean? They threw up at him his scheme to publish McClure's Journal, and the constellation of

---

* The quotation is from A Legacy to Youth, an unpublished memoir which Phillips wrote chiefly for his children.

subsidiary companies. When he objected that this was still only an idea, they reminded him that he had hired Pyle as art manager at a fancy fee. He insisted he had made no contract with Pyle without first consulting Phillips. Tiring of these details, Phillips and Miss Tarbell now produced a document and asked McClure to sign it. This contract, they informed him, provided the only possible basis for their continued association.

It provided that he turn over three hundred and sixty shares of his stock in the S.S. McClure Company and two hundred shares of his stock in McClure, Phillips & Company to be held in trust equally by Phillips, Miss Tarbell, Steffens, and Baker, and to be voted by them; it further provided that he would give them the option to buy three hundred shares of his stock in the S.S. McClure Company at one thousand dollars per share.

S.S. was not much of a businessman, but he knew when his best friends were trying to euchre him out of control of his own company. The crescendos began to reverberate con molto brio and appassionata. At last he cried out that he would rather sell his interests entirely than yield his majority control. Miss Tarbell promptly snatched up a pen and a sheet of paper and wrote as fast as she could:

> I agree to give to J.S.P. & I.M.T. an option on my entire stock in S.S. McC Co. at $1000 per share. I to receive also at a sum not exceeding $—— the S.S. McC. syndicate; this option to be exercised on demand of J.S.P. & I.M.T.
> Payment for stock to be made in terms of years not less than 10.

She plunked this down in front of him and thrust the pen into his hand. He signed. As an afterthought, she added:

> I also agree on J.S.P.'s demand to purchase his stock at $1000 per share, payable in five yrs.

McClure signed that, too. Then he burst out of the room, tears in his eyes, and walked blindly down the hall to the office of Curtis Brady, the advertising manager. "Curtis," he said brokenly, "I'm leaving here." Brady stared at him in astonishment. He knew only that McClure had just got back from Europe. "Leaving here?" he asked. "What do you mean?" McClure collapsed in a chair and struggled for composure. After a minute he managed to say that he had agreed to sell his stock to Phillips. "You will do nothing of the kind," Brady growled, and proceeded to tell him why. McClure brightened. "I'll not sell," he cried. "I'll not sell! I'll buy his stock!" And he hurried back to his own office.

But by nightfall McClure had changed his mind again. He would sell. He saw no other course. Where was he to find the money to buy Phillips's and Miss Tarbell's shares? He had no personal wealth; he had not even a personal bank account. His business was his wealth; the cashier's office was his bank. Money from the business had been regularly deposited in Mrs. McClure's bank account so that she might pay for household and family expenses; when S.S. had needed money, he had simply sent a chit to the cashier, who had sent him back either cash or a letter of credit. For years he had in this way customarily drawn more than was due him from salary and dividends, and the directors of the company had customarily met the deficit by voting him a bonus that would be entered on the books according to convenience.*

On this fateful March 24, then, McClure crept home, as miserable as can be imagined, to tell his wife that his old and trusted associates had pushed him to the wall. He was selling his business. What else could he do? He was utterly crushed. His faithful Hattie, her heart aching, gave him generously of her sympathy. Secretly she was concerned as to how this sudden reversal would affect his health. She sent off a letter to her cousin, Doctor Henry Hurd, appealing for help.†

Meantime, in his office at McClure's, Boyden was writing in haste to Baker, apparently oblivious of the fact that he was still on McClure's payroll:

> This is to tell you to get together your money—we all want to put in all we can—we'll never have as good a business opportunity—Miss Tarbell, Stef, the Bradys and I each want to put in $50,000—I hope we can keep nearly all the stock in the gang.
>
> Mr. Phillips was marvellous today—never saw him so fine & clear & firm. Mr McC of course feels terribly—but the whole thing was inevitable. . . .
>
> Yours ever,
A.A.B.
>
> I feel better than in months. It's a relief to know that the magazine is to be preserved—that's bigger & more important than any of us.

---

* The Sixteenth Amendment to the Constitution, authorizing taxes on personal income, was not ratified until February, 1913.

† Doctor Hurd seemed a likely resource in this time of her need. Besides being superintendent of the Johns Hopkins Hospital, he was also editor of The Journal of Insanity.

Boyden was too jubilant too soon. He underestimated his Chief and he overestimated the Bradys. In the spring of 1906 there were five directors of the S.S. McClure Company: McClure himself, his brother Robert, Phillips, and the two Brady brothers, Oscar and Curtis. Phillips knew he could not count upon Robert McClure, despite their warm personal friendship, but he had been confident of the support of the Bradys. They were both prudent and conservative businessmen; surely they would appreciate how sorely McClure had endangered his own property with his fantastic schemes. But on that same day of decision, March 24, 1906, the Bradys held a brief consultation. They determined to stick with McClure. And, in the days of confusion and vacillation that followed, nothing happened to make them change their minds.

The Bradys would have had no difficulty in raising their share of capital for investment. Curtis Brady, indeed, was pelted with offers of money as soon as the word got around that there was friction at McClure's. The first tender was made by J. Walter Thompson, president of what was even then the biggest advertising agency in the country. His offices were three floors below those of McClure's. Thompson called on Brady late in March, wearing a conspiratorial look. (Such a look was easy for J. Walter, who was equipped with a mustache, a full beard, and also, since he was rather deaf, a large ear-trumpet.) He closed the door of Brady's room and locked it.

"I understand," he said, "there may be an opportunity to buy stock in the McClure Company."

Brady supposed that Thompson wanted to make a personal investment and he saw no reason to encourage the idea. "That's a moot question, Mr. Thompson," he said.

"You," said Thompson, "will buy a large block of it, if it can be bought. Any time you want twenty-five thousand dollars to buy McClure stock, let me know, and I will lend it to you."

Brady stared. "Thank you very much," he said, "but what kind of collateral would you want to secure such a loan?"

"Your note, and an insurance policy on your life. If you live, you will pay it back. If you die, the insurance company will pay me." He got up to go. "Think it over," he said.

A few days later Thompson was back again, and again he carefully closed the door. "A friend of yours," he said, "has told me to tell you he is willing to underwrite one hundred thousand dollars for you to buy McClure stock, and take your note and an insurance policy as security."

Brady protested he had no friend who could spare that kind of money. "I'll tell you who it is," said Thompson. "It's Senator Dryden."

John F. Dryden, the United States Senator from New Jersey from 1902 until 1907, was president of the Prudential Life Insurance Company. Brady had met him only once, in Thompson's office, and had exchanged only a couple of dozen words of banalities with him. It seems never to have occurred to Brady, as it surely would have to one of the suspicious staff writers on McClure's, that this generous offer was made just prior to the publication of Burton Hendrick's series on life insurance. In any event, Brady smiled politely and declined.

Curtis and Oscar Brady made up their minds to stick with McClure because, as Curtis Brady said, "We knew he was the spark-plug of the editorial department, and . . . we felt that one stockholder could not and should not be compelled to purchase the holdings of others." *

With the Bradys in his corner, McClure found his spirits reviving. He had room to maneuver and time to waver, and he needed both. For more than twenty years, whenever he had been faced with a problem, he had turned to Phillips; for more than ten years, if Phillips were not there, he had turned to Miss Tarbell. Now that both had turned against him, he had to seek out new advisers. There was his brother Robert, there were the Bradys—and there was Mather.

Whatever his motives in urging McClure to launch a new magazine, Mather was an excellent ally for McClure in his present plight. He was cool, resourceful, and equally free of such distracting emotions as affection and such destructive emotions as the need to be liked and admired. Mather now appeared as S.S.'s advocate and general counsel. He was on old, familiar terrain: here would be fought a battle for control of a prosperous enterprise that had good possibilities for growth and splendid possibilities for influence over national affairs. Mather's adversary, representing Miss Tarbell and Phillips, was George W. Wickersham, who was to be appointed Attorney General by President Taft in 1909. But Mather's worst enemy was his own client.

First McClure wrote his brother Robert: "If I stay, I stay with precisely the authority conferred by my position & usage & ownership. I want no one to feel that I can in any way abate my position of authority."

---

* The quotation is from The High Cost of Impatience, an unpublished reminiscence of his days on McClure's by Curtis Brady. I have also drawn on this manuscript for the account of the two offers made to Brady by J. Walter Thompson.

Mather talked with Phillips and Miss Tarbell. Both insisted they wanted to sever their connections with McClure.

McClure thereupon advised Phillips to take a leave of absence at full salary "for a year, a year and a half or for two years." Study, rest, reflect. "When you are well rested and return here you will find . . . a prosperous business well established, a plant built and in good running order, the magazine pointed straight at the very heart of civilization. . . . It is utterly impossible for me, John, to have a position in this business different from what I have had before. When you read history you find that kings who have come to the end of their tether, as a rule suffer death rather than give up part of their power. I would dispose of the entire business before I would give up part of my power. I can do the one but I cannot do the other. . . ."

"All is well with me," S.S. told his wife on April 7. "I will not sell out." Then he wrote:

> My dear Miss Tarbell
>   I cannot leave the magazine. I *simply cannot*.
>   I would soon lose my mind with unavailing regret.
>   I can master all other matters.
>   All other disturbing matters are closed, closed on both sides. My interest in the magazine surpasses all other interests.
>   I shall not again appear in these transactions as I have turned the matter over to the others or shall Monday morning by power of att[orne]y. This is final. I am sorry, sorry.
>   Sincerely yours
>   SSMcClure

But on Monday he sent a letter to his stockholders, saying: "Such stock as I have, over fifty-one per cent, I shall be pleased to sell to other people in the office."

What did he mean? Phillips and Miss Tarbell could not be sure. They countered by proposing that he buy their interests for one hundred and eighty-seven thousand dollars. They further demanded six months' salary, to begin May 1, without prejudice to their right during that time to engage in work that would compete with McClure's.*

---

* Phillips owned one hundred and forty-six shares in the S.S. McClure Company; Miss Tarbell owned fifteen which S.S. had given her. They put a price of one thousand dollars on each of these. Phillips owned one hundred and ten shares in McClure, Phillips & Company; Miss Tarbell owned fifty; and David McKinlay, an executive of the book-publishing company, owned one hundred shares. They put a price of one hundred dollars on each of these. The total was one hundred and eighty-seven thousand dollars.

At this point everybody got childish. McClure snarled at Phillips that he wouldn't buy his stock and didn't have to. Phillips snarled back that Mc-Clure did so have to buy his stock, reminding him of the paper he had signed on the day he got back from Europe. Both men then snarled and shouted at once, threatening lawsuits.

The next day, McClure told Mather he would buy, but preferred to sell. "It is the greatest tragedy of my life," he said. "My continued wavering is caused by my utter inability to face the separation."

That same day President Roosevelt made his celebrated assault upon the muckrakers. McClure was so overwrought he scarcely noticed it.

"Nothing new," Boyden wrote to Baker a week later. "We are just as far from any settlement as we ever were." At this point McClure walked into Boyden's office, interrupting him. Presently Boyden resumed his letter: "Mr McC says to tell you it will be settled this week. I may add that I don't believe it! He's plumb crazy and it's my opinion will eventually sell to us—the Lord only knows."

April wore to a close while McClure still agonized. There were so many memories, of associations so intimate, so loyal, now being wrenched apart. There were so many conflicting desires, paramount among them the insistent desire that he never sell to his associates. But how could he find the money to buy what was theirs? In addition to all his other responsibilities, he had been for some years a trustee of Knox College and had signed notes pledging annual payments against a sizeable endowment. All his needs now wrung him. The coalition arrayed against him—Phillips, Miss Tarbell, and Boyden its leaders—knew more about his obligations than he did and confidently expected he would be forced to sell. As the days passed, the coalition hunted hard for the money to buy him out.

Meanwhile the laconic Mather had organized in Connecticut an S.S. Mc-Clure Corporation which, he had planned, would make an agreement with the Bankers Trust Company to issue three hundred thousand dollars' worth of ten-year five-per-cent gold bonds. The security for the bonds would be as much of the capital stock of the S.S. McClure Company as McClure and his friends could lay their hands on—as it turned out, nearly eighty per cent. Mather conjectured there would surely be someone, somewhere, who would buy bonds secured by the stock of a company so demonstrably successful: McClure would thus be able to pay for the stock owned by Phillips and Miss Tarbell.

But McClure still despaired. He was like a man in a maze who, shown the way out, frantically turns down the wrong corridor.

On April 27 Miss Tarbell, thoroughly exasperated, penned a formal note of resignation, again demanding six months' salary. She exacted an answer. He replied on April 30:

> My dear Miss Tarbell:
> . . . I have absolutely decided to buy you and Mr. Phillips out and to give you a six months' vacation on full salary, and to close up these matters just as rapidly as possible. I shall be under debts in this office equal to the net earnings of the last nine years when you leave, and it is therefore necessary for me to be able to give my undivided time and attention to this business. I shall agree to pay you for your stock on the most favorable terms that I can possibly hope to carry out. I have always endeavored to deal with you fairly and generously and you must understand that this separation results from no wish of mine, and that in purchasing your stock, which would not find a market elsewhere, I am simply exhibiting to you my appreciation of your long and splendid service. I feel no differently towards you and John from what I have always felt. Necessarily, in matters of this kind, many things are said and come to my ears from different sources that have been said, but I dismiss them. Even Mr. Phillips' phrase that I was headed for the insane asylum or the penitentiary, which has come to me from different sources, I forget.* I only wish that things can be settled with the least possible friction and the least possible strain upon our friendship and health.
>
> Very sincerely yours,
> SSMcClure

By this time the newspapers had begun to print rumor, conjecture, and malicious gossip about the impending split, all disguised as news. The yarn most widely broadcast was that a quarrel at McClure's had been precipitated by President Roosevelt's Man-with-the-Muck-Rake speech. The coincidence of quarrel and speech was irresistible to any journalist who, lacking facts, was obliged to speculate. According to this fable, Phillips, Miss Tarbell, Steffens, Baker, and the others were militantly committed to a policy of more and harsher muckraking; McClure was pictured in some reports as being scared, in others as being shrewd; but most accounts agreed he was anxious to muzzle his writers or perhaps to pitch the muck-rake away entirely.

As it happens McClure was, despite his travail, remarkably sensitive to the

* The phrase was, of course, Miss Tarbell's. She may have winced as she read this sentence of the letter.

mood of his readers and to the public atmosphere generally. Undeniably, there was a sentiment against what would later be called muckraking, and McClure had instinctively recorded it on his internal barometer. On April 9, two weeks before Roosevelt's public attack on the muckrakers, McClure had made a report to the stockholders of his company:

> I believe [he told the stockholders] that a study of municipal and other questions abroad would be a very good thing to do. I believe that during the present insensate wave of reaction against the magazine exposures it will be well to take up now these other constructive sides, as there will soon be a wave of reaction against reaction and we can then go on with our work. I believe to go on now with the heavy exposure articles would not convert those who disagree with us, and those who agree with us don't need conversion.

But to say, as did the newspapers, that the President's speech had caused dissension at McClure's was absurd. To suggest that McClure ever attempted to suppress or to muzzle the staff writers whom he regarded as extensions of his own intelligence was worse than absurd. Yet the fable persisted.*

And still there was no swift surgical stroke, only a long protracted anguish. At last, early in May, Mather and Wickersham were able to initial a tentative memorandum of agreement. Even then McClure hoped that by some miracle the nightmare of the past weeks would vanish and all would be as it had been before. But on May 10 Phillips, Miss Tarbell, Boyden, Siddall, and David McKinlay cleaned out their desks and departed. Steffens and Baker were both out of town, but it was clear they were quitting McClure's too. S.S. was consternated to find that his own cousin, Harry McClure, whom he had put in charge of the syndicate, had joined the exodus.

Late that afternoon Witter Bynner found McClure sitting alone in the editorial department. McClure raised a tear-stained face when he heard Bynner's steps. "Bynner," he said, "are you leaving me too?" Bynner could not speak. McClure buried his face in his arms and sobbed.

It was like the old days back in Valparaiso, thirty-eight years before.

---

* In 1919 Upton Sinclair published The Brass Check, A Study of American Journalism. "I take," Sinclair wrote in an introductory note, "the oath of a witness: the truth, the whole truth, and nothing but the truth, so help me God. . . . There are no mistakes in [this book], no guesses, no surmises; there are no lapses of memory, no inaccuracies. There are only facts." Thereafter he wrote, at page 81: "Lincoln Steffens, Ida Tarbell, Ray Stannard Baker and Finley Peter Dunne found they were no longer permitted to tell the truth in 'McClure's'."

[xx]

The palace revolution had been crushed, but the casualties had been severe. Of "the most brilliant staff ever gathered by a New York periodical," the only considerable survivors, aside from McClure, were Burton Hendrick, Witter Bynner, and Viola Roseboro'.*

Those who had left did not believe McClure's Magazine could long survive their departure. How could it? Its editor was crazy; during the previous six years he had been in Europe more than half the time and so could know nothing of what American readers wanted; he would never be able to recruit so able an editorial team. Nevertheless, they kept a wary eye on their former Chief, fearful of what surprises he might have up his sleeve.

No doubt about it, the shock for McClure's was a violent one. Apart from the departure of Phillips, Miss Tarbell, Baker, Steffens, Boyden, Siddall, McKinlay, and H.H. McClure, there were other losses.

Mark Sullivan, having completed his obligation to McClure's, had joined the staff of Collier's in March.

Finley Peter Dunne, whom McClure had personally signed to a contract, nevertheless elected to join Phillips and his associates in the purchase of The American Magazine. McClure, who despised litigation, chose not to sue Dunne for breach of contract.

Samuel Hopkins Adams, who had been for so long tied to McClure's, was now a free lance.

William Allen White was so widely advertised as having joined Phillips on The American that everybody believed it.†

---

* The superlative I have quoted belongs to Ellery Sedgwick (see p. 136 of his memoir, The Happy Profession, Little, Brown and Company, 1946), and he must be accounted a competent judge. In 1906 Sedgwick was editor of The American Magazine, *geboren* Frank Leslie's Popular Monthly, which was the magazine Phillips and his associates were to purchase in the summer of 1906 after they quit McClure's; in 1946, when he made this judgment, Sedgwick was, as he had been for nearly forty years, editor of The Atlantic.

More brilliant staffs than that on McClure's in April, 1906, may since have been assembled on American periodicals. But their departure to launch a competitive enterprise would not, I dare say, have caused as great a stir as did the split-up at McClure's, coming as it did on the heels of Roosevelt's attack on the muckrakers.

† In fact, White wrote to McClure: "The idea seems to have gained headway in your office that because I am friendly with John Phillips . . . I am at cross-purposes with you. . . . I have always felt grateful to you and also to John, and the fact that you could not arrange things

Yet there was a saving grace in the wholesale sweep of the upheaval. If only two or three had resigned, the morale of the others would have suffered sorely; but so many valuable talents had been withdrawn that the handful of loyalists could feel only an exhilarating sense of excitement and adventure. And they were confident that McClure would pull them through. "S.S. McClure always has been and will continue to be editor-in-chief of McClure's," Bynner told a reporter from The New York Times. "He is the potent factor in all editorial policy."

Bynner was thoroughly elated. Overnight he had soared to dizzy heights; he was suddenly managing editor (or desk editor, or assistant editor, depending on S.S.'s mood of the moment) and ready to shoulder his new responsibilities with zeal. Miss Roseboro' made another of her theatrical entrances into the office to hug her Chief, kiss him warmly, and bring forth another McClure's "first." This was a story spiced with slang that was fresh and vivid in 1906 (e.g. "duck soup," "kidding on the square"), told in the historical present by a first-person narrator, dealing with rough, rude characters, funny, tough, and sentimental. The master of the form had been "discovered." The by-line on the story was Alfred Damon Runyon.

For his part, McClure recognized that in this crisis he had to bring forth something like a miracle. An entire new staff was needed forthwith. In rapid-fire order, McClure hired Perceval Gibbon, George Kibbe Turner, Henry Kitchell Webster, Will Irwin, Ellery Sedgwick, George Kennan, Cameron Mackenzie, and Willa Cather. It was a very mixed bag. Judged by their contemporary celebrity, they were woefully inferior to their predecessors. McClure, however, considered that those predecessors had acquired their celebrity solely through McClure and McClure's, an opinion with which it is difficult to quarrel. He saw no reason why he should not be able to repeat the process with a new batch of writers.

Perceval Gibbon was a young Welsh journalist whom McClure hired away from The London Standard. S.S. apparently hoped he had discovered in Gibbon a second Kipling, since Gibbon's experience in Africa roughly paralleled Kipling's in India. Gibbon remained on staff only a few weeks but was thereafter a regular contributor of articles and short stories.

George Kibbe Turner was a gentle, diffident man of thirty-five, with mousy

---

amicably to conduct one magazine together seemed to me no reason why I should not do what I could to help you conduct two magazines apart. You may draw on me whenever you will for whatever you will, and if I have it it shall be yours." White continued to contribute to McClure's.

hair and a mousy personality. After graduating from Williams, Turner had gone to work as a reporter for The Springfield Republican. He had started selling short stories to McClure's in 1899, and McClure had also published his first novel, The Taskmaster. Turner was so self-effacing that his tenure on McClure's seemed doubtful. This impression was deceptive.

Henry Kitchell Webster had written several novels on contemporary subjects—Calumet K (in collaboration with Samuel Merwin), which was concerned with a corner in wheat, The Banker and the Bear, which dealt with a corner in lard, and The Copper King. He lasted as a desk editor at McClure's only a couple of months.

Will Irwin was from San Francisco, a man slight of build and impish of humor. He had succeeded Frank Norris as subeditor on The Wave, had gone on to be a reporter for The San Francisco Chronicle, and in 1904 had been lured to New York by The Sun, then the newspaperman's newspaper, where he was soon acknowledged to be the best of a remarkable staff. McClure had of course known Irwin for years; no one so promising was likely to escape his attention. At the first intimation that he might lose his own staff, McClure had at once thought of Irwin as a replacement and had begun to exert what Irwin would later call his "subtle Celtic resourcefulness." Irwin had promptly succumbed to S.S.'s blandishments and had been invited to stop by the office of McClure's to familiarize himself with the routine, against the day when he would be called on to take over. He had been thus idly occupied on the morning of April 18 when an office boy came by with the early editions of the afternoon newspapers. They were emblazoned with headlines: Disaster!—Great Earthquake in San Francisco—A City in Flames—Thousands Dead—Martial Law—All the Great Buildings in Ruins. One glance and Irwin had galloped to the city room of The Sun where he was assigned to write a running story pieced together from the scanty telegraphic reports and his own voluminous knowledge of his beloved San Francisco. In the next week he wrote nearly eighty columns of copy—a prodigious stint. On May 15 he reported for duty at McClure's, breathing easy, and a few days later S.S. told him he was managing editor. (The crestfallen Bynner learned he had been deposed when he walked into his office one morning and found Irwin established there.)

Ellery Sedgwick, the editor of The American Magazine until Phillips and his associates bought it, applied for and was given a job at McClure's in the summer of 1906 but, as he later complained, "What that job was I never knew." Sedgwick would seem to have been an expendable pawn in a most vengeful game of chess. Ignored by the group that had bought his magazine, he was bewildered to find that McClure, after hiring him, also ignored him It was a painful experience for a man who had himself been a full-fledged editor-in-chief. Still he hoped to learn something of how McClure edited. He edged up as close as he could to the white heat of S.S.'s enthusiasms. He learned to honor McClure for his thoroughness, for his passion for facts ("In McClure's, accuracy was a moral force"), for his insistence on clear, logical, forceful writing, and for his respect for the power of understatement. And he kept hoping to learn more.

George Kennan was an older man who had made his reputation in the 1880s with a series of articles written for The Century on Siberia and the Czarist practice of using those bleak wastes as a jail for political prisoners.* McClure assigned him to muckrake the politics of San Francisco.

Cameron Mackenzie, like Will Irwin, came to McClure's from The Sun. He was twenty-four years old, personable, gay, and clever, the kind of man who is the envy and despair of his rivals. Great things were expected of him. For some time he had been dancing attendance on McClure's daughter Bess, so McClure was aware of his promise.

Willa Cather was still, of course, almost totally unknown and untested. A year before, she had spent a week in New York as McClure's guest; they had got along famously, each responding to something special in the other. Now here she was again, obedient to his summons, but a little uncertain as to what was expected of her.

While these new people were still measuring each other and making each other's acquaintance, they had to put out a magazine. During the first weeks McClure himself did most of the work, spurring the others by his example. He had risen to the challenge and he was thoroughly enjoying himself. He was in his office by half-past eight in the morning and he was still hard at work after midnight. He slept in an apartment that had been outfitted for him on the top floor of his office building; here he curled up over the week-ends with a great pile of manuscripts, drinking three or four quarts of milk a day instead of going out for meals.

In the midst of the new staff of editors, eyeing their first fumbling efforts and reporting derisively to his associates on The American, was Steffens. (Before the split, McClure had assigned Steffens to write a series of articles

---

* Kennan's interest in Russia was resumed by his nephew, George F. Kennan, the diplomatist who has written extensively on Soviet-American relations.

on Judge Ben B. Lindsey, the crusader for reform in Denver; it had been agreed that Steffens would finish the job before going off McClure's payroll.) With amusement, S.S. dubbed Steffens "our friend, the enemy." S.S. was much tickled to hear that Steffens had predicted the imminent collapse of his reputation as an editor, on the grounds that he was using up all his best ideas for features at once.

The notion that McClure would ever run out of best ideas was ludicrous. His only problem, as usual, was that he had too many best ideas—more than enough to stock McClure's Magazine and the aborted McClure's Journal as well—which was no doubt why he had planned to publish McClure's Journal in the first place. Indeed, as his mood changed, S.S. was able to convince himself he was better off without Phillips: at last there was no censor to toss his best ideas aside or sweep them under the rug. "I am a free man at last," he told Irwin.

At first McClure had, to intrigue his readers, only what he had inherited: a file full of fiction and two bulky typescripts that promised to afford interesting features. One concerned Mary Baker Eddy and the new religion, Christian Science; the other concerned the brutal battles for political and economic hegemony in the raw new state of Montana. S.S. scheduled both these features for publication as soon as possible. (Hence Steffens's raised eyebrows.)

The study of Mary A. Morse Baker Patterson Glover Eddy—her antecedents, her childhood and schooling, her striking eccentricities, her various marriages, her fitful relationships with her natural son and her adopted son, her career as poetess and invalid, her ultimate emergence as full-blown theologist and architect of a new religion—had been painstakingly assembled by Georgine Milmine, the wife of a Rochester newspaperman. Mark Sullivan had spent several months in corroborating Miss Milmine's research. Her typescript had passed through other hands, for criticism and revision. In the summer of 1906 McClure gave it to Miss Cather, bidding her check the facts once again, gather supporting affidavits, and prepare it for publication. Although Miss Cather's name was not put on the final result, her hand is evident in every line; she deserves much of the credit for a remarkable portrait of a remarkable woman. As serialized, it ran through fourteen lengthy installments, and never once did it drag.

Mrs. Eddy's followers made a determined effort to have the series suppressed. At the time, Witter Bynner was still the managing editor; he has recalled how three men, identifying themselves as spokesmen for the Church of Christ Scientist, appeared one day at the office demanding to see McClure. It was one of the duties of the managing editor to shield S.S. from unwelcome visitors, so Bynner parleyed with them briefly. He then withdrew to tell McClure they insisted on speaking with him personally. S.S. scowled and fidgeted and jingled the coins in his pocket.

"Get rid of them," he said.

"I can't," said Bynner.

"Then tell them I've sailed for Europe."

"They know you're here."

"How could they know that? I might have sailed just this morning."

"I really think maybe you'd better see—"

"All right, all right," said McClure petulantly. "Bring them in."

The Christian Scientists came in. Before they sat down, they stood on chairs and closed the transoms over the two doors to the room. Then they made their demand: the series must not be published. S.S. scowled at them and said nothing. To fill the silence, Bynner began rather nervously to assure the Scientists that the articles were not sensational, not offensive; that there was no cause for apprehension; that all the facts had been most carefully verified. . . .

One of the Scientists cut in to suggest that perhaps there would be no objection to publication of the material if the Scientists were permitted to edit it as they might please.

S.S. now spoke. He flatly refused either to suppress the material or to permit the Scientists to see it in advance of publication, much less to tamper with it. "Good day, gentlemen," he said grandly, and took up some papers from his desk.

The Scientists arose. One of them announced that if McClure persisted in his course he would soon notice a distinct loss of advertising in his magazine. They then marched out.

The encounter was a silly one, but nevertheless it had its significance. It was not unusual for an advertiser to apply punitive economic sanctions. In February, 1906, Armour & Company had cancelled contracts for advertising in McClure's, as a result of Ray Stannard Baker's series, The Railroads on Trial, and in April, 1906, the Equitable Life Assurance Society and the Mutual Life Insurance Company both cancelled contracts for advertising in McClure's, as a result of Burton K. Hendrick's series, The Story of Life Insurance.* But the Christian Scientists were different. They were not advertisers. They constituted simply a pressure-group, a small but intensely vocal minority which vowed to institute reprisals if it could not have its way. This was, so far as I am aware, the first attempt by a pressure-group to force an American editor to suppress or revise.

It is not hard to see why the Christian Scientists were riled by the series. Like many other religious leaders, Mrs. Eddy was an hysteric, often a shrew, and always an egotist. Evidence of her unusual behavior abounded, in and around Boston; and there were many ex-Scientists eager to testify against her. When Miss Cather came to write about Mrs. Eddy, she was able to find many bizarre facts to buttress her characterization. For example, Mrs. Eddy, as a woman in her thirties, still desired her father to cradle her in his lap and rock her like a baby. Again, when Mrs. Eddy was asked to leave a house where she had outstayed her welcome, she retorted by trying to set the house on fire.

Her followers likewise resisted the proof that nearly all Mrs. Eddy's ideas about healing ("Disease is error," et cetera) had been cribbed from one Phineas Parkhurst Quimby, an humble practitioner of Portland, Maine, and were not, as alleged, received by divine inspiration. The Christian Scientists seem also to have been offended by the demonstration that Mrs. Eddy (Mother Eddy, as she was by then known) was singularly lacking in any maternal affection for her son, George Washington Glover.

Advertising lineage in McClure's did decrease, during and after publication of the series on Christian Science, but there was no cause-and-effect relationship. There was, however, one direct and demonstrable result of the visit by the Christian Scientists to the office of McClure's, and this had to do with what was called malicious animal magnetism, or M.A.M. for short.

M.A.M. is scarcely heard of any more, but around the turn of the century it bulked big in any circles where Christian Science or other aspects of the New Thought were discussed. Christian Science, like all new religions, was burdened with its schismatics and heresiarchs; as they appeared they were promptly charged by Mrs. Eddy with M.A.M.; as like as not, they in turn charged Mrs. Eddy and her disciples with M.A.M. (One heresiarch, Daniel Spofford, of Haverhill, Massachusetts, had the distinction of being the only American of his time to have a legal action brought against him for witch-

* Advertisements of Armour products disappeared from McClure's for only six months. By September, 1906, Curtis Brady had persuaded Armour & Company to buy four pages a month. Both life-insurance companies likewise resumed their advertising after a brief sulk.

craft; it was brought by Mrs. Eddy.) In brief, M.A.M. was the power by which one person was supposed to be capable, by mesmerism and other evil mental malpractices, of bringing injury or sickness upon another person. After word got around the office of McClure's that three eminent Christian Scientists had showed up and been turned down, there was a predictable amount of nervous joking. Would M.A.M. now be applied against the editors of McClure's? Would someone in Boston make effigies of McClure and stick pins in them? And then, sure enough, someone got sick. There followed an epidemic of every sickness known to the annals of medicine. The opportunity was irresistible: if the weather was pleasant, you simply called the office, murmured something about M.A.M., and took the day off. (Bynner suffered from tonsillitis for a whole week of sunny weather.)

McClure chuckled about M.A.M., too. But he was to hear from other pressure-groups, as time went on.

The Story of Montana, the other feature on hand at the time of the split, was a five-part series by C.P. Connolly, a young Montana lawyer who was witness of the events he described. Charges that election to the United States Senate was bought by bribes to state legislators were no longer calculated to astonish, in 1906, but Connolly had a story to tell that was more refreshing than most because in Montana the fraud was so brazen. He described a time when politics were charmingly simple. After reading The Story of Montana, one no longer needed to guess the price of a seat in the Senate; one knew it to the last penny. In 1900, the price was well over five hundred thousand dollars in old-fashioned money. Thirty-five legislators accepted bribes totaling four hundred and thirty-one thousand dollars. The greedy came as cheap as four thousand dollars a head; the more upright cost as much as fifty thousand. As insurance, another two hundred and thirty thousand dollars was offered to sixteen other legislators, but these tips were, for a wonder, refused. A grand jury was summoned to investigate what was common knowledge; each juror was allegedly paid ten thousand dollars, with fifteen thousand going to the foreman, and so the jury voted that evidence was lacking for conviction by a trial jury. After the legislature had voted, every saloon in Helena was an open house, with the victorious candidate picking up the tab. For champagne alone, the bill was thirty thousand dollars.

The victorious candidate was William A. Clark, an owner of copper mines. If Clark did nothing else, he proved that copper was a profitable commodity.

Clark's bagman was his lawyer, John B. Wellcome, and a petition was presently filed with the Supreme Court of Montana, praying Wellcome's disbarment. Clark reasoned that if he could buy dozens of legislators he could surely buy two out of three judges, even if it cost a million dollars. The attempt was made, but it failed.

The fragrant circumstances of Clark's election were subsequently investigated by the Senate Committee on Privileges and Elections. Before the committee voted, Clark decided it would be expedient to resign. But he timed his resignation in such a way that, the governor of Montana being briefly out of the state, he could at once be reappointed by the lieutenant-governor, who was his creature. When the governor howled that the appointment was illegal, Clark blandly announced that he was a candidate for re-election in 1901. The familiar process was repeated, with the bribes this time amounting to more than one million dollars; Clark won his seat in the Senate by fifty-seven votes; and Helena was treated to another free binge.

As an example of turn-of-century democracy, these events were matchless. Just so, the report of these events in McClure's was invaluable in the fight to pass the Seventeenth Amendment, which requires that United States Senators be elected by direct popular vote.

Having scheduled these two series, S.S. supposed himself to be a free man, able to invent articles as he chose. He was not, as we shall see in a moment. No editor is ever entirely free of his associates or of the stern exigencies of his balance-sheet. But at least S.S. was free of Phillips and Miss Tarbell and the others; what he would do with his freedom held interest.

[XXI]

In his prospectus of McClure's for the future, S.S. showed he had by no means struck his flag. "The object of McClure's Magazine," he wrote, "is to discuss the immediate issues of our civilization. The most urgent problems of the present time consist in bringing under the reign of law the great forces loosed upon the world in the last century."

To Will Irwin, who helped him write this prospectus, the order seemed a large one. "Do we," asked Irwin, dolefully eyeing the clutter on McClure's desk from which there had to emerge an orderly magazine, "do we have to harness the nineteenth century as well?"

"Exactly," S.S. retorted. And he went on to write: "The task of this generation is to convert into human good and happiness the miraculous inventions and discoveries and the enormous material resources made available within the past hundred years."

It was the shining dream of social perfectibility, the ignis fatuus of progressives in the years before the War of 1914–18. McClure quoted with approval the words of the British naturalist, Alfred Russel Wallace: "Compared with our astounding progress in physical science and its practical application, our system of government, of administrative justice, and of national education, and our entire social and moral organization, remain in a state of barbarism."

To which McClure added: "The great problem of government today is to organize and master the new sources of power revealed by science, and the enormous wealth created partly by inventions and partly by the development of a great virgin continent. These governmental issues will be discussed, as heretofore, by the foremost thinkers and investigators, in McClure's Magazine."

McClure more than honored this pledge. During the next five or six years he was to publish, one after another, carefully documented articles that would, in their time, cause sensations.

There was method to the way S.S. ran his magazine, and a consistency of pattern, although some of his associates could never trace it. Ellery Sedgwick, for example, insisted that S.S. was devoted to disorder, that never in American business was there a brighter talent for disorganization. "A week in the McClure office," Sedgwick said later, "was the precise reversal of the six busy days described in the first chapter of Genesis. It seemed to end in a world without form or void. From Order came forth Chaos." Sedgwick lasted at McClure's less than a year. S.S. fired him. Will Irwin lasted only a little longer. He too fell or was pushed from his uneasy perch on the edge of the editor's chair. "As a curb on genius," Irwin confessed, "I was not a success."

The editorial pattern derived from what interested McClure, and, since his interests were plural and volatile, those close to him could be easily disconcerted. When Kibbe Turner first came to work, S.S. sent him to hell and gone—all the way to Galveston, Texas—to check on the rumors trickling north that a new scheme of municipal government had been invented in that unlikely city, a scheme which was, for a wonder, both honest and efficient. Infected by S.S.'s enthusiasm, Turner went south, and what he found excited him even more. Before 1900 Galveston had groaned under government by ward aldermen, a system then typical of American cities. There were eleven aldermen in control: one saloonkeeper, one bartender, one drayman, two wharf laborers, one Negro politician, one journeyman printer, one retail butcher, one retail grocer, one curbstone real-estate broker, one political agent for a railroad which never existed except on paper. These solons had, predictably, brought the city to the edge of bankruptcy. Then, on September 8, 1900, there came the great hurricane that drowned one-sixth of the city's people, destroyed one-third of its property, and ruined the municipality. In this time of disaster, Galveston invented the city commission, a device borrowed straight from the commercial corporation—and just as liable to corruption, although this was not at first apparent. The five Galveston businessmen who were the city's first commissioners in truth worked wonders. They cut expenses, sliced political fat off the municipal payroll, eliminated graft, lowered taxes, restored the city's credit, balanced its budget, paved its streets, installed electric street-lights, and improved sanitation, water supply, and other municipal services. In short, Galveston showed that the millennium was at hand. Bursting with the glad tidings, Turner hastened back to New York, but three weeks had passed and in that time S.S. had forgotten all about Galveston. He greeted Turner with an icy stare. "Where," he said coldly, "have *you* been?"

McClure was quick to recover from this lapse. Turner's piece on Galveston evoked a remarkable response. Civic leaders all over the country scrambled to promote the commission. Topeka wanted five hundred reprints of the article, Seattle wanted twenty thousand, Philadelphia asked permission to make a pamphlet out of it, and in Des Moines two newspapers reprinted the article almost entire. The office of McClure's for a time became a headquarters for the propagation of an idea which, as McClure noted in an optimistic editorial, "may mean the regeneration of our cities." (In fact, it would take the professional politicians only a few years to figure out how to exploit the commission and convert it into a partisan device.)

Much gratified, McClure now dispatched Turner to Chicago. Throughout 1906, the newspapers of that sinful city had recorded an impressive epidemic of bloody violence and impudent crime: unprotected women clubbed down and garroted on the streets, entire apartments cleaned out by burglars who parked their trucks outside as though they were moving-men. A murder a day, a suicide a day—McClure was horrified to find that such a rate was regarded by the authorities as normal, as routine. "Human life," said a public prosecutor, "is the cheapest thing in Chicago." Faithful to his documentary technique, S.S. had scissored a fistful of clippings from Chicago newspapers and proposed to publish them as an article headed, starkly, "Chicago As She Sees Herself." All that S.S. asked of Turner was that he acquaint himself with Chicago, return to New York, and write a prefatory note for S.S.'s anthology of enormities. Turner did more.

In 1901 Josiah Flynt had filed in McClure's an underworld report on Chicago: the low-down on graft and the intimate connection between cops and robbers. In 1903 Steffens had told in McClure's an upperworld tale: how respectable reformers were trying to scrub the town clean. Now in 1907 Turner wrote for McClure's the most thorough, evidential, and convincing report of all, linking underworld of crime and prostitution to upperworld of politics and protection, and introducing to the nation for the first time in their long careers those two illustrious statesmen of the First Ward, Michael (Hinky-Dink) Kenna and John J. (Bathhouse John) Coughlin.

Turner struck precisely the note McClure most admired: a cool disgust, with no trace of flamboyance or lurid rhetoric. He totted up the revenue of dissipation—one hundred million dollars a year from alcoholic liquor, twenty million from prostitution, and fifteen million from gambling—of which he estimated forty-five million dollars a year was illegal. Hinky-Dink's First Ward, at the center of Chicago, was the capital of this illicit traffic, an enclave of thirty-five thousand savages, self-regulating and self-protecting.

> It is [Turner wrote] a region of adults—one child in every eight or nine people, while there is one in three in the general population of the city. The inhabitants neither labor regularly nor marry. Half of the men are beggars, criminals, or floating laborers; a quarter are engaged in the sale of dissipation; and a third of the women are prostitutes. A great share of the men spend most of their waking hours thoroughly drugged with cheap alcohol. Society here has lapsed back into a condition more primitive than the jungle.

This single article caused more of a rumpus than had all the earlier exposures by Steffens, and for a good reason. Steffens had stubbornly persisted in aiming his fire at the businessman; but Turner, at S.S.'s bidding, laid bare as well the traffic in vice, and his facts scraped at the raw nerve of American puritanism. Before Turner's article appeared, prostitution was discussed, if at all, only in timid, decorous generalities, and never in a general magazine. Comstockery was in fullest flower.* Legs were limbs, and a

---

* Indeed, Anthony Comstock had waged, as recently as 1905, a relentless compaign against the production in New York of Mrs. Warren's Profession, Bernard Shaw's "strenuously ethical" preachment on prostitution. It is pertinent to note that in 1905 the New York newspapers, instead of guffawing at Comstock as they would later, joined in his hue-and-cry quite as hysterically as Comstock himself.

lady wore more clothes to bathe in the ocean than she would today to walk down the street. When McClure published Turner's piece, it was as though a bright light had been turned on in a dark cellar. While nasty things scurried for cover, angry householders came pounding down the stairs to clean out the mess. A Chicago Vice Commission was appointed, a grand jury was summoned. There was a sense of outrage. At last a city had been truly shamed. It began to seem that something might be done about it.

S.S. was jubilant. He would return to this issue of prostitution later, and hammer at the venality of other city governments; meanwhile there were other forces unleashed by the nineteenth century that required his attention. For example, there were the trade unions.

Specifically, there was the Western Federation of Miners, organized in May, 1893, which had ever since been locked in mortal struggle with the Mine Owners Association all along the vast stretch of the Rockies from the Coeur d'Alene in northern Idaho to Cripple Creek and Telluride in southwestern Colorado. In this bitter conflict the owners had enjoyed something of an advantage: they had been able to get the state militia and even, occasionally, the United States Army to fight their battles for them. Union men by the hundreds had been seized without warrant and flung into bull pens guarded by Federal troops—all at the beck of mine-owners and officers of corporations with addresses in the financial district of New York City. The union men, free and angry American citizens determined to fight for their rights, had responded by grasping the weapons that lay nearest to hand—guns and dynamite. There had followed a series of pitched battles, bloody and violent.

Now, in May, 1907, the union faced another deadly battle, this time in a court of law. William D. (Big Bill) Haywood, ex-cowboy, ex-prospector, militant Socialist, charter member of the Industrial Workers of the World, and secretary-treasurer of the Western Federation of Miners, was on trial for his life, accused of complicity in the murder of Frank Steunenberg, a former governor of Idaho. Steunenberg, a union man himself, had been elected governor in 1897 as a Populist. In April, 1899, he had got President McKinley to send troops to break a strike in the Coeur d'Alene lead mines. Steunenberg realized the act was political suicide; when his term expired in 1901 he quit politics and retired to raise sheep. On the evening of December 30, 1905, as he opened the gate to his house in Caldwell, a booby-trap charged with dynamite exploded, killing him. The next day a man registered at the local hotel under the name of T.S. Hogan was arrested simply because he was so calm, where everybody else was buzzing with excitement. His manner was so reassuring that he was released, but an Oregon sheriff visiting in Caldwell had recognized him. He was identified as Harry Orchard, a member of the Western Miners Federation. He was arrested again, charged with murder, and taken to the prison in Boise. Also to Boise came James McParland, a Pinkerton detective who, long ago in the 1870s, had broken up the Molly Maguires, a syndicalist organization of coal-miners in Pennsylvania. After a week of lengthy, secret conversations with Orchard, McParland emerged with a sensational announcement: Orchard had confessed to the murder of Steunenberg and to the murder of seventeen other persons; these crimes, according to Orchard, had been ordered and paid for by the men who ran the Western Federation of Miners—Haywood; Charles H. Moyer, the president; and George A. Pettibone, a former officer and trusted adviser. All three men were at their homes in Denver, Colorado. In exceedingly high-handed fashion, without regard for the laws of extradition, the three were collared and hauled aboard a special train bound for Idaho.* Haywood, presumed the leader of the conspiracy and therefore the guiltiest, was scheduled for trial first and separately.

Even before it began, the Haywood trial sent the nation into an unprecedented state of fidgets.

The Left at once assumed Haywood was the victim of a frame-up. Orchard was scum. He was a Pinkerton agent, a bigamist, a sodden alcoholic, a psychopath, a confessed murderer; who could believe a word he said? The charge was trumped up: if Haywood had been vexed by something Steunenberg did in 1899, why should he have waited six years before ordering his execution? The Socialist weekly, The Appeal to Reason, whipped up a campaign that raised two hundred and fifty thousand dollars as a defense fund; Clarence Darrow, the ablest labor lawyer in the country, was retained as Haywood's attorney; Hearst, who still had political ambitions, swung his newspapers back of Haywood; the militant marched in the cities, waving red banners and baying out La Marseillaise.

The Right at once assumed Haywood was guilty and would be punished as he richly deserved. Orchard was a sterling chap. To be sure, there was his regrettable past, but he had been washed in the blood of the lamb and had confessed his sins, experienced a spiritual rebirth, and purged himself of the old Adam. He spoke sooth. For the sake of law, order, authority, good government, and the health of the Republic, it was imperative that Haywood

* Hence, in American slang, the term "to railroad," meaning to imprison on a false charge.

Ray Stannard Baker earned a reputation as the best reporter in the country, while working for McClure's.

Culver Pictures, Inc.

Ida Tarbell wrote three extremely successful series of articles for McClure's: a brief biography of Napoleon, a rather longer study of Lincoln, and the sensational History of the Standard Oil Company.

Harris & Ewing

This cartoon, which appeared in Puck, was published when the literature of exposure and reform was at its height. President Roosevelt had made his celebrated Man-with-the-Muck-Rake speech only a week or two before. Here they all are, outfitted as for a crusade, with McClure leading the pack, his cross-bow at the ready. Ray Stannard Baker and Samuel Hopkins Adams are at his right hand; Lincoln Steffens, mounted on a charger, is at his left; behind him, also on horseback and in the attitude of Joan of Arc, comes Ida Tarbell. The device on Baker's shield and on the trappings of Steffens's horse—the dolphin-and-anchor—was the colophon of McClure, Phillips & Company, the book-publishing house.

Lincoln Steffens wrote "The Shame of the Cities" and "Enemies of the Republic" for McClure's. He and his editor did not always get along smoothly.

Samuel Hopkins Adams went from McClure's to Collier's, for whom he wrote a blistering attack on the patent-medicine industry.

George Kibbe Turner was perhaps the most effective of the muck-rakers but he is not so well-known today. Moral: write an autobiography, if you wish to be remembered.

Willa Cather wrote the study of Mary Baker Eddy and Christian Science for McClure's, but it was published under another writer's name. Most of her time on McClure's she served as managing editor.

The McClure family sat for this portrait in 1904 or 1905. S.S. and his son Robert stand in back; Eleanor, Hattie, and Bess are seated left to right; and in front are Mary and Enrico.

This remarkable picture of McClure was taken late in 1899, when to all appearances McClure was the most successful editor-publisher in the land. See page 174.

Hattie McClure, in 1905.

In March, 1944, the National Institute of Arts and Letters announced that McClure was to be awarded its Order of Merit. Newspaper photographers found him in a corner of the library of the Union League Club. He was eighty-seven years old.

be hanged by the neck until he was dead. Only so could a revolution be averted.

In this national emergency, the Press, with glad cries, dispatched star correspondents to Boise from all over the country.

McClure was in a state of fidgets, too. How could he capitalize on all this commotion? The key to the trial was obviously Orchard: was he honest or deceitful? Who could say? (The so-called lie-detector had not yet been invented.) Doctor Hugo Münsterberg, professor of psychology at Harvard, was reputed to be versed in the arcana of the mental processes; perhaps he knew of some test—tapping the patellae or calibrating the output of the axillary sweat glands—by which the truth of Orchard's alleged confession could be measured. S.S. sent the professor from Cambridge to Boise to prod the prisoner according to approved psychometric procedures. At the same time, S.S. realized that he had to have Orchard's confession, truthful or not, for McClure's Magazine.

The trial was about to begin when Kibbe Turner slipped into Boise, unobtrusive as always, and threaded his way through the dense throng of correspondents to Orchard's cell. He came away with Orchard's confession, the story of Orchard's life, and Orchard's signature on a contract by the terms of which both confession and story of life were sold exclusively to McClure's.

Once again S.S. was delighted. Now he had a capital feature to run through the summer months. He traveled to Boise to interview Orchard personally. "A singularly marvelous mind," said the editor of the murderer, "and a most marvelous character. . . . [His] passion for telling the exact truth and [his] ability to tell the exact truth almost transcend human experience." *

From Boise McClure went on to San Francisco to see how George Kennan was coming along with his investigation of local politics. Kennan had finished the first of two articles—ten thousand words, of which at least nine thousand were libellous. (In his lead sentence, Kennan called the political boss, the mayor, and most of the city officials "blackmailers, extortioners, and thieves.") San Francisco, it appeared, was like all the other corrupt cities,

---

* Orchard could tell the truth, but not the whole truth. He was, it turned out, all things to all men. He had performed his acts of violence impartially for union and Mine Owners Association, sometimes collecting from both for the same act.

Haywood, by the way, was acquitted by a jury of Idaho farmers. Orchard, who became a Seventh Day Adventist, outlived all the other principals in the case, dying in 1956, still in prison.

except that the thieves sailed under a different flag, that of the Union-Labor Party, which had decisively trounced an alliance of Democrats and Republicans. The good union men (Mayor Eugene Schmitz had prepared for his high office by playing violin in the orchestra of the Columbia Theater) swiftly showed they were better thieves, too, than the Democrats and Republicans. They had a far better feeling for organization. They organized the so-called French restaurants, gay establishments which were in the business of renting upstairs bedrooms for private entertainments, and then extorted large sums of money to "protect" them. They organized the brothels, too, most profitably: one such house, known as the Municipal Crib, enjoyed gross receipts of about five hundred thousand dollars a year, of which about twenty thousand went to the mayor.* And of course there was the customary illicit traffic in municipal franchises, always with the most respectable of businessmen.

All this McClure read with a grim satisfaction. He would publish the piece at once. He hoped it would do good, but he doubted it. San Francisco, he wrote his wife, was "physically, financially, politically, industrially, economically & morally . . . a sort of ruin."

His magazine, however, was editorially in good shape—better than it had been for years. The reflection put him in mind of his competitors and specifically of his newest competitors. How were the editors of The American faring? It hurt him still to think of them.

July 1, 1907

My dear Miss Tarbell—
    I am so starved to see you. . . . Mr Kennan has more than justified my great hopes.
    I dreamed of you. . . . I thought I was telling you how I found out that by speaking slowly & calmly & acting calmly I found I had much greater influence on people (I am actually doing this) & I thought that I was standing by your chair & you drew me down & kissed me to show your approval.
    When you disapproved of me it nearly broke my heart. . . .
    After that breakfast at the Waldorf I saw I could not bear to see you much for a time. . . .

* A few enterprising prostitutes rented a house on Webster Street, just around the corner from St. Stephen's Protestant Episcopal Church. (The landlord, a reputable businessman, was a member of the congregation of St. Stephen's.) Whores from this house used to offer their cards to men on their way to and from church on Sunday. The rector appealed personally to the chief of police, asking that at the very least the solicitation be stopped. He got nowhere.

I want a whole half day & evening with you.

I never cease to love you as I have for many, many years. I wish you had not turned away.

With great esteem & affection
Very sincerely yours
SSMcClure

The editors of The American, meanwhile, had been having their problems. They had been thinking their second thoughts. Phillips and Steffens had quarreled; Steffens was about to resign from The American. Baker, warmly encouraged by Phillips, was in the process of transforming himself from a crusading journalist into David Grayson, a recorder of trivialities about Nature. In the summer of 1907 Phillips visited Miss Tarbell at the Narragansett Hotel in Providence, Rhode Island, where she was on a holiday. After he had gone, Miss Tarbell wrote to Boyden:

Dear Bert:—I think Mr Phillips went back a little more cheerful than he came. He wasn't exactly depressed but rather perplexed. He feels that we've come pretty near to the line but that we need a quality of effort to get over which we don't seem to have in the team. We always have lacked it. A certain hustle, ingenuity—a general energizing effect such as we used to get out of S.S. . . . It's a talent—a genius & we haven't it in the staff. It's a kind of thing which needs direction & which Mr Phillips could use feeling the need as he does & having had the experience with the most virulent type of it as he has! . . . We have not *punched* hard enough editorially. . . . J.S.P. sees it. He frets because he is not that kind & that nobody else is. . . .

Affectionately
Iderem

McClure needed them, they needed him. But what had been lost was irretrievable.

[XXII]

S.S. had his usual oversupply of hustle and ingenuity. His problem was financial, and by the fall of 1907 it was far more serious than he realized. McClure's Magazine was in fact dying.

To the casual eye, the patient exhibited no morbid symptoms. Circulation had risen steadily; it had never been higher than in the spring of 1907.

Despite the shock occasioned by the Great Secession, Curtis Brady had been able to persuade the confraternity of advertisers and their agents that Mc-Clure was the heart, soul, and brains of McClure's; as a result, advertising lineage in 1906 had actually increased over that of 1905. The magazine had nonetheless suffered a mortal wound, one which had been inflicted by its editor-in-chief, in the face of the most earnest counsel. But it is unlikely that any power could have deflected S.S. from his course, for what he did was entirely characteristic and flowed inevitably from a characteristically tangled complex of difficulties.

To begin with, there had been his obligation to buy the stock owned by Phillips and Miss Tarbell. S.S. had supposed (and so had Mather) that he could get all the money he needed by selling the bonds of the S.S. McClure Corporation, which had indeed been organized for that sole purpose. But when he offered the bonds privately, S.S. found no takers. The same men who in 1905 had professed themselves eager to back a prospective McClure's Journal were in 1906 reluctant to invest in an actual McClure's Magazine. Perhaps they were alarmed by the way his editors had deserted him; in any event, money was tighter in 1906, presaging the currency panic of 1907.

When S.S. found it impossible to sell the bonds, he was first impatient and then frantic. Where was he to find the money he needed? Until he found it, he would be saddled with three trustees, who held his stock as security for the debt to Phillips and who watched over every penny he spent. This trusteeship, intolerable to S.S., had been established at the insistence of Phillips, who feared he would never get the money owed him unless S.S.'s famous extravagances were somehow curbed. The trustees, selected after much grumbling by S.S., were Mather, Frank Doubleday, and Josiah Quincy Bennett, a Boston stockbroker. These three (or someone in their name) presently began to question plans for editorial features.* They also announced a policy of economy in the editorial department. "This is a mistake," McClure snarled. "Editorial policy must always be liberal." But the business-

---

* In 1906 S.S. contracted to buy the memoirs of Ellen Terry. (They were published in fifteen installments during 1907–08.) He was in Europe when he was handed a cable: INFORM S.S. MC-CLURE TRUSTEES OBJECT TO PURCHASE OF TERRY MANUSCRIPT. S.S. was incoherent with rage. "I shall utterly refuse," he wrote his wife, "to recognize any right to question my absolute authority as editor-in-chief. . . . I am too angry to write longer. I will hurry home."

Parenthetically, the choice of Doubleday as one of the trustees was a most curious one. Doubleday published books and magazines that competed with McClure's; moreover, in 1902 McClure had told Phillips flatly that he considered his hiring of Doubleday to have been the greatest mistake he ever made. Consistency was never one of McClure's hobgoblins.

men had moved in, and they were to serve until Phillips had been paid off. Phillips, meanwhile, proved to be a clamorous creditor. From his offices at The American Magazine he kept howling for cash.

What most exasperated McClure was his conviction that he could easily have settled his debt to Phillips from the monthly profits of McClure's Magazine—if only those profits had not been earmarked to pay for the big new printing plant in Long Island City. And was that printing plant his idea? Had he, indeed, even been consulted about the building of that plant? No! S.S. rattled the walls of his office whenever he thought about it. "That building," he stormed, "is a colossal disaster!" It was a concatenation of follies: too big, much too expensive, built in the wrong place, poorly planned; its subcellar had been dug two feet below the level of tidewater, and so required expensive waterproofing; its architect was feuding with its contractor, and both men were knaves who wasted S.S.'s valuable time; the cost had been estimated at a quarter of a million dollars but would likely top seven hundred thousand before it was done. And Phillips was responsible—Phillips and Oscar Brady. Phillips was gone: good riddance. Oscar Brady was impossible: he too would have to go. It began to seem to McClure that all his associates had been in league to wreck his company and his magazine. Why could he not find a trustworthy business manager? And how could he lay his hands on some money? He chafed, irritable and impatient, ready to clutch at any makeshift.

At this juncture Fate once again intervened, by contriving an incident that seemed wholly irrelevant. In Springfield, Massachusetts, a fire gutted the plant in which Good Housekeeping was printed, and Herbert Myrick, the magazine's publisher, arranged to have it printed in McClure's new Long Island City plant. Myrick had been thinking of selling Good Housekeeping; the prospective purchaser was a man named Harold Roberts. One day early in 1907, then, Roberts came to Oscar Brady's office to discuss the cost of manufacturing the magazine. The two men were going over the figures when McClure walked in. Quite naturally, Brady introduced McClure to Roberts. Then he made a mistake.

"Mr. Roberts," said Brady unnecessarily, "is negotiating to buy Good Housekeeping."

S.S. leaped like a trout to a fly. "Oh," he said, "is that so?" A man with money to invest in a magazine! His eyes glowed. "But," he said, "why Good Housekeeping? Why don't you buy in here?"

"I had no idea I could," said Roberts.

"Come down to my office," said McClure happily, "and let me tell you all about it."

The Brady brothers were disturbed by this turn of events. The S.S. McClure Company had always been closely held; for a stranger even with impeccable credentials to be invited to buy into it was somehow distasteful. Nor, after the Bradys had inquired into Roberts's background, were they reassured.

Roberts was a man in his middle thirties, quick-witted and charming. He had been president of the Cuban Tobacco Company, a subsidiary of the American Tobacco Company. His financial sponsor, John Cobb, was president of the American Cigar Company and vice-president of the American Tobacco Company. There was no indication that Roberts knew anything about publishing.

Anyone submitting this report card to McClure might as well have been talking to the wild, wild waves. McClure refused to see in Roberts more or less than what he wanted to see: a man with money to invest, a man who could free him from control by the triumvirate of trustees, a man who could pay the debt to Phillips and Miss Tarbell; in short, a veray parfit, gentil knight.

McClure and Roberts negotiated. It was the negotiation of a lamb with a lion. Roberts undertook to meet whatever payments would be required to buy the stock owned by Phillips and Miss Tarbell; he also engaged to buy all other available shares of stock. If after twelve months McClure and Roberts agreed to disagree, McClure would be obliged to buy from Roberts all the stock which Roberts then owned. Roberts risked nothing and stood to gain all: he had a year in which to wrest control of this splendid property from its owner. McClure risked all and stood to gain nothing: whether he would be better able to pay his debt to Phillips in 1908 than in 1907 would depend entirely on his general manager and treasurer—that is, on Roberts. Apparently McClure never realized that after a year Roberts would have him over a barrel.

McClure and Roberts signed their agreement in April, 1907. Roberts became treasurer, general manager, and a director of the S.S. McClure Company. On June 1, 1907, Phillips was handed certified checks in the amount of forty-one thousand, six hundred dollars; and McClure also signed a contract guaranteeing Phillips an additional one hundred and thirty-six thousand dollars to be paid (with accrued interest at five per cent) in monthly installments of not less than five thousand dollars. Soon thereafter the

Bradys, sorely disaffected, sold their stock to Roberts for more than one hundred thousand dollars, and resigned. Roberts appointed a new circulation manager and a new advertising manager. Both subscriptions and advertising declined, slowly at first, then faster and faster. A better example could not have been afforded of the need for loyal and efficient business management.

McClure, preoccupied with editorial matters, remained blissfully unaware of what was happening in his countinghouse.

For five years McClure's staff writers had inquired into municipal affairs, and they had showed there were two chief sources of corruption, two vast catch basins in the municipal cloaca: the traffic in franchises, and the pre-eminence of saloonkeepers in ward politics. S.S. now decided that both warranted further scrutiny.

To anatomize the traffic in franchises, S.S. called on Burton Hendrick. New York City was the archetype of this particular graft, and the story Hendrick had to tell was of the so-called Metropolitan syndicate, the informal alliance of buccaneers, two from Philadelphia and two from New York, that had stolen incredible fortunes incredibly fast by shameless exploitation of street-railway franchises. The Philadelphians—Peter A. B. Widener and William Elkins—had the experience; they were already rich from their manipulations of traction franchises in Philadelphia and Chicago. The two New Yorkers—William C. Whitney and Thomas Fortune Ryan —had the necessary political connections; Tammany Hall was eager to do their bidding. It was a combination that really cut the mustard. In the decade from 1893 to 1902 the syndicate played upon the Metropolitan Street Railway Company as upon a stringed instrument. They watered its stock, speculated in it, cornered it, and dumped it. Profits to the four men were at least one hundred million dollars. During this decade their legal adviser was Elihu Root. In 1899 Root had been summoned to more public service, first as Secretary of War to McKinley and then to Roosevelt, and later as Secretary of State to Roosevelt; in 1902 he had been succeeded as legal adviser to the Metropolitan syndicate by Paul D. Cravath, whose practice of law had begun in partnership with Charles Evans Hughes. The members of the syndicate were untroubled by these trifling interruptions in the even flow of their legal advice; they continued to siphon more millions out of the treasury of New York City and the pockets of its citizens, always thanks to an intimate alliance with Tammany Hall. Root and Cravath must have been revolted by the evidence of such Democratic venality; it is no wonder that they were good Republicans.

What the Metropolitan syndicate had got away with was, as McClure wrote in a wrathful editorial, "robbery, as clearly and certainly as the work of any footpad upon a dark street." It was even worse, for what had been involved were the securities of a corporation, "the one class of property which must be safely available for the investment of the man of moderate means." It seems never to have occurred to McClure to connect Root with Roosevelt or Cravath with Hughes. "It is the great task of America," he wrote, "already undertaken by such men as President Roosevelt and Governor Hughes, to bring these [corporations] under control; in other words, to establish an orderly and safe civilization, where the property and enterprise of the individual will be properly protected by the state."

As for the power of the saloonkeeper in American government, the more McClure thought about it, the more he found himself in sympathy with the temperance movement then beginning to sweep across the country. He would have to get someone to write about alcohol; facts, not temperance arguments; the effects of alcohol, considered scientifically. And then there was the question of prostitution, another source of revenue for the corrupt municipality. McClure was coming to realize that prostitution was a necessary end-result of poverty. He recalled that he had published a savage little tale by O. Henry, "An Unfinished Story," about a salesgirl in a department store who struggled to keep body and soul together on a wage of six dollars a week, who was given a glimpse of an easier life, who was tempted, and— If such conditions existed, how vile they were! He must have someone investigate the working-girl's budget; how could anyone live decently on such miserable pay?

In the meantime, while McClure was happily absorbed with his editorial schemes, advertising lineage was down a frightful twenty to thirty per cent from the previous year. Newsstand circulation was up, reflecting editorial vitality; but subscriptions were sharply down, reflecting—what? It was hard to say. Perhaps only the abominable condition of business. To be sure, the nation was in the throes of the panic of 1907; yet advertising in other popular magazines had not been so sorely affected. McClure, with a perseverance that would have been admirable if directed toward a better goal, continued to ignore these unpleasant details.

Only one man was alarmed by what Roberts was and was not doing. This was Michael Flynn.

Except for McClure himself, none was senior to Flynn on the staff of

McClure's; none, including McClure, was more loyal. Flynn had been hired as an office boy for the syndicate, back in the 1880s, when he was fresh off a boat from Ireland. He had gone to night school, learned accounting, and in time been appointed the company's auditor; from this point of vantage he had a clear view of what Roberts was up to. Late in 1907 Flynn came to S.S.'s office to warn him most earnestly that Hell was yawning and its tongues of fire already licking at McClure's.

S.S. patted him cordially on the shoulder. "Later, Michael," he said happily. "Later. Right now I'm too busy."

Indeed McClure was very busy, helping to hatch another of his remarkably stimulating and influential articles. He was about to ventilate one of the fuggiest institutions in the United States, to wit, the Navy Department.

As a normal editorial procedure, McClure had always maintained cordial relations with ranking naval officers like Dewey and Mahan, Caspar Goodrich and Frank Fletcher. He had come to know William Sims as soon as that officer was appointed Roosevelt's naval aide. Another invaluable source of information on naval affairs was Henry Reuterdahl, an illustrator who had done a great deal of work for McClure's and who was also the American editor of that most authoritative of naval references, Jane's Fighting Ships. From some of these men McClure had heard, in a general way, that the United States Navy was something less than a first-class fighting force, and why. He had, however, the regrettable reluctance of the civilian to criticize anything military or naval.

Then late in 1907 Reuterdahl handed him a draft of an article that had been written with the covert approval of Commander Sims. McClure read it swiftly, ordered Kibbe Turner to check it and rewrite it, and scheduled it as the leading article in the issue of January, 1908.

Publication could not have been more shrewdly timed. On December 16, 1907, just as the January issue of McClure's reached the newsstands, sixteen warships, nicknamed the Great White Fleet, steamed from Hampton Roads, Virginia, on the first round-the-world cruise ever essayed by an American flotilla. President Roosevelt, who had a boyish tendency to regard the Navy as his personal clockwork toy, to be played with, as it were, in his bath, had dispatched the fleet on this mission with a great show of secrecy and then, at the last moment, an even greater show of press-agentry. The heart of every patriotic American thrilled with pride as the Great White Fleet set out around the world. The bones of every thoughtful American were thereafter chilled to the marrow as he read the January McClure's.

Our battleships and cruisers were, said Reuterdahl, insanely designed for peacetime; in wartime they would be suicidal. The belt of armor that was supposed to protect them was underwater; they wallowed so low in the water that their guns could not possibly be aimed and fired with accuracy in any but the calmest weather; their turrets were directly connected by open shafts to the powder magazines, an arrant invitation to disaster. Indeed, as Reuterdahl pointed out, nine sailors had been killed in an explosion on board the Massachusetts in 1903, and the next year thirty-two had been killed aboard the Missouri. Each of these tragedies was the result of ghastly mistakes in design that had not yet been corrected and could not be corrected until the bureaucratic administration of the Navy Department was radically streamlined.

Newspapers from coast to coast picked the article up from McClure's; in accordance with the immemorial custom of their kind, editorial writers were on the one hand dismayed but on the other hand dubious of the accuracy of the charges. One man, more than any other, was downright cross about the article. This was the President and Commander-in-Chief. Once again, Roosevelt could pick no quarrel with the facts or with the charges. But the article had been published without his knowledge or approval. Moreover, he was in his last year of office; he was the more intolerant of criticism. Too late: an investigation by the Committee of Naval Affairs of the United States Senate was now mandatory. The hearings lasted for four weeks and, if they accomplished nothing else, they afforded incomparable publicity for McClure's.*

It was March, 1908; Roberts had been general manager for eleven months; at last the faithful Michael Flynn was able to get S.S.'s attention.

Roberts, Flynn reported, had squandered the company's cash and credit on ineffectual promotion schemes; worse, he had deliberately arranged for all the company's obligations (bills for paper, payments on the new building in Long Island City, and the like) to fall due at the same time. He had contrived to bring McClure's to the verge of bankruptcy, and he had the capital all lined up with which he hoped to force S.S. to sell out. The thing

* The hearings were rigged. Senator Eugene Hale, the chairman of the Committee of Naval Affairs, was a Republican from Maine who looked on any criticism of the status quo as contumacious. Hale tried in every way to prove that the charges made in McClure's lacked substance. When the facts overwhelmed him, he ordered his committee into executive session.
It took until 1911 to correct the more egregious errors in the design of our warships; the first battleships designed with regard to the criticism leveled by Reuterdahl were commissioned in 1914. A detailed account of the whole affair can be found at pp. 176–234 of Elting E. Morison's biography, Admiral Sims and the Modern American Navy, Houghton Mifflin Company, 1942.

was common gossip in publishing circles; Ben Hampton, the publisher of Hampton's Magazine and a friend of Roberts, was at the moment freely predicting that the next issue of McClure's would be its last.

McClure was staggered. He simply could not believe that a man he had trusted so utterly was capable of such duplicity. But Flynn had proof— bills, receipts, letters, financial statements. Roberts had even confided his scheme, in all its details, to Charles Schweinler, a prominent printer. Schweinler, who was Flynn's good friend, had promptly made it his business to warn Flynn.

McClure hung his head, his mind racing. He still owed Phillips seventy-five thousand dollars; he would have to find at least one hundred thousand more in order to buy Roberts's stock; the magazine, his only source of income, had been brought to the edge of ruin; big bills were about to fall due; Roberts would convince the creditors that the company could not pay; next he would urge that, in order to avoid receivership, McClure must be forced to sell his stock; in this emergency, he, Roberts, fortunately had the necessary capital. McClure was understandably frantic.

"Michael," he said, "is there nothing we can do?"

Flynn shook his head. He was concerned and sympathetic, but he could think of nothing. "Maybe Charlie Schweinler would have an idea," he said. McClure, grasping at straws, sent Flynn to confer with Schweinler.

What Schweinler suggested was that he take Flynn to meet John G. Luke, the president of the West Virginia Pulp & Paper Company. Luke was cordial. West Virginia Pulp & Paper had never been able to sell paper to McClure's; the S.S. McClure Company had traditionally bought its ordinary stock from Tileston & Hollingsworth of Boston, and its coated stock from the Champion Card and Paper Company of Ohio; both companies had extended valuable credit years before. Perhaps matters could now be arranged satisfactorily; it was hard to say; money was still tight; after all, the country was still gasping for its breath after the panic of 1907.

Matters were arranged. Luke and his brothers, who ran West Virginia Pulp & Paper as a family concern, agreed to provide McClure with the cash to buy all Roberts's holdings and to give the S.S. McClure Company a comfortable line of credit. In return, McClure would have to agree to buy all his paper from the Lukes; he would have to pay them six per cent interest on their loan and (since money was hard to come by) an additional ten per cent as a bonus for supplying cash readily at a difficult moment; finally, he would have to put all his stock in trust to West Virginia Pulp & Paper as security for the loan. In this way the Lukes would also control the board of directors.

Time was short. No alternative could be found. McClure agreed. The necessary papers were prepared. McClure signed them. He had never been deeper in debt, and he was now paying sixteen per cent on most of what he owed. He was fifty-one years old.

And yet S.S. showed no rancor. It was as though he was aware that he had digged his own pit, that no one else was responsible for his misfortunes. The worst he had to say about Roberts—at least out loud—was that he was "a very foolish and shallow man."

[XXIII]

In the reorganization that followed, Cameron Mackenzie bobbed to the top. At the suggestion of McClure, and with Luke's approval, Mackenzie was appointed general manager and treasurer of the company to replace Roberts. The choice of Mackenzie was Luke's way of telling McClure that he intended the friendliest cooperation, for by that time Mackenzie was McClure's son-in-law. (Mackenzie and Bess McClure had been married in April, 1907.) Luke likewise assured McClure that there would be no interference in editorial affairs. S.S. would continue as editor-in-chief, assisted by Kibbe Turner and Willa Cather.

But of course the loan from Luke only added to McClure's financial burden, and the reorganization in no way lightened it. There was still the debt to Phillips, and there were still the heavy carrying charges on the building in Long Island City. Everybody in the publishing business knew of McClure's plight. Doubleday knew of it, for he was and would continue to be a trustee of the S.S. McClure Company until the debt to Phillips was fully paid. Phillips knew of it; he had got the whole story from Roberts and, as he said later, it had made him sick to his stomach. Schweinler knew of it, and he was a printer of several magazines. This being the case, those little black specks high up in the sky could be identified as vultures, soaring motionless, ready to swoop down and pick at the carcass.

In April, 1908, Schweinler picked off all the machinery from the Long Island City plant—printing presses, binders, and the like—for seventy thousand dollars. It may have been a fair price; but it is suggestive that the sum was exactly what was owed Phillips at the time, and that the payments from

Schweinler were to be made the day before payments to Phillips were due to be paid. Schweinler also was awarded the contract to print McClure's Magazine. Schweinler was no fool.

In May, 1908, a real estate agent named William Washington picked off the Long Island City building. It was of reinforced concrete, then the most modern construction; it comprised one hundred and twenty thousand square feet of floor space, net. Washington leased the building for twenty-one years at an annual rental of seven thousand, five hundred dollars, with an option for another twenty-one years at ten thousand dollars. (This works out at six and one-quarter cents per square foot over the first term and eight and one-third cents per square foot over the second term.) Washington was no fool.

In June, 1908, the publishers of Collier's notified McClure that they were no longer interested in sharing the expenses of a London office.

In October, 1908, Frank Munsey began to interest himself in McClure's difficulties. He undertook to buy McClure out entirely, for seven hundred and fifty thousand dollars. While this king vulture hovered above the carcass, the lesser scavengers respectfully withdrew. But during the course of the negotiations, Munsey, perceiving that McClure had no room to maneuver, reconsidered. Down came his bid to six hundred thousand dollars. McClure, who had been on the point of selling, refused the final offer.

Later in October, 1908, the Crowell Company, publishers of Farm and Fireside and of The Woman's Home Companion, made another offer to buy all McClure's stock. The Crowell Company was controlled by Thomas Lamont, a vice-president of the First National Bank, then the most powerful bank in New York. Mather urgently recommended that McClure accept the offer. McClure considered, agonized, and refused. Mather thereupon resigned as a trustee of the company. The resignation was, however, tactical. A week later Mather resumed his trusteeship.

S.S. was acutely aware that he needed better advice than he had been getting on his business affairs. But where was he to get it? In his despair he even essayed to re-establish his partnership with Doubleday. To no avail; Doubleday only smiled. He was biding his time.

Meanwhile Hattie McClure was in Europe. She was first in Carlsbad, taking a cure; later she traveled to Munich to be with her son Robbie, who had been sent to the university in that city by his father. S.S. wrote her daily and cabled her almost as often, asking her to intercede with God on his behalf; she answered like a Cassandra-come-lately. "There is nothing good for you with Mr. Doubleday, I am afraid," she wrote. "Better look elsewhere." When S.S. told her Mather had resigned, she wrote him: "I commend you especially to the guidance and control of infinite wisdom and power, for the reason that we have learned that no trust can be put in any man." She was relieved to hear that Mather had rescinded his resignation, but she declined to rely on any of S.S.'s advisers or associates. "You can perhaps let [Mr. Mather] know," Hattie wrote, "how intolerable to you and how improper for all appearances it is, that Cameron [Mackenzie] should be in supreme control of your affairs. It is out of the question. It is a very bad thing for him, as well as for everybody else, and you must not let it stand so. . . . It makes me boil with indignation to know that Mr. Luke has been in consultation with Mr. Phillips, and that it was in contemplation to put him in there as business manager! Do not appeal again to Mr. Phillips. Pay Shylock the weight of your flesh and blood he demands, but leave him and those with him alone. They are quite satisfied, it seems, with themselves and with each other, and have nothing for you. Pay them, and but for the purposes of payment, forget their existence." It was excellent advice. For some months it had been obvious to everyone including McClure that any profits cleared by McClure's would amount only to a subvention for The American. In effect, McClure had for months been obliged to pay his ablest competitor to compete with him.

In November, 1908, his old friend Frank Doubleday undertook to relieve McClure of the burden of his book-publishing company. Its value was modestly appraised at some two hundred and twenty-five thousand dollars. As listed in the appraisal, the biggest single asset was what was owing the company from bookstores; this amounted to nearly eighty-two thousand dollars. Contracts with such authors as Conrad, O. Henry, Tarkington, Ford Madox Ford, Willa Cather, Conan Doyle, Arnold Bennett, Jack London, E. Phillips Oppenheim, William Allen White, Samuel Hopkins Adams, Selma Lagerlöf, Rex Beach, Mary Shipman Andrews, and Hilaire Belloc were valued, together with the firm's trade-marks and good will, at twenty-seven thousand, five hundred dollars. Doubleday generously agreed to buy this treasure for one hundred and eighteen thousand, seven hundred and fifty dollars.*

By now the carcass had been picked clean. There was left only the skeleton. But S.S. was still confident he could put flesh back on those old bones, for

* Samuel Hopkins Adams told me that Doubleday had once told him: "When I make a deal with a man, if I don't feel later that I got the better of it, then I feel cheated."

at last he had found a business manager he could trust. He had been able to persuade Curtis Brady to come back to work for McClure's again.

Brady shook his head sadly as he surveyed the remains of the once splendid property. Mackenzie, bringing him up to date, mentioned that Washington, the man who had taken a lease on the building in Long Island City, had for six months refused to pay any rent. At once Brady was more cheerful. "Oh?" he asked. "Is that so? Could I see Mr. Washington?"

Washington appeared, tearful and resentful. A number of the wire-glass windows in the building were, he said, broken; he was a poor man and couldn't afford to fix them; until they had been repaired he could pay no rent. Brady took out a handkerchief and wiped his eyes. "Mr. Washington," he said, "you have been swindled. I am ashamed of the way you have been treated, and I would like to help you. I'll tell you what I'll do. If you'll give me an option good for twenty minutes, I'll give you my personal check for ten thousand dollars, certified, and take that dreadful lease off your hands." His voice hardened. "Otherwise, you will pay me in full by noon tomorrow or I shall institute proceedings to dispossess." Washington blinked. He reached for his checkbook.*

It seemed that there might be a dance or two left in the old bones.

McClure had never doubted it. His mood was one of sunny optimism. "There is no great difficulty in managing a business of this size," he assured Luke; "it merely requires the application of common sense." He estimated that he would be out of debt by January, 1911. "All there is to a magazine business," he told Luke, "is a good magazine." And McClure was confident that no one could make a better magazine than McClure's. Even during the time of his financial travail he had continued to make a good magazine, lively and provocative. New writers: he had bought their earliest stuff from writers like Floyd Dell and Mary Heaton Vorse. New illustrators: in addition to drawings by men like Glackens and N.C. Wyeth and Benda, he was buying superb illustrations from Arthur Dove, Reginald Birch, John Sloan, and Boardman Robinson. And of course new ideas.

McClure, as usual a few months ahead of the editors of other popular magazines, was interested in what was going on abroad. He undertook to

---

* Washington subleased the building to Steinway & Sons, the manufacturers of pianos, for a rent that rose from sixteen thousand dollars in the first year to twenty-one thousand in the sixth. His net profit on the transaction rose from one hundred and thirteen per cent to one hundred and eighty per cent.

interest his readers as well. He began to publish articles dealing with the squabbles of the Great Powers.

In 1908–09 McClure printed the Kuropatkin papers, four articles mined from a lengthy memoir by General Alexei Kuropatkin, Minister of War and later commander-in-chief of the Russian armies in the disastrous Russo-Japanese War.* Here was the story of the origins of that sordid affair, a compelling proof that international power politics is only a bloodier, crueler version of ward politics, conducted in fancy dress and inspired by loftier slogans. (The initial cause of the war was the Czar's concern for his investment in a logging enterprise on the banks of the Yalu River in Korea.)

In the summer of 1909 McClure was in London and talked with various British politicians, including Sir Edward Grey, the Minister for Foreign Affairs. S.S. then commissioned H.R. Chamberlain, the London correspondent of The New York Sun, to write a chillingly prescient article entitled "The Ominous Hush in Europe." There was, Chamberlain reported, a universal dread of war in Europe, yet Great Britain and Germany were nevertheless engaged in an appalling and ruinous armaments race. (The German Navy threatened to surpass the British Navy in firepower; the British government had consequently ordered eight battleships at a cost of eighty million dollars; the Germans were therefore planning thirteen battleships; and so on, and so on; what is by now a familiar story.) War, Chamberlain suggested, was inevitable unless the United States used its good offices to intervene.†

---

* The articles were actually reconstructed by George Kennan, who also translated the manuscript for McClure. Kuropatkin's memoir had been smuggled out of Russia by the wife of one of his officers; expenses for this exploit were shared by McClure and John Methuen, the English publisher.

† Since, by a singular coincidence, Chamberlain's article precisely expressed its editor's own ideas, it will come as no surprise that S.S. now began to devote much of his excess energy to organizing an effort for peace. There were several organizations already in the field, but S.S. found them unsatisfactory; they were well-intended, no doubt, but they had no effective leadership. It was his idea that the peace movement should be led by men like Elihu Root and J. P. Morgan, and indeed he formally broached his scheme to Root, who was at this time a United States Senator from New York. McClure and Root exchanged several letters; they held several conversations. McClure also attempted to interest such men as Andrew Carnegie, Nicholas Murray Butler, and Sir William Van Horne, the capitalist who promoted the Canadian Pacific Railway.

In brief, the McClure Plan for Peace was this: that Root and Morgan form a committee of perhaps one hundred financiers, bankers, university presidents, members of Congress, and heads of great business organizations; that comparable committees be formed in the principal European countries; that all hands sign a brief document ("perhaps not more than would occupy a page of a magazine," wrote S.S., wrapped in his warm dream) agreeing to outlaw aggression, accept the status quo, submit all differences to a board of arbitration, and so "render war impossible for at least hundreds of years." "Of course," S.S. acknowledged handsomely, "there are certain difficulties, but a combined effort . . . would do a great deal."

S.S. was on surer ground when it came to inventing ideas for features on domestic politics. In the fall of 1909 he laid down a barrage against Tammany Hall in the New York mayoralty election. Kibbe Turner had warmed up by writing a piece that detailed how the alliance of professional criminals and Tammany politicians controlled New York. Like an archaeologist picking over the debris of successive civilizations, Turner showed how, in successive waves of immigration, the overlord of vice on the lower East Side of New York had been first Monk Eastman (an Irishman), then Kid Twist (a Jew), and then Paul Kelly (an Italian): pimps, thieves, and killers all, and always working for, thriving under, and protected by Timothy D. (Big Tim) Sullivan, the longtime leader on the Bowery, the principal power in Tammany Hall, the "big feller." This article, published in June, 1909, irritated Tammany chiefly because it broadcast unpleasant facts that were, however, well known to any who troubled to inquire. But in the issue of November, 1909, on the newsstands two weeks before election day, there was another piece by Turner, "The Daughters of the Poor," in which he bluntly charged that New York was a world center of the trade in prostitution and that the trade flourished thanks to protection afforded by Tammany Hall.

Here was an authentic sensation. S.S. was warned there was a warrant out for his arrest; in any event, he found it convenient to accept an invitation to join President Taft in a junket down the Mississippi.*

In the meantime Tammany had taken a trouncing at the polls, and on January 3, 1910, a grand jury was impaneled to investigate the charge that

---

Root appears to have given this notion his patient attention. Sir William, on the other hand, was frankly antagonistic. "I do not believe," he wrote McClure briskly, "that universal peace is either possible or desirable. If it were possible . . . I feel sure that it would result in universal rottenness. All of the manliness of the civilized world is due to wars . . . ; our whole civilization is the outgrowth of wars. . . . Perhaps I shall give you an article some day on 'Peace—damnable Peace.' "

* In the same November issue S.S. had printed a lengthy editorial, horrendously entitled "The Tammanyizing of a Civilization," in which he summed up his six-year effort to disinfect the cities of America. He feared it had been a losing battle. According to The Chicago Tribune, the homicide rate was up again; S.S. was informed there were two million syphilitics in the United States, and that one in every ten bridegrooms infected his bride with a venereal disease. The cause of all this misery, he insisted, was government of the cities by criminals. The remedy was the commission form of government. S.S. was prepared to nominate a slate of commissioners to save New York City from the scoundrels. He proposed: for mayor, Theodore Roosevelt; for commissioner of finance, J. Pierpont Morgan; for commissioner of police, General Leonard Wood; for commissioner of public works, William G. McAdoo; for commissioner of law, Elihu Root.

There was no sign that McClure intended these nominations humorously.

there was traffic in women, politically protected. (The foreman of the jury was John D. Rockefeller, Jr.) Its investigators, following up Turner's leads, promptly found that it was quite possible to purchase a girl from a pimp and ship her anywhere in the country. (They actually bought two girls, one for sixty dollars and the other for seventy-five dollars.) In the main, the jury sustained Turner's accusations, as had also the grand jury sitting in Chicago.

The Mann Act, approved by the Congress in June, 1910, was a logical result of agitation by the muckrakers, led once again by McClure.

While S.S. was conspicuously indifferent to the accumulation of any personal capital, he found accumulation of the stuff by others most interesting. He perceived, moreover, that the concentration of capital in the hands of a few men was the most consequential of the forces loosed upon the world by the nineteenth century; it was the issue that dominated all others, political or economic, current or conjectural.

> Fifty years ago [S.S. wrote in an editorial published in September, 1910] we were a nation of independent farmers and small merchants. Today we are a nation of corporation employees: directly or indirectly, the corporation controls our living. And, as the corporations grow greater and greater, fewer and fewer men control them, and our individual lives with them.
>
> In politics nearly every road leads back to this one point. The revolt against the change in Europe is the rising tide of socialism; in the United States, the growth of the so-called insurgent movement. The dominant note of the twentieth century is unquestionably to be the struggle for economic freedom, exactly as the fight for political freedom was that of the nineteenth.

This editorial was by way of introducing the last great series S.S. would publish. For years * he had hankered to investigate the concentration of capital and to explain, as he wrote, "the ownership, alliances, and connections between the great banks, railroads, and industries, and trace the drift of events that has brought the control of the primary activities and resources of the country into the hands of a small and constantly narrowing group of men." Once again, months had gone into the preparation of the series; once again the pains taken were justified by the result.

The series, published in seven parts and running to more than sixty thou-

---

* See his letter to Ray Stannard Baker, at pp. 278–279.

sand words, was called The Masters of Capital in America. Its authors were John Moody, a financial journalist who had for twenty years been intimately concerned with the affairs of Wall Street, and George Kibbe Turner. The series stands in approximately the same relationship to Miss Tarbell's History of the Standard Oil Company as does a graduate school to a kindergarten. It has been almost entirely ignored by the historians of the muckraking era, perhaps because it was not hostile to finance capital. Rather it was knowing, it was expository. Moody and Turner neither blamed nor excused; they simply analyzed a process, and they left no doubt that the process was inevitable. They had a dramatic story to tell, with eight principal characters— J.P. Morgan, Jacob H. Schiff, James J. Hill, Edward H. Harriman, John D. Rockefeller and his brother William, James Stillman, and George F. Baker —and a host of minor characters. Moody and Turner began by ticking off the three chief sources of capital for the development of America: English investments, which had gradually come under the control of J.P. Morgan & Company; German investments, which had gradually come under the control of Kuhn, Loeb & Company; and the huge sums that had accrued to the Standard Oil Company. They showed how the financiers, to protect their investments, had found it necessary to eliminate wasteful competition and, wherever possible, to impose a more efficient monopoly on the nation's railroads. ("A double-track railroad costs not more than two thirds as much as two single-track roads. It will do four times as much work. So every dollar of capital invested in a double-track railroad is six times as efficient as a dollar invested in two single-track roads.") Moody and Turner emphasized the formula for success common to all their principal characters: "Mind your own business, in silence; keep your money where you can get your hand on it." They traced the connection between the reorganization of the railroads and the creation of the so-called money power of Wall Street, and they defined this power: "A closer and closer central monopoly of general corporate capital invested or to be invested. It is the creation of no man's will, but of a movement going on all over the civilized world." They pointed out how in the 1880s capital had been destroyed by unrestricted competition almost as soon as it was invested and how, in consequence, the movement toward monopoly was inevitable "if a supply of money was to be continued for the development of American industry." They acknowledged that their principal characters, whenever faced with a choice between obeying the law or proceeding according to the dictates of sensible business practice, had unhesitatingly flouted the law; but they wept no tears over this collision between the legal and the pragmatic. They tracked the accumulated capital back to its two principal lairs on Wall Street, the City Bank and the First National Bank, the one loosely regarded as a Rockefeller bank and the other as a Morgan bank.* Thereafter they sniffed out the control their principal characters exerted over a few American industries. They composed a table:

PERCENTAGE OF INDUSTRIES AND RESOURCES CONTROLLED

	The Eight	Alliances	Outside
Railroads	61	25	14
Express & Pullman	93.5		6.5
Anthracite coal (supply owned)	88.5	6.5	5
Steel	82	5	13
Cement (output)	33.33		66.67
Petroleum (output handled)	67	18	15
Lead (output)		60	40
Copper (output)		60	40
Telephone	74		26

"This table," Moody and Turner wrote, "gives a general idea of the control that the seven men [Harriman having died, the number was reduced from eight to seven] and their allies have gained in certain specified industries. But it is, at best, only a rough and only a partial statement. The control of these men has gone everywhere that it is possible to create a practical working monopoly of any kind. Steamship lines, cracker-baking, the manufacture of farm machinery—these and many other industries as widely varied have been combined into the so-called 'trusts' controlled by them. And the list is always extending."

Moody and Turner (and McClure) closed on a note of fatalism, tinged with admiration:

> This central group [they wrote, having in mind their principal characters] is a perfectly natural evolution—the final product of thirty and forty years of unchecked movement toward monopoly. It has not been

---

* In 1955 these two institutions were merged; the crossbreed, called the First National City Bank, is not relatively so powerful as were its two mighty progenitors in 1910.

created by any man's or men's arbitrary acts or theories. It has risen day after day and year after year upon the progressive bankruptcy of general industry under competition. The old economic axiom has been reversed in the past twenty-five years. Competition has not been the life of trade; it has been the death of industry in the United States. Monopoly has been built up on its ruins, and it is built to stay. The last and most perfect form of monopoly is this central financial machine, now focussing in the seven men.

It is a splendid machine—never stronger than it is today. Through its various feeders, the enterprises and resources of the country are brought into it. The Northwest is constantly patrolled and watched by Hill. No new development escapes him. Through the West and Southwest the Union Pacific gathers its detailed reports from every little station. The Standard Oil Company, with its own private telegraphic system from the North Atlantic to Mexico, watches the credit and activities of its trade, and of business at large. The City Bank, with almost two thousand corresponding banks, watches the credit of the enterprises of the continent.

Through all these channels and hundreds more, the central machine of capital extends its controls over the United States. It is not definitely organized in any way. But common interest makes it one great unit—the "System", so called.

It sits in Wall Street, a central power, directing the inevitable drift of great industry toward monopoly. And as the industries of the country one after another come into it for control, it divides the wealth created by them. To the producer, steady conditions of labor; to the investor, stable securities, sure of paying interest; to the makers of monopoly and their allies, the increment of wealth of the continent, and with it the gathering control of all mechanical industry. It is a cumulative power inconceivable half a century ago. The apprehension and hostility of the whole population of the United States is directed against it. But its absorption of the machinery and resources of the country go on. The process is not only economically logical: it is now practically automatic.

The Moody-Turner series was of interest chiefly because it marked a turning point in the long and rancorous national debate about the trusts. Just as McClure had launched the debate (at least in the popular magazines, which at the time comprised the only national forum), so now he helped to change its frame of reference. By publishing the series, S.S. acknowledged that it was no longer useful to question whether corporations were good or bad; like the elements, they were here to stay. The question was, rather, whether the staggering power of corporate capital might not overwhelm a free society.

"The great struggle in the United States today," S.S. wrote in an editorial published late in 1910, "is to transfer government from the real seat of power to the legal seat of power. . . . The real power, and hence the real government, is in Wall Street. The struggle is to transfer the real power, and hence the real government, to Washington." With a sublime disregard for the fact that Taft had been President and Roosevelt presumably in retirement for nearly two years, S.S. went on: "This [transfer of power to Washington] is Mr. Roosevelt's prime object. And the interests of corporate wealth are above all things to aid him and avoid an interregnum that would be very disastrous to the general welfare. . . ."

[XXIV]

It was now 1911, the year by which S.S. had blithely estimated he would be out of debt. The circulation of McClure's had risen steadily since 1908. So, thanks to Curtis Brady, had advertising: gross revenues were once again well over one million dollars a year.

But the burden of debt was still crushing. McClure was obliged to pay more than fifty thousand dollars a year just for the interest on what he had borrowed, for the fixed charges on loans, debentures, and mortgages. It was intolerable.

Mather proposed that the company should be refinanced and its debt converted into preferred stock. The risk was that control of the magazine and its editorial policy might pass into the hands of Wall Street.

McClure proposed that he launch another magazine. To his way of thinking, a new magazine involved no risk. For example, a magazine devoted to fiction would be the simplest of editorial tasks, far easier than editing McClure's, and certain to be profitable. Frank Munsey was publishing a magazine of fiction; he called it The Argosy; it was a cheap thing, printed on pulp, and it earned three hundred thousand dollars a year. Anything Munsey could do, S.S. could do better. On a moment's notice he could go to London and find better stories than Munsey was printing. Did someone doubt it? Very well: he would prove it. Impatiently he brushed off all discussions of a possible financial reorganization. Mather had a plan—too late. S.S. had sailed for England, having first stowed two dozen quarts of fresh milk in the steamship's icebox to sustain him on his journey.

Once in London, moreover, S.S. proved his point. There was a new generation of popular writers, and he found his way to them as unerringly as he had to their predecessors. Instead of Anthony Hope, there was Jeffrey Farnol; instead of Conan Doyle and his Sherlock Holmes, there was G. K. Chesterton and his Father Brown; there was E. Phillips Oppenheim. S.S. bought all they had to offer: enough to stock the first half-dozen issues of a magazine of fiction.

Behind him the ultimate black financial thunderhead was forming over McClure's Magazine; but S.S. was heedless, he was happy, he had just conceived a notion for another bully feature.

In the spring of 1911 the Italian government was belatedly bringing to trial a gang of criminals, leaders of the notorious Camorra, whose malign influence reached across the Atlantic, affecting the politics of a half-dozen American cities. Arthur Train, who had been an assistant district attorney in New York City before he began to write short stories, knew of the Camorrist influence at first hand; he decided to attend the trial. Before travelling to Europe, he called at the office of McClure's to see if there was any interest in an account of the trial. Mackenzie was dubious. Camorra? Mafia? No. American readers couldn't care less about such matters. But Mackenzie promised to tell McClure of Train's trip.

When S.S. heard of it, he was enchanted. He foresaw a monumental history of the Mala Vita, tracing the connections between the Camorra and Tammany Hall—a detailed, documented study of the alliance of politics and crime—a big thing—a tremendous contribution to good government in American cities. And Train was the one man to write the series. Forthwith S.S. engaged the services of two English correspondents—reporters for The Morning Chronicle of London, one stationed in Rome, the other in Milan— to supply Train with research.

Only one detail was overlooked. S.S. forgot to tell Train what he was up to. Train was in Viterbo, watching the trial, when he was handed a telegram from Rome:

IF YOU ARE THE ARTHUR TRAIN CONNECTED WITH MCCLURE'S MAGAZINE I CONSIDER YOUR CONDUCT GROSSLY DISCOURTEOUS. MACDONALD.

Angry and bewildered, Train wired MacDonald, whoever he was, to go to hell, and gave his attention once again to the trial. (MacDonald was, of course, one of the two English correspondents McClure had hired.) After he had seen enough to satisfy him, he went on to Rome. Here he found that McClure was on his trail. There was a telegram—WAIT FOR ME I AM COMING

—that did not say where McClure was nor when he would arrive. Train shrugged. He knew nothing of all this. In due course he went on to Florence, where he found another telegram—WAIT FOR ME I AM COMING—from Mc-Clure.

S.S. was in hot pursuit. Accompanied by Hattie, he had caught an express for Florence only hours after Train had left Rome. Around noon, the express stopped somewhere and S.S. got off to stretch his legs. When he turned around, he discovered the train had left without him. There would not be another one along for hours. He found a seat in the waiting-room, took a pack of cards from his pocket, and began playing solitaire. On board the next train at last, he kept on playing solitaire hour after hour. Night came, the lamps were lighted, and still he played. At last his train slowed, coming into a big city. Florence at last! S.S. swept up his cards and scuttled to the platform. The train moved on. He was in Pistoia.

It was then nearly midnight. S.S. took out his cards again. A milk train finally got him to Florence in the early hours; Train found him in the garden of the Grand Hotel, wolfing down a second breakfast. "Sit down! Sit down!" said McClure, and told Train his story.

Train, who had never before met the editor, found him magnetic, most persuasive, and very urgent. S.S. was prepared to pour money out freely; the articles were to be published one a month; for years, if need be. He talked of detectives, disguises, cloaks and daggers, and spies shadowing sinister felons.

Train shook his head. "Mr. McClure," he said, "you have paid me an undeserved compliment. Personally I think there is no such interest in America in Italian criminal societies as you seem to suppose. However, that is your business, not mine. I know something about the Camorra already and I will try to learn more. I am willing to stay over here two months and I will write you three articles on the Camorra and Mafia at one thousand dollars apiece."

"Not enough! I'll give you fifteen hundred and you can spend all the money you want—"

"One thousand and my expenses," said Train firmly.

"All right! We'll draw up a contract!"

"I don't want any contract. I'll sit down now and write you a letter and you can initial it."

"Be sure and put in about your expenses!"

Train scribbled a letter of agreement. McClure read it, signed in the margin, and turning it over scrawled on the back: "This is a contract! S.S. Mc-Clure." *

A pleasant jaunt; but now once again S.S. faced the distasteful business of being a publisher. At his London office he found two letters awaiting him, one from Mather, the other from Mackenzie.

Mather wrote to tell McClure of his plan for the reorganization of the company. He had talked it over with Thomas Lamont, who was still a heavy investor in the Crowell Company (which had recently purchased The American Magazine) and who was now a partner in J. P. Morgan & Company. Lamont had offered to invest three or four hundred thousand dollars in the S.S. McClure Company. In return he would take an issue of eight-per-cent preferred stock valued at the same amount and would require, as a bonus, at least two hundred and fifty thousand dollars' worth of common stock. McClure would still own a majority of all stock, but he would be required to assign his holdings to three trustees—Lamont, Mather, and Albert Wiggin, the president of the Chase National Bank. Mather strongly urged McClure to approve the plan, pointing out that it would free him from "the disgrace as well as the expense" of paying sixteen per cent on his borrowed capital; that his fixed charges would be reduced by twenty-four thousand dollars a year; and that, by virtue of association with the Crowell Company, he would be able to effect other economies in his business department. "These financial advantages," Mather added, "can be obtained without any further limitations than exist now upon your initiative and judgment in the editorial control of the magazine."

Mackenzie wrote to tell McClure that he agreed as to the need for a financial reorganization. He knew of Mather's plan; indeed, he had been in Mather's office while Mather had dictated his letter. But Mackenzie gravely feared that financial control by Lamont would result in editorial control by Lamont. "Could you," he asked McClure, "ever convince the public at large that [control by Lamont] gave you a greater freedom than the people at the American Magazine enjoy?" † Moreover, Mackenzie was not persuaded

* When Train told the story years later in his autobiography (My Day in Court, Charles Scribner's Sons, 1939, pp. 302–306), he admitted that McClure was right in wanting more than three articles. "The subsequent development of the corrupt alliances amongst police, government agents, and racketeers throughout the United States," Train wrote, "demonstrated [McClure's] uncanny perspicacity."

† The editors of The American, who had launched a campaign against the reactionary regime of Porfirio Díaz in Mexico, had hushed their criticism shortly after the purchase of The American by the Crowell Company.

that co-operation with the Crowell Company would benefit McClure's business department. Rather, he argued, it "would undoubtedly mean the elimination of some of your best people, notably Curtis Brady and probably in time myself." Therefore, Mackenzie urged, "it is only fair that you should give me an opportunity to secure the money on terms as favorable as you will accept from Mr. Lamont. . . . I know perfectly well that this can be done. I know further that [preferred stock] can be sold to people in no way connected with the large financial interests down town. . . . I feel that I should have the first opportunity of putting the deal over as a matter of protection to you, to myself and to certain members of the organization who have given you great loyalty and affection."

What to do? S.S.'s two most trusted financial advisers both recommended reorganization, differing only in detail. When he took counsel with himself, S.S. heard two powerful arguments: Mather's plan led to Wall Street, which S.S. mistrusted; Mackenzie's plan kept matters within the family, and S.S. had a familial loyalty that surpassed both understanding and reason.

S.S. cabled Mather that he disapproved his plan. Mather promptly resigned as director of the S.S. McClure Company, and this time the resignation was not tactical. Mather meant it. "I fear," S.S. told his wife, "that Mather regards me as foolish."

S.S. cabled Mackenzie to proceed with his plan for reorganization. Mackenzie promptly conferred with Frederick Collins, the secretary of the Crowell Company and the editor of The Woman's Home Companion. Mackenzie and Collins were of the same age—twenty-nine, in 1911—and of the same ambitious disposition. In turn, they conferred with Holland Duell, a patent attorney who had married well. His wife, Mabel Hallowell Duell, had inherited a handsome legacy from her father, the treasurer of the American Tobacco Company.*

Duell agreed to put up some money. Mackenzie, Collins, and Duell then organized a new company, McClure Publications, Incorporated, with three classes of stock—first preferred, second preferred, and common. They leased (with an option to buy) a magazine called The Ladies' World, a mail-order journal with a claimed circulation of five hundred and eighty thousand. The entire issue of first preferred stock, valued at eight hundred and fifty thou-

---

* As Curtis Brady has written me, there must have been an affinity between the American Tobacco Company and McClure's Magazine. First Roberts and then Duell. And yet McClure's advertising policy was stubborn about tobacco. Tobacco advertisements were accepted but never solicited. Nevertheless, the tobacco men must have considered McClure's a lucky strike.

sand dollars, went to the owners of The Ladies' World. They leased (with an option to buy) McClure's Magazine. In return, McClure was to get five hundred thousand dollars' worth of second preferred stock (half of the entire issue) in payment for his holdings in the S.S. McClure Company. He was, moreover, assured that he would be retained as editor of McClure's under his personal contract with his own company, which stipulated a salary of twenty-five thousand dollars a year. The common stock (and the voting power) was divided amongst Mackenzie, Collins, Duell, Horace Payne (who was Collins's brother-in-law), and Arthur Moore (whose father had been publisher of The Ladies' World).

According to the articles of incorporation, the owners of the first preferred stock would pocket the first seven per cent of any dividends justified by net earnings; the owners of the second preferred would take the next seven per cent; the owners of the common stock would divide any further profits. Provision was made that if, for two years after January 1, 1914, dividends had not been paid to the owners of first and second preferred stock, they would then be given voting rights.

McClure was weary of the long fight to protect his own. The assurance that he would continue as editor was apparently all he wanted—that, and a guarantee that he would be paid enough money to support his family. In the fall of 1911 he signed the contract for the lease of his magazine (with an option for its purchase). Mackenzie and Collins took over. Miss Cather, who had been managing editor, retired. Curtis Brady, who had an ironclad contract as business manager, also retired. "What was going to happen," he said later, "was so clear a blind man could have felt it with his cane."

But McClure had no cane. "I am very happy and content and pleasantly situated here," he wrote Miss Cather, from his New York office. "I am rather enjoying the new developments, the new body of jealousies that has sprung up against Cameron [Mackenzie] and Mr. Collins among their contemporaries. It amuses me and surprises Cameron. I am rather glad to be outside of it."

Relaxed and cheerful, he wandered out to the Battle Creek Sanitarium, the curious vegetarian retreat organized and operated by Doctor James H. Kellogg. "I am content," S.S. wrote his wife from this refuge, "with the risk & burden of the magazine off my shoulders." He continued to be sanguine. "MATTERS HEALTHIEST SHAPE IN FIVE YEARS," he cabled Hattie in January, 1912.

But matters deteriorated fast.

In February S.S. was told that his salary of twenty-five thousand dollars a year would have to be assigned to reduce the debt Duell had incurred when he undertook to repay the sum owed to the West Virginia Pulp & Paper Company. S.S. was, however, still assured that everyone involved wanted him to continue as editor of McClure's.

In May the talk got tougher. Duell was suddenly intransigent; so was John Luke, the president of the paper company. For the first time it now appeared that no party to the deal wanted S.S.'s services as editor. Even the five hundred thousand dollars' worth of second preferred stock he had been promised was now sliced in half.* In blunt truth, the officers of McClure Publications, Incorporated, were planning to boot S.S. out with nothing but honeyed promises. And they almost succeeded; for at this stage of the proceedings, S.S., improvident as ever, was in Europe, at a comfortable remove from the crossroads where the dirty work was being done. His lawyer, a man of no gumption, was ready to accept any settlement, however valueless.

Luckily McClure's son Robert, then a youngster of twenty-three, was on hand and he smelled a stink. With admirable dispatch, he called on the man who, beyond all others, could petrify a pack of parvenu publishers. He called on Frank Munsey. The effect of this simple gesture was remarkable. Overnight, Duell agreed that McClure would have to be paid an absolute and unconditional ten thousand dollars a year. On this basis, McClure's lawyer, armed with his power of attorney, signed away all S.S.'s rights in McClure's Magazine.

S.S. had hurried back from Europe on the fastest ship. He arrived in New York, as usual, too late. Munsey urged him to fight, and even undertook to hold his coat. S.S. shook his head. All the fight had gone out of him. It was enough to learn that nobody thought him fit to edit his own magazine.

From Munsey's offices in the Flatiron Building S.S. walked slowly east to his own offices—or, rather, to what had once been his own. He sensed that in those rooms he was already a stranger. He was greeted with assurances that the ten thousand dollars they were to pay him would be much more, if he planned active editorial work. He looked at them sharply: he had caught the false note in their hearty welcome. He shook his head. He left

---

* This was a gratuitous insult. In terms of real income, it made no difference how much second preferred stock he was given, for the second preferred never earned one cent in dividends. But to reduce even this nominal recompense was to twist the knife in the wound.

the offices and walked back again through Madison Square and on up Fifth Avenue.

Behind him there were so many years—so many hardships, so many happy battles, so many triumphs, so many friendships, so many heartbreaks—all behind him.

What had gone wrong? Was there anyone to blame? What if he had accepted Mather's plan for reorganization rather than Mackenzie's? What if he had not hired Roberts? What if he had not insisted on starting a new magazine back in 1905? What if Phillips and Brady had never authorized that building in Long Island City? What if he had never met Florence Wilkinson? What if Doubleday had agreed to help swing the purchase of Harper & Brothers? What if Albert Brady had not died? No, it was no use asking such questions: he had only himself to blame, and if he were given it to do again he would likely do the same.

He turned into his club, the Union League, nodded to the porter in the hall, and walked into the lounge. Here he encountered an old friend, Charles Ropes, one of the two men who had put him up for membership in the club. (Munsey was the other.) "Hello, Sam," said Ropes, and then looked at him with sudden concern. "What's the matter?" he asked.

S.S. shook his head ruefully. "Does it show that much?" Then he chuckled, as though he were enjoying a private joke. "I've just been unhorsed," he said.

UNHORSED

1912-1918

[1]

What most hurt McClure was that he was out of things. When he went to Chicago for the Republican national convention, he encountered dozens of friends; a few were standing pat with Taft, most were standing at Armageddon with Roosevelt, but all were happy and busy, politicking, filing correspondence, intriguing, pretending they were making a President. S.S., all at once diffident, stood on the edges of little groups of men, listening. Shorn of his magazine, he felt like a cipher.

The greatest magazine editor of his time, having been tossed aside by his associates, was now looking around for a job. By taste, by temperament, and by talent, S.S. was fitted only for the task of editor; in any other wise he was a figure of fun, as ridiculous as a general without an army. He considered what he should do. "I am less & less inclined for editing work," he wrote his wife, "and will surely enter upon some new field."

McClure was now fifty-five years old. He had no savings; an insurance policy on his life had lapsed, owing to his inability to pay the premium due on it late in 1911; his sole income was the annual ten thousand dollars begrudged him by the new owners of his magazine. And there were dependent on him, directly or indirectly, temporarily or permanently, a dozen persons: his wife Hattie, sick in a hospital at Cannes; Hattie's aged aunt, Sophia Hurd; his mother; his brother Jack, who was crippled by arthritis, and Jack's wife and ten-year-old daughter; his own oldest daughter Eleanor; his son Robert, Robert's wife, and their two small children; and his adopted son Enrico, then a boy of ten.* His other two daughters, Bess and Mary,

---

* Enrico should have been introduced earlier. He had been informally adopted by Bess McClure in the summer of 1904, when he was an infant of two. The procedure of adoption, like many other things in this life, was far less complicated in 1904 than it is today. There were in New York many immigrant families, desperately poor; if one was sympathetic, one tried to help

were both married and no longer his immediate concern; his other two brothers, Thomas and Robert, had divided a considerable sum when they sold the syndicate in May, 1912, and so were presumably able to take care of themselves; his son Robert would presently find a job, and this would reduce the number of S.S.'s dependents to eight. Even so, he would somehow have to add to his income.

The new editors of McClure's Magazine made him an offer. If, at his expense, he would engage someone (perhaps Willa Cather) to write the story of his life, they would publish it and apply his fee for the serial rights against what he owed the West Virginia Pulp & Paper Company. In this way, the editors would get a strong editorial feature for nothing and at the same time create the illusion that McClure was still somehow connected with the magazine. S.S. would be allowed to reserve for himself any royalties that might accrue from the sale of a book, if it turned out the autobiographical articles might make a book. Even this graceless proposition depended on the co-operation of a skillful writer; Willa Cather seemed the likeliest candidate, but she was far off in the Arizona desert, exploring Pueblo towns, watching the Hopi snake-dance, and planning to ride on into Mexico.

S.S.'s letters to Miss Cather caught up with her in Lamy, New Mexico, and her heart was touched by his financial difficulties. She was, she wrote,* alarmed and pained to hear of what had happened. She could not make herself believe that S.S., at his age, with such a career behind him, and with such specialized ability, could be kept down for long. She was sure that she could help out. She bade him count on her to do anything she could. She reminded him of how generous he had always been; it made her not only sad, she wrote, but mad, fighting Irish mad, to think that he was being so tormented and deviled about money. A few days later, back home in Red Cloud, Nebraska, she assured him that she would certainly help him write the autobiographical articles, nor would she ask for any pay for the work. She could do it better, she insisted, and would feel more zest in doing it, if there were no question of payment at all. He had done more favors for her than she could count; she wanted an opportunity to do him a small favor in return. She wished she had money or influence to put at his command; fail-

---

them. At eighteen, Bess McClure was most sympathetic. She went to the proper place, where the choice, she later recalled, was as between Irish freckles and Italian curls. She chose Italian curls and took Enrico home to the McClure house at Ardsley. Hattie McClure, whose maternal affection was infinite, promptly spread a warm, protective wing over the child.

* In her will, Miss Cather requested that her letters not be directly quoted.

ing these, if her wits could help him in any way, it would indeed be a pleasure to her. She was concerned only that perhaps she might not be able to write the articles just as he would like them; the events that sang one tune to him, she wrote, might sing another to her; the *way* in which one writes a thing, she reminded him, is not altogether under one's control. As an example, she cited some of the chapters in the series about Christian Science, which she confessed she had not been able to write in the way he would have liked best. But she would gladly try the autobiographical articles. Certainly, she wrote, she was never more willing about a piece of work. Of her own affairs, she added that she had such a head-full of stories that she dreamed about them at night. She was so dark-skinned and *good humored,* after her weeks on horseback, that he would never know her. She begged him to forget how cranky she had got, when she had tired at the end of the long days in the office. Her holiday in the desert had taken all the kinks and crumples out of her; she felt as if her mind had been freshly washed and ironed; she felt, somehow, confident, as if she had got her second wind and would never again torture herself about little things. She sent him a thousand, thousand good wishes, and loyalty and hope.

S.S. was properly grateful. One, at least, of his old associates still remembered him with affection.

There remained, however, the problem of creating a new career. To trim himself for the task, S.S. decided he had to mend his health, which continued precarious. He headed again for the Battle Creek Sanitarium.

The Sanitarium was an institution unique even in the United States, where there have been launched so many daffy attempts to point the way to the perfect life. Indeed, the Sanitarium was a kind of amalgam of every Utopian fancy inherited from the nineteenth century, and to it had been added every new quirk of the twentieth. From Brook Farm the Sanitarium took the simple life; from Sylvester Graham it took vegetarianism and graham bread, adapting them and developing them into a profusion of health foods of which the best-known is corn flakes; from the Oneida Community it borrowed the notion of eugenics and transformed it into a Race Betterment Foundation. The very existence of the Sanitarium was due to a nineteenth-century perfectionist sect, the Seventh Day Adventists; and long after it had been wrested from its founders and converted into a health resort, the Sanitarium was still suffused with an ineradicable taint of moral and spiritual uplift.

The man who plucked the Sanitarium from the grasp of the godly was Doctor John Harvey Kellogg, the inventor of corn flakes and some six dozen other health foods. Although Doctor Kellogg's mind teemed with odd ideas about health, he was never exclusive; he welcomed the eccentricities of other men. Horace Fletcher, the chewer, had no sooner promulgated his doctrine that every mouthful of food should be chomped thirty-two times, once for each tooth, than Doctor Kellogg emblazoned the strange device "Fletcherize!" on a banner which he suspended in a prominent position overlooking the grand dining room of the Sanitarium. Doctor Kellogg's own pet hate was autointoxication, by which was meant the poisoning of the body by constipation. Never was there a physician more dedicated to moving American bowels. In Doctor Kellogg's view, each meal ideally should shove the previous one out; the well-tempered bowel, he argued, should move three times a day; and most of the edibles that came from his laboratory were designed to assist in the effortless accomplishment of this end-result.* Doctor Kellogg also leveled his arquebus against tobacco, alcoholic beverages, and sexual incontinence (even when the parties thereto were joined in the bonds of holy matrimony); but he reserved his gravest disapproval for those who ate meat—or, as he preferred to describe them, the flesh-eaters. To eat flesh, Doctor Kellogg insisted, was to invite autointoxication, and autointoxication in turn caused most of the thousand natural shocks that flesh is heir to, including, quite likely, heartache.

All things considered, it is astonishing that McClure did not discover Doctor Kellogg and the Sanitarium until 1909. Certainly he was predisposed in their favor. As early as 1882 S.S. had been an addict of health foods: at that time he regularly bought and ate a thing called Granula, which was the first cold cereal breakfast food.† And he had for years suspected that the source of all his physical woes was his bowel.

In any case, when they first met McClure and Doctor Kellogg had all but joined hands to dance. "I feel it is the will of Providence," the doctor told McClure, "that has brought you in contact with the work here." And McClure had written his wife: "Doctor Kellogg is right. Neurasthenia is a

---

* It was, no doubt, on account of Doctor Kellogg's flourishing practice that Sir William Osler was provoked to say: "Americans have their bowels on their brains."

† I was puzzled by McClure's reference to Granula (in a letter he wrote to Hattie in April, 1882) and the mystery was not cleared up until I read Gerald Carson's Cornflake Crusade (Rinehart & Company, 1957), a most diverting account of how evangelical religion and food faddism coupled and brought forth the breakfast-cereal industry. Granula, it seems, was a mix of graham flour and water, oven-dried, ground up, and crumbled—in short, the prototype of Grape Nuts.

great susceptibility to autointoxication. For the last two weeks I've been clean inside, not the slightest odor to my faeces, and I am growing strong."

Everything about the Sanitarium had delighted McClure—the Swedish massage; the dreadful diet; the chance to meet and talk with men like Horace Fletcher, Gifford Pinchot, Judge Ben B. Lindsey, and Irving Fisher, the professor of economics at Yale; and, most of all, the bogus aura of science that hung like a halo over the resort. S.S. had read somewhere that people in Europe ate dog meat. He put it up to Doctor Kellogg: which was worse, dog meat or cow meat? Doctor Kellogg had already studied the matter by Bouchard's urotoxic method. "I extracted the juice from beef and the juice from dog flesh," he told McClure, "treating them both alike. I injected these juices into the veins of rabbits and took careful note of the quantity required to kill the rabbits. It took just twice as much beef juice to kill a rabbit as of dog juice, showing that the dog juice was twice as poisonous."

All quite scientific; and on the strength of such nonsense McClure had even assigned a staff writer to go to Battle Creek and gather research for an article on the dangers of eating meat. Like the rabbits, the article had been killed, but McClure had become a confirmed vegetarian. Now in 1912, as he repaired to Battle Creek, his mouth watered at the thought of such delicacies as oatmeal soup, nuttolene, yogurt buttermilk, and granola fruit pudding.

In the early summer of 1912 the Sanitarium was filled with disgruntled, rancorous Republicans intent on restoring their tissues after the vicissitudes of the convention in Chicago. Taft Republicans glowered at Roosevelt Republicans; insurgents snarled at standpatters; and the insurgents were quarrelsome even among themselves, some of them declaring that, rather than split the G.O.P. by supporting Roosevelt, they would vote for Woodrow Wilson. S.S. stood with Roosevelt, no matter what. He was gratified to find that young Edward Rumely agreed with him.

Rumely was a thickset man of thirty, who had the look of a genial bulldog. He had many interests: he had taken a medical degree at a German university; he helped manage his family's business, which was the manufacture of farm equipment; and he ran the Interlaken School, a boarding school for boys near LaPorte, Indiana. It was in his capacity of headmaster that Rumely had first met McClure: Enrico had been enrolled as a student at Interlaken. Before long Rumely had interested himself in S.S.'s attempts to build an organization that would guarantee peace among the nations.

Rumely had expressed suspicion of the English. "There is a certain selfish interest," he had written McClure, "in the efforts of the English who are promoting this World Peace Movement." He had urged McClure to publish a paper by a German economist, Gerhart von Schulze-Gävernitz. McClure had read the paper and rejected it. "You made a mistake," Rumely had written him, in September, 1911. "A statement of the German point of view to the American public is a matter of great moment. Your pages," he had added reproachfully, "have been opened repeatedly to a rather full discussion of the English viewpoint."

These frictions were forgotten, however, in their common enthusiasm for Roosevelt and the Progressive party. When S.S. told him that he had been ousted from control of McClure's Magazine, Rumely was concerned and sympathetic. "I want work more than I want money," said S.S. Rumely nodded. S.S. was too able, too important a citizen to be without a job. Rumely would think of something. Not right now; but pretty soon. Right now, the job was to get Roosevelt re-elected.

So McClure still had no job, and nothing to do but work with Miss Cather on his autobiography.

As a serial feature for the magazine, the autobiography was a success all around. With the publication of each chapter S.S. could expect to find in his mail letters like these:

THE SECRETARY OF THE NAVY

Washington

Sep. 26, 1913

My dear Mr. McClure:—
Your opening chapter of your biography is charming in its simplicity and beauty. I can almost see the route you took to school and hear the voices of the children. The only good history is autobiography, and I am hungry for your next chapter.

Sincerely your friend
Josephus Daniels

Hotel Bellevue
Beacon Street, Boston

Oct. 16, 1913

My dear McClure:
I have been reading the very touching and beautiful story of your life. I cannot remember anything of more peculiar interest. As a self-

study, temperamental and social, it must stand with the great autobiographies. It makes one love you better than ever.

Yours ever
W. D. Howells

Kennebunkport, Maine
Oct. 19, 1913

Dear Mr. McClure:

We've been reading the second installment of your autobiography, and,
as you, on a time, said pleasant things of writing of mine, it strikes me
the time has come to reply in kind.

Nothing I have ever read was more touching than these early passages
in your memoirs; nor more perfectly and beautifully written. *What* you
tell is very wonderful, and the *way* you tell it is just plain noble. . . .
It's as simple as a country church—or a Greek statue.

It makes a person, reading, want to cry out to you, "God bless you!"

For my part, of course, I've *always* had ample reason for *that!*

Gratefully yours always,
Booth Tarkington

Riverside, Connecticut
Feb. 20 1914

Dear McClure: On my lecture trip in the west, I got hold of last month's
instalment of your autobiography. I wish I could tell you how great I
think that boy was and how his adventures thrilled me. Some of them
reminded me of passages in my own life, I see now how it came about
that you could keep me awake nights trying to keep up with you. It's all
very American, very inspiring. What a career you have had—so full of
honor and high success! . . .

Yours sincerely
Irving Bacheller

But—saving these friendly judgments, and saving Willa Cather's wonderfully limpid prose—what was effective as a series of magazine articles added
up to trivial autobiography. S.S. could tell the story of his early hardships
and triumphs readily enough (the account of them makes up two-thirds of
the book), but when it came to the years of his achievement he was notably
reticent. About the muckraking movement he was almost apologetic; it had
come about, he declared, quite accidentally. It was as though he were belatedly appealing to the financial community and disclaiming any critical
intent. This propitiary passage can be correctly interpreted only by those
familiar with the circumstances of his downfall.*

* Moreover, it is likely that Collins, the new editor of McClure's, urged S.S. to handle the muckraking with restraint. Collins was convinced that S.S. as editor had antagonized vast numbers
of his readers and advertisers. Collins's own editorial policy was as bland as milk toast.

Edward S. Martin, the editor of Life,* was one of those acquainted with S.S.'s misfortunes. Martin knew that S.S. had lost control of his magazine two years before. In March, 1914, Martin wrote in Life:

> It was an excellent experiment to let down McClure's Magazine till it came in contact with the bones of its prophet. It was time. The magazine had been running to a kind of phosphorescence that suggested decay. The experiment began last October with the first installment of S.S. McClure's autobiography. Since then there has been at least one live piece in every number.
>
> The October cover called Mr. McClure's discourse "The Inspiring Struggle of an Emigrant Boy, Who Became the Greatest Editor of His Time." "Editor" is a commodiously inclusive word. Among the editors of the McClure period were Pulitzer and Hearst. Whether Mr. McClure has been as great an editor as Mr. Pulitzer is a matter suitable for discussion. They were nowise alike, but there was likeness in the way they came to their destiny. The call to be a great editor is a call to a great adventure, and only comes to the desperately adventurous.
>
> Mr. McClure has been a great magazine editor; there is no doubt of that. In the three decades since he began his newspaper syndicate, nobody's hand has been more perceptible than his on the crank that turns the world upside down. If he was not the inventor of the uplift, he furnished the first considerable vehicle that it rode in. He virtually invented the ten-cent magazine. It is almost as if he had invented gunpowder or soap. He found a respectable-appearing world insufficiently fed by magazines at thirty-five cents each. He now relates the story of his life to a world struggling to escape from a vast horde of voracious and insistent magazines at any price that you can spare from five cents up. . . .
>
> He is a wonderful man; a good talker; and when he talks about himself he has a great subject. And he has done it fair justice; done it with a glow, and duly with art. It is the story of a man of genius . . . a hard, hard, hard story, pathetic sometimes, but never sad; too adventurous for that. It is something like St. Paul's tale of his sufferings in the gospel cause. They were terrific but you don't mind them, because he made so good.
>
> Nobody rides comfortably to achievement that is worth achieving; nobody presses a button and picks fame off the salver when the man brings it in; nobody knows life much without living it a good deal, and few people have lived it more than Sam McClure did between five and twenty-seven. He scrambled up the ladder, a free spirit, often in physical distress,

---

* This was the old Life, the one which, if I may borrow a quip from the late Joe Palmer, was funny on purpose.

but apparently enchanted with life, happy with the happiness of the imagination, sleeping anywhere, eating anything, clothed with what came to hand, but waking every morning with a fire lighted in him that burned all day.

That was the fire that came in due time to burn with so considerable an illumination in McClure's Magazine; that lit up our world with such a lively flare that the old magazines were wax candles beside it. That was the fire that ignited the torch with which Ida Tarbell scorched the Standard Oil, that lighted Steffens and Baker and the original muckrakers in their excavations for civic sins.

Of course, so much combustion is consumptive of a frame not all asbestos, but the kindling of it is fine to read about.

It was valedictory, it was practically obituary. But as yet McClure had no intention of saying good-by.

[II]

There was talk of S.S. going to work for Munsey, but Hattie was mistrustful of Munsey. "So far he has been only a broken staff for you to lean on," she told her husband. Later, when there was talk of his going to work for Hearst, Hattie was even sharper. "I am not pleased," she wrote S.S., in her most queenly manner, "with Hearst's reputation, personal, political, or journalistic. I should need to see that it was a right and wise thing for you to do, before I could be glad to see you at work for him." Despite this advice, McClure might have taken the job offered (as contributing editor of Hearst's Magazine, a periodical which was eventually merged with Cosmopolitan) except that Collins and Mackenzie forbade him to accept it. They reminded him that his attorney, acting with his power, had agreed that S.S. would not permit the use of his name as editor or author in any magazine other than McClure's Magazine for a period of twenty years.

By this time Hattie was again home in the United States. She urged him to concentrate on lecturing. "You have a great work to do for this country," she told him. "You must speak. Everybody needs you. God guide and bless you!"

S.S. had made his first appearance on the lecture platform, very reluctantly, in 1909, when his financial prospects had been at their most dismal. He had tried to limit his engagements to colleges; but his manager, Lee Keedick, had artfully lured him on to the Chautauqua circuit and thence, very gradually, to the dreary round of commercial and professional clubs. At every step, S.S. had protested. "This lecture business does not suit me at all," he had grumbled; "there is no pleasure in it." But his audiences had been enthusiastic, and he had needed the money. By 1913, since he had found no other way of earning a living, he had worked up a repertory of three or four lectures and was reconciled to spouting one of them out whenever and wherever he was guaranteed a hundred dollars for the job. (His pet lecture, naturally, was a sermon on the evils of municipal government and how they would be wiped out by the city commission.) But it was, at best, a dog's life.

Other evangels of the uplift, enchanted by the possibilities of motion pictures, then a strange new toy, sought to enlist McClure as figurehead for large, dreamy, cinematic enterprises by which the heathen might be converted or all mankind made literate. For a wonder, he resisted these overtures. But suddenly he saw a way to combine motion picture and lecture platform in a pluperfect educational scheme: he would use them to bring The Method to America.

In 1913, when The Method was mentioned, it did not conjure up a caricature of an ill-clad actor, grunting inarticulately and scratching his nether parts. Rather the phrase denoted the pedagogical theories of a remarkable Italian educator, Dr. Maria Montessori. A report of the Montessori Method of teaching young children had been one of S.S.'s last editorial triumphs. His associates had unanimously declared that any article on kindergarten technique would inevitably glaze the eyes of all readers of McClure's. On the contrary, the article had aroused the liveliest interest all over the country, for it explained how, by relying on permissive guidance rather than on discipline, Dr. Montessori had been able to teach three-year-olds to read and write and thirst for more. The office of McClure's had been deluged with letters of inquiry; dozens of American kindergarten teachers had headed for Rome to study The Method; Alexander Graham Bell had helped launch an American Montessori Association. In pedagogical circles, The Method had stirred up a storm.

It occurred to McClure that, if he could get the North American rights to motion pictures of Dr. Montessori working with her small pupils, he would have the basis for a fine lecture series. Certainly the motion pictures promised much, for The Method required of the pupils a great deal of creative activity, such as pretending to be swans, budding blossoms, toads, trains, trees, or whatever. (It would seem that Montessori and Stanislavsky had more than a little in common.) The films also showed children learning to read by manipulating an elaborate alphabetic apparatus, the invention of Dr. Montessori.

McClure traveled to Rome in the fall of 1913 to broach and subsequently clinch the deal. In the view of the Dottoressa, grateful for the attention given her work in McClure's Magazine, S.S. was a rich and powerful protector who could do no wrong. He was, she told him, strong and chivalrous, "comme la personne sans tache et sans peur." Carried away as usual by his enthusiasm, S.S. conceived on the spot a hasty and dubious scheme: the Dottoressa should come to the United States with him; off they would go on a joint tour of the biggest cities, beginning at Carnegie Hall in New York; they would organize Houses of Childhood, training schools for teachers of The Method, a company to manufacture the didactic apparatus, and a series of lectures and motion-picture exhibitions that would revolutionize the entire system of primary education in the United States. The Dottoressa was easily persuaded. With high hopes they sailed together for New York.

To all appearances the tour was, moreover, a triumph. When S.S. and the Dottoressa lectured at Carnegie Hall, with John Dewey presiding, more than a thousand persons were turned away; a repeat performance had to be scheduled a week later. Washington, Philadelphia, Boston, Chicago— everywhere the crowds were big and the enthusiasm for progressive education intense. When she left for home, late in December, 1913, Dr. Montessori rejoiced that she was allied with McClure "dans un idéal d'humanité, qui élève les cœurs." "I have," she assured him, "unlimited confidence in you."

But behind the scenes there had been an unseemly scramble to exploit the Dottoressa, her Method, her apparatus, and everything else involved. McClure had scrambled with the others. He claimed he sought control of the various Method enterprises solely to protect the Dottoressa from exploitation, and this may very well have been the case, but his concern was not wholly altruistic. He had pocketed twenty per cent of the net proceeds of their joint tour (she got sixty per cent and Lee Keedick, the manager, got the other twenty) and his lectures, which continued after she had left, and which made use of her films, were for his own private profit. Never had he been dishonest; but he had been naïve, which, in the circumstances, was worse. His gravest offense was his failure to make his position clear: she had imagined him to be her Maecenas, while in fact he was only a promoter diligently delving for an honest dollar.

When the Dottoressa's affectionate letters were supplanted by chilly missives from her lawyer, S.S. recognized his error. He abjured the power of

attorney she had given him, returned her films, and quit forever the battle
he should never have joined, the battle for progressive education. Four
months of exhausting work had netted him four hundred and ninety-two
dollars and ninety-nine cents.

As if this were not bad enough, his youngest and favorite brother, Robert,
shot and killed himself, late in May, 1914, in his house at Yonkers, New
York. Robert McClure was a sick man, an alcoholic, and the suicide was the
result of that illness; but S.S., in his grief, could recall only that his last
words to Robert had been spoken in anger because of a disagreement provoked by the Montessori tour.

Shocked, saddened, and sorely depressed, S.S. had recourse to his customary analgesic. He sailed for Europe early in June, 1914.

[III]

It was his intention to gather material for another lecture, one to be called
"The European Situation." It took no prescience to realize that the situation
in Europe held a certain interest; indeed, S.S. had scarcely arrived in London
before the news came of the assassination in Sarajevo of the heir-apparent
to the Austrian throne; all across the armed camp of Europe there began
the fateful interplay of forces. While S.S. was talking with politicians and
editors and cabinet ministers, sounding them on the possibilities of war, back
in the United States President Wilson was delivering a characteristically
lofty Fourth of July address at Philadelphia. "The world," he observed
plaintively, "is getting more complicated every day." It was, indeed. Not
enough that the curiously fragile chain of cause-and-effect was dragging a
civilization toward ultimate folly; at this grave moment the Irish, with their
superb gift for anticlimax, were threatening to revolt against the British
crown. Lord Northcliffe got up a party to junket through Ulster and assess
affairs at first hand; he invited McClure to come along. A pleasant interlude;
but S.S. was back in London for the thirteen tense days that began with
the Austrian ultimatum to Servia and ended with the British declaration of
war against Germany. In the midst of these great and terrible events, McClure
was once again obliged to stand aside. His old friend and associate, Walter
Hines Page, was American ambassador to the Court of St. James's; his old
friend Sir Gilbert Parker was already organizing the bureau of propaganda
that would so effectively enthrall American opinion; Kipling, Conan Doyle,

Wells, Arnold Bennett—all his old friends had enlisted their talents on behalf of the empire. To McClure it seemed that he alone was dispensable. Late
in August he sailed home, intolerably frustrated by the fact of his having no
magazine into which he could pour his ideas.

After the tension and the suspense, the excitement of the cheering, singing
crowds in London and the underlying sense of dread and grief, America
seemed strangely serene and carefree. The weather was fine; everyone bustled
about his usual business; only the newspaper headlines were black and
ominous, and even these provoked only a grateful reflection that Europe was
far away.

McClure surrendered himself to this idyllic mood. For a month or so he
and Hattie were together again, wandering through Connecticut, exploring
back-country roads, taking delight in their companionship. The days were
sunny, the nights soft and moonlit. On one of those days, they came upon a
farm that lay along the Housatonic River: a herd of dairy cattle, a big tobacco
barn, an apple orchard, and a pleasant, roomy, shingled farmhouse. They
were as enraptured as a pair of newlyweds. They bought it at once. S.S.,
after arranging to help Hattie move in, went west on another lecture tour.

More than ever he was bored and vexed by the work. He was an editor:
what was he doing out here on the plains of Kansas and Nebraska, jawing
at hostile audiences who considered him anti-German? Nor did his spirits
revive as he glanced over each succeeding issue of McClure's Magazine and
saw one after another filled with trivia.

And then, as if in answer to his prayers, there came a summons from his
old friend and rival, Frank Munsey. Like McClure, Munsey had for many
years hankered to publish a daily newspaper; unlike McClure, he had kept
a careful account of his dollars until he had enough of them to gratify his
ambition. Munsey had bought The New York Press, and now he offered
McClure a contract to edit the magazine section for a year, at a salary of
ten thousand dollars. McClure at once accepted.

And almost at once he wished he had not. Thirty years before, when he
left The Century, he had vowed that never again would he work for another
man. Even since, when he had had an idea, his next step had been to rap out
an order to execute it. Now, to his discomfiture, he was obliged to lay his
idea on some other man's desk and, standing respectfully to one side, await
that other man's capricious approval. What was even worse, that other man
might have ideas of his own and order S.S. to execute them without consultation. "I am unsure from week to week of my present job," S.S. confessed

to Hattie. "This uncertainty makes me blue. If I lost this income you know just where we would be." Meanwhile Munsey proved to be unapproachable, and his managing editor, Keats Speed, ignored McClure.

In the circumstances, it was like having the jailer toss him a ring of keys when his young friend Rumely asked to confer with him and outline a scheme. Rumely told S.S. that he proposed to buy a New York newspaper, The Evening Mail; he wanted S.S. to be editor-in-chief at twelve thousand dollars a year; how did S.S. like the idea? For once in his life, S.S. paused to reflect.

Of the many interesting considerations attaching to this offer, not the least interesting was the timing of it. In January, 1915, the sympathies of most Americans were engaged on the side of the Allies, but a substantial minority—those of German and Irish extraction, and the intransigent Anglophobes generally—still favored the Central Powers. Germany, over-confident at the outset, had belatedly recognized the value of American opinion, and German agents were making their first clumsy efforts in the battle of propaganda. They faced a formidable task; the British had all the advantages and they were exploiting them adroitly. Aside from a common language and cultural heritage, the British had on their side most of the American newspapers, which were duly filled with inflammatory tales of Hunnish atrocities visited on Belgian civilians: children with hands cut off, girls with breasts sliced off, and the like. Nobody printed the tales manufactured by the Germans, but of Allied fictions there was a surfeit.

For those who wanted to present Germany's side of the story, a New York newspaper was the most urgent need. The Sun, one heard, could be purchased; feelers were put out, but to no avail. The Evening Mail was also rumored to be on the block. Its publisher, Henry L. Stoddard, had kept it alive by means of generous subventions from George Perkins, the Morgan partner who had managed Roosevelt's Progressive campaign in 1912; but the Progressive party was dead and Perkins was no longer ladling out sugar. A syndicate of wealthy German-American businessmen, backed by the German government, tendered Stoddard a discreet offer for The Mail, but he turned them down. It was against this background that Rumely now appeared with his proposal to buy the newspaper.

McClure was probably familiar with much of this background. Certainly he remembered Rumely's importunate demands that he print an article setting forth the German point of view in McClure's, back in 1911. Even had he forgotten, Hattie was careful to warn him, as soon as she heard of Rumely's scheme. "Be sure," she wrote him on February 20, "that it is not even tacitly understood that you are to support a pro-German propaganda. Dr. Rumely has something that he wants to promote, and I am afraid that is it."

S.S. knew that Rumely had made a fair amount of money manufacturing farm equipment. But it takes more than a fair amount of money to buy a New York newspaper; moreover, Rumely was no longer connected with his family's business. Where, then, was he getting the money? Only from American citizens, Rumely assured him, and went on to outline his plan in greater detail.

Rumely proposed not that The Evening Mail should be pro-German, but that it should be neutral. He had manufactured Diesel-engined tractors; he had a contract to sell a million dollars' worth of them to Germany; but he was unable to make delivery because of the British blockade. Why should the British interfere with American commerce? Why should the American government tolerate such high-handed procedure? And why did no New York newspaper discuss such matters? The Evening Mail would discuss them; it would declare a plague on both the warring houses alike; and there would be a large, loyal, and enthusiastic readership for such a newspaper. What could be wrong with this policy? Had not even President Wilson declared that this was "a war with which we have nothing to do, whose causes cannot touch us"?

There was one difficulty. Rumely was not personally acquainted with Henry Stoddard, the publisher of The Evening Mail. Perhaps it would be best if McClure were to open negotiations for the purchase of the newspaper on Rumely's behalf. Meanwhile Rumely would set up an S.S. McClure Newspaper Corporation as a holding company which would eventually control The Mail and Express Company. It seemed an excellent procedure.

McClure was panting to edit a first-rate newspaper, especially since he was barred from editing a magazine. He had a plenitude of ideas that he wanted to use as experiments on a newspaper. He demanded the editorial page and the page opposite for his own domain. He would print many more editorial features and series of features than were customary. He would engage the best scientific, literary, and philosophical minds to fill those two pages. As for the usual newspaper editorial, he was contemptuous. "Most editorials," he said, "are scolds, many are merely namby-pamby, some are hortatory, and all fail because they combine advice with generalizations." No editorial, he insisted, had ever had the slightest effect on public opinion. Short, simple, objective articles, crammed with facts, would be far more effective. The more he thought about it, the more enthusiastic he became. He could make The Evening Mail into the finest newspaper in the country. Rumely agreed. S.S. thereupon signed a two-year contract, binding on both parties, to serve as editor-in-chief.

By the end of February, thanks to S.S.'s intercession, Rumely had an option to buy The Evening Mail. He invited Frank Parker Stockbridge to be managing editor.

Stockbridge was an experienced journalist whose most salient achievement had been to assist Walter Hines Page in pumping Woodrow Wilson up to presidential stature. Page, for his pains, had been sent to London as ambassador for the New Freedom; Stockbridge had retired to work for an obscure Chicago magazine. Stockbridge knew Rumely as one who believed Germany would win the war. He was suspicious. To reassure him, Rumely argued that McClure was to control editorial policies and McClure, of course, was pro-British. Stockbridge insisted that he be given full control of news and news features. When it was promised him, he agreed to be managing editor.

This ill-fitted team did not at once go to work. There were delays. Rumely found it difficult to raise the necessary money. Meanwhile, McClure and Stockbridge palavered, coming to tentative agreement as to how The Evening Mail might be improved. They also discussed politics, in gingerly fashion. "I love Great Britain as a son loves his mother," S.S. told Stockbridge. "The idea of a neutral newspaper is a sound one from a business point of view but I do not believe I shall be able to keep the editorial page neutral." *

While negotiations were proceeding, Rumely took Stockbridge to breakfast in a suite of the Ritz Carlton Hotel, where the host was Dr. Bernhard Dernburg. A German official of ministerial rank, Dr. Dernburg had come to New York as head of a purchasing commission, but he had perforce assumed the role of chief spokesman for the German cause in the United States. McClure was also introduced to Dr. Dernburg, but separately, at a luncheon. These social affairs perturbed McClure and Stockbridge even more, and when on May 7 the Lusitania was torpedoed and sunk by a German sub-

---

* The notion that a neutral newspaper would in 1915 constitute a sound commercial venture is so dubious that one may question whether even McClure could have believed it. So he was quoted, however, by Stockbridge, in a series of articles published in The New York Herald, July 15–24, 1918. By 1915 the neutral newspaper was, of course, a contradiction in terms, at least in New York. Any New York newspaper that did not excessively adore the Allied cause was deemed treasonable.

marine McClure was thoroughly alarmed. "I shall have to keep a strong hand on the editorial page," he told Stockbridge.

And yet the negotiations were conducted with utmost propriety. Rumely was represented by the law firm of Cravath & Henderson, a painfully respectable concern, and by W. H. Coverdale, well known as an expert in the valuation of newspaper plants. During the negotiations, Rumely made a point of congratulating Stoddard on the editorials in The Evening Mail denouncing the sinking of the Lusitania. Rumely repeatedly pledged Stoddard his word of honor that his syndicate was comprised solely of American citizens. Moreover, when McClure and Stockbridge one day met with Rumely and demanded that on international issues The Evening Mail should back President Wilson, Rumely agreed.

The sale of The Evening Mail was consummated on May 30. On the next day, a Monday, Rumely, McClure, and Stockbridge assumed control. At once there were frictions. McClure and Stockbridge wanted only to make the best possible newspaper. Rumely was most concerned that he should have the last word on editorial policy; and, since he was the publisher, his was a natural concern.

For the next few weeks there was a stubborn tug-of-war in the editorial offices of The Evening Mail, as if to illustrate the impossibility of neutrality on an editorial page. Articles, editorials, and letters-to-the-editor that seemed quite proper to Rumely seemed to Stockbridge to have been deliberately contrived to assail the English and cosset the Germans. McClure, too, protested. Time and again he threatened to have his name removed from the head of the editorial page; each time the warning sufficed for a few days. As Stockbridge viewed the developing situation, it came "as a surprise and a shock" to McClure. "His [McClure's] regard for Dr. Rumely was affectionate, almost paternal," Stockbridge wrote. "It grieved him to the heart to have letters justifying the sinking of the Lusitania printed on the same page with his own distinctly un-German articles. . . . There never was a more loyal American than S.S. McClure, nor one less capable of believing ill of those whom he regarded as his best friends."

Gradually McClure realized that he was not and never would be the real editor-in-chief.

On the afternoon of July 24, a sultry Saturday, Doctor Heinrich Albert climbed the stairs to a station of the Sixth Avenue Elevated in New York

City and took a northbound train. Albert was a Geheimrat, a principal German agent; he was subsequently celebrated as the paymaster for all German intrigue, conspiracy, and propaganda in the United States. On this Saturday afternoon Albert carried a briefcase and was accompanied on part of his journey by George Sylvester Viereck, the American editor of a weekly magazine called The Fatherland, which supported the German cause. The two men were closely followed by two Secret Service agents.* Presently Viereck got off. Albert drowsed. Suddenly aware that he had reached his stop, Albert jumped up, forgetting his briefcase, and hurried toward the rear door of the car. In a trice his briefcase was snatched up and successfully carried away. Its contents, after they had been examined by the Secret Service, were photographed, and photostats were turned over to The New York World. It was such stuff as newspaper editors' dreams are made on.

To read the contents of the sinister briefcase two generations later is to be struck by the poverty of the German intellect in the propaganda war of 1915. The agents of the Kaiser were so hopelessly naïve about the realities of American power and American opinion as to be almost endearing. Their plots could be tricked out by The World so as to seem horrific, but in truth they were merely wistful. The World trumpeted

> HOW GERMANY HAS WORKED IN U.S.
> TO SHAPE OPINION, BLOCK THE ALLIES
> AND GET MUNITIONS FOR HERSELF,
> TOLD IN SECRET AGENTS' LETTERS

across six columns of its front page, and there were dark hints of strikes, sabotage, and evil efforts to control the news; but what followed sounded more like something that Penrod and Sam might have concocted in the Schofield stable on a rainy Saturday afternoon.

In truth, the documents turned out to be singularly disappointing, at least to McAdoo. They proved nothing. The Germans had violated no law; they had, indeed, done nothing on account of which McAdoo could even trump up charges. The only lawbreakers had been McAdoo's Secret Service agents, who had stolen a foreigner's possessions with no warrant whatsoever.

---

* Viereck later said (in his book, Spreading Germs of Hate, Liveright, 1930) that the men following them were Czechoslovaks, members of an undercover group known as the Bohemian Union. Viereck's account of what subsequently occurred differs only in detail from that of William G. McAdoo in his memoir, Crowded Years. McAdoo, as Secretary of the Treasury, was boss of the Secret Service.

And yet the revelations worked serious mischief. Blameless American citizens were freely named in letters and memoranda that detailed wholly hypothetical conspiracies; and the average reader, inflamed by patriotism and hate (those interchangeable emotions), was permitted to conclude that to be suspected was to be guilty.

McClure was mentioned three times, in three different connections, and so he was thrice damned.

The purchase of The Evening Mail by Rumely and McClure was alleged by an aggrieved correspondent to have cost him money, on account of which he prayed Dr. Albert for compensation; the inference was that the German government had given the Rumely-McClure syndicate a green light and cash. McClure was also nominated by an anonymous expert as a man who would be useful in promoting an embargo on shipments of American munitions to the Allies. Finally, McClure was touted by another anonymous expert as a lecturer who could be depended upon to agitate audiences along the Chautauqua circuit.

The editor of The World, having gleefully broadcast these lies, assigned a reporter to ask McClure for his comment upon them. As usual, what S.S. had to say was remarkably free from rancor. He denied that any German money was involved in the purchase of The Evening Mail. "While I was negotiating for The Mail," he went on, "Mr. Stoddard occasionally spoke of other offers for the same paper. I know nothing of any others who may have tried to get The Mail. I heard no names and know of no people. . . . As far as remaining quiet about the Belgian atrocities is concerned, I think my position ought to be very clear. I have written several editorials both on that subject and on the sinking of the Lusitania, and it is out of the question that I should be asked to defend the German cause in that respect. The suggestion that I was to lecture is entirely new to me. . . . I have never had any communication with any of the people mentioned and have never been requested to take the lecture platform or enter the Chautauqua circuit for Germany."

The statement was, as he had described newspaper editorials generally, namby-pamby. He defended; he did not slash out. One may venture that his statement was edited, censored, and cleared for publication by some intelligence unknown. At all events, the incident showed McClure that he was involved in an enterprise that was damaging his good name. He was bound to that enterprise by contract; he could make only whatever break was legally permitted him. To attempt to control the editorial policy of The Evening Mail was fruitless. He would have to seek some other path. It was imperative:

some of his oldest and closest friends were cutting him dead on the street.

In this way, McClure became a roving correspondent. He spent the month of October on the Mexican border and in Mexico, interviewing Victoriano Huerta, the strong man who had toppled from power when President Wilson refused him recognition, and Venustiano Carranza, the revolutionary leader who replaced Huerta. By the end of November McClure was back in New York and impatient for more travel. The circumstance was perfect. Henry Ford was about to charter a ship and lead a band of pilgrims for peace across the Atlantic, in order to "get the boys out of the trenches by Christmas." McClure gladly accepted an invitation to go along.

[IV]

In a time of universal lunacy, a single distinterested act of sanity rates only a horselaugh. So it was with the Ford Peace Ship.

Ford, whose skull was alike crammed with nonsense, common sense, and a practical, workaday idealism, had noticed that, while everybody was talking about peace and the brotherhood of man, nobody was doing anything about it. He found this queer. He had done his own share of talking about peace with some old friends—John Wanamaker and Thomas Alva Edison—but the talk had got nowhere. In his simple-minded fashion, he was determined to do something. This was his frame of mind when Rosika Schwimmer and Louis P. Lochner descended upon him at his house outside Detroit. They were, to any eye, an unusual pair; to the multimillionaire industrialist they must have seemed downright exotic. Mme. Schwimmer was a Hungarian writer and lecturer, a rather dowdy, dumpy woman in her late thirties, with the glittering eye and the imperious intensity of the incorrigible zealot. She had crusaded for birth control, for trade unionism, for women's rights; peace was her present obsession. Lochner, perhaps ten years Mme. Schwimmer's junior, was a lanky, earnest, bespectacled man of a type still relatively uncommon in 1915: he was a professional executive secretary of the uplift. He had been secretary of an International Federation of Students, secretary to Jane Addams at an International Congress of Women, and secretary of a Chicago Peace Society. Just now he was secretary of a National Peace Federation.

Mme. Schwimmer professed to have documents showing that the statesmen of the belligerent nations desired to mediate their differences. Ford was easily persuaded. "Well," he said, "let's start. What do you want me to do?" In no time he was whisked to New York to confer with pacifist leaders. It was agreed that an official commission should be dispatched to Europe; if President Wilson would not appoint mediators, then a representative group of the most influential peace advocates in the country should go. But when Ford called on him in Washington, Wilson was chilly and reserved. "If you feel you can't act," Ford told the President, "I will."

Back in New York, Ford confronted a throng of reporters. "We're going to try to get the boys out of the trenches before Christmas," he said. "I've chartered a ship, and some of us are going to Europe." He was rash, he was hasty, he was ill-advised—but he was the only man to make a significant effort to stop the war. His timing, moreover, was sound. The pointless slaughter in Europe had soared far beyond the gloomiest estimates of the so-called statesmen; on all fronts Europeans were sick of the bloody conflict from which their leaders were unable to extricate them. If the scheme Ford espoused—a continuous peace conference at The Hague—were to mean anything, his gallant effort had to win either official or popular support. Wilson having denied him the one, the newspapers now closed ranks to insure he would not get the other. With remarkable unanimity and, as Walter Millis later wrote, "to the undying shame of American journalism," the newspapers gleefully whooped up a gale of ridicule.

Ford had sent telegrams to one hundred and fifteen prominent Americans, inviting them to join him aboard the Oscar II, a steamship of the Scandinavian-American Line; but the cruel mockery aimed at the Peace Ship was sufficient. The refusals flooded in: from Dr. David Starr Jordan, director of the World Peace Foundation; from William Howard Taft, Cardinal Gibbons, William Dean Howells, Louis Brandeis, Ida Tarbell, and Governor Hiram Johnson of California; from Colonel House, the President's shadowy adviser; from Ford's close friends, Edison and Wanamaker; from John Burroughs, Luther Burbank, and Helen Keller. Even Jane Addams, a tower of strength in the movement for peace, was taken sick at the last moment and obliged to send her regrets. The eminent pacifist and former Secretary of State, William Jennings Bryan, actually clambered aboard the Oscar II but stumped back down the gangplank to wave good-by from the pier. Only a pitiful few of those he had invited sailed with Ford: the governor of North Dakota, the lieutenant-governor of South Carolina, a well-known suffragist leader, a pride of Protestant clergymen celebrated only amongst their own parishioners, Judge Ben B. Lindsey of Denver, and the nation's first woman state senator, Helen Ring Robinson of Colorado. Several consecrated spirits of lesser consequence were added to the strength at the last moment, raising the total of pilgrims for peace to thirty-one. There were almost twice as many newspaper and magazine correspondents, most of whom, however, were accredited by the most obscure and transient of journals. (Two of the younger reporters, whose talents would later lift them above the ruck, were William C. Bullitt of The Philadelphia Public Ledger and Elmer Davis of The New York Times.) There were also a couple of dozen undergraduates delegated from as many colleges. Finally, a full complement of eccentrics, crackbrains, and evangelists for queer causes managed to wedge itself aboard.

Excepting only Ford himself, McClure was the best-known man on the ship. S.S. later found it necessary to explain his passage on the Oscar II rather disingenuously. "Without premeditation," he said, "and simply out of my affection for Mr. Ford, whom I had known for a long time, I concluded, when all the world sort of went back on him, to go with him to Europe on the Ford Peace Ship. Mr. Ford's plan was to leave the peace delegation at The Hague, and then he and I would travel through Europe studying the questions firsthand. So I went abroad, not in the capacity of a peace delegate, but in the capacity of a newspaper man, to report to my paper as the other newspaper men on the ship reported to their papers." In fact, McClure was invited as a delegate and accepted the invitation; moreover, his behavior on board the Peace Ship fell far short of reportorial objectivity.

Despite the bitter December weather, thousands of people packed the pier in Hoboken to see the Peace Ship off. Its departure was of slapstick all compact. Someone had let an actor on board, and this noodle, sporting a beret and a Windsor tie, elbowed up to the rail next to Ford and led "Three cheers for Henry." In the bow, another moron harangued the crowd in Yiddish. The Rev. Jenkin Lloyd Jones, a preacher from Chicago who had grown a full white beard that reached down to his umbilicus, now also appeared at the rail to invoke divine blessing on the pilgrimage. Two squirrels in a cage were handed up the gangplank as a parting gift to Ford, since he had collected so many nuts. On the pier, a band played "I Didn't Raise My Boy To Be a Soldier." * The poet Berton Braley, assigned as a correspondent for Collier's,

* The composer of this popular song was quite cross when Ford did not invite him as a peace pilgrim. The song, incidentally, was denounced by the *kaiserlich* Theodore Roosevelt, who claimed he would have been no worse offended if the composer had written "I Didn't Raise My Girl To Be a Mother."

arrived in haste, towing his fiancée behind him and requiring that they be married forthwith; and so they were, by the Rev. Jenkin Lloyd Jones, with Ford and William Jennings Bryan as witnesses. (The happy couple were subsequently spliced again on the high seas by the captain of the Oscar II, after it developed that the Rev. Dr. Jones had no license to perform his magic in New Jersey.) When, after much painful delay, the moorings were at last let slip and the Oscar II mercifully moved from the pier, there was still room for idiocy. An ultimate sap dove into the water and splashed after the ship. Unhappily, a tug came to his rescue. When he was yanked from the drink he was found to be an uplifter who insisted that he be called Mr. Zero. What else? He had, he said, been swimming "to reach public opinion."

And yet, as the Oscar II moved slowly toward the Narrows, the farewell cheer from the crowd on the pier was warm and genuine. Despite President, despite Press, the people yet hoped.

On the first day, a Sunday, McClure strolled the decks of the Oscar II, completely happy. Few things gave him more pleasure than a sea voyage. The second-class dining saloon had been made to serve as a lecture hall, and here, in the evening, the Rev. Jenkin Lloyd Jones spoke about the modern battleship. He spoke for more than an hour.

On Monday the seas were rough. Ford, walking the deck in a gray sweater, was drenched to the skin by a wave; so was Judge Lindsey. The correspondents organized themselves into The Friendly Sons of St. Vitus, an amiable society which took "Skoal!" for its password and which met frequently at the bar in the first-class lounge. In the afternoon, Ford and McClure chatted together.

Ford said: "You mean to say that Germany took Schleswig-Holstein away from Denmark?"

"Yes."

"Just took it? Just like that?"

"Yes."

"But that's an outrage! They should be compelled to give it back to Denmark right away!"

"Yes," said McClure, patiently.

A reporter came by and asked Ford what he hoped to achieve by his mission. "The main thing in this case is psychological," Ford answered. "I have implicit faith in the people, in democracy. The news will filter into the trenches and will hearten the men that someone is working for peace. Then I will request a Christmas armistice."

Later he denied that he was for peace at any price. "The Monroe Doctrine," he added, "is like an excuse to fight."

"The Monroe Doctrine," said McClure, "is a state of mind."

"Like Heaven," said Ford, smiling.

The bemused reporter, Theodore Pockman, of The New York Tribune, went away and wrote in his diary: "It is strange, but there seems nothing masterful about Ford. He is always the same quiet man, with a dreamy look in his eyes. . . . He has us all puzzled."

Monday night Mme. Schwimmer lectured at length to all those who were not seasick.

On Tuesday the seas were still heavy, but that night McClure inadvertently kicked up even stormier weather in the second-class dining saloon. As it happened, President Wilson had decided to recommend, in his annual message to Congress on the State of the Union, a limited increase in American military and naval strength—beefing the army up to one hundred and forty-two thousand men and adding a few battleships. Advance copies of this message had been routinely mailed to the newspapers; on the day before he sailed, McClure had tossed his copy into his suitcase. He let it be known that he had advance sheets of the message; he was asked to read it; he did. To an audience of dedicated pacifists, Wilson's message came as a hideous betrayal. By reading it, moreover, McClure was at once identified with it: he was assumed to be a sinister agent of preparedness; in short, a warmonger. Hell broke loose amongst the pacifists. Some assailed the munitions trust, some assailed Wilson, some assailed McClure. Ford arose and urged postponement of the discussion for a few days. The pilgrims dispersed, still grumbling. Ford strolled out of the saloon with McClure. "It'll all be forgotten in a day or two," said Ford reassuringly.

Indeed, for the next day or two there was relative calm, meteorological as well as political. Mme. Schwimmer was nevertheless perturbed. She had woven an efficient web of espionage; nothing that was said or done aboard the Oscar II escaped her; and now it was reported to her that the college students were flocking around McClure, asking questions and, what was worse, listening to his answers. This would never do. On Friday afternoon she found it necessary to summon McClure to her stateroom and admonish him, gently but firmly, for preaching preparedness. Was he trying to wreck the Peace Ship? S.S. stared at her in amazement. He was, he started to say, merely talking ordinary facts; but before he could finish the remarkable woman dismissed him.

Outside, as he walked along the deck past his fellow-passengers, he could hear snatches of conversation about the cosmic urge, prohibition, child labor, the single tax, pedagogy, vegetarianism, the co-operative movement, international ethics, suffrage, the initiative and the referendum, predestination, and the evils of smoking cigarettes—normal conversation, if one remembered where one was. Indeed, McClure was himself a sympathetic advocate of half these causes. Yet now they seemed to him fool notions, absurd ideas. What kind of company was he keeping? Was this the real world?

At the bar he found The Friendly Sons of St. Vitus in a mellow mood. Having downed their second cocktail, they were sanguine about Ford's mission; maybe, after all, it would work. All was harmony and serenity. McClure brooded. He alone, he reflected ruefully, was out of step.

Lochner had been announced as the after-dinner speaker of the evening. His subject was World Federation. The correspondents condemned two of their number to cover the lecture; the others lounged at their ease in the second-class smoking room, which had been converted into an office for their convenience. Word came that a committee on resolutions was about to make a report. The correspondents yawned and shifted comfortably in their chairs.

Stirring events were, however, about to unfold in the dining saloon. The resolutions committee * marched in to present a statement scarcely calculated to inflame any rational human. In furry, imprecise language, the resolution declared, first, that the delegates should support Ford in his effort to achieve a just and honorable peace; and, second, that they should oppose any increase of armament by the United States as threatening an extension of the war. The committee imagined that this statement would be signed by the delegates without debate. They reckoned without McClure.

No sooner had Dr. Aked finished reading the declaration than McClure sprang to his feet. "I cannot impugn the course laid out by the President of the United States," he cried. "I cannot sign anything which would place me in opposition to my government!"

At once a dozen others were on their feet, squawking like a congress of

---

* The chairman was Florence Holbrook, an educator from Chicago. Her committee comprised the Rev. Dr. Charles Aked, a natty, British-born cleric whose pulpit was in San Francisco; Mrs. Joseph Fels, widow of the soap manufacturer and a champion of the single tax; Mrs. Lola Maverick Lloyd, a Texan, a Socialist, and the daughter-in-law of Henry Demarest Lloyd; Arthur Weatherly, a professional reformer from Nebraska; and the ubiquitous Rev. Dr. Jenkin Lloyd Jones, who, by the way, was Frank Lloyd Wright's uncle.

crows. Emotions were high and hasty, for each pilgrim passionately believed, first, that his was the only way to save civilization and, second, that all who disagreed with him were benighted scoundrels intent on scuttling civilization. Responsive to this splendid hubbub, the correspondents crowded into the saloon, their pencils busily scribbling on their copy paper. Meanwhile the pilgrims cried out like the prophet Jeremiah, saying, Peace, peace; when there is no peace. McClure's last phrase, flapping and torn, soared above the brouhaha:

". . . this needless piece of meddling!"

Amid the tumult Judge Lindsey could be heard agreeing with McClure. So could the governor of North Dakota, the lieutenant-governor of South Carolina, and a half-dozen others. The coterie that had organized the expedition listened, aghast and furious.

Lochner shouted: "Anyone who accepted Mr. Ford's invitation and now refuses to sign that resolution came along on a colossal free joy-ride!"

The Rev. Dr. Jones strode toward McClure, shouting, "You have been talking armament ever since you came on this ship!"

"I have been talking facts," McClure retorted.

"Nonsense! Go to bed, sir," roared Jones, shaking his finger under McClure's nose. "Go to bed!"

"This is absurd," McClure said. He pushed his way out of the saloon and retired to the press room.

The correspondents were right on his heels, racing for their typewriters. At last they had something to report to their newspapers.

An anguished pilgrim arrived in the press room, pleaded for quiet, and begged the correspondents to refrain from sending any wireless messages until Ford could be called; surely he would be able to smooth out any slight difficulties. The press corps, genuinely fond of Ford, called a halt to its activities and waited, expectant.

In marched Dr. Aked and Dr. Jones, glaring resentfully at McClure. Presently Ford ambled in, nodding and smiling amiably, but puzzled, for he had been in his stateroom all evening and so had missed the fireworks. Even as the situation was being explained to him, tempers hotted up anew. Dr. Aked brandished in McClure's face a copy of the invitation Ford had sent to prospective delegates—proof that McClure knew, before he came on board, that the Ford expedition stood for total and universal disarmament. McClure doggedly insisted that he could support disarmament and still consistently advocate preparedness in the United States until there was international agreement on the terms of disarmament.

Tiring of these quibbles, Dr. Jones, who had a habit of rolling his r's so that he seemed to be reverberating in a barrel, now publicly accused McClure of "cor-r-rupting the college students by pr-r-reaching pr-r-repar-r-redness." Seeing that McClure was about to explode, Ford took him by the arm and led him away to a private room.

Ford said: "Some of the others think the committee was wrong to draft that resolution."

"Yes."

"But the committee is standing pat."

"Yes."

"They seem to think that if you were to change your mind then the others would change their minds and everybody would agree. But you won't change your mind either."

"No."

"I see," said Ford. "Well, then, let's go join the others."

The correspondents were once again hard at work typing their dispatches. "Mutiny aboard the Oscar II," wrote Arthur Hartzell of The New York Sun; and when his account was sent by wireless that phrase was intercepted by a passing ship, whose telegraph operator promptly flashed a message: "Are you in need of assistance?" This came to the attention of Captain Stempel, the skipper of the Oscar II, who stormed off his bridge demanding to know who was the leader of the mutiny, if any. With whoops of laughter the correspondents collared McClure and led him forward.

In the saloon, the leaders of the expedition (all except for Ford, who had retired) heard the laughter but were not amused. What was so funny? The peace party was sorely split; admittedly its chances of success had been slim at best, but now they had virtually vanished.

Presently the laughter in the press room burst out again. They were staging a mock trial: The People vs. S.S. McClure, charged with the corruption of American youth. Joe O'Neill of The New York World was Chief Justice, Judge Lindsey was Prosecutor, Elmer Davis was Counsel for the Defense. Other Friendly Sons of St. Vitus filled the jury-box, or assumed the roles of Clerk, Sheriff, Unruly Witness, and Hysterical Spectator. Apparently everything that was said was funny, for the laughter was continual. In the saloon the leaders of the peace pilgrims shook their heads and scowled.

The Sheriff, Max Swain of The New York Herald, came looking for witnesses to appear against McClure. Not a man or woman in the saloon who had not snarled a curse at McClure, but none cared to join in the romp. Soon Swain could be heard in the courtroom: "Your honor, Lochner is too busy fixing the wireless, Dr. Aked is intent on manicuring his accent, and Dr. Jones is entangled in his whiskers and seriously injured." There was a burst of applause, and then the stately brogue of the Chief Justice: "In the opinion of the court, the aforesaid Jones is in fact Santa Claus and, since Santa Claus is a mythical character, his testimony would at best be incompetent, irrelevant, and immaterial." More merriment.

In the saloon, the devoted leaders of the Peace Ship shuffled their papers together and sadly prepared to retire. Such hard work, such high hope—all for nothing, because of one man. Perhaps—the cause was so important—perhaps they might yet patch the unity of the pilgrimage. But they bitterly resented the extra effort they had now got to make. That night no man aboard the Oscar II was more cordially detested than S.S. McClure.

And with some reason. McClure was acquitted by the mock court of corrupting American youth, but he must, in retrospect, be found guilty of having helped to torpedo the Peace Ship. A sensible man of peace, confronted with the maladroit resolution, would have kept his mouth shut and so preserved what little moral force Ford's mission might yet have commanded. But McClure, still smarting from the sting of accusations that he was pro-German, felt obliged to wrap his arms around President Wilson and to protest his loyalty to his government. (In fact, the Congress, which is at least part of the government, was far more violently opposed to President Wilson's preparedness plans than were the peace pilgrims.) This is not to say that the pacifists would not, in all probability, have blighted their own expedition even without McClure's assistance. A noble cause always attracts some inept and ignoble followers. (Bullitt, after studying the pilgrims at close range, observed: "Pacifist means a person hard to pacify.")

On Sunday, December 12, the eighth day the Peace Ship had been at sea, the Friendly Sons of St. Vitus relaxed from their labors. While a church service was being conducted in the dining saloon, a newsreel photographer started a game of craps in the press room; the percentage that would ordinarily have been taken by the house was set aside so that beer might be bought for the members of the choir, to improve their voices. During the afternoon the correspondents passed the time by classifying their fellow-passengers as rather off, partly off, or wholly off. By general agreement, Ford was excluded from these categories; he had won the wholesome respect of all.

On Monday the Oscar II was intercepted by a British cruiser and conducted into Kirkwall, where it would be held for three days while the British authorities snarled themselves in red tape and then cut themselves loose again.

To his astonishment, McClure was asked to lecture to the pilgrims on Tuesday night. Pockman of The Tribune noted in his diary: "He [McClure] spoke from notes, carefully compiled, and explained the European situation in plain, cold facts. He knew what he was talking about. He did not draw a single conclusion until the end of an hour and a half of the most logical and sane speech that, in my opinion, has been delivered on this ship."

When McClure had finished, Dr. Aked said to Mme. Schwimmer: "That man's speech was nothing but ignorance and impertinence." Mme. Schwimmer replied: "I should not have added 'impertinence.'"

At Kirkwall a Boston newspaperman somehow managed to slip ashore. The other correspondents, penned aboard, were wild with suspicion and jealousy. They had good reason to believe that someone had been regularly censoring their copy; their favorite suspect was Mme. Schwimmer. Now one of their number had been set free to telegraph who knew what sort of exclusive stories back to the United States. They demanded an immediate explanation from Mme. Schwimmer.

Mme. Schwimmer had almost as poor an opinion of the correspondents as she had of McClure. They bewildered her; she feared them. But she was forced to cope with them, for, with Ford suffering from a severe cold and confined to his stateroom, she had become in name as well as in fact the leader of the expedition. When she entered the press room they accorded her a friendly round of applause. She eyed them dourly. "Don't be hypocritical," she snapped. It set the tone.

She denied, to their satisfaction, any complicity in the departure of the recreant reporter. She irritated them by accusing them of having complained to Ford that she spied and snooped on them. Finally she said: "I further deny that I am Mr. Ford's mistress." Inasmuch as her denial marked the first time the correspondents had heard of any such ludicrous intrigue, they were disgusted. And they showed it.* It was like a declaration of war. The atmosphere was electric with hostility.

---

* McClure remarked later: "She was quite right: she was not Mr. Ford's mistress. But she needn't have said so."

But as the Oscar II steamed across the North Sea toward Norway, the managers of the expedition seemed anxious to achieve harmony. Indeed, on the last night of the voyage McClure was told that Dr. Aked was to present a resolution to the effect that all the pilgrims were as one in their lofty purpose. Would McClure not add a few words? He guessed he was supposed to chime in on behalf of unity. He agreed to speak. And then, just before he took the floor, he learned that Mme. Schwimmer planned to expel all the New York newspapermen from the party as soon as they reached Christiania.

What McClure said in his brief speech was not likely to bind any wounds. He self-righteously scolded everyone in sight for bickering and indulging in petty politics and jealousies. He warned that the mission would end in disaster if the correspondents of the most important newspapers were to be expelled from the party. "If we can't keep peace in our own little party," he demanded, "how can we expect to bring peace to the terrible conflict in Europe?" Coming from McClure, these strictures were insupportable. He sat down in a terrible silence. "That ended the meeting," he confessed later. "There was no more talk about perfect harmony, but perfect hell on the ship. Nobody spoke to me for three or four days." (But the correspondents remained with the party.)

The delegates were received coolly in Oslo, warmly in Stockholm, and apprehensively in Copenhagen. Ford, a sick and confused man, had left the party in Norway. (Lochner, the Rev. Dr. Jones, and others tried to block his departure. "This is mur-r-rder," Jones said. "This is mur-r-rder, taking this man away in this condition." One of Ford's bodyguards hit Jones on his nose and bloodied it. Ford managed to get safely away.) But, to the considerable discomfiture of Mme. Schwimmer and the others, McClure was still very much one of the group. In fact, he had remained at the personal request of Ford himself. "All right," McClure said, when he was asked to stay; "I suppose I have lost all the little reputation I have, I don't suppose I can lose any more."

At Copenhagen, however, McClure called it quits. The pilgrims faced the problem of how to get to The Hague and, since Germany was a belligerent, this seemed to require a journey by sea, through waters lavishly sown with mines. To charter a ship for the voyage would cost twenty-five thousand dollars; another twenty-five thousand would be charged for insurance against the uncertainties (or "certainties," as McClure called them) of the North Sea. Some of the delegates argued that it would be glorious to drown in such a cause. McClure chuckled, genuinely amused for the first time since he had left New York. At length pressure was brought on the German government to permit a train to carry the delegates from Denmark through to Holland, but by that time McClure had already made his own private arrangements. He was on his way to Berlin.

S.S. stopped over at Hamburg. Here he was told that the peace pilgrims were to pass through in the evening; he went to the station to watch them go past. There they were, tightly sealed in their train; and here he was, strolling cock-a-hoop along the platform. He caught the eye of Mme. Schwimmer, a portly goldfish in a bowl. He bowed sardonically; she turned away. It would be hard to say which was happier that he was at last shut of the Peace Party.

[v]

Enterprise and a respect for facts can be estimable qualities in a journalist, if exercised sparingly, but in wartime they are fearful liabilities. In wartime the prudent journalist rarely ventures beyond the nearest official in charge of propaganda and public enlightenment; facts are superseded by what the public wants to be told, or at any rate by what some exalted personage imagines they want to be told. This is a truism, but McClure came to appreciate its force only very slowly.

McClure showed his enterprise when he ventured into Germany, but at the same time he provoked the Department of State of the United States of America and he sent a thrill of anger through His Britannic Majesty's entire establishment. Before S.S. left New York on the Oscar II his unrestricted passport had been taken from him and instead he had been handed one that was valid only for Norway, Sweden, Denmark, and Holland. The British authorities would not have allowed him an inch beyond Kirkwall if they had for an instant supposed that he meant to go to Germany; when he did so it was a lapse from grace viewed, as the diplomatists say, with utmost gravity.

This was bad enough, but when McClure gave his respect for facts full rein he made enemies all over the landscape. He chose to investigate a sensitive subject, to wit: how well the German people were eating.

At the outset of the war the Allies had announced they intended to starve the Central Powers into capitulation by blocking the sea routes to Germany; civilians were to be enfeebled quite as much as the armed forces. The policy, having been publicly proclaimed, of course had to prove successful. Sure enough, before long American newspapers began to carry reports of shortages of food in Germany, even of riots over food in German and Austrian cities. By January, 1916, many compassionate Americans were grieved about the plight of German babies, the pathetic little innocents, who were alleged to have been deprived of milk by the pitiless British blockade. Belgian babies were said to be in even more doleful circumstances. Committees for the relief of these infants were formed in the United States. In the offices of The Evening Mail, Rumely launched what seemed a most promising little propaganda.

In Copenhagen, as he was preparing to leave for Germany, McClure read fresh accounts of the shortages, especially of fats and milk. Being curious, he made a thorough investigation, in both Germany and Belgium. He found that, while there was indeed less milk in Germany than before the war, rationing had been organized so efficiently that pregnant women, babies, and small children were actually healthier than ever; infant mortality had been reduced, even in Belgium; and the families of the poor were at last being properly fed. S.S., who had for some time believed that most people eat too much, and who was a recent convert to the vegetarian diet, was delighted to find that the health of the German people generally had improved as a result of the wartime pinch. "The babies of Belgium & Germany are today better off than [those] in America," he wrote his wife in February. "People here all like the two meat-less days, & there will soon be four. The health of the people is improving. . . . No one in America need worry about the babies here."

Cheerful news; tidings, it might be supposed, of great joy. Yet McClure, when he published his findings in The Evening Mail, was universally damned. The British were discomfited to have it broadcast that their blockade was unavailing; the Americans were furious when their propaganda—on behalf of starving Belgians or starving Germans, as the case might be—was deflated; the Belgians were fearful that the flow of American dollars for relief would subside to a trickle; and the Germans, while proud that the achievements of their wartime socialism had been praised, were nonetheless dismayed to find their good works transformed into a boomerang that severely damaged their hopes of alerting the world to the perfidies of Albion.

As for McClure, when he was assailed alike by those who were pro-German and those who were anti-German, he cried out from within his fortress of facts and statistics, "I love truth!" Too late; on both sides of the trenches it was agreed: he had put his foot in it.

In the meantime, S.S. was taken on a tour of the eastern front, to Poland, where few bullets were being fired in anger. The anniversary of his birthday arrived. To celebrate it, he was invited aloft in a German aeroplane piloted by a mischievous youngster who gave him the full treatment—loops, Immelmanns, and rolls—and brought him back to earth green in the gills but still game. "Well," McClure said as he clambered from the plane, "I have got *that* finished."

He was dined by the commanding officers of the Imperial Twelfth Army; there was champagne. McClure proposed a toast: "To the Kaiser!" Everybody rose, applauded, drank, and sat down.

McClure stayed on his feet and raised his glass again. "To President Wilson!" Again everybody rose, applauded, drank, and sat down.

McClure was still standing. He refilled his glass and raised it once again. "And," he cried, "to King George of England!" There was the hush of the tomb. "May they all unite together," McClure went on, "for peace and the advancement of civilization." Once again there was a burst of applause and everybody drank.

A few days later McClure traveled to Constantinople in the Balkanzug. His companion, assigned to him as interpreter, was Professor von Schultze Gävernitz, the prorector of the University of Freiburg and a member of the Reichstag. (It was Gävernitz who wrote the article that Rumely had tried to get McClure to publish in his magazine five years before.) On the train, Gävernitz introduced McClure to a Dr. Jaeckh, a functionary of the German Ministry of Foreign Affairs who was a specialist in Turkish and Near Eastern politics. The three men got to talking. Dr. Jaeckh told McClure of a treaty that had been concluded between England and Germany in June, 1914, and initialed by the negotiators. McClure was most interested. This was indeed news. England and Germany, now flying at each other's throats, had come to formal agreement only a few weeks before Armageddon?

S.S. knew, of course, that England had made a treaty with France in 1904 and another with Russia in 1907, for these were the alliances invoked by English statesmen to justify the English declaration of war against Germany. But he had heard no whisper of any treaty binding England and Germany.

In the most confident way, however, Dr. Jaeckh rattled off the terms of the agreement: the Bagdad railway from Constantinople to Basra to be built by German capital, and English capital to stay out of the area; Basra to be made into a sea harbor by a capital investment of which sixty per cent would be German and forty per cent English; German capital to have a twenty-five per cent share in the oil fields of Mesopotamia, previously the sole property of English finance capital; et cetera, et cetera. In short, Germany was to be granted her "place in the sun," her share of colonial loot.*

McClure checked his information carefully: first with Count von Metternich, the German ambassador to Turkey, and later in Berlin with Zimmermann, the Undersecretary of Foreign Affairs. Zimmermann, after penciling a few minor corrections, authorized McClure to use his information as he chose. S.S. promptly headed for the American embassy and showed his notes to Ambassador Gerard, who made a copy of them for transmission to Washington. S.S. next sought passage to England, but it was denied him.

At this time, McClure considered the war "a world-madness." He perceived no lofty idealism in the aims of either set of belligerents. While he instinctively favored the Allies, their more hypocritical protestations did not impose on him. The Anglo-German treaty of 1914 seemed to him to emphasize more than ever the useless, wicked folly of the war. Apparently it never dawned on him that the Allies might be embarrassed by publication of the treaty. Once again, he let his independence and his respect for facts run away with him.

Early in May, 1916, he left Copenhagen, bound for New York, once again aboard the Oscar II.

McClure found things in the United States most distasteful. The pro-German label had been firmly pasted on him; it seemed there was nothing he could do to peel it off. The issue dearest to Republican hearts, preparedness, had been swiped by President Wilson, blandly and in broadest daylight. General Leonard Wood and Colonel Theodore Roosevelt, the prophets of preparedness and the Republican champions most adored by McClure, were gurgling down the political drain. S.S. was obliged to sweat out a few editorials on behalf of Charles Evans Hughes, the Republican candidate in 1916; but he begrudged every moment devoted to domestic politics, for he

---

* The Anglo-German treaty of 1914, while it was never consummated, was in no way more sordid than earlier treaties which had operated to maintain the peace of Europe. The Anglo-French treaty of 1904 similarly defined the exploitation of Egypt and Morocco; the Anglo-Russian treaty of 1907 similarly defined the exploitation of Afghanistan and Persia. These pacts were made by England, according to Sir Edward Grey, "to pave the way to permanent peace."

had become obsessed by the need to get to England. Why should blocks have been placed in his road? How could anyone doubt that his heart was with England?

At length McClure got a passport to visit England, France, and Switzerland. Officials of the State Department warned him, however, that the British embassy had refused to guarantee that he would be welcome in England. Unmindful of the threat, S.S. sailed for Liverpool in July, aboard the U.S.M.S. Philadelphia. It was his fifty-fourth passage to England.

At Liverpool, while officials were routinely examining the other passengers, McClure was taken aside for a long, extraordinary inquiry. "I answered every question truthfully and fully," McClure said later, adding, "I am such a poor liar that in an emergency I have to tell the truth." The other passengers left for London; on orders from the Home Office, McClure was detained. After Ambassador Page had intervened, McClure was finally allowed to go ashore and sojourn at Buxton, an inland watering place, until the Philadelphia should be ready for her return passage to New York.

All this naturally made front-page headlines in the American newspapers, the readers of which were permitted to conclude that, sure enough, McClure was a German agent. If they had any lingering doubts on this score, John Rathom, the editor of The Providence Journal, removed them by running an article which was duly reprinted in the New York press.* Rathom charged that, by "taking advantage of the latitude allowed him to pass unmolested between England and Germany, [McClure] has given to German officials under the guise of 'observations' important and valuable information," and that "he has also been responsible for bringing into the United States propaganda moving picture films which have been handed to him by German officials for that purpose." These wicked charges were, of course, wholly false.

The Hartford Times commented, in a leading editorial:

> The British empire may send S.S. McClure home as an undesirable alien. It may even detain him; perhaps lock him up for a time. The mighty British empire is sufficiently powerful for that.
>
> But that is all. The mighty British empire is not sufficiently powerful to make Sam McClure sidestep one principle, tolerate in silence as right

---

* From 1914 onward, no journalist brandished the Stars and Stripes with more vigor than Rathom; but his banner was an ensign with the British Union Jack in the corner, for he was an Australian.

what he believes wrong, back away through fear from a goal once intended, abandon one ounce of conviction, one shred of purpose, one atom of conscience.

Perhaps the mighty empire doesn't wish to do this. Anyway, it can't.

The mighty empire, however, was determined to force McClure to think and write as it pleased he should think and write—or to boot him out.

S.S. was permitted to go to Buxton on the understanding that he would come straight back to Liverpool as soon as the Philadelphia was ready for her return passage. He was expressly instructed to stay away from London. In Buxton, however, McClure found that the chief constable was unaware of his peculiar status; S.S. was told that, so long as he let the police know what he was up to, he might go away overnight. He at once wrote to William Archer, the critic, asking to be invited to Archer's house at King's Langley, twenty-some miles from London. Archer was an old friend, and had a great deal more sense than the Home Secretary; he told McClure to come ahead. McClure informed the Buxton police he could be reached at King's Langley, and headed straight for London. He reached the Euston station just before dusk, checked his baggage (except for one small valise), and paused to consider where he would spend the night. He was as jumpy as a thief.

He ruled out his club (which was, appropriately, the British Empire Club), for he was too well known there. He ruled out the hotels, for he knew he would be required to fill out an official form which would go straight to the police. He decided to look for lodgings in Jermyn Street. After two or three unsuccessful attempts to get a room, he remembered there was a French hotel, the Dieudonné, in the neighborhood; perhaps there his American accent would pass unnoticed. He went in and asked the boy at the desk for a room.

"I can't give you a room with a bath, sir."

"That's quite all right. I've just left a place where one bathes every few minutes."

He was given a key, and went upstairs to wash and change his linen. When he strolled down again a few minutes later, he found the porter with a list of names in his hand.

"I don't see your name on this list, sir."

"Why, of course not. I haven't had time to put my name down."

"But," said the porter severely, "I don't believe you are a member of the club."

"Club? I haven't come to a club. Isn't this a hotel?"

"Oh, no, this hasn't been a hotel for years. This is a club."

"Which club is this?"

"The Eccentrics Club, sir."

McClure smiled knowingly. "I think I can qualify for membership," he said. "I'm sure I must know some of the members."

"No, sir," said the porter stolidly, "you cannot stay here."

So McClure fetched his bag and went out into the blackout of wartime London and thought of Stevenson's story, "A Lodging for the Night," and wandered along through the gloom feeling miserable and homeless and friendless. By chance he turned into Duke Street and pressed the bell at Number 31-A, an old-fashioned lodging house where, for a wonder, the people were devoid of curiosity. At last he had his rooms, but his troubles were just beginning.

Every friend McClure looked up on Saturday was scandalized to find him in London, against the express orders of the government; some, to prove their loyalty, closed their doors in his face. Saturday night he went with Archer to the theater and on Sunday with Archer to King's Langley. Tuesday night he was back in London at Archer's house in Fitzroy Square for dinner. A man called and asked: "Is Mr. McClure here?" McClure acknowledged his presence. The man eyed him. "The commissioner of Scotland Yard," he said, "would like to see you tomorrow morning at half past ten o'clock." There was a pause. "Shall I come after you," asked the sleuth, "or will you go by yourself?" McClure said he thought he could get there alone.

Now S.S. recalled the anxiety of his friends in London, and reflected on the imperturbable, inexorable methods of Scotland Yard, so well known to him from his constant reading of detective stories. He had no appetite for dinner.

He slept little. He ate little breakfast. At half past ten, on the mark, he was at Scotland Yard. He was led to a room where a policeman sat at a desk. "Special case, sir," said his guide. McClure sat down uneasily. Presently a man and woman were led in. "Special cases," said the first policeman to the second. Before long the room was filled with special cases, and to McClure they seemed a disreputable crowd. There was a long silence. Everybody gazed steadily at McClure.

At eleven o'clock a policeman appeared and beckoned to McClure. As he followed the officer down the corridor, S.S. kept up a nervous chatter. "I have often intended to visit Scotland Yard and study it," he said, "but now that I am here I find I am quite ignorant as to its organization. All I know about it really," he went on, chuckling at his own stupidity, "is what I know from reading novels and detective stories. Why," he prattled on, "I don't even know if I'm being taken to meet the commissioner of all Scotland Yard or not."

"No," said the policeman. "You're being taken to the commissioner of the Criminal Investigation Department."

McClure felt no better.

But he was handled gently at this first interview. His chief inquisitor was only a youngish assistant commissioner; and while he was not told he could stay in London, neither was he severely taxed for being there. As he left the Yard, S.S. was met by reporters, who had of course been alerted to the fact of his having been summoned. S.S. treated his case lightly. He was returning to the United States, he said, because of questions that had been raised about his passport; it bore a visa for travel in Switzerland, a country in which he had for many years enjoyed a summer holiday, but the English apparently suspected him of wanting to go to Switzerland only so that he might proceed on to Germany. The whole affair, he added, had been blown up out of all proportion.

Next day he was back at Scotland Yard, again summoned by the commissioner, but this time he was less apprehensive.

The commissioner of the C.I.D., Basil Thomson, was perfectly typecast for his job. His father had been Archbishop of York, but Thomson had chosen to police more material things than souls. He had risen steadily until he was governor of Dartmoor Prison, then of Wormwood Scrubs; along the way Eton had left its mark on him, and Oxford, and the colonial service. At fifty-five he was a trim, conventionally lean-faced man whose hair was conventionally cropped close to his head; his glance was conventionally keen and his voice had the proper note of command. He was, in short, the perfect Junker type. When in 1913 Thomson had been appointed His Majesty's top cop, he had scaled the summit of his ambition. Since then his days had been provokingly cluttered with suffragettes and conscientious objectors and rumors of spies and vexatious Irishmen like Sir Roger Casement. Now here was this Irish-American McClure, another headache.*

* There is evidence that Thomson actually believed McClure was a German agent, at least until he met him. In his autobiography, The Scene Changes (Doubleday, Doran & Company, 1937), Sir Basil refers (at page 327) to one X, an Irish-American who was "declared to be a German agent" by "our agent in America." In all particulars but one, Sir Basil would seem to have been describing McClure.

McClure was closeted with Thomson for nearly two hours. One may surmise what they talked about.

On the continent S.S. had been invited to talk with all the leading statesmen: from von Bethmann-Hollweg, the chancellor of Germany, and his foreign minister; through Count Tisza, Count Apponyi, Baron Burian, and Count Berchtold, the principal spokesmen of Austria-Hungary; all the way down to Talaat Bey, the scoundrelly dictator of Turkey. He had reported his interviews with these men fairly and impartially, as a neutral should. But in fact he was not neutral, he was eagerly sympathetic to the Allies. What he wanted was an opportunity to meet and talk with the leaders of the British and the French—nothing more than he had been granted by the leaders of the Central Powers. Why should his path not be smoothed?

Yes; but S.S. had preached peace. He had joined the pilgrimage aboard the Ford Peace Ship; he had found it difficult to justify England's holy war against the Prussian militarists; he had not followed the English all the way in deploring the odious atrocities visited on Belgium by the Huns; he had even urged the belligerents to join with the United States in some sort of world congress to achieve a lasting peace, quite as though the Allies and the Huns were on the same moral footing. So long as his public expressions on the war were so conciliatory, no right-thinking Englishman would dream of talking to him, least of all the Prime Minister or the Minister for Foreign Affairs. Under the circumstances, why should his path be smoothed?

Basil Thomson smiled and rose. The interview was over.

When he was intercepted by the reporters, S.S. announced he was staying in London for at least a month. There was no longer any fuss about his passport, he was free to move about as he chose. He cleared his throat. "All talk of peace efforts now," he said, "is pure idiocy. Ford's peace expedition was a sheer phantasm. I only went for the fun of the thing. I wanted the trip to Europe to see how things were going."

On August 7 he wrote his wife that all was well. "I can set myself right with the world now," he wrote. *"I am just happy."* But in fact he was wretched, the more so as the days wore on. At last he erupted.

Friday Sept 8

My dearest Hattie:
    . . . By Monday the 11th I will have been here *7 weeks. I've not yet got permission to do anything or see anything.* Conan Doyle refused to see me. Kipling never answered my letter. I met Frederick Palmer *

* Palmer was an American war correspondent.

yesterday in the office of Curtis Brown. He showed me an unsmiling face of iron. Brown urged him to lunch with him at the Devonshire Club, where I am [staying]. I suggested to Palmer to lunch there with me or I would sit at the table. I was eager to hear. No. He said he had so much to talk with Brown. Now. I heard them make the engagement. I was right there & it was casual & unexpected.

Once in these seven weeks, I've been invited to dinner—& that by an American. Once to a country house.

People generally fail to answer me. I had a similar experience in the New York clubs. When I return my resignation [from The Evening Mail] will be cabled all over the world.

The magazine income is unsure, but death or destitution are sometimes the lesser evil.

This is absolute. Yesterday I got a note from Sir Gilbert Parker, asking me not to sail Saturday, as he was hoping to do something [to help me get to France].

If I can get to France & to Verdun, I will have the greatest material anyone has had.

I will not resign in a corner. The world will know it & know why. I am keeping vigorous. I am greatly homesick for you. Yesterday was the end of 40 years since that Friday afternoon when we agreed to marry. You can count on me for hard & intelligent work to re-establish myself

Your loving husband
SSMcClure

A few of McClure's old friends were still clement. Arnold Bennett lifted his latch when McClure called and talked with him briefly; Mrs. Belloc Lowndes used her influence on his behalf. Meanwhile S.S. peppered the Foreign Office, the Home Office, and Sir Gilbert Parker's propaganda bureau with carbon copies of his dispatches to The Evening Mail, inviting official attention to some of his phrases. (In one dispatch, after reporting the severity with which talk of peace was discountenanced, the unhappy man wrote: "A neutral is an enemy." In manuscript, he scratched this out and revised it to read: "A neutral attitude is inconceivable.") As always, he had nothing but praise for the gallant British war effort; but now there crept into his dispatches a note of contempt for the Germans, whom he had earlier accorded a measure of compassion.

These efforts presently convinced the authorities he had learnt his lesson. There was a sudden thaw in the official climate. He was invited to talk with members of the War Cabinet; he was taken on tours of munitions factories; he was allowed to go to France, to interview Prime Minister Briand, even to visit the embattled fortress of Verdun. "A most wonderful two weeks in France," he wrote to Mrs. Lowndes, in thanking her for her kindness to him during his stay in London. Late in October he landed again in New York and at the first opportunity consulted his lawyer on the question of resigning from The Evening Mail. The lawyer advised him that his two-year contract of employment was binding until May, 1917.

S.S. thereupon went off on a lecture tour, expounding the obstacles to peace in Europe, of which, as he saw it, the greatest was emotional: "the extraordinary hatreds, contempts, and horrors that divide the warring nations." Before long it occurred to him that this lecture, pieced out by diplomatic documents and by his dispatches from Europe to The Evening Mail, might make a book; moreover, for him to publish a book would enable him to make it clear where he stood on all the questions raised by the war and so to purge himself of the pro-German taint. In much excitement, he hurried home and got out his scissors and paste.

His book, Obstacles to Peace, was not so much written as compiled.* It was documentary; its tone was dispassionate. A later fashion has decreed that international politics should be portrayed as racily as, say, the amorous enormities of some libertine Hollywood couple; but it is not a fashion that would have been to McClure's taste. He was austere, he was didactic. He was also partial. He believed the verdict of history would rank the amiable Sir Edward Grey as "the foremost statesman of his time," a judgment that history has been notably reluctant to affirm. On the other hand, McClure insisted, with what must have required some courage at the time, that both the Kaiser and the German government had tried to avert the cataclysm. As forcibly as he could, McClure argued that stupid men had fumbled the world into war. On balance, however, Obstacles to Peace was an indictment of Germany, German leaders, and the German methods of warfare.

The book got a good press ("The book of the year"—The Nation; "Lucid and convincing"—The New York Tribune; "More absorbing, more thrilling than the skilled artisan in best selling fiction can ever hope to achieve"— The New York Sun), but advance copies sent to the directors of The Evening Mail failed to arouse any such enthusiasm. McClure, all unaware of their disapproval, was again on the wing. He had planned a trip to report con-

* Obstacles to Peace was published by Houghton Mifflin Company at the end of March, 1917. A few days later the United States declared that a state of war existed with Germany; this event can hardly have helped the sale of a book that dealt with the problems of making a peace. Nevertheless, the book went through four cautious printings and ultimately sold a modest six thousand, two hundred and thirty copies.

ditions in the Far East for The Mail; he was in San Francisco; indeed, he was just about to step on a steamer bound for Honolulu when he was handed a telegram from Rumely summoning him back to confer in Chicago. Ostensibly he was recalled to discuss the revolution in Russia and whether he should not now plan to visit that country as well; but the real reason was so that Rumely might ask him to resign as editor-in-chief of The Mail as of September 1, 1917, when his assignment in the Far East should have been completed. McClure owned two thousand, seven hundred and fifty shares of stock in The Mail, nominally worth twenty-seven thousand, five hundred dollars; Rumely agreed to buy fifteen hundred shares for twenty-five hundred dollars and to try to sell the remaining twelve hundred and fifty shares for another twenty-five hundred. McClure quite cheerfully accepted this proposition. Once again he headed west for San Francisco.

Bohemian Club,
San Francisco.

March 30th 1917

My dearest Hattie:

All the way across the continent . . . the feeling I find everywhere is an eagerness to go into war, & a great hatred of Germany. Also, everywhere there is despair, apprehension & exasperation as to our national government. . . .

I want you to see Dr Rumely as to removing my name from the [editorial] page. I am heart-broken whe[ne]ver I look at our editorial page. I am feeling as I felt in London. . . .

It cuts me and angers me to have such continual slaps at England & it hurts my standing & reputation.

. . . I do not think that the book will sell widely enough to do me a great deal of good. The two last copies of the Mail I saw . . . one on Saturday & one on Sunday in each case sickened me. I could hardly eat my dinner in one case, & my lunch in the other. The editorial policy of the Mail is terribly offensive to me & to the vast majority of the people of the United States & practically to *all* the people I know or who liked me because of McClure's Magazine. In this war the Mail has utterly failed to convince a single person or to change the country's policy a hairsbreadth. Its pro-German policy prevents it from being much use in good policies & it could do so much for Dr Rumely has a splendid intellect. I like him & admire him more & more, but in this matter he uses the worst & most harmful judgement. . . . I am really glad to be free at last from the Mail because I was not earning my salary. Dr Rumely

. . . read the book & he sent copies to all the directors. . . . I can imagine Mr Kaufmann & Mr Anhelt! *

If we fail to enter the war, our future as a nation will be very uncertain. In fact I feel that we are heading for a great national disaster . . . & we have four years of the most incompetent & harmful government any nation has ever had. . . .

This whole country is for action. I will write again before I sail. . . . I am very lonely for you. . . .

Your loving husband
SSMcClure

S.S. sailed on April third. His name was removed from the masthead of The Mail a fortnight later. In May an item appeared in The Fourth Estate, a trade paper:

> The name of S.S. McClure, which has been at the head of the editorial page of the New York Evening Mail for nearly two years as editor, disappeared a few days ago. Inquiry by The Fourth Estate at the Mail office as to the reason, brought the information that Mr. McClure is now on a long trip to Japan and his name was removed until his return on account of the many people who stop in daily to see him or write letters.
> It was stated plainly that Mr. McClure is still editor of the Mail.

McClure had a fine time in Japan, speechifying, banqueting, touring the country, meeting all the important personages, lunching with the Foreign Minister and dining with the Prime Minister, and getting dolled up in top hat, white tie, and tailcoat to attend the morning ceremony at which the Emperor convened the Imperial Japanese Diet. He ran into Walter Weyl, the radical economist of The New Republic, who was already reflecting on the despair of the tired radicals in this war that was to end war. But S.S., once again busy and important in an exotic land, was in no mood for the anguished sighs of bereft reformers. To S.S. the world seemed good. Already he had begun to plan a new magazine.

If he had been content in Japan, in China he was ecstatic. He thrived on hardships that would have stunned the ordinary traveler into apoplexy. Two hundred miles south of Peking his railroad drowned in a flood: he waded, walked, heaved on a hand-car, picked his way from one tie to another over

---

* S. Walter Kaufmann was a New York lawyer, a partner in the firm of Hays, Kaufmann & Lindheim. William P. Anhelt was president of the Pictorial Review Company. Both were directors of the company that published The Evening Mail.

tracks that sagged, perilous and unsupported, forty feet over swollen streams, and arrived in Hankow feeling splendid. "The best time I have had since I peddled," he wrote his wife. "I slept out doors, was naked a great deal, got an appetite perfectly incredible. I've gained about ten pounds & learned a lot." On the river boat down the Yangtze to Shanghai he smote his chest with his fist. He was a man of iron. He would make a new magazine. It would combine the best features of All-Story, the old McClure's, The Outlook, and The Literary Digest. He would make it *universal*. He would call it The Universal Weekly. He had never felt so confident.

S.S. was one day out of Honolulu, bound east for San Francisco, when another passenger showed him a copy of the most recent issue of Life. He glanced at it carelessly and then froze. There he was, lampooned in a cartoon as pro-German. It was malicious, it was libelous, and it was all over the country. He felt sick. In San Francisco he announced he was suing Life for fifty thousand dollars. Life printed an apology several weeks later, but there was no repairing the damage. And there was worse to come.

After six months abroad, S.S. was anxious to hurry home to his wife. The war had worked many changes in his family: his son Robert had been drafted and, because of his fluency in French, was already bound overseas as a military interpreter; his adopted son Enrico had lied about his age (he was only sixteen) and had been recruited into the cavalry; of his six nephews, four were already in service. But S.S. could not go straight home, for he had been booked for a series of lectures that kept him busy all the way across the country. His friend Archibald Henderson, the professor of English literature at the University of North Carolina, had written to ask him to speak to the students at Chapel Hill; McClure was reluctant to swing so far south, but then something happened that made his presence at Chapel Hill imperative. A Tarheel patriot got the governor of North Carolina to intervene and force the cancellation of McClure's lecture engagement.* Once again McClure's name was smeared over the front pages of newspapers across the country; once again newspaper readers were invited to draw their ugliest conclusions.

In the event, S.S. spoke twice in North Carolina: first at Raleigh, to the North Carolina Literary and Historical Association, and the next night at Chapel Hill to a university audience. At Raleigh he was introduced by an apologetic governor; a resolution was voted by the association, condemning the fact that McClure's loyalty had been questioned. At Chapel Hill a

---

* Such a vigilant champion of the rights of free speech should be memorialized, if only in a footnote. He was a lawyer called, if contemporary newspapers can be credited, James Pou.

capacity audience in Gerard Hall listened attentively for an hour and a half. "I have two sons and four nephews at the front," S.S. declared, somewhat stretching the truth, "and I say to you now in the sight of God that I would rather, having seen what I have seen, that they never came back than that they had not gone." Later, outside the building, the undergraduates gave him college cheers. But still there was no repairing the damage.

"It will likely take me a year or two to get fully clear of the *Mail* stigma," McClure wrote his wife. He underestimated his plight.

At that point McClure may be said to have utterly exhausted his reservoir of public good will. His reputation had been irrevocably tarnished. Those who did not know him dismissed him either as a fool or a knave. His behavior aboard the Peace Ship had alienated the pacifists and reformers generally; those who uncritically favored the Allies would never forgive his connection with The Mail; those who uncritically favored the Germans had for some time despised his correspondence in The Mail and now found his lectures inexcusable. Those few thoughtful folk who, neither pacifist nor radical, still viewed the war as insensate and horrible folly mourned McClure's surrender to hysteria and his departure from their inconsiderable number.

What, then, was he to do? He could only scribble away for George Creel's Committee on Public Information, the propaganda factory of the New Freedom. Creel was a journalist whose stuff had been contemptuously rejected when McClure was still editor of McClure's Magazine. But times had changed: Creel was now the supreme jackanapes of all American publicity, advertising, and promotion, licensed to harness every imaginative talent that might boost the war effort. Creel was the national wizard: he manufactured hate; he spread the germs of spy fever; he mobilized writers, artists, actors, opera singers, college professors, and other deep thinkers; he coined slogans; he wrote speeches; he inspired songs. Having invented, as he liked to think, a new kind of war, the war for the minds of men, he was determined to win it. Creel could find room in his ranks for any new recruit, however humble. In January, 1918, S.S. went to Washington to write a book for Creel. "I am to get $35 a week as an expense account," he wrote Hattie. "My book is to contain the material to show why we cannot make peace with Germany— her lack of faith in agreements, her terrorism, etc—just the exact line I've been working on."

It was like the approach of a damned soul to purgatory.

AT THE END

❧❧❧❧❧❧❧❧❧❧❧❧❧❧❧❧❧❧❧❧❧❧❧❧❧❧❧❧❧❧❧❧

1918-1949

[1]

After the war, there were so many changes. Europe, an untidy litter of overturned thrones and discarded crowns, was crisscrossed by new and unlikely boundaries, exhausted, cynical, and contemplating with an uneasy and certain dread the ominous fact of the socialist revolution in Russia. Could the Red contagion be stamped out or—if worst came to worst—at least quarantined? The United States had soared gloriously into the pratfall of Prohibition; the nation was, moreover, wracked by strikes, Red scares, race riots, and the recrudescence of the Ku Klux Klan; good citizens and bad alike suffered from the jitters. The pre-war mood of security and serenity had forever vanished, and with it the complacent dream of man's potential perfectibility.

Everyone agreed that the world was a quite different place; the only variance was in the moment of awareness, the moment of certainty that from then on there would be universal uncertainty. "I doubt if I can ever again go back into public place," Theodore Roosevelt wrote to Rider Haggard late in 1918; "like you, I am not at all sure about the future." In December, 1920, William Allen White wrote to Ray Stannard Baker: "What a Goddamned world this is! . . . If anyone had told me ten years ago that our country would be what it is today . . . I should have questioned his reason." And Willa Cather was to speak of how the world had broken in two, but for her the moment came in 1922, or thereabouts.

Personal misgiving, dismay at the nation, rue for the world that had been. So his friends, and McClure, too, had these thoughts thrust upon him; he, too, eyed the new world sourly. He was cheered by the advent of Prohibition, but he was appalled by the so-called Bolshevik outrages.* For

---

* A favorite nephew, Colin McClure, was killed when a bomb exploded just before noon on September 16, 1920, at the corner of Wall and Broad Streets in New York City. The bomb was touched off by some unknown maniac amidst the buildings that housed the Sub-Treasury,

S.S., however, the world was the same bad old world, at least in the only particular that mattered. Before the war he had controlled no magazine; now the war was over and he still controlled no magazine. With all the cunning of a confidence man stalking an easy mark, S.S. set about finding a man of means who would be foolish enough to back him in his heart's desire.

His need persisted. Still hanging about him was a tribe of dependents, doleful relics from the days of his magnificent extravagance; although he was meeting his own needs for a few dollars a day, his pride required that he keep these parasites in comparative luxury. Meanwhile his wife and brother Jack, acting in all kindliness, managed to waste his income by investing gaudy sums in chickens and chicken-houses at the farm in Connecticut.

"Unless I can get a new magazine business," S.S. growled to Hattie, "all the rest of my life will be spent in a hand-to-mouth struggle, with what money I earn going through a sieve."

Later he told her: "Mr. Munsey has been paying me some good attention. If he would only buy McClure's and put me in charge!" But Munsey declined to do more than cheer him from the side lines.

At the Peace Conference in Versailles, to which he had wangled an accreditation as correspondent for the McClure Syndicate, S.S. was glum. "I must either get into a magazine," he wrote his wife, "or withdraw from mingling with real newspaper men. I really am nobody here." In London, he was sure he had found a man willing to stake him to two hundred thousand dollars, to found a McClure's Weekly. "The best magazine executive I know is Miss Cather," S.S. wrote to Hattie in much excitement. "She knows the editorial field. She is no amateur. So I want you to see her at your earliest opportunity." He fondly believed the scheme would be settled within two weeks. Four months later it had at last collapsed. "I've come to the end of my string," he confessed to Hattie, adding: "I feel like a dog that's got run over & is trying to run away from his injury!"

Back again in New York, the bewildered man took stock. He was sixty-three years old, he was in debt, his income—the ten thousand dollars pledged him annually by the owners of McClure's Magazine—was precarious, and his reputation was at a low ebb. In publishing circles he was dismissed as erratic, impossibly extravagant, hot-tempered, and unreliable. Even his great-

---

the United States Assay Office, J. P. Morgan & Company, and the New York Stock Exchange; it would seem to have been directed impartially at every tentacle of the octopus of capitalism.

est asset, his editorial judgment, had been contemptuously put in question by the bright young men of the shoddy post-war world. None sought him as adviser, even as editor emeritus. He was ignored by almost all those who had not forgotten him.

Almost, but not quite all. Robert Joseph Cuddihy remembered him. Cuddihy had become publisher of The Literary Digest in 1905 when S.S. was still king-of-the-mountain of American magazines; now he offered S.S. the chance to create a syndicate—The Literary Digest Newspaper Syndicate. For a man to take up again what he had invented and long since discarded was a humbling proposition, but McClure was grateful.

And when McClure called on him to solicit material for syndication, Frank Doubleday remembered S.S., too, and wrung his hand warmly. Doubleday was distressed that S.S. was reduced to peddling syndicate stuff again; it was shameful that he was not editing his magazine as in the old days, with John Phillips at his side. Suddenly Doubleday advanced the suggestion that he might buy McClure's Magazine and place S.S. back at its helm. S.S. pinched himself: was it possible? Of course, said Doubleday thoughtfully, there were complications; he could not permit McClure's to compete with his own magazine, The World's Work; but that aspect of the matter could doubtless be resolved. He urged S.S. to talk it over with Phillips at once.

Phillips had long since sold The American to the Crowell Publishing Company, but he was still its consulting editor. Without much hope, S.S. told him of Doubleday's offer and begged him to consider it. He had, he handsomely admitted to Phillips, made mistakes in the past. "One was entering upon the Long Island building and the other was selling the magazine to Collins and Cameron Mackenzie rather than to Mr. Munsey or Mr. Lamont. But these mistakes of judgment do not change the fact of the great success of our editing policy."

"I am sorry," Phillips wrote Doubleday, "but I cannot go into the scheme."

"I am sorry," Doubleday told McClure. "I regarded John as the working editor who would make the plan possible. Since he feels that the idea is impracticable, I am convinced that the only thing to do is to forget it."

S.S. was sorry, and bitter too. If as old and close a friend as Doubleday would not trust him unless Phillips were involved, he might as well forget the magazine business entirely.

Then there came news that plucked him from trough of despondency to crest of elation. McClure's Magazine, Incorporated, successor to The McClure

Publications, Incorporated, had gone into receivership and filed a petition in bankruptcy. The magazine was on the block, and it was just possible that S.S. might once again get control of it.

The course of McClure's Magazine, following on the forced departure of its maker, had led steadily down. For a time Collins and Mackenzie were able to publish articles that S.S. had planned and stories that the perceptive Viola Roseboro' had recommended. Long after S.S. had been booted out, his successors were still publishing fiction—such as the G.K. Chesterton stories about Father Brown—that he had bought and put in the safe. But neither Collins nor Mackenzie was a creative editor; and after Mackenzie left, in the summer of 1915, to be replaced by Charles Hanson Towne, the magazine was vapid. It became a kind of second-rate woman's magazine, lacking personality, character, conscience, soul, or guts. Towne was of the breed that McClure most despised—an armchair editor, whose notion of how to get good stuff was to sit on his tail and wait for the mailman to bring it to him. Towne lamented the lack of new young talented writers. "McClure's is waiting to discover you," he besought all such authors, in the issue of August, 1916. "We cannot go to every garden spot of the world; but fortunately, in the game of editing, every garden spot can come to us. A two-cent stamp . . . will bring [us your story]." How McClure would have snorted! But, mercifully, S.S. was out of the country when Towne printed this confession of his inadequacy.

In vain its publishers tinkered with McClure's. They gave it a new format; they lowered its price to ten cents, then raised it back to fifteen cents, to twenty, to twenty-five; they tailed editorial matter in amongst the advertisements; they hauled it into footling circulation wars and boasted of their empty victories. Nothing could conceal the fact that its editors were lazy, uninspired hacks. Circulation rose to a high of five hundred and sixty-three thousand in 1918; but that was during wartime, when every magazine circulated widely. In the summer of 1919 Collins was looking for a buyer; in the summer of 1920 he found him. He was a glad man, a peppy man, called Herbert Kaufman.

Kaufman was a kind of bush-league Arthur Brisbane. He wrote snappy, inspirational editorials, heavily leaded, in which the key words were printed in italics or capitals or boldface. He was an editorial writer who would invoke perseverance, initiative, neatness, nobility, application, courage, loyalty, and enthusiasm, and then point out that the first letters of these words spelled

PINNACLE and that, taken in sum, they would likely lead to success. What was more important, his brother was president of the American Safety Razor Corporation, and so there was money. Kaufman was of the breed that Mc-Clure next most despised—a checkbook editor, whose notion of how to get good stuff was to hunt out the authors being published by his competitors and offer them more money. This policy having brought him, within nine months, to the edge of bankruptcy, Kaufman subsided into receivership. The receivers announced a public auction of the property. S.S. blocked the sale. He pointed out that, since Kaufman had failed to make the necessary payment of ten thousand dollars annually for the use of McClure's name, the right to use that name had now reverted to him.

S.S. then introduced Moody B. Gates, publisher of a mail-order magazine called The People's Home Journal.* Gates handed over money; the receivers handed over McClure's Magazine. S.S. was once again its editor, and chairman of the board of directors of a new corporation, the McClure Publishing Company.

[II]

Now that he was once again in command of his magazine, S.S. was deluged with messages of good cheer. Writers who for ten years had avoided him now pressed upon him warm assurances of their loyalty; they were, they added, available for any assignment he might have in mind. Doubleday hired a hall at the Yale Club to celebrate the occasion with a banquet; there were present thirty or forty men who had, in one way or another, helped McClure to make McClure's. (But Phillips was not there; but none of the women who had helped to make McClure's was invited.) In the face of this bonhommie, S.S. maintained a cautious reserve. It was as well; for within a fortnight he was having his troubles with Moody Gates.

In theory, S.S. was to be editor-in-chief of McClure's: he was to hire an editorial staff, Gates was to take care of the business and the advertising.

---

* The mail-order journal, so-called, was a cheap, poorly printed competitor of the great women's magazines. The distinguishing stigma of the mail-order journal was the plenitude of advertising of cheap cosmetics, proprietary medicines, soaps, jewelry, and so on, which were sold by mail. A few mail-order journals for a time threatened even the most prosperous women's magazines. The Ladies' World, which was bought by Collins and Mackenzie in 1912, eventually claimed a circulation of more than seven hundred thousand. By 1920 Gates had whipped the circulation of The People's Home Journal to better than a million.

In fact, S.S. was merely the desk editor: Gates made all editorial decisions, large and small, and no one took care of business and advertising except to watch over and growl at every dollar S.S. spent. He was allowed less than three thousand dollars a month for stories and articles. With a budget that was a small fraction of what his competitors had available, with a staff that was small, overworked, and undistinguished, S.S. was expected to produce miracles. Gates's penny-pinching policies chained S.S. to his desk, obliging him to do what any journeyman could have done better. Writers whose stuff he bought went unpaid for months; some were never paid.

After a short time, McClure and Gates communicated only by inter-office memorandum; both men grew chillier, more elaborately polite, more savagely sarcastic. Gradually Gates arrogated more of the editorial functions. McClure bought an amusing story, "Polly Say Damn", about a parrot. Gates entered his veto: "I don't believe any magazine will take this story on a/c of it being a story about a so-called swear word—Damn." McClure urged a series of articles about the Ku Klux Klan. Gates replied: "I think personally, that if we cover the Ku Klux Klan we ought not to take sides—we ought to give both sides. I personally know we have readers among its membership—and I personally know of some good things it has done."

Clearly the new McClure's was not to be the old McClure's.

S.S. lost interest. In December, 1922, he sailed for Europe, telling Gates he meant to hunt up fresh material; but in truth he was drawn by what he had heard about a French apothecary called Émile Coué, who professed to cure mental and physical diseases by autosuggestion. Coué instructed the sick to repeat, over and over again: "Every day in every way I am getting better and better." Any such simple quackery was bound to attract McClure's attention and guaranteed, as well, to make eager believers of a vast audience in the United States. When S.S. got back to New York in January, 1923, he had Coué in tow. He turned the healer over to Lee Keedick, the lecture manager, who arranged a tour that was to delight the discriminating, vex the clergy, provoke the medical profession even more sorely, and pack halls with the gullible in city after city.

Meanwhile S.S., refreshed by his round trip across the ocean, resumed the tedious struggle with Gates over how McClure's Magazine should be edited. Neither could win. Where the titular editor-in-chief was reduced to a reader of manuscripts, where the publisher shrank from the controversial and adored the insipid, the product was certain to be execrable. Gates hung on for another twelve issues, stubborn, timid, yet hopeful, and then finally surrendered.

McClure's Magazine, by then mired deep in debt, was handed back to its founder. It was worthless, but it was all his. "I wouldn't take half a million dollars for it," S.S. announced bravely. Nobody was disposed to call this bluff.

At S.S.'s request, Curtis Brady came to see him. S.S. told Brady he meant to revive the old McClure's in the old royal-octavo format, but printed on cheaper paper, maybe even on pulp, and with fewer illustrations, at least to begin with, because—to be frank—he couldn't afford much art work. He couldn't afford to hire the staff writers he needed to write the kind of articles he had in mind, either, so for a time he'd be using more fiction than in the old days. But the magazine wouldn't cost much to produce; so little, in fact, that he wouldn't need much advertising to pay the bills. The one man he desperately needed was a sensible business manager. Would Brady take the job again? Brady, remembering McClure in the days of his spendthrift glory, tried to imagine him editing the magazine he had just described. He started to say something, failed, shook his head miserably, and left the office.

McClure was able to publish his magazine from May through August of 1924. Then he ran out of money. There was no issue for September.

But the sun had not quite set, the snake still twitched.

When the prospects were gloomiest—nineteen thousand dollars' worth of pressing debt and only enough cash to pay salaries for one week—Doctor Rumely once again appeared, and to S.S. he seemed like the Good Fairy. "He has defects," S.S. wrote to Hattie, "but he has great qualities & he is the only man in the world that would have saved me. He is great & sympathetic & above all understanding & very sympathetic. I am sure he is meant to be my salvation."

With Doctor Rumely to advise him, S.S. snared his last patron. This was Lewis E. Myers, creator and president of a thing called The Children's Foundation, and manufacturer of books and Chautauqua equipment which were designed for the use of pre-school children and sold on the installment plan.

Myers was a small man with big, Napoleonic ideas. One of his notions was that his squads of salesmen—field secretaries, he called them—could peddle subscriptions to McClure's Magazine while peddling Chautauqua desks. The scheme was as simple as two-plus-two. His field secretaries visited six thousand families every day; they could easily sign up two or three thousand subscribers a week; to be conservative, say fifty thousand a year. This was the kind of commercial fluff that S.S. himself was used to inventing:

for him to listen to Myers was as soothing as to tune in on his own most beguiling daydreams. S.S. introduced Myers to Hattie. "While the situation is perhaps piled high with difficulties," Myers told her, "they do not appear to be insurmountable." She beamed.

There was money available at once, but Myers proved to be more interested in the packaging than in the product. Tens of thousands were spent to lease, decorate, and furnish glossy offices at 250 Park Avenue; more thousands were spent on full-page advertisements in the newspapers. A managing editor, hired by Myers, turned out to have had no experience whatever with any kind of editing or publishing. (S.S. told this man: "You give me the impression of being a moron.")

Meanwhile, as editor-in-chief S.S. was paid a salary half that of the business manager, and he was allowed a magnificent fifteen hundred dollars a month for manuscripts and art work. When he protested, Myers told him his judgment on business matters was unreliable. When he protested further, arguing that three thousand dollars was owed for manuscripts, the response was: "What! Are the authors howling again?"

In the face of these frustrations, S.S. grew peevish. His temper, rarely governable, soared at times to the heights, and on the most trivial provocation. George Brooks, who was managing editor of McClure's after S.S. had got rid of Myers's moron, was standing beside his chief one evening when an elevator operator with a full car closed the door in S.S.'s face. At once S.S. went into a childish tantrum, kicking at the elevator door. His blue eyes were furious and ice-cold. At that moment, Brooks reflected, S.S. could have killed a man without half trying.

Brooks was a young reporter on The Rochester (N.Y.) Tribune when S.S. first heard of him. He had sold some stories to Scribner's; he sold three more to McClure's while Gates was its publisher. (S.S. bought them, but Gates never paid for them.) In 1924 S.S. went to Rochester and sang a siren song: "All my successes have been due to young men and women like you whom I discovered. . . ." Brooks wanted badly to believe him, and took the job of managing editor. In New York, Brooks soon found that S.S. had three reputations, depending upon whom he listened to. S.S. was (a) careless in financial matters, or (b) unfortunate in some of his transactions, or (c) a goddamned crook. Brooks also learned that McClure's Magazine was the joke of the business and that McClure was considered a low-comedy has-been. (The reigning monarch of magazine editors was Ray Long of Cosmopolitan, a checkbook editor.)

None of this fazed Brooks, who liked McClure, respected him, and got along famously with him. The only serious row the two men ever got into was over Prohibition. S.S. was a dry and Brooks was a practicing wet, a sufficiently serious student of the matter to have established that there were twenty-one speakeasies on Forty-sixth Street beween Park Avenue and Broadway.* One day S.S. got to wagging his head over the gang wars waged by some rival beer barons. Conditions, he said, were like those just before the Civil War. Brooks agreed. The drys, S.S. went on, could be compared to the abolitionists.

"Oh, no," said Brooks. "The drys are like the slave hunters, chasing fugitive slaves toward Canada, with all the power of the Fugitive Slave Act and the Dred Scott decision to back them up."

S.S. went into one of his rages. His eyes got hard. He rattled the change in his pocket. "You mean to infer that the people who ran the Underground Railroad were like the bootleggers today?"

"In certain ways, yes, sir."

"You don't know what you're talking about."

"I know more about it than you do."

"What do you mean?"

"My grandfather organized the underground through western New York. The house where I was born was a station on the Underground Railroad." Brooks grinned. "When you get right down to it," he added, "there's no gang war over beer any worse than John Brown's murders of Southern sympathizers in Kansas."

S.S. kicked his way out of the office. That day and the next he raged and fumed, for another two days he sulked, but on the fifth day he was able to talk to Brooks about other matters. After a week or so he took Brooks to lunch at the Union League Club. S.S. ordered Guiness's stout, for self and guest. Brooks arched an eyebrow. "Well," said S.S., "I do not consider stout intoxicating."

Strange and wonderful people came into the office of the newest McClure's. One day it was a Grand Kleagle of the Ku Klux Klan of Indiana, out on bail while appealing a conviction for second-degree murder. S.S. told Brooks this man was a gold-mine. "You ought to be able to get material out of him for something or other."

"I've known murderers before," Brooks said. "I used to write police."

---

* This was in 1924. Five years later a census would have turned up three times that number.

"Well," said McClure. "Well." He jingled the change in his pocket. "You never knew a murderer who kept his head in a pillow-case, did you?"

On another day Boyden Sparkes dropped into the office. Sparkes was a successful journalist who looked (at least to Brooks) like a bond salesman. He sold his stuff chiefly to The Saturday Evening Post and he dressed the part. McClure talked to Sparkes about Herbert Hoover, one of S.S.'s favorites. There was general talk about American politics. Sparkes was reminded of a story. One evening, Sparkes said, he had had lucky dice. He had been on vacation in Vermont, only a few miles from Plymouth, when the telephone rang and it was Fate calling, to tell him he should scramble over to Plymouth to witness the ceremony by which Calvin Coolidge was to be sworn as President. Harding, it appeared, was dead, and the Republic lacked a leader. So Sparkes sped to Plymouth, only to discover that the Coolidges, simple, God-fearing folk, unused to city ways, were willing to let the world spin on its axis and the Republic float rudderless, because of their determination that their Calvin should not be sworn until photographers should have arrived to properly record the historic moment. Hence, Sparkes insisted, the superfluity of pictures of the spare Yankee farmhouse, its parlor, its kerosene lamps, the family Bible, the charcoal portraits of ancestors, and the ectoplasm of Ethan Allen riding herd over the entire scene. Sparkes told the story well. S.S. and Brooks were alike helpless from laughter. Suddenly S.S. pulled himself together.

"Wasn't there a golden-haired little girl of five or six in her night clothes, waked up to see Grandpa swear in Uncle Calvin?"

"No," said Sparkes, "or, if there was, I missed her."

"Didn't she lisp, 'Why, that isn't the President, that's just Uncle Cal'?"

"No," said Sparkes. "They missed that."

"Well," said S.S. "Well. Just for that they don't deserve to ever have another President in their family."

Another frequent visitor was Willa Cather. Once she came at S.S.'s request; he hoped she would help him persuade Brooks to write a series of short stories based on a character in a story that Brooks had written and that S.S. had much admired. It was the old editorial precept: what a writer has once done well, he can and should do again. But Brooks was reluctant. While S.S. talked at him, Miss Cather nodded and smiled. A few moments later, however, she privately invited Brooks to come to her apartment for tea; and on that occasion she all but made him swear he would never attempt such a series. She understood the editor's viewpoint thoroughly and so, as a writer talking to a writer, she was the more sensibly concerned. "You'll wish you were dead every morning you live," she told Brooks, "if you let yourself get identified with a series of stories about the same character."

Miss Cather also warned Brooks that McClure's Magazine faced a difficult future, but on this score he needed no caveats. By that time he had already attended a sales meeting of the Myers organization—his "family," as Myers preferred to call it—and had witnessed how the salesmen joined in pep songs, prayers, and hymns. He had formed his own dubious estimate of how many subscriptions to McClure's Magazine they would be able to sell. He had gone from the sales meeting back to his own office, to be confronted by Hattie McClure, who desired to know why he did not run six-color prints of the saints in miniature, since children loved pictures. Brooks was unhappily aware that S.S. was trying to sell a 1912 product or, worse, a 1906 product, in 1925, and that the reading public wanted no part of it.

After nine issues, Myers wanted no further part of it either. He had dropped one hundred and fifty thousand dollars, and he was stuck with a lease for office space that cost two thousand a month. Thousands more were owed to authors and never paid. There was some talk that Herbert Hoover might buy Myers's interests and keep the magazine alive with S.S. as its editor, but these negotiations collapsed in rather bizarre circumstances when one of the parties to the transaction was attacked by his son-in-law, who subsequently killed himself. The magazine was sold to Hearst early in 1925.* S.S. had a contract with Myers under which he was to be paid one hundred dollars a week for five years, but it was not honored. S.S. had paid several hundred dollars out of his own pocket in an effort to meet obligations to writers; this debt, too, was ignored.

As an editor, S.S. McClure was finished.

[III]

"I have entered on my seventieth year in a humble mood," McClure told his wife in February, 1926. "I will take any chance that comes."

---

* Hearst's International Publications made the magazine over into McClure's, The Magazine of Romance; it was a sordid and vulgar thing, filled with leering fiction fit to be read only by adolescents behind the barn. Louella O. Parsons became a regular contributor, and the covers were by John Held, Jr. After a time it was sold to James R. Quirk, the publisher of Photoplay, who rechristened it The New McClure's—A Man's Magazine! It died in the barber shops in 1930, unmourned.

His plight presents the moralist with a sore temptation. All about him were authors and editors who had got rich and fat thanks in part to his effort and his acumen; many of them, having reached the age of retirement, were comfortably coasting downhill on annuities or royalties he had helped make possible. Yet he had not saved against this rainy day; yet he was now, at seventy, and through his own pluperfect improvidence, confronted with the need to hustle a dollar. His mother was still alive, lodged in the Connecticut State Hospital, anile and crazy; his wife continued in poor health; he had sold the farmhouse on the Housatonic, retaining only a small cottage without plumbing as his entire estate; he felt himself responsible for the support of a widowed daughter and her infant son. His prospects were nil. He wrote his wife: "I am so ashamed & sorry that I havent a home for you!"

Yet he remained sanguine. "I feel an endless and sure energy," he told Phillips. "I suppose I am in as nearly perfect health as is possible, and by inheritance I should have twenty good years in front of me. My mother is still in good health and vigor. I can count for some years on doing as good work as I ever did."

Another old associate—Edward Rumely—keenly regretted S.S.'s enforced idleness. Rumely suggested that S.S. seek to become an associate editor of The Dearborn Independent, the newspaper owned by Henry Ford. At the time The Independent was surely the most scurrilous journal in the country. Its editors were conducting a violent, vile, and fraudulent campaign against Jews; despite the horrified protests of conservatives and liberals alike, The Independent published the spurious Protocols of Zion as solemnly as if they were the tablets entrusted to Moses on Mount Sinai by God. "Its [The Independent's] fundamental viewpoint coincides with yours," Rumely wrote McClure. McClure was quite willing to take a job on The Dearborn Independent. But its editor politely ignored his overtures.

Rumely came up with another helpful suggestion that S.S. duly reported to Hattie. "I am working on a big idea," he wrote his wife in June, 1926, "that I got from Dr. Rumely, namely, to get a series of signed articles by Mussolini. I am pulling all the wires to get the right influences, & if I succeed I will go on to Rome." Armed with letters of introduction, he arrived in Italy a month later.

Fascism bowled McClure over. It was "a new and dawning civilization," the Italians were "the one free people" in the world, Mussolini was "solving the problem of democracy." The fascist state, the corporate state, the strong centralized government led by the masterful man who had brought the trade unions to heel and who promised the same for industry—all this seemed to

S.S. the fulfillment of the dream he had fought for back in the days of Theodore Roosevelt.* When S.S. was invited to the Chigi Palace for an audience
with the Duce late in 1926, he was thrilled. He assured Mussolini he was
wholly at the Duce's service, as he had been at Roosevelt's. Later S.S. wrote
to Hattie: "We had a beautiful talk. . . . [Mussolini] is full of force & charm
& kindliness. It made my heart beat hard for a long time after I left him."

To serve the Duce, S.S. got him to agree that he would put his name to a
series of articles about his rise to power. Mussolini imposed only the condition
that the articles would have to be approved by Signora Margharita Sarfatti,
a curious female who had once been his mistress, who had composed an
adoring biography of him, and who was apparently still his Egeria. McClure
had to promise the Sarfatti ten thousand American dollars to wring from
her her co-operation, but he was then able to sell the series to The Saturday
Evening Post for a handsome fee. It appeared in 1928 and was later published
as a book.†

To serve the Duce further, S.S. came home to engage in a public debate on
the merits of fascism. The arena was the Selwyn Theatre, just off Times
Square in New York; the time was the ides of March, 1928; his opponent
was Dr. Vincenzo Nitti, son of the man whom Mussolini had deposed as
premier. In fact, there were two debates in the Selwyn Theatre that night:
one was had with some decorum on the stage and the other was contested
—with rude noises, fist fights, and Latin passion—amongst fascists and anti-
fascists in the audience. "The working man," McClure declared, "feels safe
and happy in Italy." This remark was greeted with hoots and shouts of
laughter from the anti-fascists sitting in the orchestra, but the fascists in the
balcony cheered when McClure insisted, "I know what I am talking about,"

---

* If one may judge by their autobiographies, Steffens and Miss Tarbell seem to have been
likewise flimflammed into an admiration of fascism, either by the swagger of hoodlums in
uniform or by the tyrant's dimple.

† George Horace Lorimer of The Post tried to persuade Kenneth Roberts to ghost the articles.
Roberts, who was about to blossom forth as an author of successful historical romances, resented
the spectral aspects of the job, regarded McClure as a garrulous old bore, and detested the
Sarfatti, whom he considered "a dumpy, hard-voiced, coarse-skinned bleached blonde from
North Italy." Roberts told S.S. that to write the series as S.S. wished it to be written (i.e., in
the painstaking fashion McClure had decreed for the staff writers of the old McClure's) would
take twice too long. When S.S. suggested that he might revise his own contract with The
Post so as to make an additional five thousand dollars available for expenses, Roberts chose
to construe the offer as a bribe.

Mussolini's so-called autobiography was eventually written by Richard Washburn Child, a
journalist who had served in the early 1920s as ambassador to Italy. As a series for The Post,
it was dreadful. As a book, published by Charles Scribner's Sons, it is still awfully remembered
in the rooms of that firm, and is mentioned only in the hushed whispers reserved for catastrophes
of the first magnitude.

and went on to say that during his eighteen months in Italy the trains had always arrived on time.* Fights broke out during the period allotted for rebuttal; one combatant had to be ejected from the theater. At the stage door S.S. found a throng of fascists waiting for him. They lofted him to their shoulders and bore him in triumph to Times Square, cheering and singing a fascist song. S.S. waved his hat as he was carried along. Just as the anti-fascists were about to dispute this celebration, the police intervened.

And now what was left for McClure? Only the steady erosion of his public character, as he permitted himself to be used by others. Some were sincerely anxious to help him, others were more nakedly greedy, but all joined in exploiting what was left of his reputation. He signed a testimonial for some sort of health food, he was a speaker at banquets of the Italy America Society, he fronted for a speculation in South Carolina real estate.

During this time Hattie McClure saw little of her husband. For several months she lay in the American Hospital in Paris, desperately sick of anemia, exhausted and feeble. When she came back to the United States, she shared a small apartment in Waterbury, Connecticut, with her sister Mary and her adopted son Enrico (who was now called Henry McClure). Here S.S. visited her from time to time, but only briefly, for he was driven by the need to earn more money. His son Robert contributed a generous monthly check, and so did Frank Doubleday, but S.S. was still trying to support a full complement of necessitous dependents.

Hattie McClure, in a gallant and futile effort to add to the family's income, ransacked volumes of inspirational verse in quest of selections she hoped might be bought by The Golden Book, an eclectic magazine of the time. She tired easily, but her courage was strong. Early in May, 1929, she undertook, as she had so often before, to cheer her despondent husband. "I well know," she wrote him, "how deeply concerned you have been for my health and well-being, at all times, through all my deep troubles. I'll never forget it. Now I am going to be less of a care to you, I hope. . . . Best love—best wishes—" She signed her name, folded her letter into an envelope, sealed it, found a stamp, licked it, and stuck it on. Everything was such a trouble, even the simplest tasks were so hard.

There were two flights of stairs from her apartment to the street. She was

---

* This fascist boast, so swiftly transformed into an anti-fascist gibe, is, so far as I have been able to ascertain, another McClure "first."

used to taking them slowly. The letterbox was a block away. She was anxious to mail her letter, for she wanted her husband to know she was feeling better, that all would yet be well. The truth was, she was feeling poorly. She should see a doctor, but that would mean a trip by bus, too much for one day.

A few days later she managed the trip to the doctor's office. He gave her a prescription and she began the journey home. (The careful foot on the step into the bus, the firm grip of the hand on the rail.) On the way was a drug store where she had the prescription filled. (The clasp of the handbag, the clasp of the change purse, then everything back in place, just so.) From the drug store, she walked home. It was uphill, but there was a park where she sat for a time. She stayed only a few minutes, for there was a chill in the air. Back in her apartment, she suffered the first of several mild heart attacks. A swift attack of pleurisy followed. The pain was agonizing; she lapsed into a coma. S.S. was at her side when she died, on May 29. Fifty-three years before, on May 30, he had picked a handful of wild flowers and brought them to her; they had gone for a walk together, alone with each other for the first time; the anniversary of that day had been more important to them, down through the years, than even that of their wedding day.

Now she was gone. In the months and years that followed, S.S. would be suddenly reminded of her and would have to withdraw to a room apart from everybody so that he might weep, alone and unrestrained. He had, he knew, often treated her shabbily, often ignored her, often gone kiting off to leave her alone and miserable; and the memory of these wrongs was painful, for he had loved her deeply and, perhaps more than even he realized, needed what she had given him.

But if she was gone, at least S.S. had the letters she had written him, thousands of them, the chronicle of a singularly faithful devotion that had persisted for more than a half century, through every imaginable vicissitude. He gathered the letters together, put them in order, and, as the months went by, read them over and over again with unflagging absorption. She had loved, she had admired, she had encouraged, she had sustained; rarely had she reproached or complained; never had she nagged or scolded. From the first moment she met him she had been convinced of his special destiny, of the great work he would surely do; and at the end she had still been certain of the excellence and the permanence of his achievements.

Of course she had been prejudiced, but nevertheless S.S. sorely wanted to agree with her judgment. He had never been a contemplative man—he had always been too busy, rushing here and there, his mind flooded with impressions and sudden, dazzling perceptions, some daffy, some shrewd and acute—but now for the first time he began to reflect upon his life and its value, if any, to his time and his fellow man. McClure took such matters quite seriously. Just as, in the first days of his editorship, he had fixed his gaze on the edge of the future, so now in his old age his thoughts were sometimes troubled by what lay ahead, just beyond the edge of final consciousness.

Would the record of his achievements be lasting and lustrous? Or had all his energy, all his eager enthusiasm, gone for nothing? He had described himself to Doctor Rumely as a wretched failure: Doctor Rumely had protested that S.S. had rendered tremendous service to his time and his country and, smoothly adapting the words of Pericles, had insisted that S.S. had erected memorials in the minds of people in many lands. S.S. had taken comfort from these assurances.

S.S. liked to recall, too, that back in 1910 William Archer had written an essay for The Fortnightly Review in which he had credited McClure with having invented and developed "the vital and stimulating" cheap American magazine. S.S. had a copy of that article among his papers; he had read it so often that he had it almost by heart.

> Mr. McClure is a very remarkable personality [Archer had written]. There is, indeed, something that lends itself to caricature in his feverish fertility of ideas, his irrepressible energy, his sanguine imagination. But besides being an editor of genius, he is a staunch and sincere idealist. When he determined to make his magazine a power in the land, he also determined that it should be a power for good; and he has nobly fulfilled that resolve. . . . His method is to present facts, skilfully marshalled, sternly compressed, and let them speak for themselves. And they *have* spoken for themselves, to the no small enlightenment, and to the lasting good, of the American people. The historian of the future may determine how much of the "uplift" that distinguished the Roosevelt administration was due to the influence of the McClure type of magazine. We cannot, at this distance of time, see things quite in proportion; but it seems to me certain that Mr. McClure both paved the way for President Roosevelt and potently furthered the movements with which his name will always be identified.

For S.S. to reread his dog-eared tear sheets of this piece was an immense satisfaction. Archer had put the matter just as he would himself. Perhaps after all the historians would have a good word to say for him.

But he was presently dismayed to find that the historians who have dealt with the muckraking era were off on a quite different tack.

The first such history to come to his attention was Harold Faulkner's The Quest for Social Justice. Professor Faulkner had written: "The public response to the articles of Miss Tarbell and Steffens was immediate and McClure discovered his circulation mounting rapidly. Although more interested in this than in reform, he . . ." At about this point McClure slammed Professor Faulkner's book down in disgust. Where had the professor got the idea that he, McClure, was more interested in circulation, in profits, than in reform? Where, indeed, had the professor got the idea that circulation *had* risen? S.S. sent off a testy note to the professor, asking by what authority he had presumed to divine his, McClure's, motives for publishing the muckraking articles without so much as inquiring of McClure himself as to those motives. Professor Faulkner replied tactfully and apologetically. "My chief authority," he wrote, "was the manuscript of Regier which had not yet been published."

By then McClure had read C.C. Regier's book, The Era of the Muckrakers, and considered it shot through with error and absurdity. Professor Regier had written that *"McClure's* had stumbled on muckraking without premeditation"; he had told how McClure would bring "a score of projects" to meetings of the editorial staff and "would grow indignant and desperate as they were one by one picked to pieces by his associates"; he had observed that "McClure was sceptical of the value of the historical approach, but allowed himself to be convinced" that Miss Tarbell's notion of a history of the Standard Oil Company might make a good feature; he had concluded—and here he threw a cue to Professor Faulkner—that McClure, "though not himself in any way a reformer", realized that in muckraking "he had found a field with great possibilities for his magazine."

It was hard for S.S., who as editor had always been so devoted to accuracy, to decide which was the most preposterous of these statements. Where had Professor Regier got his misinformation? The professor himself, in answer to another of S.S.'s tart inquiries, confessed that he could not remember exactly. "I think," he wrote, "that it was from your former associates, possibly from Hamlin Garland." Professor Faulkner was more specific. He wrote McClure that Regier's manuscript, prior to its publication, had undergone extensive revisions by still another young professor, Granville Hicks. Faulkner had told Hicks of McClure's complaints and Hicks had responded: "I don't see why Regier isn't adequate authority [as to McClure's motives]. And Steffens is, of course, even better, though, if I remember correctly, you hadn't seen his book when you wrote yours. You could, if you wanted to, quote me as saying that McClure's associates gave me that impression when I talked to them. That's rather vague, but it's true. Steffens, Ida Tarbell, Phillips, and, to some extent, Baker, all stressed the fact that McClure was primarily interested in circulation. And I think they'd back you up on that, though they might not."

McClure was interested by the idea that Regier was an adequate authority as to his, McClure's, motives and that Steffens was, of course, even better. He turned with equal interest to an examination of The Autobiography of Lincoln Steffens.

S.S. was fascinated—in the precise sense of that word—by Steffens's book. When Steffens described the four years he had spent on the staff of McClure's Magazine, his memory, it seemed to McClure, had been powerfully assisted by his imagination. Steffens had consistently imputed motive to McClure, saying, for example, that the article on Minneapolis had sent both newsstand circulation and subscriptions zooming, and that in consequence McClure, his mind on profits, had ordered Steffens to increase the sensationalism of his articles so that they might "hold and reap" their advantage. (Reading a little further on, McClure was amused to note that Steffens had written: "Men expose their own psychology when they attribute motives to others.") Much of what Steffens had invented McClure found harmless enough. Some was even comical, as when Steffens told of the time Phillips had hired him as managing editor. Steffens had Phillips ask him: "What will your policy be on the magazine?" And he had himself answer: "Put news into it." It was as though the Vice-President of the United States, on hiring a doorman for the White House, were to ask him how he proposed to administer the government and the doorman were to confidently answer: "Get the country moving again."

But a few of the stories Steffens had invented roused S.S.'s temper, for they demeaned and discredited S.S.'s work as editor. There was a maliciously witty tale of how S.S. had got to talking with some unnamed Antarctic explorer and had so enchanted himself with his own vivid account of the explorer's journey that he had promised the explorer a fat fee for a series of articles. "We all hated serial articles," Steffens had commented; "they tied us up, and S.S. knew that." As Steffens told it, S.S. fled to Europe to avoid the mess he had made; but Steffens cleverly saved the magazine from the chore of having to publish a great wad of dull matter by telling the explorer where in Europe he might find McClure. "S.S. either put him off," Steffens concluded, "or settled with him out of his own pocket."

The notion that his associates had hated serial articles struck McClure as most curious. All the magazine's greatest successes had come from series of articles; two such, indeed, The Shame of the Cities and Enemies of the Republic, had been written by Steffens himself. What was the man talking about?

As for the explorer, McClure could remember no such man. To be sure, he had published accounts of several polar expeditions—those headed by Andrée, Nansen, and Peary jumped to his mind—but he could recall none during the brief period Steffens had worked for the magazine. Nor, when he put the question to him, could Phillips remember any. S.S. dispatched a note to Steffens: Who was this explorer?

April 25, 1933

Dear S.S:

I don't remember what that explorer was that I write of on p. 362; I didn't at the time I related the anecdote. And you say Phillips doesn't. Ask Miss Tarbell.

But what do you want to know for? You wouldn't spoil a good story, would you? And make me dig around for another like it? Somebody told me you didn't like my picture of you; that you said that "if you were as I described you, you could never have made McClure's." If you said that, I [am] astonished at you & will agree that, not you, but we (the rest of us) made McClure's.

Let me see you some time, S.S. We'll laugh together, as we used to; didn't we? I can't remember that for sure, either.

Yours affectionately
Lincoln Steffens

Once again S.S. reached the boiling point. He sent off an indignant letter: How dare Steffens suggest that he had not made his own magazine? What did he mean?

May 15, 1933

Dear S.S.

I mean that you have lost or forgotten your sense of humor. My book contains a laughing sketch of you that makes other people like & appreciate & understand you. And you kick. Why not talk to Phillips or

Miss Tarbell about it? And then paint a self-portrait. You can do one of me, too; & of them.

And do come along this way some day & let us have a talk. My memory is emptied. I dumped it into my autobiography so that, now, I am interested only in the future which I see coming with both feet & both fists. But with you here, I'll bet I could recall a lot of things.

Meanwhile I'm

Yours as ever, S.S.

Steffens

By that time McClure had already determined that the proper way to answer Steffens and the professors was to write another book—to update his own autobiography. Phillips agreed. Perhaps, McClure thought hopefully, perhaps one of his old friends might be free to help him. In turn he cautiously sounded out Willa Cather, Burton Hendrick, Ida Tarbell, Kibbe Turner. All were preoccupied with their own schemes. If the book were to be written, S.S. would have to write it himself.

In his cottage on the Housatonic he set up a long deal table; on it he spread Hattie's letters to him and his to her; near at hand he stacked bound volumes of the old McClure's; he sharpened pencils and covered dozens of pages of paper with notes; he hit upon a title for his book: My Life and Work. He would do more than simply set the record of his editorship straight, he would go on: he would include his study of the techniques of government which he had been pursuing over the last twenty years; he would call it The Science of Human Self-Organization or, even better, The Influence of Human Organization in History.

He set to work. He wrote a twelve-page introduction. It was all he could manage.

He was then seventy-seven years old.

[IV]

The round of his days took on a pattern, strangely circumscribed for a man who had always delighted to hop from one continent to another as most men cross the street. Thanks in part to his children, in part to some friends who arranged for a small monthly sum to be paid him anonymously through the Banker's Trust Company, he survived the lean years of the

great depression. His demands were few. He had a small room in a venerable hostelry, the Murray Hill Hotel; someone who visited him in this room
later recalled that outside, on the window sill, S.S. had perched a half loaf
of some sort of dark peasant bread, a bit of butter, an orange, and a con-
tainer of acidophilus milk. He spent long hours every day in the Union
League Club, in which he had a life membership. He held squatter's rights
to one corner of the library, and here he kept a great tangle of research,
books and papers and notes and cuttings from newspapers stuffed higgledy-
piggledy into file folders, the raw material of the book he was interminably
at work upon. He took his meals at the Horn & Hardart Automat on Forty-
second Street. Every day he bought a large Idaho potato from a grocer on
Third Avenue and took it to the automat where it was baked for him and
set out on the steam table to await his arrival—and the girl back of the
counter would rap the knuckles of any customer who tried to make off with
"the old gentleman's potato."

He was still a trustee of Knox College and whenever he could he attended
commencement ceremonies. These trips to Galesburg were his only lengthy
travels. When the weather was fine, he liked to go back to his cottage on
the Housatonic and spend the day in bed, sipping milk and reading pulp
magazines. (He had become addicted to stories of the Wild West.) He had
slipped so far from the public eye that the newspapers referred to him only
as "the late S.S. McClure." It was a natural mistake; so many of his contemporaries were dead: Munsey long since, Cyrus Curtis in 1933, Doubleday
in 1934, Kipling and Steffens in 1936, John Finley in 1940.

But Phillips was still alive, and Miss Tarbell, and Miss Roseboro'; and
S.S. tried to keep in touch with them. Once, in 1936, he had managed to
round them all up for a luncheon at the Union League Club, to celebrate
his birthday. Something like fifty letters had to be exchanged before the four
old crocks could find a day that was mutually convenient. By the time they
were all propped up around one table, S.S.'s birthday was three months gone.
No matter: he was so delighted to see them; to tell them all about his new
project, his great work, The Science of Human Self-Organization; to be
with three old associates who could remember the days when their magazine
was proconsul of the Republic, and who would listen to everything he had
to say with affection and respect. He gave to each of them copies of an
outline of his great work-in-progress and prayed for their good opinions of
it. Later, with much delicacy, each of them wrote him a careful letter, prais-

ing, hopefully criticizing, but never revealing the harsh truth, for that would have been too cruel. The truth was that McClure, as a writer, was a great editor, and each of his old friends knew it.

By cherishing the illusion that what he was doing was important, S.S. kept on working. Indeed, he had supporters to subsidize his work. Doctor Rumely, who had been profoundly disturbed by the advent of the New Deal, had helped to found something called the Committee for the Nation and later something called the National Committee to Uphold Constitutional Government; he was convinced that what McClure was up to would assist in the great patriotic work of baying at the heels of the New Deal. Doctor Rumely undertook to pay McClure a modest weekly fee so that he might pursue his scholarly researches, looking toward the eventual publication of a book.

But S.S.'s energy was at last beginning to flag. On a September day in 1941 he and his daughter Eleanor drove from the cottage on the Housatonic down to Bethel to visit Miss Tarbell. Later Miss Tarbell wrote to Phillips:

Last Day of Summer—1941
Dear J.S.P.,
. . . S.S. telephoned from up-country, might Eleanor bring him down. They came only for a call. He is almost gone, I think—undernourishment. White, shaky, frail. Exhausted voice, except when he speaks of [Franklin] Roosevelt. He says he is earning $15.00 a week defending the Constitution. The story we have heard so often. . . . He talked of the early McClure's. Seems puzzled that he did it. "A man makes mistakes about himself. He sees himself as people think he is, then as he thinks he is. But when you are old you see yourself as you are." He cant live long on two baked potatoes a day. . . .
I felt I was saying good-bye to a dying man. . . . It seems so a part of things, like the coming of fall. . . .
Faithfully
I.M.T.

But the leaves fell, and the snows came, and S.S. persisted in his endless task of collecting and arranging the material for his work-in-progress.

After a little while he was saddened to hear that Miss Tarbell had died.

Suddenly S.S. was once again in the public eye. In March, 1944, Arthur Train, who was then the president of the National Institute of Arts and Letters, wrote him that he had been awarded the Institute's Order of Merit for his work "in the furtherance of arts and letters, particularly in the recognition of new talent and in the creation of a new type of journalism in McClure's Magazine." The award meant a gold medal and a check for one thousand dollars, and that was good; but what was far better was the heartwarming knowledge that he had been honored by the country's most distinguished company of authors and artists. He was not, after all, entirely forgotten. The award, Train wrote him, had been voted unanimously: "You would, I feel sure, have been proud and pleased at the tributes that were showered upon you last evening, in which I am glad to say I participated." As he read those words, S.S.'s eyes were stinging.

Then there was the public announcement. "The American people," Train told the reporters, "owe a great debt to this man, once famous, now almost forgotten." S.S. had an appointment at Memorial Hospital for treatment of a lip cancer, but he had to cancel it. All afternoon there were reporters and photographers around him in his corner of the library of the Union League Club. It was like old times.

Then, on a May afternoon, there was the ceremony. A splendid speech by Train and, when S.S. stepped forward to receive the medal, there was Willa Cather, on hand to be awarded the Institute's Gold Medal for fiction, and, before all the members of the Institute and their guests, Miss Cather flung her arms around him and hugged him affectionately. He had been asked to say something in acknowledgment of his award; he could manage only a few halting words. He clutched his medal and went back to his chair in the front row. He was as happy and excited as he had been seventy-eight years before, when he had tasted his first lemonade and heard his first firecrackers. This was a wonderful land, and he had realized all its wonderful promises.

And then back into obscurity again. There were so many changes; he grew confused. The Murray Hill Hotel, where he had lived so long, was torn down; he was obliged to move. The library committee of the Union League Club wrote to tell him he must remove all his notes, clippings, books, and utensils. "Outside garments," the committee added sternly, "should be left in the check-room." His health, so sturdy for so long, began to fail. He celebrated his ninetieth birthday at his son's house in New Rochelle; he was surrounded by children, grandchildren, and great-grandchildren. Who were they all? It was hard to keep them straight. Talk and laughter and smoke, people drinking, children listening to The Green Hornet on the radio, young women he could swear he had never seen before. . . . He shook his head in bewilderment and retired to his own little room, apart, and began picking nervously at his notes, shuffling them about, mixing them up beyond all hope of order. He no longer knew where he was.

He was taken to St. Barnabas Hospital in the Bronx. Word was brought to him that John Phillips had died. Had he understood? At any rate, he wept. In the long months of his final illness his thoughts turned all the way back to his childhood, and the person of whom he spoke most often was his father, who had plunged to death in the hold of a ship so many long years before. What would have become of Samuel McClure, if his father's neck had not been broken? It is with such speculations that novelists begin and biographers end.

S.S. McClure died at nine-thirty on the night of March 21, 1949, in his ninety-second year. His body was coffined and taken to Galesburg, Illinois, where it was buried next to that of his wife. Galesburg was not his home but, after all, there really was no place that had been his home. "The feeling of homelessness," he had told Hattie in 1883, "has been upon me ever since my father died." It may be doubted that he ever shook it off. His Galesburg friends remarked that on the day of his funeral the town was struck by the worst cyclone in its history. S.S. McClure, they agreed, went out with a bang.

Author's Note and Bibliography

The principal resource for this book was a great mass of papers, letters, diaries, journals, bills, circulars, canceled checks, letter-books, and cuttings from magazines and newspapers which, when I first came upon them in 1956, were stuffed higgledy-piggledy into more than forty trunks, crates, and great boxes, variously disposed in the cellar and attic of a small house in New Milford, Connecticut, then occupied by Eleanor McClure. These were the McClure Papers, now in the Lilly Library of the University of Indiana.

In 1956 the McClure Papers were a bewildering trove of trash and treasure. Apparently neither S. S. McClure nor his wife had ever thrown anything away. The first handful from a crate or trunk would include a 1921 laundry list, a gossipy letter of 1876 to Hattie Hurd from a girlhood chum in Galesburg, a holograph manuscript of an article by William Dean Howells, a medical prescription made out by a Swiss physician in 1902, and a letter to McClure from Theodore Roosevelt. While I would be carefully unfolding what turned out to be a receipt from the butcher, my wife would be carelessly whisking mouse dung off a letter from George Bernard Shaw.

The McClure Papers have irritating gaps. I came upon a box of correspondence, alphabetically filed, that turned out to be letters from newspaper editors to the infant McClure Syndicate; but the file included only N–Z, and I never found A–M. Letters exchanged by McClure and his wife mounted into the thousands, but McClure only occasionally wrote to his wife about his business affairs. Much material, and especially that dealing with McClure's Magazine, had to be found elsewhere.

Happily, most of those to whom I turned were most helpful. I was given invaluable assistance by relatives of two of McClure's earliest associates, John S. Phillips and Albert A. Brady. Phillips's daughter, Mrs. Dorothy S. P. Huntington, graciously made available many letters; she also loaned me her father's unpublished memoir, A Legacy to Youth. Brady's younger brother Curtis, who was advertising manager and business manager of McClure's Magazine for many years, wrote me scores of lengthy letters to help me puzzle out some of McClure's financial difficulties; after he died, his nephew, Albert A. Brady, Jr., generously turned over to me the unpublished typescript of Curtis Brady's memoir, The High Cost of Impatience, which deals only with his association with McClure's Magazine.

To have worked on McClure's seems to have been a provocative experience. A remarkable number of those who did so wrote their autobiographies. It would seem they were under an obligation to justify how they came to McClure's, what they did there, and how they came to leave it. In witness, here is a partial list of these reminiscences:

BAKER, RAY STANNARD. *American Chronicle:* Charles Scribner's Sons, 1945.
BRADY, CURTIS P. *The High Cost of Impatience:* unpublished.
DOUBLEDAY, FRANK N. *Secret Memoirs of a Publisher:* unpublished.
IRWIN, WILL. *The Making of a Reporter:* G. P. Putnam's Sons, 1942.
MCCLURE, S. S. *My Autobiography:* Frederick A. Stokes, 1914.
PHILLIPS, JOHN S. *A Legacy to Youth:* unpublished.
SEDGWICK, ELLERY. *The Happy Profession:* Little, Brown, 1946.
STEFFENS, LINCOLN. *Autobiography:* Harcourt, Brace, 1931.
SULLIVAN, MARK. *Education of an American:* Doubleday, Doran, 1938.
TARBELL, IDA M. *All in the Day's Work:* Macmillan, 1939.

Even more helpful were the collected letters and papers of some of these people. I have to thank the Library of Congress and Miss Katherine Brand for making available the papers of Ray Stannard Baker; Douglas M. Black, president of Doubleday & Company, for making available several ancient contracts and sales agreements, and Mrs. Nelson Doubleday for permitting me to read F. N. Doubleday's memoir and many letters from Kipling; the Butler Library of Columbia University for making available the papers of Lincoln Steffens, and Ella Winter for permitting me to quote from them; the Reis Library of Allegheny College and the Drake Memorial Museum in Titusville, Pennsylvania, for making available the papers of Ida M. Tarbell, and Mrs. Paxton Price for permission to quote from them.

The librarian of Knox College sent me material bearing on McClure's undergraduate days at that institution; C. Waller Barrett most generously permitted me access to his remarkable collection; the Yale University Library, by making available many items in the Beinecke Collection, helped me to piece together McClure's relationship with Robert Louis Stevenson;

Frederick Anderson of the General Library of the University of California at Berkeley sent me material dealing with McClure's attempt to get Mark Twain to edit a magazine; William A. Jackson of the Houghton Library at Harvard University sent me letters and contracts dealing with McClure's scheme for a magazine to be edited by William Dean Howells; Robert W. Hill, the Keeper of Manuscripts at the New York Public Library, was helpful in many ways; and A. P. De Weese, the chief of the information division at the same library, who knows everything, often was good enough to help me ferret out an obscure fact. To all of these I am indebted. And I must express my particular gratitude to the New York Society Library and to Sylvia Hilton and Helen Ruskell, who gave me a liberty amounting to license with the books and magazines on the shelves of that library.

Of McClure's associates, some wrote to me, some were good enough to give me of their time, some did both. I spent four pleasantly acerb hours with the late Samuel Hopkins Adams; the late George Brooks wrote me sharp and funny accounts of his days as managing editor of McClure's Magazine in the 1920s; Witter Bynner, both in correspondence and in conversation, gave me invaluable stuff; Earnest Elmo Calkins was most helpful; the late Elmer Davis contributed his memories of the Ford Peace Ship; the late Arthur S. Moore told me about the sale of McClure's Magazine in 1912; the late Kenneth Payne recalled his brief tour of duty as managing editor of McClure's in 1923; Doctor Edward A. Rumely was always most obliging and considerate; and the late Ellery Sedgwick was so kind as to invite me to his home in Beverly, Massachusetts, so that he might reminisce about his brief tenure on McClure's.

I also pestered Josephine Dodge Dascom Bacon, whose first stories were written for McClure's and who spent a summer with the McClures in Switzerland; Anna K. Bean, sister of Mary Cloud Bean, who loaned me family letters and gave me permission to quote from them; Mrs. Ino M. Burton, literary executrix for Viola Roseboro', who loaned me valued letters; Ruby Douglas Evans, who worked for the McClure Syndicate more years ago than she cares to remember; Elsie K. Frank, who was McClure's secretary in the 1920s; B. W. Huebsch, who loaned me material dealing with the Ford Peace Ship; Inez Haynes Irwin; Thayer Jaccaci; Mrs. Percy Jackson, who turned over to me material having to do with law suits entered against McClure's Magazine; George F. Kennan; the late Lee Keedick; Edwin Lefevre, Junior; Mrs. Isabel Garland Lord, literary executrix for Hamlin Garland; Mrs. Jameson Parker and Mark Sullivan, Junior, who had in charge Mark Sullivan's papers; and Mary Heaton Vorse, whose first stories were published in McClure's. All these people were most obliging.

I have also to thank Jonathan Daniels for permission to quote a letter from Josephus Daniels, Mrs. George Bambridge for permission to quote from two letters of Rudyard Kipling, Frank C. Preston, Jr. for permission to quote from a letter by Frank Norris, Mrs. Austin Strong for permission to quote two letters of Robert Louis Stevenson, Mrs. Susannah Tarkington for permission to quote from two letters of Booth Tarkington, William L. White for permission to quote from two letters of William Allen White, and W. W. Howells for permission to quote two letters of William Dean Howells. (Mr. Howells asks me to note that these letters cannot be re-quoted without express permission from the heirs of William Dean Howells.)

I must express particular gratitude to McClure's daughters—Eleanor McClure, Elizabeth McClure Mackenzie, and Mary McClure Lyon—who were helpful with reminiscence and in other ways.

Anyone attempting a book like this one is able to stand on the shoulders of his predecessors, learning from them and occasionally profiting from their errors. My predecessors include:

ABBOTT, CHARLES D. *Howard Pyle, a Chronicle:* Harper & Brothers, 1925.
ALDINGTON, RICHARD. *Portrait of a Rebel, the Life and Work of Robert Louis Stevenson:* Evans Brothers, 1957.
ARCHER, C. *William Archer, Life, Work, and Friendship:* Yale University Press, 1931.
BACHELLOR, IRVING. *From Stores of Memory:* Farrar & Rinehart, 1938.
BARR, AMELIA. *All the Days of My Life:* D. Appleton, 1913.
BARRETT, JAMES WYMAN. *Joseph Pulitzer and His World:* Vanguard Press, 1941.
BARRIE, JAMES M. *Letters.* Edited by VIOLA MEYNELL: Charles Scribner's Sons, 1947.
BEACH, REX. *Personal Exposures:* Harper & Brothers, 1940.
BEER, THOMAS. *Stephen Crane, a Study in American Letters:* A. A. Knopf, 1923.
BERRYMAN, JOHN. *Stephen Crane:* William Sloane Associates, 1950.
BISHOP, JOSEPH B. *Theodore Roosevelt and His Time:* Charles Scribner's Sons, 1920.
BOK, EDWARD. *The Americanization of Edward Bok:* Charles Scribner's Sons, 1920.
BOROUGH, REUBEN. *See* Lindsey, Ben B.
BRALEY, BERTON. *Pegasus Pulls a Hack:* Milton, Balch, 1934.

BRITT, GEORGE. *Forty Years—Forty Millions: The Career of Frank A. Munsey*: Farrar & Rinehart, 1935.

BROOKS, VAN WYCK. *The Confident Years: 1885–1915:* E. P. Dutton, 1952.

—— *The Ordeal of Mark Twain:* E. P. Dutton, 1920.

—— *The Time of Melville and Whitman:* E. P. Dutton, 1947.

—— *William Dean Howells, His Life and World:* E. P. Dutton, 1959.

BROWN, E. K., and EDEL, LEON. *Willa Cather, a Critical Biography:* A. A. Knopf, 1953.

BRYAN, WILLIAM JENNINGS, and MARY B. *The Memoirs of William Jennings Bryan:* John C. Winston, 1925.

BURNETT, VIVIAN. *The Romantick Lady* [Frances Hodgson Burnett]: Charles Scribner's Sons, 1927.

CADY, EDWIN H. *William Dean Howells, Dean of American Letters:* Syracuse University Press, 1957–1958.

CALKINS, EARNEST ELMO. *"and hearing not—":* Charles Scribner's Sons, 1946.

—— *They Broke the Prairie:* Charles Scribner's Sons, 1939.

CARR, JOHN DICKSON. *The Life of Sir Arthur Conan Doyle:* Harper & Brothers, 1949.

CARRINGTON, CHARLES E. *The Life of Rudyard Kipling:* Doubleday, 1955.

CARROLL, JOHN CHARLES. *See* Leech, Harper.

CARSON, GERALD. *Cornflake Crusade:* Rinehart, 1957.

CHAMBERLAIN, JOHN. *Farewell to Reform:* Liveright, 1932.

CHARTERIS, EVAN. *The Life and Letters of Sir Edmund Gosse:* Yale University Press, 1931.

CLEMENS, SAMUEL L. *Mark Twain's Letters.* Edited by ALBERT BIGELOW PAINE: Harper & Brothers, 1917.

CLEVELAND, GROVER. *Letters.* Selected and edited by ALLAN NEVINS: Houghton Mifflin, 1933.

CLOUGH, FRANK C. *William Allen White of Emporia:* Whittlesey House, 1941.

Corporation of Trinity Church—*Correspondence with McClure's Magazine:* New York, 1905.

CRANE, STEPHEN. *Letters.* Edited by R. W. STALLMAN and LILLIAN GILKES: New York University Press, 1960.

DAVENPORT, WALTER, and DERIEUX, JAMES. *Ladies, Gentlemen & Editors:* Doubleday, 1961.

DAVIS, RICHARD HARDING. *Adventures and Letters of Richard Harding Davis.* Edited by CHARLES BELMONT DAVIS: Charles Scribner's Sons, 1917.

DAVIS, ROBERT H., and MAURICE, ARTHUR B. *The Caliph of Bagdad, a Biography of O. Henry:* D. Appleton, 1931.

DELL, FLOYD. *Upton Sinclair: A Study in Social Protest:* Doran, 1927.

DORAN, GEORGE H. *Chronicles of Barabbas:* Harcourt, Brace, 1935.

DOYLE, ARTHUR CONAN. *Memories and Adventures:* Little, Brown, 1924.

DUNBAR, ELIZABETH. *Talcott Williams, Gentleman of the Fourth Estate:* Brooklyn, 1936.

DUNLAP, ORRIN E. *Marconi, the Man and His Wireless:* Macmillan, 1938.

EARHART, MARY. *Florence Willard:* University of Chicago Press, 1944.

ELIAS, ROBERT H. *Theodore Dreiser, Apostle of Nature:* A. A. Knopf, 1949.

ELLIS, ELMER. *Mr. Dooley's America, a Life of Finley Peter Dunne:* A. A. Knopf, 1941.

ELLSWORTH, W. W. *A Golden Age of Authors:* Houghton Mifflin, 1919.

FAULKNER, HAROLD U. *The Quest for Social Justice:* Macmillan, 1931.

FILLER, LOUIS. *Crusaders for American Liberalism:* Harcourt, Brace, 1939.

FLYNN, JOHN T. *God's Gold, the Story of Rockefeller and His Times:* Harcourt, Brace, 1932.

FLYNT, JOSIAH. *See* Willard, Josiah Frank.

FORD, FORD MADOX. *Return to Yesterday:* Liveright, 1932.

FURNAS, J. C. *Voyage to Windward:* Sloane, 1951.

GARLAND, HAMLIN. *Companions of the Trail:* Macmillan, 1931.

—— *Daughter of the Middle Border:* Macmillan, 1926.

—— *My Friendly Contemporaries:* Macmillan, 1932.

—— *Roadside Meetings:* Macmillan, 1930.

—— *Son of the Middle Border:* Macmillan, 1917.

GEORGE, HENRY, JUNIOR. *The Life of Henry George:* Doubleday, McClure, 1900.

GILDER, RICHARD WATSON. *Letters.* Edited by ROSAMOND GILDER: Houghton Mifflin, 1916.

GILKES, LILLIAN. *Cora Crane:* University of Indiana Press, 1960.

GOLDMAN, ERIC. *Rendezvous with Destiny:* A. A. Knopf, 1952.

GORDAN, JOHN D. *Joseph Conrad, the Making of a Novelist:* Harvard University Press, 1940.

GRAHAM, JANE K. *Viola, the Duchess of New Dorp, a Biography of Viola Roseboro':* Dansville, Illinois, 1955.

GREENSLET, FERRIS. *The Life of Thomas Bailey Aldrich:* Houghton Mifflin, 1908.

GRIFFIN, MARTIN I. J. *Frank R. Stockton, a Critical Biography:* University of Pennsylvania Press, 1939.

GURKO, LEO. *Joseph Conrad, Giant in Exile:* Macmillan, 1962.

HAPGOOD, NORMAN. *The Changing Years:* Farrar & Rinehart, 1930.

HARPER, JOSEPH H. *The House of Harper:* Harper & Brothers, 1912.

HARRIS, JULIA COLLIER. *The Life and Letters of Joel Chandler Harris:* Houghton Mifflin, 1918.

HARTE, BRET. *Letters.* Edited by GEOFFREY BRET HARTE: Houghton Mifflin, 1926.

HENDRICK, BURTON J. *The Life and Letters of Walter Hines Page:* Doubleday, Page, 1922–1925.

—— *The Training of an American: The Earlier Life and Letters of Walter Hines Page:* Houghton Mifflin, 1928.

HINSHAW, DAVID. *A Man from Kansas, the Story of William Allen White:* G. P. Putnam's Sons, 1945.

HOFSTADTER, RICHARD. *The Age of Reform:* A. A. Knopf, 1955.

HOLLOWAY, JEAN. *Hamlin Garland, a Biography:* University of Texas Press, 1960.

HOWE, FREDERIC C. *The Confessions of a Reformer:* Charles Scribner's Sons, 1925.

JAMES, HENRY. *The American Essays.* Edited by LEON EDEL: Vintage Books, 1956.

JEWETT, SARAH ORNE. *Letters.* Edited by ANNIE FIELDS: Houghton Mifflin, 1911.

JOHNSON, ROBERT UNDERWOOD. *Remembered Yesterdays:* Little, Brown, 1923.

JOHNSON, WALTER. *William Allen White's America:* Henry Holt, 1947.

KIPLING, RUDYARD. *Something of Myself:* Doubleday, Doran, 1937.

LA FOLLETTE, BELLE, and FOLA. *Robert M. La Follette:* Macmillan, 1953.

LANGFORD, GERALD. *Alias O. Henry, a Biography of William S. Porter:* Macmillan, 1957.

LEECH, HARPER, and CARROLL, JOHN CHARLES. *Armour and His Times:* D. Appleton-Century, 1938.

LEECH, MARGARET. *In the Days of McKinley:* Harper & Brothers, 1959.

LINDSEY, BEN B., and BOROUGH, REUBEN. *The Dangerous Life:* Liveright, 1931.

LINSON, CORWIN F. *My Stephen Crane:* Syracuse University Press, 1958.

LONDON, CHARMIAN. *The Book of Jack London:* Century, 1921.

LOW, WILL. *A Chronicle of Friendships:* Charles Scribner's Sons, 1908.

MacMANUS, SEUMAS. *The Rocky Road to Dublin:* Macmillan, 1938.

MARBURY, ELISABETH. *My Crystal Ball:* Boni & Liveright, 1923.

MARCOSSON, ISAAC F. *Before I Forget:* Dodd, Mead, 1959.

—— *David Graham Phillips and His Times:* Dodd, Mead, 1932.

MASSON, ROSALINE O. *The Life of Robert Louis Stevenson:* Stokes, 1923.

McADOO, WILLIAM G. *Crowded Years:* Houghton Mifflin, 1931.

McCLURE, S. S. *Obstacles to Peace:* Houghton Mifflin, 1917.

MILLIS, WALTER. *Road to War:* Houghton Mifflin, 1935.

MITCHELL, E. P. *Memoirs of an Editor:* Charles Scribner's Sons, 1924.

MORISON, ELTING E. *Admiral Sims and the Modern American Navy:* Houghton Mifflin, 1942.

MOTT, FRANK LUTHER. *A History of American Magazines:* Harvard University Press, 1938–1957.

—— *Golden Multitudes, the Story of Best Sellers in the United States:* Macmillan, 1947.

NEVINS, ALLAN. *Henry Ford:* Charles Scribner's Sons, 1954–1957.

—— *Study in Power, a Biography of John D. Rockefeller:* Charles Scribner's Sons, 1959.

ODELL, RUTH. *Helen Hunt Jackson:* D. Appleton-Century, 1939.

PAINE, ALBERT BIGELOW. *Mark Twain, a Biography:* Harper & Brothers, 1912.

PEARSON, HESKETH. *Conan Doyle:* Walker, 1961.

PEMBERTON, T. EDGAR. *The Life of Bret Harte:* Dodd, Mead, 1903.

PHELPS, ELIZABETH STUART. *Chapters from a Life:* Houghton Mifflin, 1896.

PINCHOT, GIFFORD. *Breaking New Ground:* Harcourt, Brace, 1947.

POOLE, ERNEST. *The Bridge, My Own Story:* Macmillan, 1940.

PRINGLE, HENRY F. *Theodore Roosevelt:* Harcourt, Brace, 1931.

REGIER, C. C. *The Era of the Muckrakers:* University of North Carolina Press, 1932.

RICE, ALICE HEGAN. *The Inky Way:* D. Appleton-Century, 1940.

RICE, CALE YOUNG. *Bridging the Years:* D. Appleton-Century, 1939.

RICH, EVERETT. *William Allen White, the Man from Emporia:* Farrar & Rinehart, 1941.

RICHARDS, GRANT. *Author Hunting:* Coward McCann, 1934.

—— *Memories of a Misspent Youth:* Harper & Brothers, 1933.

RIDEING, WILLIAM. *Many Celebrities and a Few Others:* Doubleday, Page, 1912.

RIIS, JACOB. *The Making of an American:* Macmillan, 1901.

ROOSEVELT, THEODORE. *Letters.* Edited by ELTING E. MORISON and others: Harvard University Press, 1951–1954.

RUSSELL, CHARLES EDWARD. *Bare Hands and Stone Walls:* Charles Scribner's Sons, 1933.

SCHLESINGER, ARTHUR M. *Political and Social History of the United States, 1829–1925:* Macmillan, 1927.

SEITZ, DON C. *Joseph Pulitzer, His Life and Letters:* Simon & Schuster, 1924.

SERGEANT, ELIZABETH SHIPLEY. *Willa Cather, a Memoir:* J. B. Lippincott, 1955.

SINCLAIR, UPTON. *American Outpost, a Book of Reminiscences:* Farrar & Rinehart, 1932.

—— *The Brass Check, a Study of American Journalism:* Pasadena, 1919.

SINGLETON, FRANK. *Tillotsons, 1850–1950, Centenary of a Family Business:* Tillotson & Son, Bolton, 1950.

SMITH, CHARLES ALPHONSO. *O. Henry Biography:* Doubleday, Page, 1916.

STEFFENS, JOSEPH LINCOLN. *Letters.* Edited by ELLA WINTER and GRANVILLE HICKS: Harcourt, Brace, 1938.

—— *The Shame of the Cities:* McClure, Phillips, 1905.

—— *The Shame of the Cities.* Introduction by LOUIS JOUGHIN: Hill and Wang, 1957.

STEUART, JOHN ALEXANDER. *Robert Louis Stevenson, a Critical Biography:* Little, Brown, 1924.

STEVENSON, LIONEL. *The Ordeal of George Meredith:* Charles Scribner's Sons, 1953.

STEVENSON, ROBERT LOUIS. *Letters.* Edited by SIDNEY COLVIN: Charles Scribner's Sons, 1911.

—— *Letters to Charles Baxter.* Edited by DE LANCEY FERGUSON and MARSHALL WAINGROW: Yale University Press, 1956.

STONE, IRVING. *Sailor on Horseback, the Biography of Jack London:* Houghton Mifflin, 1938.

SULLIVAN, MARK. *Our Times:* Charles Scribner's Sons, 1927–1935.

TARBELL, IDA M. *All in the Day's Work:* Macmillan, 1939.

TAYLOR, CARLISLE. *Life of Alfred Thayer Mahan:* Doran, 1920.

TEBBEL, JOHN W. *George Horace Lorimer and The Saturday Evening Post:* Doubleday, 1948.

THOMSON, BASIL. *The Scene Changes:* Doubleday, Doran, 1937.

TOWNE, CHARLES HANSON. *So Far So Good:* Julian Messner, 1945.

TRAIN, ARTHUR. *My Day in Court:* Charles Scribner's Sons, 1939.

TREVELYAN, JANET PENROSE. *The Life of Mrs. Humphrey Ward:* Dodd, Mead, 1923.

VANDERLIP, FRANK A., and SPARKES, BOYDEN. *Farm Boy to Financier:* D. Appleton-Century, 1935.

VIERECK, GEORGE SYLVESTER. *Spreading Germs of Hate:* Liveright, 1930.

VORSE, MARY HEATON. *A Footnote to Folly:* Farrar & Rinehart, 1935.

WALKER, FRANKLIN. *Frank Norris, a Biography:* Doubleday, Doran, 1932.

WASHINGTON, BOOKER T. *Up from Slavery:* Doubleday, Page, 1901.

WATSON, ELMO SCOTT. *A History of Newspaper Syndicates in the United States, 1865–1935:* Chicago, 1936.

WHITE, WILLIAM ALLEN. *Autobiography:* Macmillan, 1946.

—— *Selected Letters.* Edited by WALTER JOHNSON: Holt, 1947.

WHITLOCK, BRAND. *Forty Years of It:* D. Appleton, 1914.

—— *Letters and Journal:* D. Appleton-Century, 1936.

WHITMAN, WALT. *Complete Prose Works:* David McKay, 1897.

WHYTE, FREDERIC. *William Heinemann, a Memoir:* Jonathan Cape, 1928.

WILEY, HARVEY W. *An Autobiography:* Bobbs-Merrill, 1930.

WILLARD, JOSIAH FRANK. *My Life:* The Outing Company, 1908.

WOODRESS, JAMES LESLIE. *Booth Tarkington, Gentleman from Indiana:* J. B. Lippincott, 1955.

Magazines of the period were extremely helpful. Naturally, McClure's Magazine itself was most useful of all: I had at my hand a complete set of bound volumes, most of them including the advertising (of which Rudyard Kipling once said that he found it at least as interesting as the fiction and articles), from 1893 through 1913; bound volumes for the later years of publication I found in the New York Public Library.

Other magazines—Harper's Monthly and Harper's Weekly, Life, Printer's Ink, Scribner's, The American, The Bookman, The Century, The Critic, and The Wheelman—I consulted extensively. The files of The Critic were especially helpful for the years when McClure was running his syndicate; those of The Bookman were most helpful for the gossip of the literary world from 1900 to 1908. I skipped through the complete files of The Wheelman more because of a kind of archaeological curiosity than because they were particularly rewarding.

Still other magazines—Ainslee's, Collier's, Editor and Publisher, Everybody's, Frank Leslie's Popular Monthly, Munsey's, Success, The Arena, The Atlantic, The Cosmopolitan, The Independent, The Knox Student, The Ladies' Home Journal, and The Review of Reviews—I consulted ad hoc.

A word about the circulation of McClure's Magazine. The first to interest himself in ascertaining accurate circulation figures of American periodicals was George P. Rowell, the publisher of Printer's Ink. Until 1905 or there-abouts, Rowell's American Newspaper Directory, an annual that reported on magazines as well, was the most trustworthy compendium of this sort of data. Since 1908 the directory published by N. W. Ayer has been standard in the field. Inasmuch as the Audit Bureau of Circulation was not formed until some time later, both Rowell's and Ayer's directories must be used with some skepticism; but I have found no evidence that they have been used at all by any of the historians of the muckraking period.

I have one final acknowledgment.

Carolyn G. Heilbrun and Harry Sions read the typescript and made many suggestions, most of which I was delighted to heed.

My greatest debt is to Jane D. Lyon, who took many hours from her own work not only to help sort the McClure papers and to assist in research but also to give expert editorial advice and finally to act as copy editor.

INDEX

Adams, Samuel Hopkins, 186, 189, 192 fn, 195, 243, 248, 249, 295, 322
Addams, Jane, 360–61
Advertising, development of, 114
Ainslee's Magazine, 216, 219
Aked, Charles, 365, 366, 368, 369, 370
Albert, Dr. Heinrich, 357–58, 359
Alden, Henry Mills, 67, 68, 163, 169
Aldrich, Nelson W., 225, 226, 248, 249
Aldrich, Thomas Bailey, 41, 67, 68
Alger, Horatio, 8, 10, 35, 254
All-Story, 384
American Medical Association, 248, 249
Ames, Albert Alonzo, 217–18, 222
Ames, Fred, 217–18
Anderson, Melville, 27, 28 fn, 31, 76
Andrée, Salomon, 407
Andrews, Mary Shipman, 322
Anhelt, William P., 383
Apponyi, Count, 379
Archer, William, 94, 376, 377, 404
Armour, J. Ogden, 238, 239, 243
Armour, P. D., 236, 243
Armour & Company, 236, 241, 242, 243, 244, 300, 301 fn
Art Interchange, 46
Astor, John Jacob, 137
Atherton, Gertrude, 86
Ayer's Directory, 252

Bachellor, Irving, 54, 66, 70 fn, 75, 76, 78, 80, 129 fn, 347
Baker, George F., 327–29
Baker, Newton D., 229
Baker, Ray Stannard, 151–53, 159, 163, 167–68, 181, 190, 193, 194, 195, 198, 200, 202–03, 204, 205, 206, 209, 228 fn; as muckraker, on labor, 232; on lynchings, 232–33;

on railroads, 233–44, passim; 249, 251, 253, 257, 259, 269, 278–79, 280, 281; breaks with McClure, 286–94, passim; 295, 311, 326 fn, 349, 389, 406
Balestier, Beatty, 103, 105
Balestier, Wolcott, 98, 102–03, 104, 105
Bancroft, Edgar, 283
Bancroft, Frederick, 28, 56
Bangs, John Kendrick, 164
Bangs, Mr., 23, 24–25
Barr, Robert, 122
Barrie, James M., 85, 159
Bate, Florence, 175
Battle Creek Sanitarium, 335, 343–46
Baxter, Charles, 89, 107 fn
Beach, Rex, 254, 322
Bean, Mary Cloud, 188, 194 fn
Beardsley, Aubrey, 72 fn
Bell, Alexander Graham, 132, 134, 175, 195, 350
Bellamy, Edward, 69, 86
Belloc, Hilaire, 322
Benda, Wladyslaw, 323
Bennett, Arnold, 322, 353, 380
Bennett, Josiah Quincy, 312
Bennett, Malvina, 34
Berchtold, Count, 379
Berkman, Alexander, 116
Besant, Walter, 85, 92, 128
Bethmann-Holweg, Theobald von, 379
Beveridge, Albert, 15 fn, 168, 249
Bey, Talaat, 379
Bicycle craze, 34
Birch, Reginald, 323
Bishop, W. H., 59
Bisland, Mary, 195–96, 262–63, 265–66, 270
Bismarck, Prince, 142
Blaine, James, 56, 60

S. S. McClure Newspaper Corporation, 355

Stanton, Theodore, 104, 117

Stead, William, 94, 151, 152

Stedman, E. C., 72

Steele, Frederic Dorr, 179

Steffens, Lincoln, 157, 159, 193, 194, 195, 202, 204, 206, 209; writes The Shame of the Cities and Enemies of the Republic, 215–30; at White House, 222; 231, 249, 251, 257 fn, 263, 276, 280, 283; breaks with McClure, 286–94 passim; 295, 298–99, 306, 311, 349, 401 fn, 405, 406, 407, 408, 409

Stempel, Captain, 367

Stetson, Francis Lynde, 163

Steunenberg, Frank, 307–08

Stevenson, Robert Louis, 70, 77, 80, 85; encounters with McClure, 86–94; 96, 98, 99–100, 105; sends letters from the South Seas, 106; caricatures McClure in The Wrecker, 107–08; 123, 131, 136, 141, 377

Stillman, James, 327–29

Stimson, Frederic J., 57, 58

Stockbridge, Frank Parker, 356–57

Stockton, Frank, 80

Stoddard, Henry L., 354, 355, 357, 359

Stoddard, W. O., 58

Stoker, Bram, 159

Stone, Ellen, 194, 196–98, 202

Stone, Harlan F., 229

Stone, William, 223

Success, 206, 238

Sullivan, Mark, 234, 243, 246 fn, 247, 249, 281, 295, 299

Sullivan, Timothy D., 325

Swain, Max, 368

Swinburne, Charles Algernon, 86

Symons, Arthur, 178

Syndicates, early history of, 53–55

System, the, defined by Steffens, 223; 224, 225, 229, 282, 329

Taft, William Howard, 207, 259, 290, 325, 330, 341, 345, 361

Tarbell, Ida M., 117, 131; writes series on Napoleon, 132–34; on Lincoln, 134–35; 150, 152, 155, 166; editing McClure's, 169; 170, 174, 175; plans series on U.S. Steel Corporation, 185; discusses trusts with McClure, 190; and Standard Oil, 191; writes to Baker about trusts, 191–92; decides to tackle a history of the Standard Oil Co., 193–94; 195–96, 199, 201, 202, 204–05, 206; History of the Standard Oil Co. and its effect, 210–14; 215, 218, 226, 231, 243, 244, 249, 251; and McClure's emotional problems, 255–66; 270, 274–75, 276, 277, 278, 280, 281, 283, 284–85; breaks with McClure, 286–94; 295, 303, 310–11, 312, 314, 349, 361, 401 fn, 405, 406, 407, 408, 409, 410

Tarkington, Booth, 154–56, 159, 322, 347

Tauchnitz, Baron, 102

Taylor, Charles, 61

Templeton, Herminie, 159

Tennyson, Alfred, 85, 97

Terry, Ellen, 312 fn

Thanet, Octave, 128

The American Magazine (McClure's version), 184; (Phillips's version) 295, 297, 298, 310, 311, 313, 322, 333, 391

The Appeal to Reason, 237, 238, 308

The Arena, 177

The Argosy, 330

The Atlantic Monthly, 41, 67, 69, 109, 126, 134, 141, 166, 167, 234, 295

The Black Cat, 158

The Boston Globe, 58, 61

The Century Magazine, 36, 38, 40, 47, 48, 55, 56, 60, 67, 69, 97, 109, 113, 121, 122, 126, 132, 134, 135, 136, 141, 146, 167, 264 fn, 298, 353

The Chautauquan, 117

The Chicago American, 237

The Chicago Daily News, 283

The Chicago Inter-Ocean, 29, 125

The Chicago Record, 151

The Chicago Tribune, 267, 325 fn

The Continent, 46

The Cosmopolitan, 109, 126, 134, 136, 206, 208, 250, 274 fn (See Cosmopolitan)

The Coup d'Etat, 29

The Critic, 71 fn, 73, 78

The Davenport Times, 119

The Dearborn Independent, 400

The Eclectic Magazine of Continental Periodical Literature, 40, 42

The Emporia Gazette, 149

The Fatherland, 358

The Fortnightly Review, 404

The Fourth Estate, 383

The Galesburg Register, 26

The Golden Book, 402

The Hartford Times, 58, 61, 375–76

The Hoosac Valley News, 61

The Idler, 122

The Independent, 136, 249–50

The Journal of Insanity, 288 fn

The Knox Student, 14, 28, 36, 37

The Ladies' Home Journal, 126, 206, 233, 246–47, 248